Truth and Pluralism

Truth and Pluralism
CURRENT DEBATES

Edited by Nikolaj J. L. L. Pedersen
and
Cory D. Wright

UNIVERSITY PRESS

Oxford University Press is a department of the University of Oxford.
It furthers the University's objective of excellence in research, scholarship,
and education by publishing worldwide.

Oxford   New York
Auckland   Cape Town   Dar es Salaam   Hong Kong   Karachi
Kuala Lumpur   Madrid   Melbourne   Mexico City   Nairobi
New Delhi   Shanghai   Taipei   Toronto

With offices in
Argentina   Austria   Brazil   Chile   Czech Republic   France   Greece
Guatemala   Hungary   Italy   Japan   Poland   Portugal   Singapore
South Korea   Switzerland   Thailand   Turkey   Ukraine   Vietnam

Oxford is a registered trademark of Oxford University Press
in the UK and certain other countries.

Published in the United States of America by
Oxford University Press
198 Madison Avenue, New York, NY 10016

© Oxford University Press 2013

All rights reserved. No part of this publication may be reproduced, stored in a
retrieval system, or transmitted, in any form or by any means, without the prior
permission in writing of Oxford University Press, or as expressly permitted by law,
by license, or under terms agreed with the appropriate reproduction rights organization.
Inquiries concerning reproduction outside the scope of the above should be sent to the Rights
Department, Oxford University Press, at the address above.

You must not circulate this work in any other form
and you must impose this same condition on any acquirer.

Library of Congress Cataloging-in-Publication Data
Truth and pluralism / edited by Nikolaj J.L.L. Pedersen and Cory D. Wright.
p. cm.
ISBN 978–0–19–538746–9 (alk. paper)
1. Truth.   2. Pluralism.   I. Pedersen, Nikolaj J. L. L., 1978–   II. Wright, Cory D., 1975–
BD171.T7135 2013
121—dc23
2012016470

ISBN 978–0–19–538746–9

1 3 5 7 9 8 6 4 2
Printed in the United States of America
on acid-free paper

{ CONTENTS }

Contributors — vii
Acknowledgments — ix

1. Introduction — 1
   NIKOLAJ J. L. L. PEDERSEN & CORY D. WRIGHT

PART I Varieties of Pluralism

2. Three Questions for Truth Pluralism — 21
   MICHAEL P. LYNCH

3. Lynch's Functionalist Theory of Truth — 42
   MARIAN DAVID

4. Alethic Functionalism and the Norm of Belief — 69
   PASCAL ENGEL

5. Pluralism about Truth as Alethic Disjunctivism — 87
   NIKOLAJ J. L. L. PEDERSEN & CORY D. WRIGHT

6. Truth, Winning, and Simple Determination Pluralism — 113
   DOUGLAS EDWARDS

7. A Plurality of Pluralisms — 123
   CRISPIN WRIGHT

PART II Pluralism, Correspondence, and Descriptions

8. Forms of Correspondence: The Intricate Route from Thought to Reality — 157
   GILA SHER

9. The Synthetic Unity of Truth — 180
   ROBERT BARNARD & TERENCE HORGAN

10. Alethic Pluralism and the Correspondence Theory of Truth — 197
    RICHARD FUMERTON

11. Naturalizing Pluralism about Truth — 213
    WOLFRAM HINZEN

12 On Describing the World 238
DOROTHY GROVER

PART III **Pluralism, Deflationism, and Paradox**

13 Deflationism, Pluralism, Expressivism, Pragmatism 263
SIMON BLACKBURN

14 Should We Be Pluralists about Truth? 278
MAX KÖLBEL

15 Deflationism Trumps Pluralism! 298
JULIAN DODD

16 Deflated Truth Pluralism 323
JC BEALL

17 Pluralism and Paradox 339
AARON J. COTNOIR

Index 351

{ LIST OF CONTRIBUTORS }

Michael P. Lynch is Professor of Philosophy, University of Connecticut, United States.

Marian David is Professor of Philosophy, University of Graz, Austria.

Pascal Engel is Professor of Modern and Contemporary Philosophy, University of Geneva, Switzerland.

Nikolaj J. L. L. Pedersen is Assistant Professor of Philosophy, Underwood International College, Yonsei University, South Korea.

Cory D. Wright is Assistant Professor of Philosophy, California State University, Long Beach, United States.

Douglas Edwards is Lecturer and Marie Curie Research Fellow (2011–2013), Northern Institute of Philosophy, University of Aberdeen, United Kingdom.

Crispin Wright is Professor of Philosophy, New York University, United States, and Director, Northern Institute of Philosophy, University of Aberdeen, United Kingdom.

Gila Sher is Professor of Philosophy, University of California, San Diego, United States.

Robert Barnard is Associate Professor of Philosophy, University of Mississippi, United States.

Terence Horgan is Professor of Philosophy, University of Arizona, United States.

Richard Fumerton is F. Wendell Miller Professor of Philosophy, University of Iowa, United States.

Wolfram Hinzen is Professor of Philosophy, University of Durham, United Kingdom.

Dorothy Grover is Adjunct Professor of Philosophy, University of Canterbury, New Zealand, and Professor Emeritus, University of Illinois at Chicago, United States.

Simon Blackburn is a Fellow of Trinity College, University of Cambridge, United Kingdom, Research Professor, University of North Carolina, Chapel Hill, United States, and Distinguished Professor at the New College of the Humanities.

Max Kölbel is ICREA Research Professor, University of Barcelona, Spain.

Julian Dodd is Professor of Philosophy, University of Manchester, United Kingdom.

Jc Beall is Professor of Philosophy, University of Connecticut, United States, and Professor of Philosophy (2011–2013), University of Otago, New Zealand.

Aaron J. Cotnoir is Lecturer, University of St. Andrews, United Kingdom.

{ ACKNOWLEDGMENTS }

It would not have been possible for us to get to the finish line without a number of people, most notably the contributors themselves. They have thought long and hard about the issues involving truth pluralism, and their articles have come together to form the groundbreaking collection on this subject. Participants in the *Truth: Current Debates* conference at the University of Connecticut in May 2009 also helped shape this volume in many ways, and we are grateful to Michael Lynch, Jc Beall, Marcus Rossberg, Lionel Shapiro, and Connecticut's Humanities Institute for their support of the event. The volume was also helped along by discussions or assistance from Maria Baghramian, Bob Barnard, Eric Carter, Sharon Coull, Doug Edwards, Kamper Floyd, and Michael Horton. We are also grateful to Jeremy Wyatt for compiling the index, and to Peter Ohlin from Oxford University Press for not only recognizing the value of this collection in the first place, but also for being very patient while it was being assembled. Finally, we are most grateful to our respective teachers: Michael Lynch, Gila Sher, and Crispin Wright. This project would not have been possible without their grace and patience with each of us as students, and their generous and unwavering support of our endeavors thereafter. A special thanks is owed to Michael in particular for his advisory role and encouragement of this volume from beginning to end. The friends that we have made along the way have made the journey all the more worthwhile.

Nikolaj Jang Lee Linding Pedersen & Cory D. Wright
Seoul & Long Beach, 2011

{ 1 }

Introduction
Nikolaj J. L. L. Pedersen & Cory D. Wright

1. Three debates

The relative merits and demerits of historically prominent views such as the correspondence theory, coherentism, pragmatism, verificationism, and instrumentalism have been subject to much attention in the truth literature and have fueled the long-lived debate over which of these views is the most plausible one. Another big debate—one of a more recent vintage—concerns the issue of whether truth is merely a logical 'device' that finds its use in generalizations and in expressing semantic ascent. Deflationists endorse the idea, whereas inflationists reject it. As deflationism has become increasingly prominent, so has the divide between the two camps and the debate between them. More recently still, a third debate has started to emerge in the truth literature, centered around the issue of whether truth is one or many. Put in slightly different terms: is there only one property in virtue of which propositions can be true, or are there several? The truth monist holds the former view, while the truth pluralist adheres to the latter.

Truth pluralism is often associated with Michael Lynch, Gila Sher, and Crispin Wright, who have expressed sympathy toward the view in a number of writings. Several criticisms have been leveled against pluralism in the literature. Defenses have been offered, as have attempts to develop the view further.[1] The literature on truth pluralism has been growing steadily for the past twenty

---

[1] C. J. G. Wright touched on pluralism in passing in a variety of work in the 1990s (1992, 1994a, 1994b, 1996, 1998a, 1998b, 1999, and 2001). Criticisms have been formulated by a wide range of commentators, including Blackburn (1998), Horton & Poston (2012), Jackson (1994), Nulty (2010), Patterson (2010), Pettit (1996), Shapiro (2009, 2011), Sainsbury (1996), Sher (2005), Tappolet (1997, 2000, 2010), Williamson (1994),and C. D. Wright (2005, 2010, 2012). For defenses, applications, or attempts to develop the view further, see, e.g., Beall (2000), Cotnoir (2009, forthcoming), Dorsey (2006, 2010), Edwards (2008, 2009, 2011, 2012), Kölbel (2008), Lynch (2000, 2004, 2005a, 2005b, 2006, 2009, 2012), Pedersen (2006, 2010), Sher (1998, 2004), and C. D. Wright et al. (2012).

years, and has enjoyed a recent burst of research. This volume, however, is the first of its kind—the first collection of papers focused specifically on pluralism about truth. This is an interesting topic in its own right. Part I of the volume is thus dedicated to the development, investigation, and critical discussion of different forms of pluralism. An additional reason to look at truth pluralism with interest is the significant connections it bears to other debates in the truth literature more generally—the debates concerning traditional theories of truth and the deflationism/inflationism divide being cases in hand. Parts II and III of the volume connect truth pluralism to these two debates. In the next three sections, we give a very short overview of the different parts of the volume. The overview highlights only selected aspects of the individual contributions, and as such, betrays their richness and level of detail. However, our hope is that the reader will come to appreciate these on her own.

2. Varieties of pluralism (Part I)

Although there are various ways to articulate the core pluralist thesis, it has typically been construed thus: what property makes propositions true may vary across domains, or from subject matter to subject matter. Corresponding with reality might be the alethically potent property—the property that can make propositions true—when it comes to discourse about ordinary, concrete objects. On the other hand, cohering with the axioms of Peano arithmetic and being endorsed most widely might be the relevant properties for discourse about respectively arithmetic and the goodness of consumer goods.

Certain issues give rise to divisions within the pluralist camp. In particular, although pluralists agree that several properties are alethically potent, they diverge in their understanding of alethic potency. The issue is how precisely to articulate the thought that different properties can make propositions belonging to different domains true. Suppose that the property of being F_i is the property that makes propositions in domain D_i true. Then one way to understand alethic potency is along reductionist lines:

(R_1) In domain D_i, the property of being true is identical to F_i.
(R_2) In domain D_i, the property of being true is constituted by F_i.

Since identity is stronger than constitution, (R_1) is stronger than (R_2). However, given the shared reductionist nature, both (R_1) and (R_2) intimate a very strong link between being true and having one of the alethically potent properties. On either account of alethic potency, there is nothing to being true in a given domain D_i over and above being F_i. This leads to a radical or strong form of pluralism. Truth is many, and just that. There is no overarching unity to truth. This is reflected in the relativization of the identity or constitution thesis that is part of reductionist versions of pluralism: truth-as-such is lost—truth-in-a-domain is what remains.

Strong pluralism is not a position widely held within the pluralist camp. The contributors of Part I of the volume (Michael Lynch, Nikolaj Pedersen & Cory Wright, Douglas Edwards, and Crispin Wright) all advocate a form of moderate pluralism, a position intermediate between strong pluralism and monism.[2] The moderate pluralist grants something to each of the two views by taking truth to be both many and one. Truth is many because different properties make propositions true in different domains, and it is one because all these propositions have something in common, truth-as-such.

What sets moderate and strong pluralists apart is their take on alethic potency. As seen, on the strong pluralist's view, truth-as-such drops out of the picture since there is nothing to truth in each domain over and above the property that is alethically potent within that domain. To preserve the idea that propositions can be true-as-such—and not just true-in-a-domain—the moderate pluralist gives a non-reductionist account of alethic potency.[3] The accounts on offer in the contributions to Part I of the volume differ significantly in detail, but can all be regarded as incorporating the idea that alethic potency is a kind of dependence relation. Being true-as-such is a property distinct from—and over and above—the properties that are alethically potent within their respective domains. However, a proposition's being true-as-such depends on its having one of the locally alethically potent properties.

Lynch (ch. 2) spells out dependence in terms of what he calls 'manifestation'. A property F manifests a property F* just in case it is a priori that the set of conceptually essential features of F* is a subset of F's features. One way to think of this is to think that part of being F is to be F*. Applied to the case of truth, Lynch takes alethically potent properties like correspondence (in a suitably naturalized version), superwarrant, and coherence to manifest truth. Truth's conceptually essential features are given by three so-called 'core truisms'. Roughly, these describe true propositions as objective, correct to believe, and aimed at inquiry. The appeal to the core truisms makes Lynch's proposal functionalist in nature: the core truisms pin down the 'truth-role', or the functions that truth has. The properties of corresponding, being superwarranted, and cohering manifest truth because propositions that possess these properties are objective, correct to believe, and should be aimed at in enquiry. To be true is part of what it is to correspond, be superwarranted, and cohere.

---

[2] However, see Max Kölbel's contribution (ch. 13) for a form of strong pluralism; see also Cotnoir (forthcoming) for a defense.

[3] The debate between moderate and strong pluralists over relativization of truth to a domain has some unnoticed parallels with an older debate between Davidson and followers of Tarski's over the consequences of relativization of truth predicates to a language.

Pedersen & Wright (ch. 5) propose a form of moderate pluralism called 'alethic disjunctivism'. On this view truth-as-such is a certain disjunctive property, characterized as follows: a proposition is true-as-such just in case it possesses the alethically potent property of domain$_1$ and pertains to domain$_1$, or . . . , or possesses the alethically potent property of domain$_n$ and pertains to domain$_n$. A proposition's possessing the disjunctive property depends on its having one of the alethically potent properties in the sense that the former is grounded in the latter. Grounding is (strongly) asymmetric, that is, if x's being F grounds x's being F*, then it is not the case that x's being F* grounds x's being F. For this reason, for alethic disjunctivism, while a proposition is true-as-such because it has the property that is alethically potent within its domain, the converse does not hold. Given this asymmetry between truth as one (truth-as-such) and truth as many (the alethically potent properties), alethic disjunctivism gives metaphysical priority to the many over the one. At the same time, claim Pedersen & Wright, the alethic disjunctivist can maintain a high degree of unity because the disjunctive truth property—the one possessed by all true propositions—satisfies certain core principles. Pedersen & Wright support this claim by arguing that the disjunctive truth property satisfies Lynch's three truisms.

Edwards (ch. 6) bases his account of dependence on an analogy with winning. Edwards observes that an instance of the following schema holds for games: if one is playing game x, then if one possesses property F, one has won the game. For example, in the case of chess, the conditional is this: if one is playing chess, then if one checkmates one's opponent, one has won the game. Edwards takes the relationship between the game-specific property and the property of winning to be one of determination. Thus, in the case of chess, checkmating one's opponent specifies what it takes to win, and so, having that property determines a win. Transposed to the truth case, Edwards suggests that domains of discourse can be treated as being associated with a certain truth-determining conditional. For example, assuming that corresponding with reality is the alethically potent property for discourse about the material world, the conditional would be: if p pertains to the material world, then if p corresponds with reality, then p is true. Possessing the property of corresponding with reality is what it takes to be true for discourse pertaining to the material world, and so, correspondence determines truth for this kind of discourse.

Wright's *Truth and Objectivity* (1992) is widely cited as one of the works with which pluralism originated. While the book contains passages that mention 'pluralism', the view is not developed in detail. The same applies to Wright's later work (see references in fn. 1). Wright's contribution to this volume (ch. 7) contains his most extensive and worked-out version of pluralism to date.

The starting point of Wright's proposal is a platitude-based approach to the characterization of the concept of truth, just as in his (1992, 2001) earlier works.

Introduction 5

This commitment is supplemented by a commitment to moderate pluralism, or the idea that truth is both one and many. In spelling out his view, Wright registers a fundamental agreement with Edwards: the most promising way to think about the relationship between truth-as-such and the multitude of alethically potent properties like correspondence and coherence is to endorse a range of domain-specific 'determination conditionals'.

However, while Wright agrees with Edwards that there are insights to be gleaned from the analogy between winning and truth—crucially, the domain-specific conditionals—he thinks that the epistemological status of the conditionals is significantly different in the two cases. Both types of conditional rank as conceptual truths. The correctness of any given game conditional "leaps at you" or is obvious. Furthermore, this immediate recognition of correctness seems to be constitutive of knowing what the relevant game is. For instance, it would appear reasonable to doubt that someone knew chess if she were to deny or doubt the correctness of 'If one is playing chess, then if one checkmates one's opponent, one has won'. However, the same point does not appear to apply to the conditionals in the truth case. For the sake of illustration, suppose that 'If p pertains to morals, then if p is superassertible, then p is true' is correct.[4] This conditional does not seem immediately obvious in the way that the chess conditional is, and it would seem unreasonable to charge someone who did not immediately endorse it with not knowing what morals are. Against the background of this disanalogy, Wright subjects the domain-specific conditionals to further discussion. The discussion aims to accomplish two things: first, to reconcile the status of the domain-specific conditionals as conceptual necessities with the air of controversiality that surrounds them, and second, to account for how the domain-specific conditionals can do the intended metaphysical work, that is, how a proposition's possession of the property relevant to its domain makes the proposition true-as-such.

The pluralist contributions just touched on are complemented by critical pieces by Marian David (ch. 3) and Pascal Engel (ch. 4). Both contributions target Lynch's functionalist view.

David subjects two of the major components of Lynch's view—functionalism and alethic-potency-as-manifestation—to critical scrutiny. As we have seen above, Lynch's functionalism derives from the idea that the core truisms pin down the truth role, and that truth is to be characterized in terms of this role. David suggests that the Lynch-style functionalist is most naturally understood as operating with an absolute notion of the truth-role, meaning that a property's playing the truth-role requires it to satisfy the core truisms in relation to all (truth-apt) propositions. However, this has the untoward

---

[4] A statement is superassertible just in case 'it is, or can be, warranted and some warrant for it would survive arbitrarily close scrutiny of its pedigree and arbitrarily extensive increments to or other forms of improvement of our information' (Wright 1992: 48).

consequence that none of the locally potent properties can play the truth-role (since each of them only satisfies the core truisms for propositions belonging to a specific domain). In light of this, David urges the functionalist to relativize the truth-role to individual propositions or to domains.

David likewise thinks that the Lynch-style functionalist has work to do with respect to the other major component of her view: the notion of manifestation. In order for a property F to manifest truth-as-such, the essential features of truth-as-such must be among F's features. However, truth-as-such has several properties essentially that are not shared by any of the properties supposed to manifest it—for example, the property of playing the truth-role for all propositions and the property of being identical to truth-as-such. In light of this, contrary to Lynch's own contention, it would appear that correspondence, superwarrant, and so on cannot manifest truth-as-such. David concludes that the notion of manifestation cannot do the work that Lynch intends it to do, but that the functionalist is free to replace it with some other—and better—account of alethic dependence.

Lynch claims that the normativity of truth is straightforwardly accounted for on the manifestation functionalist view: it is an essential feature of truth to be the standard of correctness for belief, and as such, true beliefs are ones that ought be held (all things being equal). Engel critically discusses this aspect of the functionalist position by developing a dilemma: the multiple manifestability of truth does not harmonize with the idea that the normativity of truth is both uniform and substantive. To hold on to multiple manifestability, the functionalist has to give up either the uniformity of alethic normativity or its substantiveness. To do the former would be to give up on the idea that there is a single norm of truth that applies across all truth-apt discourse—a part of Lynch's view. Instead, there would be a multitude of local norms. To do the latter would bring the functionalist story close to deflationism in certain respects; yet, the functionalist view is precisely meant to be a polar opposite of deflationism.

3. Truth pluralism, correspondence, and descriptions (Part II)

The core pluralist thesis—that there are several alethically potent properties—gives some credit to traditional theories of truth: any theory that focuses on one of the alethically potent properties gets things right, at least locally. The qualification 'at least locally' is important. Traditional theories of truth commit to the monist idea that one and the same property is alethically potent across the board, or within all truth-apt domains of discourse. According to the pluralist, by taking on board this monist commitment traditional theories extend the applicability of their favored property too far. None of the favored properties can plausibly be thought of as applying globally, or within every truth-apt domain of discourse. This issue has become known as the 'scope problem' in the literature.[5]

Which among the traditionally prominent theories of truth is the most plausible one? If the scope problem is a compelling one, the extensive debate over this question would appear to rest on the misguided supposition that one theory must get things right across the board. Several contributions to Part I of the volume take the scope problem to motivate a move away from monism and traditional theories of truth (as they incorporate monism) to a pluralist position that accommodates a range of alethically potent properties. The papers by Lynch, Pedersen & C. D. Wright, Edwards, and C. J. G. Wright are cases in hand.

However, matters may not be as simple as they seem at first. Gila Sher (ch. 8) and Robert Barnard & Terence Horgan (ch. 9) adhere to a version of the correspondence theory, but propose a way to deal with the scope problem. Both papers are premised on the need to account for the diversity of our truth-apt thought—and so acknowledge the force of the scope problem—but at the same seek to preserve its unity. In their own ways, they do so by suggesting that there are different forms of correspondence. This move results in views that go beyond traditional versions of the correspondence theory, that rest with the reduction of truth to correspondence. According to Sher and Barnard & Horgan, however, there is correspondence, *and* correspondence is a genus that subsumes different species or forms.

The proliferation of correspondence into different forms makes the correspondence views in Part II significantly similar to the kinds of moderate pluralism presented in Part I: on all views truth is both diverse and unified. Moderate pluralists think so because truth is both one and many. There is truth-as-such, but likewise—and importantly—there are several properties that can ground truth-as-such for propositions belonging to different domains. For the correspondence views in Part II, what we have is this: truth is diverse because there are *different* forms of correspondence, and at the same time, truth is unified because they are all forms of *correspondence*.

The moderate pluralist views and the correspondence views of Sher and Barnard & Horgan are also significantly dissimilar. As mentioned earlier, pluralists do not think that traditional monist theories are completely off the mark. They get it right locally, or within certain domains. In this sense pluralists do give some credit to traditional theories of truth. Matters are somewhat different when we consider multitudinous correspondence views. They give much credit to one traditional theory of truth, and one theory only: the correspondence theory. No credit is given to coherence, superassertibility, pragmatic expediency, or any other candidate properties. It is correspondence across the

---

[5] The label is from Lynch (2004). Other labels are used in the literature as well, but 'scope problem' seems to be used most widely.

board. However, crucially, as we have seen, different forms of correspondence may hold sway over different domains or subject matters.

Sher (ch. 8) distinguishes between direct and indirect forms of correspondence. Direct correspondence covers simple cases where language straightforwardly represents reality (e.g., via causal links), while indirect correspondence obtains in cases where the route between the two is more intricate. Sher's methodology is to proceed inductively on a case-by-case basis. Not until a domain has been extensively and thoroughly examined will the exact nature of correspondence for that domain be known. Thus, further and more fine-grained distinctions may be drawn under the umbrella of respectively direct and indirect correspondence—only careful examination of specific domains will show how many and how diverse subdivisions of the two forms of correspondence are.

Consonant with her favored methodology, Sher's contribution contains an investigation into the nature of correspondence for the specific domain of mathematics. Very roughly, Sher takes mathematics to be concerned with certain kinds of formal properties of reality (i.e., the properties that are invariant under isomorphism, such as identity). She restricts attention to basic arithmetic, taking cardinal numbers to be certain second-level properties (i.e., properties of properties). The standard formulation of arithmetic is first-order, meaning that numerals—the linguistic expressions meant to denote numbers—are treated as singular terms, that is, a type of expression that usually refers to individuals. Subsequently, Sher proposes that we think of arithmetical truth in terms of indirect rather than direct correspondence. The world contains no numbers at the level of individuals, and so there is no way for arithmetical statements—with their ingredient-singular terms—directly to correspond to reality. However, since mathematics is a human activity, and since it is cognitively more straightforward to engage in reasoning about individuals and their properties, human cognizers posit individuals and first-level properties when doing arithmetic. These posited entities represent the arithmetical features of the world. Given the vital representative role played by the intermediate entities, we are dealing with an indirect form of correspondence—an illustration of how, for some domains, the route from thought to reality is quite intricate.

Like Sher, Barnard & Horgan (ch. 9) draw a distinction between direct and indirect correspondence. For them, both forms of correspondence are 'ideologically mediated' relations between language and the world, and different domains of discourse will involve different ideological commitments or posits. These are elements of language and thought. While posits often figure in language or thought whose surface grammar is existentially committing, only some posits correlate with entities or properties that really exist or are part of the ultimate ontology. When language maps entities and properties in the ultimate ontology, the relevant kind of correspondence is direct. In other cases the relevant kind of correspondence is indirect.

For the sake of illustration, consider Barnard & Horgan's example where we suppose that the ultimate ontology contains many trees, but just that. In that case, the statement 'there are trees' directly corresponds to the world: the relevant posit—the lexeme *tree*—maps something in the ultimate ontology. On the other hand, 'there exist forests' does not correspond in a direct way because the relevant posit—the lexeme *forest*—does not map something in the ultimate ontology. Nonetheless, the statement is true in virtue of indirectly corresponding to the world. The semantic standards operative for discourse about trees and forests are such that 'there are trees' mediates between language and a world in which trees are within close proximity of each other.

Barnard & Horgan grant minimal realism as a background assumption for their correspondence view. (Let 'minimal realism' name the thesis that there is a world and that it has a definite nature.) Beyond this minimal realism, they maintain that the correspondence view ought to be metaphysically neutral; being a correspondence theorist should be compatible with being just about any metaphysical view whatsoever.

In his contribution to the volume, Richard Fumerton (ch. 10) argues that, in several respects, the correspondence theory might be more accommodating or flexible than often thought. First, continuing the thread of metaphysical neutrality, Fumerton suggests that the correspondence theory is compatible with not just realism of various stripes, but likewise with anti-realism of different kinds (including idealism). Second, the correspondence theory can allow for degrees of truth. He rehearses the claim that the correspondence relation works very much in the way pictures do, as representations; and just as pictures are naturally thought of as being more or less accurate representations of what they depict, it is natural to think of truth bearers as representing or corresponding to reality to a higher or lower degree. Third, the correspondence theory can accommodate a kind of relativism in the sense that there can be alternative equally correct descriptions of reality. Just as different pictures can succeed in representing the same thing, different descriptions or conceptualizations can correspond equally well to reality. Considering two descriptions q_1 and q_2, one description might include a truth not included in the other. However, Fumerton maintains that, while p might be true in q_1 and not be included in q_2, the reason is never that not-p is true in q_2. Equally correct descriptions of the world are always compatible. Furthermore, they can always be conjoined into one big description of what the world is like. Fourth, considering the pluralist idea that there are different truth properties $F_1, \ldots, F_n$ (coherence, utility of belief, etc.), Fumerton goes on to argue that the only way to make sense of $F_1, \ldots, F_n$ is to understand these properties in terms of correspondence. The effect of doing so, however, would be to deprive pluralism of much of the initial plausibility it might be thought to possess (due to, e.g., the scope problem). Ultimately, Fumerton reverts to a neoclassical view of correspondence as the only viable way to think about truth.

For his part, Wolfram Hinzen (ch. 11) takes an approach radically different from any correspondence approach to truth. Hinzen proposes a (methodologically) naturalistic inquiry into truth, which eschews the metaphysical approach of developing grand alethic stories about the nature and constitution of truth independent of the cognitive creatures who conceptualize it. While Hinzen endorses a kind of naturalism that is widely regarded as being one of the chief motivations for adopting some version of the correspondence theory, he thinks that the theory goes wrong by treating truth in an externalist fashion—as having a source that is external to language and mind. He develops a novel view that pulls in the opposite direction: truth emerges as a product of the mental organization of human beings, and so naturalistic studies into its nature must be directed inward or take as their focus the internal structure of our mind and language.

Hinzen's view has mixed consequences for all three major kinds of conceptions: traditionalist, deflationist, and pluralist. With respect to pluralism, he aims his criticisms at both the main consideration in its favor—namely, the scope problem—and the view itself. The scope problem says that no uniform treatment can plausibly be given of truth across all truth-apt domains of discourse. Reminiscent of Sher's view about the indirect correspondence of first-order arithmetic and mathematics as a cognitive activity, Hinzen also counters by arguing that moral properties are part of moral cognition and mutatis mutandis for other domain-specific properties and types of cognition. But these kinds of cognition are all activities of mind and as natural as mind itself. Since truth is rooted in the internal structure of mind and language, truth across all domains emerges as having an internalist-naturalistic nature. And it does so in a domain-general way, argues Hinzen, analogous to sense in which language is domain-general. Hinzen does take seriously the idea that there may be disunification in what might be called the 'alethic mode of cognition' (Sher & Wright 2007), given the inherent structure of human language and the role that our concept of it plays in human cognition. But while he considers the pluralist intuition that there is considerable variation when comparing discourse across domains, he is unable to trace this variation to anything more than differences in the conceptual structure in domains of human cognition. Thus, contra the pluralist, domain-related variation is not a natural indicator of alethic variation.

Dorothy Grover (ch. 12) has long been one of the foremost exponents of prosentialism, which is a radical form of deflationism and which is incompatible with the key pluralist idea that there is a multitude of substantive properties that are alethically potent within specific domains. Grover is also therefore a detractor of truth pluralism, so construed. However, Grover also engages with the issue of truth pluralism from the alternative route of descriptions: is there more than one true way of describing the world? The pluralist about descriptions answers in the affirmative, the monist in the negative.

Grover rightly points out that the question of pluralism must be supplemented by a specification of what kind of description is relevant to answering the question. She doubts the coherence of the notion of a complete description of the world and thinks that the question can only be interestingly asked when the relevant kind of descriptions of the world are not required to be complete. Against this background, and perhaps consonant with Fumerton's view (were he a prosententialist), Grover develops a perspectivalist view according to which different incomplete descriptions of the world provide a multitude of perspectives that are needed for rational decision-making. She argues that her perspectivalism supports what Lynch (1998) refers to as 'vertical pluralism', or the thesis that there are different kinds of non-reductive facts (e.g., moral facts and mathematical facts, neither of which are reducible to the other). She then explores the issue of whether her perspectivalism likewise supports 'horizontal pluralism' (in Lynch's sense), a more radical form of pluralism according to which there can be incompatible facts within the same discourse. For example, according to this kind of pluralism, it is possible for there to be incompatible moral facts. Grover rejects Lynch's own attempt to support horizontal pluralism and does not think that considerations from Quine on distinct empirically equivalent systems suffice either. She identifies the existence of two genuinely irreconcilable, fact-stating languages as something that would support horizontal pluralism. However, she leaves open the question of whether there are indeed two languages of this kind.

4. Truth pluralism, deflationism, and paradox (Part III)

As we have seen in the previous section, truth pluralism connects with the correspondence theory—and cognate themes such as descriptions—in significant and interesting ways. The same can be said about truth pluralism and the debate between inflationists and deflationists. To see this we note that there is a fundamental methodological point of convergence between deflationists and pluralists. Both camps approach the task of characterizing the concept of truth by laying down certain basic principles that capture its functions.

The deflationist maintains that there is a small set of principles that completely characterize the concept of truth, the favored principle being the disquotational schema ('p' is true if, and only if, p) or some similar principle.[6] Such T-schemata enable truth predicates to serve as a vehicle of generalization, semantic ascent, and certain other logical or expressive functions. According

---

[6] Compare the equivalence schema (⟨p⟩ is true if, and only if, p) or the operator schema (it is true that p if, and only if, p).

to the deflationist, there is nothing else to say about truth other than what truth predicates do (which is not much).

Like the deflationist, pluralists take the concept of truth to be characterized by certain fundamental principles that capture its functions. This is the approach taken by Lynch, Pedersen & Wright, Edwards, and C. J. G. Wright in Part I of the volume. Unlike the deflationist, however, pluralists think that it takes more than one principle to fully to characterize the concept of truth. They agree with the deflationist that the disquotational schema (or some similar principle) must be part of any adequate characterization, but also deny that such a schema exhausts what can be said and endorse a number of additional principles that inflate truth beyond what the deflationist is willing to accept.

Simon Blackburn (ch. 13) discusses deflationism, pluralism, expressivism, and pragmatism. First he turns to deflationism and pluralism. The pluralist claims that differences in domains track differences in truth. In Blackburn's view, it is clear what the deflationist ought to say in response to this claim: the pluralist is double-counting. Differences in domain or subject matter are simply differences in content. However, once this kind of difference has been taken on board, there is no need to endorse an additional kind of difference in terms of truth. Blackburn thinks that a recent objection against deflationism—due to Bar-On & Simmons (2007)—poses more of a challenge. Bar-On & Simmons argue that the deflationist cannot account for the Fregean thought that to assert is to present as true. Here, 'is true' cannot be disquoted away, contra deflationism. Blackburn considers a pragmatist-deflationist response due to Brandom: assertion is to be accounted for in terms of socio-deontic commitments, or normative commitments incurred by participation in a social practice of reason-giving (e.g., reproach if you have asserted p and not-p turns out to be the case). Even with an account of the truth norm of assertion that is acceptable by deflationary lights, the question remains whether the deflationist can offer a satisfactory account of assertoric content. Here Blackburn returns to the theme of differences in domain or subject matter. His contention is that in order to account for such differences we need 'pragmatist pluralism'—a number of local pragmatisms, each giving a theory of use that is based on our everyday practice and explains why we employ the terms of some specific domain of discourse. In turn, given the focus on explanation and everyday practice and needs, Blackburn thinks the plurality of local pragmatisms is best understood in an expressivist way.

Max Kölbel (ch. 14) continues the discussion of various '-isms', although his attention is restricted to deflationism and inflationism. He sets out to examine two kinds of pluralism about truth. According to the first kind, the truth predicate expresses several distinct concepts. According to the second kind, the truth predicate expresses a single concept, but this concept is the concept of something that can be realized by different properties. Kölbel endorses the first kind of pluralism, regarded as a thesis about the use of the truth predicate in ordinary language. Ordinary language users acknowledge uses of 'true' that support a deflationary truth concept—one that is characterized completely by one T-schema. However, they also acknowledge uses of 'true' that support a substantive truth concept—one characterizable in terms of some T-schema plus a requirement of objectivity (which, as a bare minimum, involves the idea that, if it is correct for anyone to apply the truth concept to p, then it is a mistake for everyone to deny applying the truth concept to p). Kölbel's 'concept pluralism' gives credit to both deflationism and inflationism: each carves out a legitimate truth concept. Interestingly, as Kölbel himself emphasizes, on this view ordinary uses of 'true' come out ambiguous between expressing the deflationary truth concept and its substantive counterpart. In this respect the proposed form of pluralism is different from the pluralist views considered above. On all these other views, there is one truth concept—characterized by a set of inflationary core principles—that is expressed by uses of 'true'.

Kölbel also discusses the prospects of the second form of pluralism (one concept, several properties). He suggests that a stable form of pluralism about truth properties is likely to call for a corresponding pluralism about propositions. More specifically, the pluralist cannot take truth properties to apply solely to structured propositions; rather, she must be willing to accommodate different types of propositions to which the various truth properties can apply.

While Kölbel is moved to endorse a form of pluralism by giving simultaneous credit to inflationism and deflationism, Julian Dodd (ch. 15) credits only the latter. Dodd endorses deflationary monism: truth is one, and it is deflationary. He maintains that this view is the default position, owing to its theoretical simplicity, and that a compelling argument is needed to balk from it to anything more substantive. Moreover, the usual lessons learned from the scope problem fail to shoulder the burden of proof, argues Dodd, simply because the scope problem itself is a psuedo-problem. Like Blackburn's 'double-counting' response, Dodd's claim is prompted by the so-called 'Quine-Sainsbury' objection, which suggests that taxonomical differences among kinds of true statements in different domains can be accounted for simply by doing basic ontology in object-level languages rather than proliferating truth properties:

> There are philosophers who stoutly maintain that 'true' said of logical or mathematical laws and 'true' said of weather predictions or suspects' confessions are two uses of an ambiguous term 'true'. [. . .] What mainly baffles me is the stoutness of their maintenance. What can they possibly count as evidence? Why not view 'true' as unambiguous but very general, and recognize the difference between true logical laws and true confessions as a difference merely between logical laws and confessions? (Quine 1960: 131)
>
> [E]ven if it is one thing for 'this tree is an oak' to be true, another thing for 'burning live cats is cruel' to be true, and yet another for 'Buster Keaton is

funnier than Charlie Chaplin' to be true, this should not lead us to suppose that 'true' is ambiguous; for we get a better explanation of the differences by alluding to the differences between trees, cruelty, and humor. (Sainsbury 1996: 900)

However, rather than treating the objection as being disdainful of ambiguity claims about the predicate 'is true', such as Kölbel's, Dodd suggests that Quine-Sainsbury objection should be generalized to truth properties.

Dodd then turns his attention to criticizing arguments by Wright and Lynch, respectively, that are meant to support a move to pluralism. Wright's motivation for pluralism is that it enables us to understand the sustained discussions between realists and anti-realists in such a way that neither party comes out as being *generally* misguided. Realism gets it right with respect to some domains, anti-realism with respect to others.

Lynch's argument in favor of pluralism is the scope problem: no monist theory plausibly applies across all truth-apt discourse. Against Wright, Dodd argues that the deflationist, too, can make sense of the dispute between realists and anti-realists. Since deflationism is the default position, other things being equal, deflationism trumps pluralism. Against Lynch, Dodd observes that the scope problem is best conceived as an argument against *inflationary* forms of monism, and as such, deflationism still has to be ruled out as a viable option. Lynch tries to do just that by offering two independent considerations against the view: first, deflationism cannot give a truth-conditional account of meaning and content because the view denies that truth does any genuinely explanatory work, and second, deflationism cannot account for the normativity of truth. Dodd argues that both replies miss their mark; in both cases the deflationist has a response ready at hand. Given these responses, deflationism trumps pluralism once more.

Beall (ch. 16) explores what he calls 'deflated truth pluralism', a certain kind of pluralism about truth predicates. A truth predicate T for a language $\mathcal{L}$ is transparent just in case, for any sentence p in $\mathcal{L}$, $T(p)$ and p are intersubstitutable in all (non-opaque) contexts. For Beall, a deflationist is someone who holds both that transparent truth is our fundamental truth predicate, and that it serves only certain logical and expressive functions. Of course, there may be other truth predicates too; but they are all parasitic on the transparent truth predicate in the sense that they are derived from the transparent truth predicate using only logical resources.

Subsequently, one way to motivate the need for several truth predicates is the search for an adequate solution to the Liar Paradox and other semantic paradoxes. Beall outlines a response to the paradoxes that involves a transparent truth predicate, but also at least one non-transparent predicate. The response carries a commitment to truth pluralism because there are several truth predicates, each of which designates something different, and to deflated truth pluralism because the transparent truth predicate is taken as fundamental and the non-transparent predicates as derived through reliance on logical resources only. Like Hinzen's internalist deliberations on methodological naturalism about truth and the possibility of pluralism, Beall's contribution adds variety to the pluralist landscape: not only are there inflationary versions of pluralism— one might also be a deflationary pluralist. Furthermore, Beall's paper provides a response to Dodd's argument that pluralism is always trumped by deflationism. Again, according to Dodd, deflationary monism is the default position; however, if Beall is correct, perhaps the best way to deal with the paradoxes is to endorse a form of deflationary *pluralism*. So, if a solution to the semantic paradoxes is thought to be a pressing task (as Beall and many others would have it), this would seem to support a move away from deflationary monism.

Aaron Cotnoir (ch. 17) notes that the paradoxes have been largely neglected in the literature on pluralism, and like Beall, urges pluralists to start paying attention to them because they are as much a problem for pluralists as they are for anyone else. Indeed, the paradoxes might even serve as a hard constraint on the adequacy of candidate versions of pluralism. Cotnoir suggests that several versions of pluralism about truth predication are subject to paradox on fairly minimal assumptions, and so should be abandoned or considerably modified. Consider first any moderate form of (predicate) pluralism according to which there is a truth predicate T_U that applies across all truth-apt discourse, in addition to a range of domain-specific truth predicates $T_1, \ldots, T_n$, and then suppose that T_U satisfies the T-schema. This will be the case on the views of prominent pluralists like Wright and Lynch, and perhaps Beall. Then it is straightforward to derive a paradox. Suppose that the pluralist rejects T_U and endorses only the domain-specific truth predicates $T_1, \ldots, T_n$ (but thinks that there are infinitely many such properties, i.e., that there is some T_i for every $i \in \omega$). Does this free her view from paradox? Not necessarily. Many pluralists would grant that the T-schema holds for the domain-specific properties $F_1, \ldots, F_n$. However, the universal truth predicate T_U is definable in terms of $T_1, \ldots, T_n$ and disjunction (any sentence p is T_U just in case it is T_1 or ... or T_n), and if the T-schema holds for each of $T_1, \ldots, T_n$, it holds for T_U too. But that means that paradox has returned. Cotnoir sees no need for the pluralist to give up on the T-schema for any truth predicate or to adopt a non-classical logic in order to deal with the paradoxes. Instead Cotnoir suggests rejecting infinite disjunction, which is needed to obtain T_U from the infinitely many domain-specific properties $F_1, \ldots, F_n$.

5. Concluding remarks

The contributions to Part I of the volume raise a range of issues internal to the pluralist camp. In particular, how are we to understand the idea of alethic potency that is so fundamental to pluralism? Part II of the volume explores the issue whether the unity of truth and its wide range of applicability can be accommodated by the correspondence theory, a traditionally very prominent view in the truth debate. Part III connects pluralism with deflationism and paradox.

Our goal in this introduction has been to provide an overview of the volume. The overview no doubt betrays the richness and level of detail of each contribution. Even so, our hope is to have said enough to convince the reader that the present volume makes for a valuable contribution to the truth literature—that, indeed, truth pluralism is interesting in its own right, but likewise connects with several other views and fundamental themes or issues in significant ways. Much work remains to be done, of course, but the present volume should make for a good start.

References

Bar-On, D. & Simmons, K. (2007). The use of force against deflationism: assertion and truth. In D. Greimann & G. Siegwart (eds.), *Truth and Speech Act: Studies in Philosophy of Language* (61–89). London: Routledge.

Blackburn, S. (1998). Wittgenstein, Wright, Rorty and minimalism. *Mind* 107: 157–181.

Cotnoir, A. 2009. Generic truth and mixed conjunctions: some alternatives. *Analysis* 69: 473–479.

Cotnoir, A. (forthcoming). Validity for strong pluralists. *Philosophy and Phenomenological Research*.

Dorsey, D. (2006). A coherence theory of truth in ethics. *Philosophical Studies* 117: 493–523.

Dorsey, D. (2010). Truth and error in morality. In C. D. Wright & N. J. L. L. Pedersen (eds.), *New Waves in Truth* (235–248). New York: Palgrave Macmillan.

Edwards, D. (2008). How to solve the problem of mixed conjunctions. *Analysis* 68: 143–149.

Edwards, D. (2009). Truth-conditions and the nature of truth: re-solving mixed conjunctions. *Analysis* 69: 684–688.

Edwards, D. (2011). Simplifying alethic pluralism. *Southern Journal of Philosophy* 49: 28–48.

Edwards, D. (2012). Alethic versus deflationary functionalism. *International Journal of Philosophical Studies* 20: 115–124.

Horton, M. & T. Poston. (2012). Functionalism about truth and the metaphysics of reduction. *Acta Analytica* 27: 13–27.

Jackson, F. (1994). Realism, truth, and truth-aptness. *Philosophical Books* 35: 162–169.

Kölbel, M. (2008). 'True' as ambiguous. *Philosophy and Phenomenological Research* 77: 359–384.

Lynch, M. P. (1998). *Truth in Context*. Cambridge, MA: MIT Press.

Lynch, M. P. (2000). Alethic pluralism and the functionalist theory of truth. *Acta Analytica* 15: 195–204.

Lynch, M. P. (2004). Truth and multiple realizability. *Australasian Journal of Philosophy* 82: 384–408.

Lynch, M. P. (2005a). Functionalism and our folk theory of truth: reply to Cory Wright. *Synthese* 145: 29–43.

Lynch, M. P. (2005b). Précis to *True to Life,* and replies to commentators. *Philosophical Books* 46: 289–291, 331–342.

Lynch, M. P. (2006). ReWrighting pluralism. *Monist* 89: 63–84.

Lynch, M. P. (2009). *Truth as One and Many*. Oxford: Oxford University Press.

Lynch, M. P. (2012). The many faces of truth: a response to some critics. *International Journal of Philosophical Studies* 20:255–269.

Nulty, T. J. (2010). The metaphysics of mixed inferences: problems with functionalist accounts of alethic pluralism. *Metaphysica* 11: 153–162.

Patterson, D. (2010). Truth as conceptually primitive. In C. D. Wright & N. J. L. L. Pedersen (eds.), *New Waves in Truth* (13–29). New York: Palgrave Macmillan.

Pedersen, N. J. L. L. (2006). What can the problem of mixed inferences teach us about alethic pluralism? *Monist* 89: 103–117.

Pedersen, N. J. L. L. (2010). Stabilizing alethic pluralism. *Philosophical Quarterly* 60: 92–108.

Pettit, P. (1996). Realism and truth: a comment on Crispin Wright's *Truth and Objectivity. Philosophy and Phenomenological Research* 56: 883–890.

Quine, W. v O. (1960). *Word and Object*. Cambridge, MA: MIT Press.

Sainsbury, M. (1996). Crispin Wright: *Truth and Objectivity. Philosophy and Phenomenological Research* 56: 899–904.

Shapiro, S. (2009). Review of Michael P. Lynch, *Truth as One and Many. Notre Dame Philosophical Reviews*. URL = http://ndpr.nd.edu/news/24169/?id=17487.

Shapiro, S. (2011). Truth, function, and paradox. *Analysis* 71: 38–44.

Sher, G. (1998). On the possibility of a substantive theory of truth. *Synthese* 117: 133–172.

Sher, G. (2004). In search of a substantive theory of truth. *Journal of Philosophy* 101: 5–36.

Sher, G. (2005). Functional pluralism. *Philosophical Books* 46: 311–330.

Sher, G. & C. D. Wright. (2007). Truth as a normative modality of cognitive acts. In D. Griemann & G. Siegwart (eds.), *Truth and Speech Acts: Studies in the Philosophy of Language* (525–574). New York: Routledge.

Tappolet, C. (1997). Mixed inferences: a problem for pluralism about truth predicates. *Analysis* 57: 209–210.

Tappolet, C. (2000). Truth pluralism and many-valued logics: a reply to Beall. *Philosophical Quarterly* 50: 382–385.

Tappolet, C. (2010). Review of Michael P. Lynch, *Truth as One and Many. Mind* 119: 1193–1198.

Williamson, T. (1994). A critical study of *Truth and Objectivity. International Journal of Philosophical Studies* 30: 130–144.

Wright, C. D. (2005). On the functionalization of pluralist approaches to truth. *Synthese* 145: 1–28.

Wright, C. D. (2010). Truth, Ramsification, and the pluralist's revenge. *Australasian Journal of Philosophy* 88: 265–283.

Wright, C. D. (2012). Is pluralism inherently unstable? *Philosophical Studies* 159: 89–105.

Wright, C. D., I. van Rooij, & T. Wareham (2012). Truth pluralism and the problem of domain individuation. Unpublished manuscript.

Wright, C. J. G. (1992). *Truth and Objectivity*. Cambridge, MA: Harvard University Press.

Wright, C. J. G. (1994a). Response to Jackson. *Philosophical Books* 35: 169–175.

Wright, C. J. G. (1994b). Realism, pure and simple? *International Journal of Philosophical Studies* 30: 147–161.

Wright, C. J. G. (1996). Précis to *Truth and Objectivity*, and response to commentators. *Philosophy and Phenomenological Research* 56: 863–868, 911–941.

Wright, C. J. G. (1998a). Truth: a traditional debate reviewed. *Canadian Journal of Philosophy (suppl.)* 24: 31–74.

Wright, C. J. G. (1998b). Comrades against quietism: reply to Simon Blackburn on *Truth and Objectivity*. *Mind* 107: 183–203.

Wright, C. J. G. (2001). Minimalism, deflationism, pragmatism, pluralism. In M. P. Lynch (ed.), *The Nature of Truth: Classical and Contemporary Readings* (751–787). Cambridge, MA: MIT Press.

{ PART I }

Varieties of Pluralism

{ 2 }

Three Questions for Truth Pluralism
Michael P. Lynch

1. Three questions

Truth pluralism, as I understand it, is a *metaphysical* theory about the nature of truth. It is therefore concerned with that in virtue of which propositions are true, when they are lucky enough to be true. Monists hold that there is only one property of propositions in virtue of which they are true. Deflationists can be understood as denying that there is any such property (or any interesting property). In contrast, the pluralist seeks to widen the playing field.[1] She endorses

> *Pluralism*: there is more than one property of propositions in virtue of which propositions (that have that property) are true.

While there are, as we'll see, a range of pluralist positions on truth, the basic idea behind most versions is that while some propositions are true in virtue of say, corresponding to reality, others may be true by virtue of possessing some epistemic property, such as:

> *Superwarrant*: p is superwarranted just when believing p is warranted at some stage of inquiry and would remain warranted without defeat at every successive stage of inquiry.[2]

One basic motivation for pluralism—not the only motivation, but an important one—is that it has certain theoretical benefits that its rivals lack. Monist theories have always seen truth as an explanatorily rich notion: understanding the nature of truth helps us understand the nature of knowledge, content, and

---

[1] Crispin Wright is the most important advocate of pluralism. His original statement is Wright (1992); some important revisions to his view were made in his 2001 essay: there, as here, the position is presented in terms of properties.

[2] This notion is obviously derivative of Crispin Wright's notion of superassertbility. For a related epistemic notion of truth, see Putnam (1981).

the norms of thought. But traditional theories face counterexamples, and counterexamples of a particular form. Such theories work well enough as accounts of how some propositions are true, but fail with regard to others. The most plausible correspondence theories, for example, are plausible when applied to propositions about the color of snow, but generate problems when applied to normative and mathematical propositions.[3] Epistemic theories—whether they are unpacked in terms of superwarrant or coherence—seem on firmer ground when applied to normative propositions, but less plausible when applied to propositions about middle-sized dry goods.

These patterns of failure have motivated many philosophers who think about truth for a living to pursue deflationism. The basic deflationary insight is that we can know all we need to know about truth by looking at its function. And that function, says the deflationist, is really very simple: our concept of truth doesn't work to pick out an interesting property of propositions, it simply serves as an expressive device: it allows us to overcome our biological limitations and generalize over infinite strings of propositions. But as most deflationists will acknowledge, they pay a price for this simple account of truth: they remove truth from our explanatory resources. We can no longer use it to help explain content, or meaning, or the norms of thought.[4]

Prima facie, the pluralist seems poised to take advantage of the other approaches' shortcomings. She claims that different propositions can be true by virtue of distinct properties. So, like the traditionalist, the pluralist can seemingly allow, if she wishes, that truth can have explanatory value. We might even be able to appeal to the different kinds of truth to explain the different kinds of content our propositional attitudes enjoy.[5] And as I will argue below, pluralism—seen in its best light—also shares a key commitment with deflationism: the idea that the key to truth's nature is through its function.

Naturally, pluralism's theoretical advantages (and its costs) are best appreciated after we get a clear sense of the view itself. Indeed, as with any new view, making sense of it is half the battle. So in this essay, I aim to clarify pluralism by concentrating on three questions any pluralist theory of truth must answer:

- How do we identify the properties in virtue of which propositions are true?
- How are those properties related to truth?
- What determines which of these properties a given proposition must have in order to be true?

---

[3] By a 'plausible' correspondence theory of truth I mean a correspondence theory that goes beyond simply affirming the correspondence, or Objectivity, platitude about truth and explains this platitude by appeal to a theory of correspondence, or what in contemporary terms is called 'representation'. See Wittgenstein (1922) and Russell (1912/2001). See also Lynch (2009a).

[4] For explicit acknowledgments of this sort, see Horwich (1990/1998) and Williams (2001).

[5] See Lynch (2009a) for just such an attempt.

Clearly, these aren't just questions for pluralists. Any substantive view of truth must face them. Nor are they the only questions facing pluralists. Yet they are certainly among the most basic. Consequently, it pays for anyone sympathetic to the view to give these questions serious attention. But my aim will not be solely clarificatory. I will make a case for a specific answer to each, building on some of the views I defend in *Truth as One and Many* (hereafter *TOM*).

2. What makes a theory a theory of truth?

Alethic pluralism is a metaphysical view of truth. Like any other metaphysics of truth, it is distinct from views about the concept of truth, or the meaning of the truth predicate, and again from an account of how we fix that predicate's reference. Nonetheless, it is clear that something needs to be said about an issue that, at the very least, is in the neighborhood of these other questions. Any non-deflationary view of truth takes it that there is some property F of true propositions in virtue of which they are true. Some of those views will take it that F *is* truth. Others may hold that truth supervenes on F. But whichever way we end up going on that question, we will need to be given some reason for thinking that F has—to put it bluntly—anything to do with truth. And that means we need some way of narrowing down the candidates for F—one that rules out obvious nonstarters.

As it turns out, this is not a question that only the pluralist must answer. Any view of truth must say something about what would qualify as a property in virtue of which propositions are true. This is because our first question is really just an instance of a more general issue. What makes a given metaphysical theory of truth a theory of *truth,* rather than a theory of some other thing?

In doing metaphysics, we are looking for real essences—we seek to understand the nature of causation, identity, mind. Yet in order to search for something, you must already know something about it—otherwise you won't know if you have found it. So in searching for the real essence of something, we must already have some beliefs about it. Call these beliefs its nominal essence. The nominal essence of something, in the sense I intend here, is the set of largely tacit beliefs we folk have about it. By appealing to those folk beliefs, or truisms, we won't learn *everything* about the object or property in which we are interested. And our later discoveries may force us to revise our preconceptions of it. But however these questions play out, keeping one eye on our folk beliefs about the thing about which we are curious will hopefully tell us whether our subsequent theories of its nature address the topic we were concerned with when our theorizing began.[6]

---

[6] The strategy is, of course, familiar. See Jackson (1998) and Wright (1992).

What applies in metaphysics generally applies to the metaphysics of truth. This suggests a simple answer to our question. A theory is about truth as opposed to something else if it incorporates most of what I will call the 'core truisms' about truth—the nominal essence of truth. So what are these? Well, one obvious contender is the truism celebrated by correspondence theories of truth: the idea that truth is objective. To speak truly is to 'say of what is, that it is', as Aristotle said.[7] And since what we say, at least when we are sincere, is an expression of what we believe or judge, a parallel truism holds about true propositions we believe. That is,

> *Objectivity*: True propositions are those that when we believe them, things are as we believe them to be.[8]

Two more obvious contenders are platitudes celebrated by epistemic theories of truth such as classical pragmatist theories:

> *End of Inquiry*: True propositions are those we should aim to believe when engaging in inquiry.
>
> *Norm of Belief*: True propositions are those that are correct to believe.

There are doubtless many other obvious and fundamental platitudes about truth, but the historical importance of these three suggests they are among the most central. They connect truth to inquiry, belief, and objective being—how things are. It is difficult to deny that truth has these relations in the platitudinous sense identified by the truisms. We would find it puzzling, to say the least, if someone claimed to believe truly that roses are red but denied that this is how things are. We would ask for an explanation, and if none was forthcoming, we would suspect that that they mean something different by 'believing truly' than what we mean. Likewise, with *End of Inquiry*: if you don't think that truth is, other things being equal, what we are trying to get at when asking questions, then you are probably using 'truth' to talk about something other than what the rest of us use that word to talk about.

Call such truisms 'core truisms'. Core truisms about truth cannot be denied without significant theoretical consequence and loss of plausibility. If you do deny any one of them, you must be prepared to explain how this can be so in

---

[7] *Metaphysics* Γ. 7.27, (1993).

[8] Together with some further and reasonably obvious assumptions, *Objectivity* underwrites further derivative principles which are typically highlighted by philosophers. One related principle is that when, for example, I believe that roses are red, things are as I believe them to be just when roses are red. That is,

With respect to the belief p, things are as they are believed to be if, and only if, p.

With this point in hand, we can derive, together with the idea that it is the proposition which is believed that is primarily true or false, instances of the equivalence schema

ES: The proposition p is true if and only if p.

the face of intuitive opposition. And denying *many or all* would mean that, at the very least, other users of the concept would be justified in taking you to be changing the subject.[9]

Two points to allay misunderstanding. First, in saying that these principles are truisms, I don't mean that they are consciously endorsed by all the folk. They are the sorts of principles we believe tacitly. And what someone tacitly believes is more often revealed in action than in verbal reports. So the fact that, for example, many college freshman would appear to deny *Objectivity* by saying that 'what is true for me might not be true for you' doesn't mean that they think that believing makes it so. Most freshmen, I think, are not going to *act* consistently with the idea that belief is sufficient for truth. Second, the fact that there is disagreement among experts about which are the *core* truisms doesn't imply that there are no such truisms, or that we don't tacitly believe some rather than others. Nobody ever said it would be easy to specify the content of our tacit beliefs about matters as complicated as truth.

On the view I am suggesting, then, what makes a theory about truth rather than something else is that it incorporates the core truisms, in the sense of either including them among the principles of the theory or including principles that directly entail them. And we'll count it as a *theory* of truth (as opposed to just a chat about it, say) just when it *explains* those truisms. And an obvious way to do that is to show why they are true by pointing to some property or properties that all true propositions have that results in those propositions satisfying the truisms. Such a property will have the features described by the core truisms. Features of this sort could obviously be called core features. But in the present case we might as well call them the 'truish features'.

3. A functional analysis

Our first question for a pluralist theory of truth was: how do we identify the properties in virtue of which propositions are true? We now have an answer. A property determines that a proposition is true when it has the truish features. That is:

> *Truish*: A property determines that propositions are true just when it is such that propositions that have it are objective, correct to believe, and those we should aim to believe in inquiry.

The truish features are relational; they specify that truth has a role in a structure of interrelated properties, revealed by the folk truisms—what we called its nominal essence. There may be other features that are part of truth's nominal

---

[9] For an earlier, and somewhat different, discussion of truisms, see the exchange between myself and C. D. Wright (Lynch 2005; Wright 2005).

essence, of course, features that—while possibly going beyond the core—also help to demarcate truth in a structure of relations. These include relations to assertion, negation, and logical consequence. But at its heart, that structure connects truth with belief, inquiry, and objective being.

This, in effect, is the basic insight and starting point of what I've elsewhere called the functionalist theory of truth. The guiding idea of that view is that we think of the core truisms as revealing what truth does—its functional role. That is,

(F) ($\forall x$) x is true if, and only if, x has a property that plays the truth-role.

In effect, our discussion above tells us what constitutes playing the truth-role. A property plays the truth role when it has the truish features. Moreover, this idea—the idea that true propositions have a property that has the truish features (or we can now say: 'plays the truth-role')—is a consequence of what it takes for a theory to *even count* as a theory of truth. These features tell us what a property *must* be like to play the truth-role.[10] Thus while we initially appealed to the truish features only to help *identify* that property or properties that plays the truth-role, it seems warranted to go further and take those truish features as defining that role. This means treating the truish features as features of truth's nominal essence that are conceptually essential—essential by way of the very concept of truth.[11]

Understood in this way, our functional understanding of truth is presupposed in our grasp of the concept.[12] Not surprisingly, then, the major metaphysical theories of truth's nature are perfectly consistent with it. Take a standard

---

[10] As just noted, there will be other features, and possibly other core features, that will help us demarcate the truth-role. Specifying the extent and limits of these features of truth, and determining which are more centrally weighted than others, is an important further project for the alethic functionalist, just as it is for functionalists in the philosophy of mind. But however those questions are decided, the basic functionalist idea is that truth's conceptually essential features jointly define the truth-role. See Lynch (2009a, ch. 1) for more discussion.

[11] Obviously, not every essential feature of a property is conceptually essential. Being identical to itself and being distinct from the number 1 are both features of truth, for example. But neither serves to identify truth (they don't distinguish truth from other properties) and certainly neither is a conceptual truth about *truth*. Compare David's remarks (2013).

[12] In a recent article, C. D. Wright (2010) argues that functionalist views face a problem of epistemic circularity. Wright has in mind versions of the view that explicitly employ Ramsification techniques for making an implicit definition of truth (see Lynch 2001, 2004b). Such techniques are useful, but as our discussion illustrates, they are not necessary to make the functionalist's basic point. Nonetheless, Wright may suspect his worry is more general; he writes: 'But any implicit definition proceeds on the basis of explicit decisions that the principles constitutive of [the relevant Ramsey sentence] are themselves true. Hence the circularity. In turn, making any explicit decisions that they are true requires already knowing in advance what truth is. Hence the epistemic circularity" (Wright 2010: 272). This is a general problem—but it is, I would suggest, too general to be just a problem for the pluralist. Any attempt to define—or even fix the reference of—'true' by appeal to what I've called 'truisms' will face such a problem. But then the problem is one for any view.

monist theory such as the correspondence theory of truth. Understood from a functional perspective, this is the view that there is only one property that has the truish features and that therefore plays the truth-role: the correspondence property. Even deflationist theories can be understood in this way. Indeed, deflationists are obviously functionalists: they tell us that truth's nature is exhausted by its function, which by their account is quite thin: truth functions as an expressive device, and that is all. Consequently, on their view, truth does have a functional role, and that role, insofar as it is played by any property at all, is played by the property of being an expressive device.

So the functionalist theory itself is not a metaphysical theory of the nature of truth. It doesn't tell us what truth is. But it does give us a way of answering a question that any metaphysics of truth must answer, and a question that is particularly important for pluralism. It tells us how to identify the properties that make judgments true. They are the properties that they play the truth-role or have the truish features.

Indeed, it is difficult to see what other sort of answer a pluralist *can* give to our question. Pluralism is the view that there is more than one property, $F_1, \ldots, F_n$, in virtue of which propositions are true. Either $F_1, \ldots, F_n$ possess the truish features or they do not. If they do, then they all have something in common: they all satisfy the truisms—which is to say that they all fall under the same (functional) description. If they do not, then, for reasons adduced above, we should not regard the position as a theory of *truth* at all. It is the view, instead, that the word 'true' picks out various properties, none of which have anything truish in common. This would, in effect, be a form of eliminativism about truth, not pluralism.

A similar dilemma confronts anyone who takes 'true' to be straightforwardly ambiguous like the word 'bank'—that is, as a word with more than one meaning and referent. Either the properties referred to by the predicate bear the nominal essence of truth in common, or they don't. If they do, then why not take that shared nominal essence as the common meaning of 'true'? If they don't, then it is misleading to say that 'there is more than one way to be true'. There is not more than one way to be a bank. Riverbanks and the Bank of America are not two ways of being the same thing. There are simply different meanings to the word. Analogously with an ambiguity view about 'true'. What we believed was in common between the different uses has, on this view, been eliminated.[13]

So we now have a way for the pluralist to identify those properties in virtue of which propositions are true. But we still need address our second question: to say what truth is—and how it is related to those properties that determine it. Here the functionalist faces some options.

---

[13] For further problems with such a view, see Lynch (2009a), Pedersen (2006), and Tappolet (1997).

4. The nature of truth: four initial options

If the above remarks are right, pluralists must be functionalists about the concept of truth, or at least about how we identify the referent(s) of that concept. But that still leaves open our second question, which is how to relate the various properties pluralists are pluralists about to the property of truth itself. Here are four options for the pluralist cum functionalist:

Truth is the realizer property. On this view, there is a single functional concept of truth, but it picks out different properties when ascribed to different kinds of propositions.[14] This is the version of pluralism defended by C. J. G. Wright (2001). The concept acts as a nonrigid definite description. In this way, 'true' is like 'the color of the sky at noon'. The latter phrase expresses a single uniform concept, but it denotes different properties in different environmental contexts. Analogously, 'true' expresses a single description (as given by *Truish* above) but that description applies (or can apply) to distinct properties. Hence on this view, we might say that truth *just is* whatever property plays the truth-role for a given kind of proposition.

Realizer functionalism is reductive in nature, and thus akin to other reductive functionalisms, such as those championed by Lewis (1980) and Kim (1998) with regard to psychological properties. On this sort of view, there is no fact about whether, for example, *x* is in pain over and above whether *x* has some physical property P, and so 'there is no need to think of [pain] itself as a property in its own right' (Kim 1998: 104). Realizer functionalism is parallel: there is no fact of the matter whether a proposition is true over and above whether it has some lower-level property like superwarrant or correspondence. Consequently, 'truth' does not name a property shared by all truths.

Realizer functionalism has its attractions, but it faces some by-now familiar problems. One of the most discussed concerns the truth of 'mixed' compound propositions.[15] Consider the proposition

(*Water*) Waterboarding is painful and waterboarding is wrong.

Intuitively, the conjuncts of this proposition are of distinct kinds. One is normative, the other not. So according to realizer functionalism, the truth concept expresses one property when ascribed to one conjunct (some correspondence property, say) and another property (superwarrant, say) when ascribed to the other. But if so, what property does it pick out when ascribed to (*Water*) as a whole?

This is a significant problem, and not just for realizer functionalism, as we'll see below. But it is particularly damning for any view, like realizer

---

[14] A lengthier discussion of Wright's position can be found in Lynch (2006).
[15] A sampling of the literature, here, includes Williamson (1994), Tappolet (2000), Pedersen (2006), Edwards (2008, 2009), and Cotnoir (2009).

functionalism, which denies that there is a 'global' truth property—a property expressed by the truth concept that applies across the board to propositions of every type. Indeed, as a number of authors have argued, it seems that any satisfactory resolution of the problem will require just such a property (Tappolet 1997; Lynch 2006; Pedersen 2010; Cotnoir 2009).

A second problem for realizer functionalism is that it undermines one of the motivations for adopting pluralism in the first place. As we just noted, the analogous position in the philosophy of mind implies that pain is not a real psychological kind. There is nothing in common, in other words, between the states we describe as pain-states in dogs and the states we describe as pain-states in humans. Consequently, the view gives up the ability to appeal to pain as such in general psychological explanation. And this is a loss. For we do find it useful and informative to talk about pain as such in order to explain other things of psychological interest, such as fear or anger. A similar loss occurs with realizer functionalism about truth. It implies that true propositions do not form a real kind. The only property shared by all and only true propositions is one that is not, by the lights of the theory itself, ascribed by our use of 'true' or denoted by 'truth'. Consequently, there is no property we ascribe by 'true' that can be appealed to in order to explain certain general facts. One such general fact, for example, we might wish to explain is:

> *Unity*: beliefs with radically distinct kinds of content are equally apt for one kind of normative assessment.

We might put this by saying that they are open to being assessed as correct or incorrect in the same sort of way. What explains this? The simple explanation is that beliefs are correct when they have the property *truth*. Of course, to those who already believe that truth as such has no general explanatory role to play—who believe that it does not figure in explaining anything else of interest such as belief, or content, or meaning—this will not be troubling. But then they will not have needed realizer functionalism to reach that conclusion. But to those who see truth as at least a potentially valuable explanatory resource, realizer functionalism remains dissatisfying.

Truth is the role property. This view (Lynch 2001, 2004b, 2006) attempts to avoid the above problems by identifying truth with what is sometimes called the 'role' property: or the property of having a property that plays the truth-role. This allows one to say that there is a single property of truth. Hence there is no barrier to *Unity*: any proposition is correct just when true—that is, just when it has the property of having a property that plays the truth-role.

But this position is ultimately unsatisfying. First, like its cousin 'realizer functionalism', it says nothing about mixed conjunctions other than they are true when they have the property of having a property that plays the truth-role. But it doesn't tell us what property a mixed conjunction has that plays the truth-role.

Second, the property of having a property that plays the truth-role does not obviously have the truish features that define truth's functional role. Is the property of having a property that plays the truth-role the property that we aim our beliefs to have in inquiry? It doesn't look like it.

Truth is a disjunctive property. A third option is to take the functional concept of truth to denote a single disjunctive property.[16] Suppose, for simplicity's sake, that some propositions are true when superwarranted and all other propositions are true when they represent things as they are. If so, then we might say that our functional description of truth just picks out a property defined like this:

> A proposition is true$_D$ just when it is either superwarranted or represents things are they are.

If we can accept that a proposition is correct just when it is true$_{D,}$—when it is either superwarranted or representing, this view allows us to grant the simple explanation of *Unity*. But it too seems to founder on mixed conjunctions like *Water* above. For again the question is what makes the conjunction *itself true*. And the conjunction itself is surely not true because it has the property of, say, being either superwarranted or representing the facts. For that to be the case, *Water* must have one of the disjunct properties; but it is not clear what property that would be. The proposition that waterboarding is painful might represent some fact (or object/property pair). It is far from clear that the proposition that waterboarding is painful and waterboarding is wrong itself represents any fact.

Truth is a disquotational property. A final possibility is that truth itself is a merely disquotational property: that is, the property of being an expressive device.[17] This would the result if we took it that the function of truth was as thin as the deflationists typically take it to be. On this view, the concept of truth would be the concept of the property whose only feature is that it is *a device for generalization via disquotation*. There is nothing else to say about truth itself other than that.

The problem with this view becomes apparent once we remember it is to be combined with the metaphysics of pluralism. The combined view is odd, to say the least: truth itself is a disquotational property. If a proposition p has that property, you can infer p, and if p, you can infer it has that property. But whether a proposition has that property is determined by whether it has some more substantive property, like correspondence. But *why* would a proposition's having the disquotational property depend on its having some other,

---

[16] See Pedersen (2010) for discussion of versions of this alternative. In a forthcoming paper, he suggests that there are properties specific to the various compounds in virtue of which they can possess the disjunctive property. This leads, as he acknowledges, to a multiplication of truth determining properties.

[17] A variant is tentatively suggested by Cotnoir (2009).

presumably non-disquotational, property? Moreover, the view would rule out appealing to truth itself to explain phenomena like *Unity* above. So like the realizer view, it is not clear that it would have virtues over and above those of deflationism simpliciter.

5. Truth as immanent

Recall where we are: I've said that pluralists should be—indeed, have to be-functionalists. The properties in virtue of which propositions are true are those that play the truth-role. What constitutes a property playing that role is its having the truish features. But our second question is still outstanding: what do these properties have to do with truth?

In order to answer this question, the pluralist cum functionalist needs two things. She needs an account of what functionalists sometimes call 'realization' and she needs an account of the property truth itself.

I think we can meet both demands at once. Start with the thought that properties can have their features essentially or accidentally. A functional property is defined by its functional role, which, I've suggested, is best seen as the sum of those relational features implicit in the nominal essence of the property. Those features can therefore be thought to be essential to it. Thus, for the functionalist, the natural suggestion is to *equate* the property of truth with the property *that has the truish features essentially* or that plays the truth-role *as such*. It is the property that is, necessarily, possessed by believed contents just when things are as they are believed to be; possessed by propositions believed at the end of inquiry and that makes propositions correct to believe.

This gives us a straightforward account of what truth is. Yet once we understand truth this way, we can go on to say that the property can be *immanent* in other properties.[18] An immanent property is a property that can be manifested by other properties. M manifests an immanent property F just when it is a priori that F's conceptually essential features are a subset of M's features. Again, a conceptually essential feature of F is an essential feature of F that (a) is part of the nominal essence of F; (b) holds as a matter of conceptual necessity; and so, (c) helps to distinguish F from other properties. Since every property's conceptually essential features are a subset of its own features, every property manifests itself. So immanence, like identity, is reflexive. But unlike identity, it is nonsymmetric. Where M and F are distinct—individuated by nonidentical sets of conceptually essential features and relations—and F is immanent in M, M is not immanent in F. Intuitively put, where F is immanent in M, it will be the case that *part of being M is being F*.

---

[18] Why talk of manifestation and immanence rather than realization? To avoid confusion; 'realization' is generally understood by philosophers of mind to be an a posteriori, nonrational relationship.

Applied to truth, the initial thought is this: for some propositions, truth is manifested by, or immanent in, their correspondence to various bits of reality. Part of what is for those propositions to correspond is for them to be true. Just as the psychological functionalist will claim that which physical property *realizes* pain in a given organism is determined by facts about the organism, the alethic functionalist will claim that which property *manifests* truth for a particular proposition will depend on facts about that proposition. Two kinds of facts are clearly relevant. The first is what the proposition is about. The second is the proposition's logical structure.

This second point is not surprising. That a proposition's logical structure should help to determine how it is true is familiar from traditional correspondence views, according to which the only sort of propositions that correspond to facts are atomic. Similarly, which property manifests truth for a proposition depends on whether it is atomic or not. How we understand this, however, depends on how we understand the first sort of fact.

In *TOM*, I suggested that pluralists hold that truth for atomics is always manifested relative to what I called a domain of inquiry. As I defined it, a propositional domain is a subject-matter: mathematics and ethics are two examples. How do we know whether a proposition is about one subject rather than another? How else? By looking at the objects and properties that the concepts that compose that proposition are about.

I still take this to be fairly straightforward. Almost any philosopher will think that there are different kinds of content and will take it for granted that we believe all sorts of propositions: propositions about ethics, about mathematics, about the sundries of everyday life. No one, presumably, will deny that these propositions concern not just different subjects, but *fundamentally* different subjects. And *any* philosopher who wishes to claim that we should treat propositions about these subject matters differently—for example, by saying that they aren't representational, or are all false—must have a way of distinguishing propositions of different kinds from one another. Nothing about pluralism distinguishes it in this regard.

Nonetheless, talk of 'domains', does suggest, if it does not imply, that subject matters come in natural kinds, and that as a result, we can sort them into these kinds with little difficulty. That is implausible. We can admit, as is obvious, that beliefs have different kinds of content, but we needn't say that the propositions that are those contents divide into natural or rigid kinds.

So why the use of the term 'domain'? One reason was this. There are doubtless propositions that correspond but are not superwarranted. For example, consider

(*Star*) At this very moment, the number of stars in the universe is odd.

Presumably, either this proposition or its negation is true. But neither is superwarranted. No matter how many stages of inquiry we go through, we are never going to possess warrant for or against *Star*. Yet presumably there either are or are not an odd number of stars in the universe at this moment.

If both correspondence and superwarrant manifest truth—play the truth-role—for *Star* then we have a problem. Assume that falsity is truth of negation. Assume that *Star* is not superwarranted, but that it does correspond with reality. Conclusion: it is both true and false. In *TOM*, I solved this by drawing a page from the philosophy of mind. Just as a given neural property only realizes pain relative for a given organism, so a given semantic property like correspondence only realizes truth for a domain. But this was more theory than I needed. All I really needed to say was this: properties like correspondence manifest truth for some propositions and not others, *and* only one property of a proposition manifests truth for that proposition.[19]

Let's unpack this. We can say that where M is a property distinct from truth,

> If p is an atomic proposition, then: p is true if and only if it has the property M that manifests truth for p.

And

> If p is atomic and p is M, then: M manifests truth for p, if and only if it is a priori that the truish features are *a proper subset* of M's features.

So an atomic proposition is true when it has the distinct *further* property that manifests truth *for* p.[20] Not being true consists in lacking that property, either because there is no property that manifests truth, in which case the content in question is neither true nor false, or because there is such a property, but the proposition in question fails to have it, in which case it is false.

But if it is not the facts about the domain to which a proposition belongs that determine which property manifests truth for a proposition, what does? The very same facts as before. Think about it this way. No matter what your theory of truth might be, the question of what makes a particular proposition true (or even truth-apt) will depend on the facts about that proposition. What is it about? What concepts does it employ and so on? These are the questions we will ask when confronting this issue. It would be curious if our answers didn't sort themselves into groups, since, as I've already noted, it is obvious that propositions do come in at least rough kinds—kinds that are individuated by differences in the sorts of properties and objects that the various sorts of propositions are about.

---

[19] A number of commentators have suggested this point to me, including, most recently, David (2013).

[20] David (2013) complains that I must relativize playing the truth-role, not manifestation. But playing the truth-role means having the truish features, and properties that have those features manifest truth. It is manifestation that is in the metaphysical driver's seat.

If this is right, there is no need for the pluralist to sort (atomic) propositions into strict domains. She takes each proposition as it comes, finding that, in fact, they come in groups, in bunches, in mobs.[21]

6. Plain truth

Our third question concerns what determines which property manifests truth for any given proposition. We have an answer now for atomic propositions. But what about logically complex propositions? In particular, if more than one property plays the truth-role, then what plays it for compound propositions like two and two is four and murder is wrong? A significant benefit of understanding truth as an immanent property is that that answer drops right out of the metaphysics. The functionalist can say that compounds, mixed or not, are *plainly* true. Nothing manifests their truth other than truth; so nothing plays the truth-role other than truth.

The picture here is familiar from older correspondence theories of truth, according to which atomic propositions like grass is green were thought to correspond to the facts, and the truth of compounds was understood as derivative. Likewise, in *TOM*, I suggested that the truth of compounds is grounded in atomics in a certain sense: 'there can be no change in the truth-value of a compound proposition without change in the truth-value of at least *some* atomic propositions'. (2009a: 90). I called this the weak grounding principle. It is weak for two reasons: it doesn't require that propositions in question depend for their truth-value only on atomics, and it doesn't require that the atomics they depend on (in the case of compounds) are those that directly compose them. But it does reflect a general intuition, and one that Shapiro (2011) has challenged in a recent article: that plain truths/falsehoods will always depend on some unplain truth/falsehood.[22]

Shapiro's question is whether there might be some plain truths that don't supervene on any unplain truth. One example he considers is truth attributions such as

(1) The proposition that grass is green is true.

This is an atomic proposition. It ascribes a property—truth—to an object, a proposition. In virtue of what is it true? There are various answers available to the functionalist; sorting them clearly reveals their relative merits.

---

[21] So does the pluralist believe that we always know what subject we are talking about? No. Are there interesting philosophical problems about when we are talking about ethics and when the law, when we are talking about mathematics and when physics? Sure. But they aren't special to pluralists.

[22] Shapiro is right to point out that in *TOM*, I only consider the plain truth of compounds. I say that if a compound's truth-value is weakly grounded then it is plainly true. That leaves open that some atomics might also be plainly true (see Lynch 2009a: 90).

One possibility is the *inheritance view*: Truth attributions are true in the same way as the proposition to which truth is ascribed. Thus (1), for example, is true; however

(2) Grass is green

is true. So if (2) is true because it corresponds to reality (however that is cashed out) then so is (1). Truth attributions *inherit* the property that manifests their truth from the proposition to which they attribute truth. Thus (1) will be correspondence true, and so will any proposition that attributes truth to *it* and so on up the ladder of semantic ascent.

There are two reasons the functionalist should not hold this view. First, it implies that truth attributions are true in different ways. But that means that it is in tension with the idea that which property manifests truth for a proposition depends on the subject matter it is about. There would be no tension if (1) and (2) are the same proposition. But they are not.

The second problem is that the inheritance view is hopeless in the generalizations like

(3) Everything Stewart says is true.

The inheritance view says that a truth attributer inherits the way it is true from the truth attributee. But obviously Stewart may say all sorts of propositions, about all sorts of things. Given functionalism, they might have their truth manifested in distinct ways; (3)'s truth would inherit too many manifestations of truth.

Another possibility is *a levels or hierarchy view*.[23] The idea here is to hold that every level of truth attribution is made in a different domain, and hence that every truth attribution is true in a different way than the one preceding it on the semantic ladder. For reasons having to do with the paradoxes, you might add that no domain has the resources to make truth attributions about itself. As Shapiro (2011: 40) notes, the shade of Tarksi is close). But this position also faces significant problems. Here are three. First, *why* think that (1) and an attribution of truth to (1) manifest truth differently? Second, given that we can continue to attribute truth to the truth attribution to (1) and so on, this seems to imply that there are an indefinite number of different properties that manifest truth. And finally, note that the levels view implies that (1) and an attribution of truth to (1) are not cognitively equivalent. As with an inheritance view, this may or may not be a bad thing, depending on one's view about how to read the T-schema.

Given these considerations, I favor the *plain truth view*. Truth attributions are plainly true. This seems particularly sensible in the case of a proposition

---

[23] Shapiro (2011) himself suggests a similar line; Cotnoir (2013) independently develops it in detail.

like (1). For it is intuitive that (1) is true because (2) is true. While (1) and (2) are both atomic, (1) is clearly true *because* of (2), and (2)'s truth will be manifested by correspondence. The plain truth of (1) is founded on the unplain truth of (2). This is clearly consistent with the general picture I defend in *TOM*.

So far so good, admits Shapiro. But what about (3)? Again, it seems that this too is an excellent candidate for plain truth. Shapiro is not so sure. One issue he raises is complexity:

> The problem is that there is no limit to how complex these propositions can be [. . .] as we chase down the various propositions that [(3)] depends on, we [may] end up considering more and more complex propositions, with no upper limit. (2011: 42)

Fair enough. The truth-value of (3) depends on what Stewart says. But I don't see the problem. The weak grounding principle only requires that there be some unplain truth-values (such as the truth-values of some atomics) that the plain truth-value of (3) depends on. Given that (3) is a universal generalization, if Stewart utters any unplain truth, then this constraint is satisfied. Whatever else he utters is irrelevant as far as the principle goes.

I think a similar response is merited to another example Shapiro considers, a truth-attribution to a generalization of the T-schema, or:

TS': It is true that for every proposition p, p is true if and only if p.

Here too, I am inclined to say that the truth of *TS'* is plainly true. But, says Shapiro, one of the proposition *TS'* generalizes over is *TS'* itself. We are caught in a loop, and so 'it is simply not true that the truth-status of any given proposition depends *solely* on the truth-status of atomic propositions' (2011: 7). Granted. But again, that does not violate the weak grounding principle: for it does not claim that the truth-value of compounds supervenes on only atomics. It claims that their subvening base must include at least some atomics. And the truth-value of *TS'* certainly does.

But Shapiro may insist that there is still a problem. Thus Stewart, in our version of the example,

> might have said that most of what his disciples say is true, and one of those disciples (or all of them) may have said that [(3)], that everything [Stewart] says is true. So, the process of unpacking the various pronouncements, to figure out which truth-realizers are invoked, goes on forever.

Note the epistemic language here and in the earlier quotation: the process of 'figuring out' what properties play the truth-role never stops. Doubtless. But, of course, how difficult it is for us to *know* what plays the truth-role for a given proposition isn't the question. The issue is whether there *are* any unplain truths on which the truth-value of (3) depends. I don't see that Shapiro's actual example does the trick: if only one of the things that Stewart says is that what his disciples say is true, then the subvening class on which the truth of (3) depends may well include some unplain truths. But put that aside. Abstracting from the details, the fundamental question Shapiro is asking still stands: might there not be some propositions whose plain truth (value) doesn't depend on any unplain truth (value)? The question is whether the functionalist can allow for this possibility.[24]

I submit that the functionalist can grant two points. Some atomic propositions are plainly true. That much, as I have already noted, is completely consistent with what was said in *TOM*, which applied the weak grounding principle to compounds while leaving it open that some atomic propositions might also be plainly true. The other point is perhaps more interesting. There may, after all, be propositions that are plainly true but whose truth (value) does not depend on the truth-value of any unplain truth (value).

Indeed, there are reasons to consider this over and above those suggested by Shapiro's comments. Consider, for example, logically necessary truths, such as an instance of the propositional version of the T-schema, or even any instance of:

(4) If p, then p.

This is again not atomic. But its truth-value does not depend on the truth-value of its atomic components; p could have any truth-value and (4) would still be true. Indeed, it doesn't depend on the truth-value of any proposition in the actual world. For this reason it seems curious to say that it corresponds to reality either. What reality, exactly? And being a necessary truth, it seems less than plausible to say that its truth is somehow epistemically constrained and hence that its truth is manifested by its being superwarranted. It seems much more plausible to simply say that (4) is plainly true—but not because its truth depends on some other truth, but simply because its truth is basic and ungrounded on the actual truth-value of any proposition. Indeed, that very fact is what helps to explain what makes necessary truths a distinct kind of truth. Part of what makes the content of such propositions distinctive is that their truth, in a sense, needs no metaphysical explanation.

Here's the point I wish to emphasize in light of Shapiro's comments. The key move of functionalism is to allow that sometimes—that is, for certain types of propositions—a property other than truth can play the truth-role, and in so doing manifest or realize truth. It is not—at least it should not—be part of the view that every true proposition has its truth manifested by some property distinct from truth. Moreover, as I have already argued, I think that in a wide spectrum of cases—including truth attributions—plain truth is weakly grounded in unplain truth. But I am also perfectly happy to admit that in other

---

[24] Consider: if what I assert is (3) and the only thing Stewart asserts is that everything Lynch says is true, then our mutual admiration society really does form a closed loop.

cases—such as (3)—this might not be so. But whether it is or isn't really doesn't hang on whether the weak grounding principle is true. It hangs on the nature of the type of content in question, and what sort of theoretical apparatus is needed in order to explain that nature.

The functionalist will insist that for some kinds of beliefs and assertions, understanding their propositional content will require understanding that those contents are true in virtue of having some distinct property that manifests truth. For such contents, the property that plays the truth-role has explanatory value.

Compare identity. Suppose we think that some things, like necessarily existing objects, are just plainly identical across time. Their identity is not manifested by any other property. That hardly means that some things might not be identical in a particular way. Personal identity across time might well be manifested by psychological continuity. It all depends—not only on what we think we must say in order to account for personal identity, but more importantly, on what we think we must say about personal identity *in order to explain other phenomena of interest*—such as personal responsibility and human rights. The same holds in the case of truth. The reason I think that there is more to say about truth in some domains is the same reason other substantivist theorists of truth think this: we must say more about it in order to explain *other phenomena of interest: such as the differences in content between moral, mathematical, and physical-object propositions*.

So, for example, I have argued that if we want to understand the content of our moral judgments, then we need to understand the truth of those judgments as epistemically constrained (2009a). And we can do that only if we think there is more to say about moral truth than plain truth—if we think that it is an epistemically constrained property that manifests truth in the moral domain. Given that posit, we can say that what differentiates ethical judgments from other kinds of judgments is that they have a different kind of truth-condition, and hence a different kind of content. Likewise, even when there may *not* be more to say about what manifests truth for a given class of propositions—say logically necessary conceptual truths—that fact itself can, as we've seen, be informative. The very fact that there *isn't* more to say about their truth is part of what explains why those propositions are the kind of propositions they are. Thus the possibility of ungrounded plain truth, far from being a problem to be explained away, offers the possibility of new explanations.

But isn't plain truth just deflationary truth? No. Think again about what deflationism involves. Broadly speaking, deflationary views involve two commitments. First, the concept of truth is considered as an expressive device of generalization. Second, whatever property, if any, that concept denotes is itself metaphysically transparent. A property is metaphysically transparent just when all the essential facts about the property can be known via grasp of the ordinary folk concept alone. This makes, on the deflationist view, *being true* very unlike the property *being water*, say. We can't know all the essential facts about being water from grasping the ordinary concept of water. But we can grasp all the essential facts about truth, says the deflationist, from grasping the ordinary, expressive concept of truth.

Plain truth is not deflationary truth. The property of being true, I claim, is the property that has the truish features essentially. The truish features are those conceptually necessary features of truth described by our folk platitudes about truth. That is, the property of truth is the property propositions have when they are objective, correct to believe, and the sort of propositions we aim at in inquiry. These features go well beyond the mere expressive device imagined by deflationists. So truth is not just an expressive device on my view. Indeed, I'm not sure it is even essentially such a device. Moreover, truth is not metaphysically transparent either. While you can know the truish features of truth just by grasping the concept of truth, you can't know all the essential features of truth that way. Here is one essential feature of truth you can't know that way: that it is open to multiple manifestation.

Functionalists get to keep truth in their philosophical tool-kit. Not so the deflationist; if truth is a merely expressive device, then we better be able to explain everything we want to explain without appealing to any substantive facts about its nature. This is like hoping to solve all carpentry problems with a hammer. Some jobs call for complicated tools; sometimes you need complex notions like truth in order to get a grip on the nature of content or knowledge.

In sum, Shapiro is of course right that any truth theory must confront that which brings us to the edge of paradox—if only because what brings us to the edge can sometimes throw us over. But these phenomena don't raise special problems for the functionalist. Indeed, they suggest that functionalism has the resources to offer some new explanations for how certain truths are true.

7. Conclusion

We have put three questions to the pluralist. We now have three answers.

- How do we identify those properties by virtue of which propositions are true? Answer: by seeing which properties play the truth-role, and hence have the truish features.
- How are those properties related to truth? Answer: Truth as such is the property that has the truish features essentially. But truth can be immanent in distinct properties, properties that have the truish features accidentally.
- What determines which of these properties a given proposition must have in order to be true? Answer: two things. First, the logical

structure of the proposition and second, the subject matter of the proposition.

These are not the only three questions a pluralist must answer. Nor, perhaps, are these the only answers available. But if the pluralist wishes to make sense of her view, some such answers must be given. Avoiding them is not an option.[25]

References

Aristotle (1993). *Metaphysics*, trans. C. Kirwan. Oxford: Oxford University Press.
Cotnoir, A. (2009). Generic truth and mixed conjunctions: some alternatives. *Analysis* 69: 473–479.
Cotnoir, A. (2013). Pluralism and paradox. In N. J. L. L. Pedersen & C. D. Wright (eds.), *Truth and Pluralism: Current Debates* (339–350). New York: Oxford University Press.
David, M. (2013). Lynch's functionalist theory of truth. In N. J. L. L. Pedersen & C. D. Wright (eds.), *Truth and Pluralism: Current Debates* (42–68). New York: Oxford University Press.
Edwards, D. (2008). How to solve the problem of mixed conjunctions. *Analysis* 68: 143–149.
Edwards, D. (2009). Truth conditions and truth: resolving the problem of mixed conjunctions. *Analysis* 69: 684–688.
Field, H. (2001). *Truth and the Absence of Fact*. Oxford: Oxford University Press.
Gupta, A. (1993). A critique of deflationism. *Philosophical Topics* 21: 57–81.
Horwich, P. (1990/1998). *Truth*. Oxford: Oxford University Press.
Jackson, F. (1998). *From Metaphysics to Ethics: A Defense of Conceptual Analysis*. Oxford: Oxford University Press.
Kim, J. (1998). *Mind in a Physical World*. Cambridge, MA: MIT Press.
Lewis, D. (1980). Mad pain and Martian pain. In N. Block (ed.), *Readings in the Philosophy of Psychology*, vol. 1 (216–222). Cambridge, MA: Harvard University Press.
Lynch, M. P. (1998). *Truth in Context*. Cambridge, MA: MIT Press.
Lynch, M. P. (2001). A functionalist theory of truth. In his (ed.), *The Nature of Truth* (723–749). Cambridge, MA: MIT Press.
Lynch, M. P. (2004a). Minimalism and the value of truth. *Philosophical Quarterly* 54: 497–517.
Lynch, M. P. (2004b). Truth and multiple realizability. *Australasian Journal of Philosophy* 82: 384–408.
Lynch, M. P. (2004c). *True to Life*. Cambridge, MA: MIT Press.
Lynch, M. P. (2005). Alethic functionalism and our folk theory of truth: a reply to Cory Wright. *Synthese* 145: 29–43.
Lynch, M. P. (2006). ReWrighting pluralism. *Monist* 89: 63–84.

---

[25] Sections of this paper were presented at the *Truth* Workshop at UConn in May 2009; at a conference honoring Crispin Wright at the Australian National University; at a meeting of the Society of Realist/Anti-realist Discussion; and at the 2010 Central APA. Thanks for helpful discussion to: Aaron Cotnoir, Marian David, Patrick Greenough, Henry Jackman, Claire Horisk, Stewart Shapiro, Jeremy Wyatt, and Crispin Wright. A special thanks to Cory Wright and Nikolaj Pedersen for their helpful comments.

Lynch, M. P. (2009a). *Truth as One and Many.* Oxford: Oxford University Press.
Lynch, M. P. (2009b). The value of truth and the truth of values. In A. Haddock, A. Millar, & D. Pritchard (eds.), *Epistemic Value* (225–242). Oxford: Oxford University Press.
Pedersen, N. J. L. L. (2006). What can the problem of mixed inferences teach us about alethic pluralism? *Monist* 89: 103–117.
Pedersen, N. J. L. L. (2010). Stabilizing alethic pluralism. *Philosophical Quarterly* 60: 92–108.
Putnam, H. (1981). *Reason, Truth, and History.* Cambridge: Cambridge University Press.
Russell, B. (1912/2001). Truth and falsehood. In M. P. Lynch (ed.), *The Nature of Truth* (17–24). Cambridge, MA: MIT Press.
Shapiro, S. (2011). Truth, function, and paradox. *Analysis* 71: 38–44.
Tappolet, C. (1997). Mixed inferences: a problem for pluralism about truth predicates. *Analysis* 57: 209–211.
Tappolet, C. (2000). Truth, pluralism, and many-valued logic: a reply to Beall. *Philosophical Quarterly* 50: 382–385.
Williams, M. (2001). On some critics of deflationism. In R. Schantz (ed.), *What is Truth?* (146–160). Berlin: Walter de Gruyter.
Williamson, T. (1994). Critical study of *Truth and Objectivity*. *International Journal of Philosophical Studies* 30: 130–144.
Wittgenstein, L. (1922). *Tractatus Logico-Philosophicus*, trans. C. K. Ogden. London: Kegan Paul.
Wright, C. D. (2005). On the functionalization of pluralist approaches to truth. *Synthese* 145: 1–28.
Wright, C. D. (2010). Truth, Ramsification, and the pluralist's revenge. *Australasian Journal of Philosophy* 88: 265–283.
Wright, C. J. G. (1992). *Truth and Objectivity.* Cambridge, MA: Harvard University Press.
Wright, C. J. G. (2001). Minimalism, deflationism, pragmatism, pluralism. In M. P. Lynch (ed.), *The Nature of Truth* (751–788). Cambridge, MA: MIT Press.

{ 3 }

Lynch's Functionalist Theory of Truth

Marian David

In his new book, *Truth as One and Many* (2009), Michael Lynch presents a theory of truth with two main components. The first is a *functionalist account of truth*, saying that a proposition is true just when it has some property that plays a certain characteristic role, the truth-role. The second is the thesis that truth is *multiply realizable*, saying that truth can be realized by different properties for propositions belonging to different domains of discourse. In this chapter, I want to look at the structure of Lynch's functionalist account of truth while keeping a close eye on his multiple realizability thesis. It will turn out that it is not a straightforward matter to understand how the two components of his theory fit together. The main aim of the chapter is to provide constructive criticism and clarification. I will scrutinize relevant aspects of Lynch's view in considerable detail, hoping that this will tell us something interesting about functionalism concerning truth, and maybe even about functionalism in general.

1

Lynch summarizes the functionalist component of his theory, stating its general account of truth together with a definition of the key notion employed in the account:

> [c]all this the *functionalist theory of truth* [. . .] A proposition is true just when it has a property that plays the truth-role [. . .] A property plays the truth-role when it has the truish features specified by the truisms' (2009: 73).

Lynch has adopted a strategy familiar in outline from certain versions of functionalism in the philosophy of mind. First he identifies a set of basic principles, 'the truisms', which, he claims, are constitutive of our folk-conception or folk-theory of truth. Then he employs these principles to introduce the key notion of 'playing the truth-role': a property is said to play the truth-role if and only if it has a set of characteristic features, 'the truish features', that can be extracted from the principles constituting our folk-theory of truth.[1] Finally, he employs the notion of playing the truth-role to state his general account of truth.

Since the whole structure rests on the principles Lynch calls 'the truisms', we should look at them first. Our folk conception of truth, according to Lynch, comprises a fair number of principles. For simplicity, he often limits attention to the three most important ones, referring to them as *the core truisms about truth* (2009: 70):

Objectivity: The belief that p is true if, and only if, with respect to the belief that p, things are as they are believed to be.

Norm of Belief: It is prima facie correct to believe that p if, and only if, the proposition that p is true.

End of Inquiry: Other things being equal, true beliefs are a worthy goal of inquiry.

The account of truth will be based on these truisms via the notion of *the truth-role*, or rather, *playing the truth-role*. By way of introducing this crucial notion, Lynch asks, '[w]hy not see [the truisms] as telling us what the property of truth does so to speak—about its function?', and then says that 'the truisms tell us that true propositions are those that have a property that has a certain function in our cognitive economy'—that they reveal 'truth's functional role', or 'the truth-role', for short (2009: 71).

Lynch thus introduces the notion of playing the truth-role using quasi-causal language, talking about what truth 'does' and about its 'functional role'. This is not to be taken quite literally: he is using causal metaphors to make non-causal points. A functionalist theory of truth naturally reminds us of functionalism in the philosophy of mind. There are some similarities, but there is also this noteworthy difference. When functionalists about mental states talk about properties playing a functional role, say, the pain-role, they take functional role to be causal role: to say that a property plays the pain-role means that it has certain characteristic causal powers, or rather, that its bearers, token brain-states or events, have certain characteristic causal powers in virtue of having that property. When Lynch calls the truth-role a functional role, he means this to be understood in an extended sense. He does not specify the truth-role in causal terms, nor does he think

---

[1] That the second thesis of the quoted passage is indeed meant as stating a necessary as well as sufficient condition is clear from what Lynch (2009: 72) has said earlier.

that a property playing that role has causal powers, or that possessing such a property endows propositions with causal powers.

Playing the truth-role is a matter of having certain (non-causal) features that are said to be 'picked out' or 'specified' by the truisms: '[o]ur core folk truisms pick out certain relational features—call them the *truish features*—which a property must have in order to play the truth-role' and '[a] property plays the truth-role when it has the truish features specified by the truisms' (2009: 72, 73). Lynch does not say what exactly these features are, but there appears to be a natural way of figuring out what they ought to be. Let us follow his instructions and see what the truisms can be taken to tell us about truth: the properties they ascribe to truth ought to be the truish features. However, as one tries to do this, one runs into certain obstacles stemming from the truisms, or rather, from the ways in which Lynch has formulated them. His formulations are, I think, in need of some repairs.

The second truism applies the term 'true' to *propositions* whereas the first and third apply it to *beliefs*. This is awkward. Lynch argues that propositions and not beliefs are the primary bearers of truth (2009: 129–32); and indeed his account of truth is stated in terms of propositions rather than beliefs. Since the account is supposed to be based on the truisms, they should be reformulated so that they uniformly apply 'true' to propositions. This is easily done in case of *End of Inquiry*: just take it to say that, other things being equal, if the proposition that p is true, then believing it is a worthy goal of inquiry. Finding a satisfactory reformulation of *Objectivity* is more difficult. Let us put it like this: the proposition that p is true if and only if, were the proposition that p to be believed, then things would be believed to be (with respect to the belief that p) as they are. This is far from perfect. But a similar formulation is suggested by Lynch himself at one place (2009: 29), and it will do for present purposes, since I am really concerned with the form of the truisms rather than the details of their content.[2]

It is usually held that the term 'true' is ambiguous, expressing different properties when applied to truthbearers of different types (propositions, beliefs, sentences). Lynch's multiple realizability thesis, on the other hand, says that 'true' is *not* ambiguous, although the one property it expresses, *being true*, can be realized by various other properties. Note that Lynch's thesis is concerned with truthbearers of *one type*. When considering truthbearers of different types, it has to be taken distributively, that is, 'true' is not ambiguous when applied to propositions; 'true' is not ambiguous when applied to beliefs; and so on. This does not mean that the term is univocal when applied

---

[2] But does the notion of a *proposition* occur in our folk-theory of truth? Lynch holds that the truisms are 'preconceptions' that can be extracted from 'the set of largely implicit beliefs we folk have' concerning truth (2009: 7–8). The notion of a proposition can then be regarded as being implicitly, if not explicitly, involved in our folk-theory of truth.

across propositions and beliefs. On the contrary, Lynch appears to hold that it is ambiguous in this sense. When arguing that propositions are the primary truthbearers, he implies that 'true', when applied to beliefs, can be defined to mean 'has a true proposition as its content' (2009: 129–32), which makes 'true' ambiguous, because that is not what it means when applied to propositions. Of course, as applied to beliefs, the term is still univocal on Lynch's view; and it is a consequence of his view that the property it then expresses, having a true proposition as content, is multiply realized, because propositional truth is multiply realized. But this property is obviously not the same as the one expressed by 'true' when applied to propositions. This shows that the truisms should apply 'true' uniformly to bearers from one ontological type. Otherwise there would not be any one property expressed by 'true' as it occurs in the truisms such that they could be understood as telling us something about that property; and since Lynch's account of truth is put in terms of propositions, the truisms should be reformulated to apply 'true' to propositions.[3]

We are not done yet with the truisms. Lynch's formulations require some more repairs. The third truism is formulated as a *universal generalization* whereas the first and second are presented as mere *schemas*, employing the schematic letter 'p'. As such, they do not really say anything (not anything truth-evaluable at any rate) and are not really truisms but schemas of truisms at best. This is strange. Lynch needs genuine principles here, for he holds that his truisms are constitutive of our folk-theory of truth—that is, they are (implicit) beliefs we have involving the concept of truth (2009: 7–8). But mere schemas do not really express anything we could believe. More importantly, we want to identify the truish features (hence the truth-role) by seeing what the truisms can be taken to tell us about truth. But mere schemas do not really tell us anything about truth. They ought to be formulated not as schemas but as generalizations. This point is of some importance and will resurface at times. In the meantime, I observe that it is clear from what Lynch says later in the book that the schematic formulations are merely for ease of exposition: all three truisms are intended as universal generalizations.[4]

---

[3] The ambiguity-view of 'true' as applied to different types of truthbearers is the traditional one. But there seems to be room for an alternative, multiple realizability view here too, at least in principle. One might maintain that 'true' expresses one property that is realized by different further properties for truthbearers of different types: one for true propositions, one for true sentences, another for true beliefs. On this view, 'true' would be univocal even as applied across types of truthbearers. To my knowledge, this position has not been officially advocated, at least not yet. Lynch might want to adopt it, extending his multiple realizability thesis from applying to individual types of truthbearers to applying across types of truthbearers. If so, difficulties that arise with respect to the proper formulation of his functionalism will be exacerbated. For instance, it will take considerable effort to formulate the truisms in such a way that they are neutral between different types of truthbearers.

[4] The generality of the truisms is crucial to his argument against deflationism; see Lynch (2009: 111–3).

Taking this point together with the previous one (that all three truisms should apply the term 'true' to propositions), we can rewrite the three truisms as genuine principles, that is, as universal generalizations over propositions:

Objectivity: For every proposition x, x is true if and only if, were x to be believed, things would be believed to be as they are.

Norm of Belief: For every proposition x, it is prima facie correct to believe x if and only if x is true.

End of Inquiry: For every proposition x, other things being equal, if x is true then believing x is a worthy goal of inquiry.

Having amended Lynch's formulations, we can proceed to see what those truish features might be that the truisms are supposed to specify. The truisms are most naturally taken as talking about propositions. But, following Lynch's instructions, we can look at them differently, namely as talking about the property being true and ascribing certain properties, or features, to this property. The *Objectivity* truism then tells us that being true is such that a proposition has (instantiates) this property if and only if, were the proposition to be believed, things would be believed to be as they are. Since this is cumbersome and I am not much concerned with the actual text of the truisms anyway, I abbreviate this to: "BEING TRUE is a property ϕ such that $(\forall x)(\phi O x)$," where "ϕ" is a property-variable and "x" ranges over propositions. For convenience, we can read this as saying that BEING TRUE stands in the O-relation to every proposition. The other truisms can be given a similar treatment. *Norm of Belief* tells us that being true is a property such that it is prima facie correct to believe a proposition if and only if it has that property, which abbreviates as: 'being true is a property ϕ such that $(\forall x)(\phi N x)$'. *End of Inquiry* tells us that being true is a property such that, other things being equal, if a proposition has this property, then believing it is a worthy goal of inquiry, which abbreviates as: 'being true is a property ϕ such that $(\forall x)(\phi E x)$'.

For still more convenience, we can consolidate the three truisms, in their new guises, into a single one by stripping each of its quantifier, forming the conjunction of the resulting open formulas, and putting a single $(\forall x)$-quantifier in front of that conjunction. Thus taken together, the three truisms can be further abbreviated as: 'being true is a property ϕ such that $(\forall x)(\phi ONE x)$', which ascribes a rather complex relational feature to the property being true. The feature thus ascribed is expressed by '$(\forall x)(\phi ONE x)$', which is quite a mouthful when spelled out. We can abridge it like this: standing in the ONE-relation to every proposition.

This is the natural way to construe the truish features—having consolidated them into a single feature—that can be said to be specified by the truisms. It is what we get from the truisms when we follow Lynch's advice and extract the truish feature from what the truisms, taken together, can be understood to tell us about truth. But the truish feature, thus construed, will cause difficulties when we employ it to spell out what it is for a property to play the truth-role.

2

The two main principles of Lynch's functionalist theory of truth presently under consideration are his general account of truth in terms of playing the truth-role and his definition of playing the truth-role in terms of the truish feature(s):

T A proposition is true iff it has some property that plays the truth-role.
PR A property plays the truth-role iff it has the truish feature(s).

The task at hand is to find out how *T* and *PR* are best understood, specifically, to find out what it is for a property to play the truth-role, which, in turn, requires us to understand what the truish features are supposed to be.

According to the straightforward method of extracting the truish features from the truisms, discussed in the previous section, the truish features (consolidated into a single feature) are expressed by '$(\forall x)(\phi ONEx)$'. This leads to a simple interpretation of Lynch's *PR*:

PR1 ϕ plays the truth-role iff $(\forall x)(\phi ONEx)$,

saying that a property ϕ plays the truth-role iff it stands in the ONE-relation to every proposition. If we use this to spell out the right-hand side of Lynch's account of truth, we get the claim that, for every proposition *y*,

T1 T*y* iff $(\exists \phi)(\phi y \ \& \ (\forall x)(\phi ONEx))$,[5]

saying that a proposition is true iff it has some property that stands in the ONE-relation to every proposition.

The account is appealingly simple, but it has unwanted consequences. Sure enough, truth plays the truth-role in the sense of *PR1* (taking for granted, if only for the sake of argument, that what Lynch's truisms tell us about truth is correct). But the properties Lynch claims can realize truth won't play the truth-role, because they do not stand in the ONE-relation to *all* propositions, which means that *PR1* does not leave any room for Lynch's multiple realizability thesis. To see why, we have to take a look at this thesis.

The second component of Lynch's theory, his multiple realizability thesis, is best approached via a slight detour. Remember the traditional

---

[5] I use a different variable, '*y*', merely to avoid potential confusion that might arise from the presence of '*x*' in '$(\forall x)(\phi ONEx)$', though '*x*' is of course bound by the $(\forall x)$-quantifier anyway. Note that 'T*y*' is short for '*y* is true', whereas 'ϕy' is to be read as '*y* has (or: instantiates) ϕ'; this is because 'ϕ' is a property-variable, taking the place of the *name* of a property. I will continue to gloss over this detail.

correspondence theory of truth: a proposition is true iff it corresponds with some fact. It faces a number of objections. The one Lynch takes most seriously is this. The correspondence theory may be plausible for claims about certain subject matters, for instance claims about everyday physical objects and their properties. But for claims concerning moral matters the theory is not plausible at all: *there are no moral facts*, according to this objection, not in any serious sense. Morality is not the only domain of discourse that has provoked objections of this sort: aesthetics, mathematics, the law, and various others have been similarly 'flagged' as problem areas for the correspondence theory. Some would defend the theory, maintaining that discourse from flagged domains, despite linguistic appearances to the contrary, is not truth-evaluable to begin with (non-cognitivists), others by embracing the consequence that all claims from flagged domains must be false because the required facts are missing (error theorists). Lynch does not consider such defenses to be promising (2009: 2). He favors a pluralistic reaction to the problem.[6]

Pluralism holds that claims from flagged domains are truth-evaluable and that some, even many, may well be true. It thus rejects the correspondence theory, at least in its original form. It doesn't have to reject it entirely though. A pluralist may advocate a limited version of the correspondence account of truth, restricted to appropriate *domains of discourse*. For claims from some domains, truth may well consist in correspondence with facts, but for claims from various other domains, flagged domains, truth consists in the possession of properties other than correspondence with facts. In effect, pluralism offers a bunch of domain-restricted conditionals generated from the pattern:

$$(\forall x)(x \in \Delta \to (x \text{ is true} \leftrightarrow x \text{ has } \phi)),$$

by successively replacing 'Δ' with names for the various domains of discourse and 'ϕ' with names of the associated truth-constituting properties.

It is tempting to conceive of pluralism as the thesis that truth is defined differently for propositions belonging to different domains of discourse. But this amounts to the view that the term 'true' is ambiguous, expressing different properties when applied to propositions from different domains—a view Lynch wants to resist. His theory is designed to show that a form of pluralism can be defended without succumbing to the view that 'true' is multiply ambiguous. He advocates a *monistic* pluralism: the term 'true' is univocal, expressing one concept that picks out one property—truth is one. But truth is also many—in a sense: the one property, being true, can be *realized* by various other properties for propositions belonging to different domains of discourse. In short, rather

---

[6] For some recent alternative attempts to address this problem that try to stay within a correspondence framework, see Sher (2005, 2013) and Barnard & Horgan (2006, 2013).

than claiming that 'true' is multiply ambiguous, Lynch's pluralism claims that truth is multiply realized.[7]

Officially, Lynch's pluralism can remain neutral about which properties realize truth in which domains of propositions. It will, however, be helpful to have some concrete examples. Lynch himself suggests that for propositions concerning everyday physical objects, truth is indeed realized by the property of corresponding with a fact (assume some account of correspondence and of facts sufficiently robust for this to be a substantive property), and that for propositions concerning ethical matters, truth is realized by a strong epistemic property he calls 'being superwarranted' (cf. 2009: 50).[8] When it comes to propositions concerning other subject matters, truth may be realized by one of these two or by some further properties—Lynch does not provide additional examples of potential realizers, but he mentions aesthetics, mathematics, and the law as domains for which it is plausible to hold that truth is realized by some property other than correspondence with facts.

I want to remark in passing that the notion of a *domain of discourse* may well be a serious liability for pluralism about truth—for Lynch's version as well as most other versions I am aware of, including the one presented by Wright (1992), which Lynch acknowledges as an important influence. Pluralism wants to sort propositions into different domains according to the subject matter they are about (2009: 79). Giving a principled account of how this is to be done is likely to be difficult. Indeed, I am inclined to think that issues concerning domain individuation (by subject matter) will be the most difficult for Lynch to work out.[9] Nevertheless, I will set these issues aside for

---

[7] These claims are to be understood as being concerned with 'true' when applied to propositions. As we saw in the previous section, Lynch allows the term to be ambiguous when applied across bearers of different types.

[8] Lynch (2009: 21–32) sketches a robust account of correspondence, and he defines superwarrant, albeit for beliefs, as follows: '[t]he belief that p is superwarranted if and only if the belief that p is warranted without defeat at some stage of inquiry and would remain so at every successive stage of inquiry' (2009: 38)—only a slight modification is required to make this applicable to propositions: a proposition is superwarranted if and only if believing it is warranted [. . .] etc. It turns out later in the book (ch. 8) that Lynch actually takes truth in the ethical domain to be realized by a property he calls 'being concordant', a complex property that involves the epistemic property being supercoherent, which is a more specific version of being superwarranted.

[9] What if there are 'mixed propositions' that are concerned with more than one subject matter? They will cause problems, as can be seen from the pluralist's domain-restricted conditionals indicated above. If the pluralist says such propositions do not belong to any domain in the relevant sense (because they are not concerned with *one* subject matter), the pluralist account of truth threatens to be incomplete. If the pluralist takes the more intuitive option and says that mixed propositions belong to more than one domain, an even more serious consequence threatens. Take two domains Δ associated with two different truth-constituting properties ϕ (say, correspondence and superwarrant). A mixed proposition belonging to both domains may well have one of these properties but lack the other: the pluralist's conditionals will then rule this proposition to be both true and not true. Are there such mixed propositions? Yes—most obviously, propositions compounded from simpler propositions, such as the proposition that torture is wrong and the book is on the table. Lynch addresses such mixed compounds with

the most part. I want to reflect on the overall shape of Lynch's functionalist theory of truth, that is, on the form this theory takes rather than the details of its content.

Let us return to our present interpretation of Lynch's functionalist account of truth, *T1* plus *PR1*. The properties Lynch claims can realize truth, such as correspondence and superwarrant, won't play the truth-role in the sense of *PR1*, not according to Lynch's pluralism anyway. This is because their truth-making power is supposed to be restricted to their respective domains, which means that they won't stand in the ONE-relation to *every* proposition, as required by *PR1*. In case this is not already obvious, take just one of the truisms, say *Norm of Belief*. Put 'corresponds with a fact' in place of 'is true'. The result does not hold, because corresponding with a fact is not supposed to be generally necessary for being true. More precisely, according to Lynch's pluralism, it is not the case that, for every proposition x, it is prima facie correct to believe x *only if* x corresponds with a fact: as long as x is a proposition about, say, ethical matters, it can be correct to believe x even though it does not correspond with any fact, namely when it is superwarranted. We get a similar result putting 'is superwarranted' in place of 'is true', because being superwarranted is not supposed to be generally necessary for being true either: as long as x is a proposition about physical objects, it can be correct to believe x, according to Lynch, even if it is not superwarranted, namely when it corresponds with a fact.

So, on our present simple account of playing the truth-role, properties such as correspondence and superwarrant do not play the truth-role, not on Lynch's view; consequently, they do not realize truth. That last move rests on a point that, though not made entirely explicit by Lynch, is sufficiently obvious from his discussion (2009: 69–78): the notion of playing the truth-role is supposed to be the *locus* at which the two components of his theory connect, which means (at the very least) that in order to realize truth, a property must play the truth-role. Since our present account does not allow for correspondence and superwarrant to play the truth-role, it does not allow them to be realizers of truth either: it leaves no room for Lynch's multiple realizability

---

an extension of his theory (2009: 90–1), restricting its core to propositions that are 'atomic' in the sense of not being compounded from other propositions. But aren't there also mixed atomic propositions? Lynch himself cites the proposition expressed by 'the number seventeen is beautiful' as a problem case (2009: 79); or take the proposition expressed by 'this crystal is beautiful' or the proposition that immoral acts happen in space-time. They are atomic in Lynch's sense. Yet each appears to be concerned with more than one subject matter and should be assigned to more than one domain. Lynch himself seems to admit as much when he suggests that membership in a domain is determined by 'the kinds of concepts (moral, legal, mathematical) that compose the proposition in question' (2009: 80). But being a pluralist, Lynch cannot allow mixed atomic propositions. He is committed to the doctrine of 'domain specificity', according to which every proposition not compounded from simpler propositions belongs to one and only one domain (2009: 81). Sorting such propositions into different non-overlapping domains according to their subject matter is going to be a difficult business.

thesis. It thereby prevents the two components of his overall theory from fitting together. The moral to be drawn is that playing the truth-role in the sense of *PR1* must not be the right notion of playing the truth-role for Lynch's purposes.[10]

3

The simple account of playing the truth-role, stated above as *PR1*, was constructed from the way in which Lynch introduces the notion of the truth-role. But I have not yet looked at how Lynch himself spells out *PR*. This is because his own official proposal presents certain difficulties. What Lynch says is this:

> Where p is a proposition, and T a property,
> T plays the truth-role if, and only if: p is T, if and only if, where p is believed, things are as they are believed to be; other things being equal, it is a worthy goal of inquiry to believe p if p is T; it is correct to believe p if and only if p is T. (2009: 72)

Put into the present format (with 'ϕ' in place of Lynch's 'T' and 'x' in place of his 'p', and noting that the righthand side of his biconditional just spells out the ONE-relation), this suggests:

> *PR2* ϕ plays the truth-role iff ϕONEx

As it stands, this is difficult to interpret because of the dangling variable 'x', which fails to occur on the left-hand side.[11] In view of the point that the truisms ought to be universal generalizations, one might think the variable is to be bound by a ($\forall x$)-quantifier preceding 'ϕONEx'. But we have already looked at this interpretation: it is *PR1*, which is not the right one for Lynch's purposes. Lynch's introductory words, 'Where p is a proposition, and T a property', might be taken to indicate that he means the dangling variable to be bound from the outside, so that *PR2* would say: ($\forall x$)(ϕ plays the truth-role iff ϕONEx).[12]

---

[10] It would not be right to say the present account does not allow for *any* properties other than truth to play the truth-role, ruling out multiple realization entirely. The account allows for properties to play the truth-role as long as they are coextensive with truth (or, depending on modal issues that I do not want to go into now, as long as they are necessarily coextensive with truth). However, this point does not make a difference because truth-realizers such as correspondence and superwarrant are *not* coextensive with truth on Lynch's view. Note that those who advance multiple realizability theses in the philosophy of mind likewise take it for granted that the relevant realizing properties do not have the same extension as the properties they realize.

[11] Note that Lynch's 'p', just like my 'x', is an objectual variable ranging over propositions, not a schematic letter; note also that 'p' is missing from the left-hand side of Lynch's biconditional.

[12] The introductory words are probably just meant to inform us about the intended ranges for the variables, but they might also indicate universal quantifiers.

However, this formulation would not provide an account of playing the truth-role at all. It is equivalent to the following conjunction:

[φ plays the truth-role → (∀x)(φONEx)] & [(∃x)(φONEx) → φ plays the truth-role],

which merely offers a necessary condition and a different sufficient condition. Moreover, the necessary condition is too demanding, taking us back to the problem with *PR1*.

The problem with the *PR1* notion of playing the truth-role derives from the universal quantifier heading the truish feature expressed by '(∀x)(φONEx)', which leaves no room for the sort of multiple realizability Lynch wants. It is natural to try to circumvent this problem by doing something about this troubling quantifier. But Lynch's proposal, as it stands, is not the way to do it. Simply taking off the quantifier leaves 'φONEx', with the 'x' left dangling, which does not express a feature of φ. It's like uttering: 'Philadelphia has the feature of being larger than it', without indicating what the 'it' is supposed to refer to. An alternative idea about what to do with the troubling quantifier is suggested by the pattern for the pluralist's conditionals, '(∀x)(x ∈ Δ → (x is true ↔ x has φ))': restrict the quantifier to domains of discourse.

4

The problem with the *PR1* notion of playing the truth-role comes out in the order of the quantifiers in *T1*: it requires that there be a property, at least one, that does the job for *every* proposition. But, as we know from Lynch's pluralism, the properties that he says realize truth do so not for every proposition, but only for propositions belonging to certain *domains* of discourse. Correspondence with a fact realizes truth throughout the domain of physical-object propositions and maybe some others; being superwarranted realizes truth throughout the domain of ethical propositions and maybe some others; and so on, for whatever other domains of (atomic) propositions and whatever other truth-realizing properties there are.

Remembering that in order to realize truth a property must play the truth-role, it is natural to take note of the realizers' restriction to domains by building the same restriction into the account of playing the truth-role—something that our *PR1* and Lynch's *PR2* neglected to do. Instead of saying that a property plays the truth-role iff it stands in the ONE-relation to every proposition, let us say that a property plays the truth-role iff it stands in the ONE-relation to every proposition belonging to some domain Δ of propositions; more precisely:

PR3 φ plays the truth-role iff (∃Δ)(∀x)(x ∈ Δ → φONEx).

The attendant account of truth comes out as saying that a proposition is true iff it has some property φ that stands in the ONE-relation to every proposition from some domain Δ; that is, for every proposition y,

T3 Ty iff $(\exists\phi)(\phi y \,\&\, (\exists\Delta)(\forall x)(x \in \Delta \rightarrow \phi ONEx))$.

The new account requires that we revise our understanding of what is meant by 'the truish feature' in Lynch's *PR*. The relevant feature must now be the one *PR3* says is shared by the properties that play the truth-role, in other words: standing in the ONE-relation to every proposition from some domain—expressed by '$(\exists\Delta)(\forall x)(x \in \Delta \rightarrow \phi ONEx)$'. This feature is not actually specified by the truisms, for they do not mention domains at all. Still, one might concede that it can be 'extracted' from the truisms in an extended sense. For one can get the new truish feature from the truisms, taken as telling us something about truth, plus the thesis (not part of our folk-theory) that every proposition belongs to a domain in Lynch's sense: if what the truisms say about truth holds for every proposition and if there are such domains at all, then trivially there is some domain such that what the truisms say about truth holds for every proposition of that domain.

PR3 looks like a plausible account of what it is for a property to play the truth-role, and it seems to provide what Lynch wants. It obviously allows for different properties, such as the ones Lynch says are realizers of truth, to play the truth-role. Moreover, it exhibits something the different realizers have in common. This is important because Lynch wants the truth-role to provide for unification amid his pluralism. The truth-role, he says, 'gives truth its unity' (2009: 5). He employs it to answer the question how we are to identify the truth-determining properties (the realizers): 'the properties that can determine that propositions are true are those that play the truth-role' (2009: 71); and he indicates that playing the truth-role is the property common to the realizers that explains why they realize truth: 'There are some properties that play the truth-role and, in virtue of that fact, make propositions that have them true' (2009: 72).[13] Consider also truth itself. Pursuing unification, Lynch wants an account of truth that vindicates the monistic thesis that 'there is a single property named by "truth" that all and only true propositions share' (2009: 67). The account of truth based on *PR3* given above, *T3*, offers just that. On the face of

---

[13] One might raise the following objection to Lynch's strategy: You say the property being true has a certain characteristic property ψ (the truish feature); you claim that some other property, φ, also has ψ; you then infer that propositions having φ are thereby true. This would follow, if ψ were to pin down truth uniquely, but then we would have φ = being true, and there would be no multiple realization; but if ψ does not pin down truth uniquely: What's the proof? How does it follow that propositions having φ are true just because φ is a property that has a property that truth also has? Isn't that a fallacy? I take it the answer must be that there is no proof because it is not supposed to be an *inference* but a *proposal*. The proposal is that φ's having ψ explains why φ is such that having it makes propositions (of certain domains) true. The proposal is to be born out by its fruitfulness, its unifying virtues, etc., not by proof.

it, the *PR3* notion of playing the truth-role looks like it might be the right one for Lynch's purposes.[14]

Though it has many virtues, the present account is not good enough for Lynch either. The problem this time is that *PR3* does not cooperate in the right way with the attending account of truth. This is because of an important point about realization and domains that I have not mentioned yet.

Lynch's pluralism allows for a property that realizes truth in one domain to be present among propositions from another domain without realizing truth there. This is a good thing, as can be brought out by our examples: a physical-object proposition may be superwarranted but fail to be true because it fails to correspond with any fact; moreover, a physical-object proposition that is superwarranted *and* true is not true *in virtue of* being superwarranted; it is true in virtue of corresponding with a fact (2009: 42). As Lynch observes, this is 'parallel to the thought, familiar from the philosophy of mind, that whether a given neural property realizes pain depends on the kind of organism whose neural property it is. (Thus a neural property that realizes pain in one kind of organism may not realize it in another kind of organism even where members of the latter kind have that property)' (2009: 76). The same point applies to playing the truth-role.[15] Because of this, *T3* delivers wrong verdicts; it is too weak. Say some physical-object proposition has the property being superwarranted. It then has a property that plays the truth-role in the sense of *PR3*, because being superwarranted plays that role in the domain of ethical propositions, hence in *some* domain. *T3* now tells us that the proposition must be true. But Lynch tells us that, being a physical-object proposition, it may fail to be true, namely if it does not correspond with any fact. The present account is not sensitive to the point that a truthmaking property may be present in various domains but exert its truthmaking powers only in some of them. The fault seems to lie with *PR3*; at least, I cannot see how to revise *T3* in a manner faithful to Lynch's intentions while still employing the *PR3* notion of playing the truth-role.

---

[14] Note, however, that the account does not address the problem posed by mixed propositions. Consider what account of falsehood would come along with *T3*. There are some options. One could say *y* is false iff it *lacks* a property that plays the truth-role (2009: 77); or one could say *y* is false iff it *has* a property that plays the falsehood-role (where the latter would require identifying a falsish feature via additional folk-truisms about falsehood). Say *y* is mixed and belongs to the domain of physical-object propositions as well as to the domain of ethical propositions: if *y* corresponds with a fact but lacks superwarrant, it comes out both true and false on the first account; if *y* corresponds with a fact and also possesses whatever property plays the falsehood-role in the domain of ethics, *y* comes out true and false on the second account. If, finally, one says *y* is false iff it lacks *every* property that plays the truth-role, one gets the wrong result for propositions belonging to one domain: if *y* belongs only to the domain of physical-object propositions, its having or lacking superwarrant should have no bearing on whether it is false.

[15] Lynch puts it like this: '[j]ust as a single neural property may play the pain-role for one kind of organism and not for another, a single property like superwarrant may play the truth-role for propositions of one domain but not for propositions of another' (2009: 77).

5

Lynch's official account of playing the truth-role, *PR2*, says: φ plays the truth-role iff φONE*x*. As I pointed out earlier, this is deficient: 'φONE*x*', with the '*x*' variable left free, does not ascribe a feature to φ; it certainly does not ascribe a feature φ has just when it has the property expressed by the one-place predicate 'plays the truth-role'. This last observation, however, is suggestive. Let us try to turn it around: maybe the expression 'plays the truth-role', despite its appearance, is not best construed as a one-place predicate expressing a property; maybe it is better to construe it as expressing a relation.

PR1–PR3 have in common that they treat the notion of playing the truth-role as an *absolute* one, that is, they attempt to spell out what it is for a property to play the truth-role, period. Since they run into difficulties, one naturally turns to the thought that it might be better to construe this notion as a *relative* one—and this will indeed turn out to be more promising. There are two ways in which this might be done. First, treat the notion of playing the truth-role as being relativized to individual propositions *x*. Second, treat it as being relativized to whole domains of propositions Δ. Note that, either way, statements where Lynch appears to employ an absolute notion of playing the truth-role—and there are quite a few, especially *T*, *PR*, and *PR2*—will have to be replaced by statements employing one of the relativized notions.

The first method of relativizing—to individual propositions—makes for a fairly simple account. A property plays the truth-role relative to, or let us say *for*, a proposition iff it stands in the ONE-relation to that proposition:

> *PR4* φ plays the truth-role for *x* iff φONE*x*

This might be what was intended by Lynch's formulation of *PR2*—if so, he forgot to put in the crucial relativizing parameter 'for *x*' on the left-hand side. At any rate, *PR4* requires that his account of truth be revised. The new account says that a proposition is true iff it has some property that plays the truth-role *for* that very proposition. That is, for every proposition *x*,

> *T4* T*x* iff (∃φ)(φ*x* & φONE*x*).

On this account, we (again) have to revise our understanding of the truish feature. It turns out not to be a feature at all, not even a relational feature. Instead, it is a relation between properties and propositions, expressed by 'φONE*x*': it should be referred to as *the truish relation*. This relation can be said to be specified by the truisms in a fairly straightforward sense. For they surely specify the original truish feature, expressed by '(∀*x*)(φONE*x*)', and the expression for the truish relation results from simply taking off the initial quantifier.

The truth-role, Lynch says, 'gives truth its unity' (2009: 5); it provides for unification in the theory of truth, because playing the truth-role is something the different realizers of truth are supposed to have in common. Does the truth-role in the present sense provide for this? Well, on *PR4*, playing the truth-role is itself a relativized notion. So it is not accurate to say that the realizers of truth have in common that they play the truth-role in the sense of *PR4*. On the other hand, a common property is nearby, for the different realizers of truth have in common the relational property of playing the truth-role relative to some proposition or other—expressed by '$(\exists x)(\phi$ plays the truth-role for $x)$'.

I mentioned earlier that, pursuing unity, Lynch wants an account of truth vindicating the thesis that 'there is a single property named by "truth" that all and only true propositions share' (2009: 67). The present account of truth is a bit unusual in this regard. Looked at from a distance, *T4* has the form 'Tx iff xRx', having a one-place predicate on its left-hand side and a two-place predicate on its right-hand side, albeit one where 'x' occurs in both places. Should we then say that the righthand side of *T4* expresses a *property* that all the true propositions share (the property of having some property that stands in the ONE-relation to oneself) or should we say it expresses a *relation* that all the true propositions bear to themselves (the relation expressed by 'has some property that stands in the ONE-relation to')? The latter seems more accurate, though it sounds a bit odd to call something a relation while at the same time equating it with a property such as *being true*. But the oddity seems largely verbal. The important point is that *T4* does appear to exhibit something that all and only the true propositions share.[16]

The present account does not mention *domains* at all. This may be surprising since they seemed rather important earlier. However, it is actually an advantage. Lynch wants there to be a clear line between the two components of his overall view, the functionalist account of truth, on the one hand, and his 'pluralist metaphysics of truth', on the other hand (2009: 84). The functionalist account is supposed to provide an analysis of our ordinary concept of truth, telling us that it is the concept of a functional property. The account is supposed to stay close to our folk-conception of truth, as encapsulated in the truisms, remaining neutral on issues that go significantly beyond what is already implicit in the truism. The pluralist metaphysics is supposed to be the component of Lynch's view that adds various theses concerning the property picked out by our concept of truth, substantive theses that go significantly beyond what's already implicit in our folk-conception (2009: 82–4).

Our present interpretation of the functionalist account, *PR4* plus *T4*, fits this picture fairly well (much better than *PR3* plus *T3*). For *PR4* remains entirely neutral on the issue of domains. Indeed, as far as *PR4* is concerned, the

---

[16] Accounts of the same general form are not all that unusual; compare 'x is self-identical iff $x = x$'; and 'x commits suicide iff x kills x' and 'x is prime iff x is divisible only by 1 and x'. There does not seem to be anything disreputable about such accounts.

truth-role could be played by different properties for each and every proposition, or it could be played by one single property for every proposition, or it could be played by a number of different properties that play the role for propositions belonging to certain domains. The functionalist account remains silent on such issues. We can then see Lynch's claims concerning domains as additional, substantive theses of his pluralism. There is, first of all, the thesis that there are domains in his sense, that is, non-overlapping domains of (atomic) propositions individuated in terms of *the* subject matter these propositions are about—as I remarked earlier, I would rate this as a serious trouble-spot in Lynch's theory. Then there is the multiple realizability thesis, saying that truth can be realized by different properties, such as correspondence and superwarrant. There is the thesis that the truth-realizers play the truth-role throughout whole domains of propositions (i.e., if correspondence plays the truth-role for any physical-object proposition, then it plays the truth-role for all physical-object propositions). And there will be some other theses, especially the one that brought down the PR_3-plus-T_3 account of truth: a property that plays the truth-role for propositions from one domain may be instantiated by other propositions from other domains without playing the truth-role for these other proposition.

Concerning the last thesis, one may observe that T_4 does not generate the wrong results. Say x is a physical-object proposition that is superwarranted. It does not follow from T_4 that x is true, since PR_4 does not imply that being superwarranted plays the truth-role for x. Nor does PR_4 imply that being superwarranted does not play the truth-role for x. The latter is an additional thesis advocated by Lynch. That superwarrant, even though it can be instantiated by physical-object propositions, does not play the truth-role for them (does not stand in the ONE-relation to physical-object propositions) but does play the truth-role for ethical propositions (does stand in the ONE-relation to ethical propositions) is a thesis that properly belongs to Lynch's pluralist metaphysics—together with an explanation of *why* this should be so.[17]

---

[17] Why is it that some truth-realizing properties that are present in different domains exert their truthmaking powers in some domains but not in others? I take this to be a fairly deep question for Lynch. I won't go into it here, but I want to note that Lynch offers some considerations that bear on the issue. The picture is, briefly, this (2009: 1–3, 32–6, 41–9). Beliefs about everyday physical objects (whose contents are physical-object propositions) are by and large causally responsive to mind-independent objects and their properties, which is why corresponding with a fact is the relevant truth-realizing property in that domain. There are various other subject matters such as morality, where we have genuine beliefs (having truth evaluable contents), but where our beliefs are not (plausibly understood as being) causally responsive to mind-independent objects and their properties. If our beliefs concerning such matters are still apt for rational assessment, subject to constraints of rationality (as is the case with moral beliefs), the relevant truth-realizing property will be some epistemic property, such as being superwarranted. One might still ask, though, why it is that correspondence *dominates* superwarrant when it comes to beliefs about everyday physical objects, beliefs that are both causally responsive to facts and apt for rational assessment.

In sum, the *PR4*-plus-*T4* version of the functionalist account of truth appears to be well suited for Lynch's purposes. I suggest that Lynch's originals, *PR* (and *PR2*) and *T*, which are expressed with an absolute notion of playing the truth-role, are best replaced by *PR4* and *T4*, which employ a relativized notion of playing the truth-role, the one that is relativized to individual propositions.

The second method of relativizing the notion of playing the truth-role relativizes to whole *domains* of propositions. I should point out that Lynch himself advocates relativizing to domains, albeit only after he has laid out the main ingredients of his functionalist account, *T* and *PR*, in absolute terms. Moreover, the notion he explicitly says needs to be relativized to domains is not the notion of playing the truth-role but the notion of *manifestation*: 'For atomic propositions, ontologically distinct manifestations of truth are manifestations *relative to a domain*' (2009: 76). I must admit that I find Lynch's use of 'manifestation' difficult to understand. Early on, he indicates that he is going to use it for what among functionalists is usually referred to as the relation of realization, but the way he later officially characterizes the notion of manifestation does not seem to bear this out (2009: 3, 74). Moreover, his official characterization does not introduce a relativized notion anyway, so that it is not quite clear how it fits with the passage just quoted. I will set aside this notion for the moment, returning to it later.

Relativizing the notion of playing the truth-role to domains makes for an account somewhat more complex than the previous one. A property plays the truth-role relative to, or let us say *in*, a domain Δ iff it stands in the ONE-relation to every proposition belonging to Δ:

> *PR5* ϕ plays the truth-role in Δ iff $(\forall x)(x \in \Delta \to \phi \text{ONE} x)$.

On this account, the truish feature is (again) not a feature at all but a relation, this time a relation between properties ϕ and domains Δ. It is not directly specified by the truisms, but it might be said to be 'extracted' from the truisms in an extended sense similar to the one mentioned with respect to PR3. A common property shared by the realizers lies again just around the corner, namely the relational property of playing the truth-role relative to some domain or other—expressed by '$(\exists \Delta)(\phi$ plays the truth-role in $\Delta)$'.

PR5 requires that Lynch's account of truth, *T*, be revised accordingly. But it should *not* be revised to say that a proposition is true iff it has some property that plays the truth-role in some domain. That would take us back to 'Ty iff $(\exists \phi)(\phi y \; \& \; (\exists \Delta)(\forall x)(x \in \Delta \to \phi \text{ONE} x))$', which is just *T3* with its attendant problems. Instead, we now need a more substantial revision of Lynch's original, along the following lines:

> *T5** $(\forall y)(y \in \Delta \to [Ty \leftrightarrow (\exists \phi)(\phi y \; \& \; (\forall x)(x \in \Delta \to \phi \text{ONE} x))])$.

As it stands, though, this is not an account of truth at all. It is merely a pattern which doesn't actually say anything, because of the unbound domain-variable 'Δ'.

One way $T5^*$ can be turned into something that says something is by successively replacing 'Δ' with names referring to domains in Lynch's sense. Take 'DP' as a name for the domain of physical-object propositions and 'DE' as a name for the domain of ethical propositions. The resulting account of truth will be a bunch of conditionals, such as:

T5.1 $(\forall y)(y \in \text{DP} \rightarrow [Ty \leftrightarrow (\exists \phi)(\phi y \ \& \ (\forall x)(x \in \text{DP} \rightarrow \phi\text{ONE}x))])$,

$(\forall y)(y \in \text{DE} \rightarrow [Ty \leftrightarrow (\exists \phi)(\phi y \ \& \ (\forall x)(x \in \text{DE} \rightarrow \phi\text{ONE}x))])$,

and so on, until all domains of (atomic) propositions are covered.[18] We have encountered similar domain-restricted conditionals before, namely when I described pluralism concerning truth. While there is nothing wrong with such conditionals (not on Lynch's view anyway, for he takes the notion of a domain of discourse to be a viable one), they will not be good enough for Lynch's purposes. He wants a general account of truth that vindicates the monistic aspect of his pluralism, the idea that truth is one. But domain-restricted conditionals lend themselves to the multiple ambiguity version of pluralism, that is, to the view that truth is many rather than one realized by many.

The second way to turn $T5^*$ into an account of truth is by generalizing over domains. For every domain Δ, for every proposition y, if y belongs to Δ, then y is true iff y has some property standing in the ONE-relation to every proposition belonging to Δ:

T5.2 $(\forall \Delta)(\forall y)(y \in \Delta \rightarrow [Ty \leftrightarrow (\exists \phi)(\phi y \ \& \ (\forall x)(x \in \Delta \rightarrow \phi\text{ONE}x))])$.

This is more suitable for Lynch's purposes because it offers a single generalization rather than a bunch of conditionals. It also comes close to some of the things Lynch says when talking in domain-relative terms after he has laid out his functionalist account in absolute terms.[19]

---

[18] As I mentioned in fn. 10, because of the issue of mixed compound propositions, Lynch restricts attention to (domains of) atomic propositions when laying out the core of his functionalist account of truth. I will continue to gloss over this point for the sake of simplicity.

[19] At one point Lynch writes: '[a]n atomic proposition is true when it has the distinct *further* property that plays the truth-role—manifests truth—*for the domain of inquiry to which it belongs*' (2009: 77, his italics). In this passage, Lynch seems to think of playing the truth-role as domain relative. I am not happy with the passage, though, for a number of reasons. (a) It indicates that Lynch is thinking of one of the T5-type accounts of truth, but it doesn't make quite clear which one. (b) He seems to equate playing the truth-role (for a domain) with manifesting truth (for a domain), but that can't be right, given how Lynch defines manifestation (see below). (c) He employs a definite description: '*the* distinct *further* property that plays the truth role'. Since truth also plays the truth-role, on any notion of playing the truth-role, Lynch has to exclude it, saying in effect that a proposition is true when it has *the* property, *other than truth*, that plays the truth-role for the domain of inquiry to which the proposition belongs. This makes the passage quite unsuitable for a general account of truth.

However, it seems that *T5.2* is not quite as suited for Lynch's purposes as *T4*. Though it does offer a single generalization, it does not clearly identify anything that is shared by all and only the true propositions, because it does not take the form of an explicit account of truth, that is, the form '$(\forall y)(Ty \leftrightarrow \ldots y \ldots)$'. Consequently, it does not quite live up to the monistic aspirations of Lynch's pluralism. Since it merely generalizes over the bunch of domain-restricted conditionals in *T5.1*, *T5.2* still lends itself to the multiple ambiguity version of pluralism, which Lynch wants to resist.

Moreover, *PR5* and *T5.2* tend to blur the distinction between the two components of Lynch's theory by building the notion of a domain of discourse, which properly belongs to his pluralist metaphysics, into the functionalist account of truth, which was supposed to remain neutral with respect to theses that go beyond what is already implicit in our folk-conception of truth as given by the truisms. Thus, taking *PR5* plus *T5.2* to constitute the functionalist account of truth would come uncomfortably close to what Lynch says would be silly: '[i]t would be silly to say that the grasp of our folk concept of truth requires a tacit understanding of a pluralist metaphysics of truth' (2009: 84).

I suggest that Lynch's purposes are best served by taking *PR4* plus *T4* to constitute his functionalist account of truth. They are not in conflict with *PR5*, *T5.1*, and *T5.2* anyway. Lynch can advocate the latter in addition to the functionalist account of truth, namely as belonging to the second, the pluralist component of his overall view. Of course, this would mean that the overall view employs at least two somewhat different notions of playing the truth-role, one relativized to individual propositions, the other relativized to whole domains of propositions.

6

At the beginning, I presented the functionalist component of Lynch's theory as comprising two main claims, his *T* and his *PR*, and I went on to refer to the former as Lynch's functionalist account of truth. This is a bit misleading, for Lynch's functionalist theory contains a third central claim, a claim intended to tell us what truth itself is. Take Lynch's generalized biconditional,

> *T* A proposition is true iff it has some property that plays the truth-role,

which, according to Lynch, exhibits something that all and only true propositions have in common. One might now think that this biconditional is supposed to offer us an 'account of truth' in the sense that it can be upgraded to a property identity, telling us that truth itself just is the property expressed by the right-hand side of *T*:

> *T** the property being true = the property having some property that plays the truth-role.[20]

But Lynch rejects this: while *T* provides 'truth-conditions for the application of the truth concept' (2009: 72), it does not tell us what the property being true is, according to Lynch. This is the job of the third main claim of his functionalist theory:

> *TL* The property *being true* (or the property of truth) is the property that has the truish features essentially or which plays the truth-role as such. (2009: 74)

Note that, unlike *T**, Lynch's *TL* does not, as it were, aim to acquaint us with the property being true; it does not present an alternative *name* for this property, but instead presents a *definite description*. Lynch's functionalism about truth is thus a form of 'specifier functionalism' rather than a form of 'identity functionalism'.[21]

I postpone consideration of why Lynch rejects *T**. I want to take a closer look at *TL* first. On Lynch's view, truth plays the truth-role, but other properties, the realizers, play the truth-role too. Lynch now tries to single out truth by claiming that it is the sole property that has the truish features *essentially*, which amounts to the claim that it is the sole property that plays the truth-role essentially. The realizers, properties such as correspondence and superwarrant, may also play the truth-role, but they do so only accidentally (2009: 78).

I find this attempt to single out truth by way of a *modal* difference unconvincing. What is the problem? Note first that Lynch needs one of the relativized notions of playing the truth-role. Let us take the one that seemed most apt for Lynch's pluralism, the one that relativizes to individual propositions, *PR4*, expressed by 'φ plays the truth-role for *x*'. Since this is a relation, it is not quite clear what it even means to say that a property plays the truth-role, in

---

[20] Where, of course, the words 'plays the truth-role' abbreviate a much longer expression, extracted from the truisms and not containing the terms 'truth' or 'true'.

[21] *T** is like '(the property) being human = (the property) being a rational animal'. Note that the parenthetical phrase 'the property' can be dropped from both sides of *T**. The phrase is redundant, merely serving to prepare us for what sort of thing is going to be named next. *TL*, on the other hand, is like '(the property) being human is the property that Commander Data would like to possess the most'. The phrase 'the property' can be dropped from the left-hand side of *TL*, but not from its right-hand side, where it functions as an indispensable part of a definite description of a property. Why not regard *TL* as a kind of identity functionalism too? Because, unlike *T**, *TL* is not a genuine identity claim, of the form '*x* = *y*', at least not according to standard Russellian accounts of definite descriptions on which *TL* comes out as an existential generalization.

this sense, essentially.[22] Still, I think we can see what the problem is if we look at some examples.

Take two physical-object propositions, say the proposition that snow is white and the proposition that snow is green, and an ethical proposition, say the proposition that killing is wrong. Truth plays the truth-role for each one. Moreover, it is plausible to hold that it does so essentially or necessarily.[23] Now consider one of the intended realizers, say correspondence with a fact. It does not play the truth-role for the ethical proposition at all, according to Lynch, so the modal difference he adverts to does not show up here. What about the physical-object propositions? Correspondence does play the truth-role for each of them. But it is hard to see why there should be a modal difference in this case: Why would Lynch claim that correspondence plays the truth-role for these propositions but doesn't do so essentially?[24] Maybe he thinks that, though these propositions exist in our world, there are some worlds in which they do not exist. But if this were a reason for saying that correspondence does not play the truth-role for these propositions essentially, then it would equally be a reason for saying that truth does not play the truth-role for them essentially (which tells us that 'φ plays the truth-role for *x* essentially' ought to be understood in terms of 'φ plays the truth-role for *x* in every world in which *x* exists'). Maybe Lynch thinks that, though these propositions belong to the domain of physical-object propositions in our world, there are worlds in which they belong to some other domain, say the domain of ethical propositions, for which correspondence does not function as a truth-realizer. But this would be a very odd view. Moreover, it is one Lynch explicitly rejects: '[b]elonging to a particular domain is an essential fact about an atomic proposition' (2009: 80). I see no further reason why Lynch might claim there to be this modal difference between truth and correspondence: they both seem to play the truth-role essentially for the propositions for which they play the truth-role at all.

Lynch's *TL* also contains the claim that truth is the sole property that plays the truth-role *as such*. Lynch seems to think this just says the same thing again in other words. But I do not think it does. He tells us that other properties that may also play the truth-role, such as correspondence and superwarrant, play the truth-role 'only accidentally'. He then elaborates on this, writing: 'That is,

---

[22] Given a relativized notion of playing the truth-role, the reference to 'the truish features' in Lynch's *TL* must be replaced by a reference to the truish *relation*. It is equally unclear what it means to say that a property stands in the truish relation essentially.

[23] Form the relevant instantiations of the truisms from the first section: they are plausibly taken to express necessary truths—certainly Lynch will take them to express necessary truths. (For present purposes, we don't need to discuss whether that's really sufficient for saying that truth plays the truth-role for these propositions *essentially* as opposed to *necessarily*. Lynch doesn't raise the issue either.)

[24] Form the relevant instantiation of the truisms (instantiating them to the physical-object propositions) and replace 'is true' with 'corresponds with a fact'. Why should the results not express necessary truths, if they express truths at all?

they may have the truish features, but only when they are possessed by [. . .] propositions of a certain domain' (2009: 78). By my lights, the elaboration does not point to a modal difference at all: it does not really indicate that correspondence and superwarrant play the truth-role only accidentally. Instead, it points to another difference: correspondence and superwarrant play the truth-role only *relative* to certain domains, while truth plays the truth-role *absolutely*. Of course, we have seen that Lynch's official notion of playing the truth-role should be a relativized one, so it would be ill advised to suddenly invoke an absolute notion to single out truth. However, one can use a relativized notion to get the import of an absolute one: while correspondence and superwarrant play the truth-role relative to some domains of propositions but not relative to all domains, truth plays the truth-role relative to all domains of propositions. Alternatively, using the *PR4*-notion of playing the truth-role: while correspondence and superwarrant play the truth-role relative to some but not to all propositions, truth plays the truth-role relative to all propositions.

If Lynch really wants to reject T^*, if he really does not want to identify truth itself with the property of having some property that plays the truth-role, then, I suggest, he should single out truth in this manner, through its *range*. The modal difference he adverts to in *TL* is too hard to find—as far as I can see, there is no such difference at all.

Why does Lynch reject T^*? Given that T is one of the central claims of his functionalist theory of truth, wouldn't it be natural to propose that truth is the property of having some property that plays the truth-role? Lynch himself made this proposal in an earlier publication.[25] But now he rejects it: '[t]hat [i.e., T^*] would imply that truth is the property of having some property that has certain features. But does the second-order property itself have those features? That is, it seems that we want to say that *truth itself* is objective and a goal of inquiry. But now is my belief's having the property of having some property that is a goal of inquiry a goal of inquiry? [. . .] Not obviously; indeed, obviously not' (2009: 66).

So the idea is this: since being true plays the truth-role (has the truish features), the property having some property that plays the truth-role does not play the truth-role (does not have the truish features). On the face of it, this has the ring of plausibility. But at the same time one might be worried whether there is not some illusion involved here. The issue is a bit confusing. In the following, I want to present an argument suggesting that Lynch's point, despite its seeming plausibility, does indeed involve an illusion.

Lynch makes his point in terms of his functionalist account of truth, *PR* plus *T*, which employs an absolute notion of playing the truth-role. We have

---

[25] See Lynch (2001). Lynch (2009: 63–5) says that one might be tempted to advance something akin to T^* on behalf of the view advocated by Wright (1992).

seen that he should be employing one of the two relativized notions. Since the PR4-notion of playing the truth-role seemed the one better suited to Lynch's purposes, we should be looking at the functionalist account of truth that employs this notion, that is, at

T4 Tx iff $(\exists\phi)(\phi x \ \& \ \phi ONEx)$.

If it can be shown that the property expressed on the right-hand side plays the truth-role for x, then Lynch's point rests on an illusion and does not provide a reason against identifying truth with that property.

I think this can be shown—well, at least a fairly good stab can be made at showing it. But to run the argument with T4, we would have to look at what the truish relation actually says when the abbreviations in '$\phi ONEx$' are spelled out. This would make things very complicated. So I will engage in a simplifying pretense.

Pretend there is only one truism about truth, say *Norm of Belief*, so that the truish relation can be expressed more simply as 'ϕNx'. Continuing this pretense, the relevant T4-style account of truth will then be:

t4 Tx iff $(\exists\phi)(\phi x \ \& \ \phi Nx)$,

and our task will turn into the simpler task of showing that the right-hand side of *t4* plays the relevant (pretend) truth-role for some given proposition. So, take some sample proposition and call it 's'. Unpacking 'N' tells us what it is for a property ϕ to play the truth-role for s: $\phi Ns = (\phi s \leftrightarrow$ it is correct to believe s). Let us consider the two parts separately:

N.1 $\phi s \rightarrow$ it is correct to believe s,

N.2 It is correct to believe s $\rightarrow \phi s$.

Consider N.1 first. Replace 'ϕ' with the expression from *t4*'s right-hand side, that is, '$(\exists\phi)(\phi x \ \& \ \phi Nx)$', applied to s:

$(\exists\phi)$ $(\phi s \ \& \ \phi Ns) \rightarrow$ it is correct to believe s.

Unpacking 'N', we get:

$(\exists\phi)$ $(\phi s \ \& \ (\phi s \leftrightarrow$ it is correct to believe s$)) \rightarrow$ it is correct to believe s.

Instantiate 'ϕ' to some property, say the property corresponding with a fact. The antecedent of the resulting conditional trivially entails its consequent. So the property expressed on the right-hand side of *t4* satisfies N.1: it plays one half of the relevant truth-role. Now consider N.2. Again replace 'ϕ' and unpack 'N':

It is correct to believe s $\rightarrow (\exists\phi)(\phi s \ \& \ \phi Ns)$,
It is correct to believe s $\rightarrow (\exists\phi)(\phi s \ \& \ (\phi s \leftrightarrow$ it is correct to believe s$))$.

Assume, for conditional proof, that it is correct to believe s. Then s, on Lynch's view, must have one of the properties that realizes truth, that is, s corresponds with a fact or is superwarranted or . . . ; using obvious abbreviations:

Cs or Ss or . . .

From this, together with the assumption that it is correct to believe s, we get (fairly trivially):

(Cs & (Cs ↔ it is correct to believe s)) or (Ss & (Ss ↔ it is correct to believe s)) or . . .

from which we get the consequent: (∃ϕ)(ϕs & (ϕs ↔ it is correct to believe s)). So the property expressed on the right-hand side of *t4* satisfies *N2*: it plays the other half of the relevant truth-role too. So it looks like the property expressed by '(∃ϕ)(ϕx & ϕNx)' does play the truth-role for *x*, pretending that role is given by 'ϕNx'.

There seems to be no obstacle against identifying the property that appears on the right-hand side of the pretense-account *t4* with the property that appears on its left-hand side. And as far as I can see at the moment (but I admit that I am not entirely sure), the pretense is not essential to the argument. When the pretense is lifted, an argument of the same sort—though it would be considerably more complex—should still work to show that the property expressed on the righthand side of *T4*, the property expressed by '(∃ϕ)(ϕx & ϕONEx)', plays the truth-role for some given proposition. This suggests that the obstacle Lynch perceives against identifying being true with the property having some property that plays the truth-role (at least in the *PR4*-sense of playing the truth-role) does indeed involve an illusion.

7

I have described the main claim of the second component of Lynch's view as his multiple realizability thesis, the thesis that truth can be realized by different properties. Though Lynch at times employs the term 'realization', familiar from functionalism in the philosophy of mind, he actually prefers another term: '[t]ruth is a functional property that can be realized—or, as I shall say in the book "manifested"—in more than one way' (2009: 3). Lynch would put what I called his multiple realizability thesis as the claim that truth can be *manifested* by different properties. At first, this appears to be no more than a matter of terminological preference. There is, however, a bit more involved, for Lynch also offers his own, special account of manifestation (and he may well have chosen the alternate term to signal that he has his own, special account of realization/manifestation). Unfortunately the account appears to be flawed:

> Let us say that where a property F is immanent in or *manifested by* property M, it is a priori that F's essential features are a subset of M's features. (2009: 74)

Note first that this characterizes the general relation of manifestation—the claim that some given property, such as correspondence or superwarrant, manifests truth will then come out as an instance of this general relation of manifestation that can hold between properties. I have already hinted at one problem with this account: Lynch will say later that properties like correspondence and superwarrant manifest truth relative to certain domains (2009: 76), yet his account does not characterize manifestation as a domain-relative notion. This, however, is not the main problem. The main problem is that the basic idea behind the account appears to be on the wrong track.

Lynch holds that the property being true can be manifested by, for example, the property corresponding with a fact. On the account given above, this can be the case only if *all* the features essential to the first are also features of the second. But we have already encountered some properties of being true that appear to be essential to it but are not properties of corresponding with a fact at all, not on Lynch's view. The property playing the truth-role for all propositions (standing in the truish relation to all propositions), and the property playing the truth-role in all domains are two examples: they appear to be essential to being true, but corresponding with a fact does not have these properties, according to Lynch. As it stands, the account of manifestation does not allow that properties such as correspondence and superwarrant can manifest truth: it undermines what was supposed to be the main selling point of Lynch's version of pluralism concerning truth.

There is a still more general problem here. We can see that Lynch's account of manifestation does not work, even when we disregard all issues concerning the question which properties play the truth-role in which sense of the notion of playing the truth-role and focus solely on the idea that lies at the very core of Lynch's pluralism. Being true surely has the property being identical with being true and has it essentially. But it is crucial to Lynch's pluralism that various properties can manifest (realize) being true without being identical with it. Such properties will thus lack a property truth has essentially. The fault lies entirely with Lynch's account of manifestation, which does not work for any sort of multiple realizability thesis. Those who advocate such a thesis in the philosophy of mind, about pain, for example, will want to say that being in pain can be realized by, say, C-fiber agitation. Yet, being in pain has a property, namely the property being identical with the property being in pain, that C-fiber agitation is precisely supposed to lack; hence, it cannot be manifested by C-fiber agitation—not on Lynch's characterization of manifestation.

What has gone wrong? I think it has to do with the term 'feature', which appears in Lynch's account of manifestation. Lynch generally uses this term to mean 'property', so that a feature of a property will simply be a property of a property (he even emphasizes this explicitly (2009: 78 fn. 6). However, at times he seems to slip into thinking of a 'feature' of a property differently, namely along the lines of what is sometimes called a 'mark' of a property, in the sense in which one might say that being an animal is a mark of being human, because being human = being a rational animal. On this use of 'feature of a property', Lynch's account of manifestation does make some sense: it makes sense to say that being an animal is manifested by being human because every mark of being an animal is also a mark of being human (i.e., whatever properties are constitutive of being an animal are also constitutive of being human). Note that at a point where Lynch wants to illustrate his manifestation relation, he writes that 'the essential features of redness, whatever they are, are a subset of the features of being scarlet' (2009: 75). This works for 'feature' in the sense of 'mark of a property', but not in the sense of 'property of a property,' because being red has a property being scarlet lacks, namely being identical with the property being red. Unfortunately, Lynch's account also needs the first, original sense of 'feature of a property', because on his view, playing the truth-role is a property, but not a mark, of the property being true.

How serious is this problem? In one sense, it is of course very serious: Lynch's account of manifestation (realization) does not work at all; it is on the wrong track entirely. On the other hand, Lynch's functionalist theory of truth can be stated without it, and even his pluralism can be developed for quite a while, employing the notion of manifestation (or realization) without taking on board his special account of this notion. I see no reason why Lynch could not simply replace this faulty account with another one. So, ultimately, the problem does not seem all that serious, not for the overall shape of his theory.

8

Let me take stock and summarize the points that Lynch—and others with a functionalist-pluralist agenda—should take to heart and be guided by in their attempts to pursue and develop the pluralist program. Bearing in mind that functionalism in general continues to be of some interest and that its proper formulation tends to present difficulties (especially if one is prepared to look at the details), I have devoted considerable attention to the proper formulation of the variety of functionalism under discussion in this chapter, Lynch's pluralist functionalism about truth. It turns out that the role-playing notion crucial to Lynch's functionalism, the notion of playing the truth-role, is best construed as a relativized one—relativized to propositions, as in *PR4*, or maybe relativized to domains of propositions, as in *PR5*, though the latter seems second best.

Lynch now advocates a form of specifier functionalism about truth, offering a description of the property being true. In previous publications, he advocated a form of identity functionalism about truth, identifying the property being true with the (second-order) property having some property that plays the truth-role. The argument motivating this change of mind is interesting—if successful, it would show all forms of identity functionalism to be untenable. But the argument does not appear to be successful. Finally, Lynch offers a special account of the important notion of realization (or manifestation). The account is flawed; however, this does not seem to seriously threaten the overall shape of his functionalist theory of truth.[26]

References

Barnard, R. & Horgan, T. (2013). The synthetic unity of truth. In N. J. L. L. Pedersen & C. D. Wright (eds.): *Truth and Pluralism: Current Debates* (180–196). New York: Oxford University Press.

Barnard, R. & Horgan, T. (2006). Truth as mediated correspondence. *Monist* 89: 31–50.

Lynch, M. P. (2001). A functionalist theory of truth. In M. P. Lynch (ed.), *The Nature of Truth* (723–749). Cambridge, MA: MIT Press.

Lynch, M. P. (2009). *Truth as One and Many*. Oxford: Clarendon Press.

Sher, G. (2013). Forms of correspondence: the intricate route from thought to reality. In N. J. L. L. Pedersen & C. D. Wright (eds.): *Truth and Pluralism: Current Debates* (157–179). New York: Oxford University Press.

Sher, G. (2005). Functional pluralism. *Philosophical Books* 46: 311–330.

Wright, C. J. G. (1992). *Truth and Objectivity*. Cambridge, MA: Harvard University Press.

---

[26] Thanks to JC Beall, Pascal Engel, Patrick Greenough, Michael Lynch, and Crispin Wright for helpful objections to a talk based on an earlier draft of this paper, and thanks to Nikolaj Pedersen and Cory Wright for their helpful comments.

{ 4 }

Alethic Functionalism and the Norm of Belief
Pascal Engel

1. Alethic functionalism and the norm of truth

Deflationists take truth to have no essence and to be nothing more than an expressive device encapsulated in the equivalence schema

(*ES*) ⟨p⟩ is true if and only if p.

A familiar objection to deflationism is that truth contains more than this platitude. The extra element that it contains is that truth is the norm of assertion, what our assertions aim at, and in this sense it involves a substantive property (Dummett 1959; Wright 1992). To that objection, deflationists have answered either by denying that truth involves any normative dimension or by agreeing that truth is a norm of assertion, while denying that this can be a substantive property. Truth, the deflationist argues, is indeed desirable and valuable, but this evaluative dimension is not part of the concept of truth itself (Horwich 1990/1998, 1999, 2001). But is it clear that all there is to say about the normativity of truth can be drawn from the deflationist platitudes? And are we forced to choose between a 'lightweight' and a 'heavyweight' conception of the normativity of truth? Perhaps there is some middle ground between these extremes, which would both allow us both to grant that the normative dimension of truth is a substantive property—contra deflationism—and which nevertheless would not entail that truth has an essence—contra nature traditional theories (correspondence, coherence, and the like). Functionalism about truth seems to suit that purpose. According to alethic functionalism, truth is a complex functional property identified by various properties playing jointly a certain role. These properties are the platitudes or truisms that we commonly associate with truth: the disquotation principle, that to be true is to correspond to the facts, that truth is distinct from justification, that truth is objective, that truth is the correctness condition of belief, that truth is the end of inquiry. Together these truisms compose the functional role of truth, just as for analytic functionalism in the philosophy of mind, the various properties associated to being in pain compose the functional role of pain. To be true for a proposition is to have a property that plays the truth-role. Just as the functional property of pain is realized differently in various organisms, the functional role of truth is realized differently in different domains and discourses where truth applies. Although there is a common role that all truths play, all truths are not of the same sort: moral truths, mathematical truths, truth about ordinary, physical, medium-size objects, or truths about aesthetic matters, if such there be, are each of a distinctive kind. This view has been suggested by Wright (1996, 2001) and further elaborated by Lynch (2009). My objective, in this article, is not to discuss the ontological and logical difficulties that alethic functionalism encounters (C. D. Wright 2010; Pedersen 2010), but to concentrate on the specific issue from which much of this discussion started, that of the normative role of truth. In particular, I want to concentrate on the two following so-called 'truisms':

(NT) *Norm of belief*: it is prima facie correct to believe that p if an only if the proposition that p is true.

(EI) *End of inquiry*: other things being equal, true beliefs are a worthy goal of inquiry.

The question that I want to raise is the one that Lynch asks directly in his essay: how does alethic functionalism account for the normativity of truth (Lynch 2009: 153–5)? According to Lynch, his form of pluralism accounts for both truisms and makes them part of what plays the truth-role. One of the tenets of functionalism about truth, thus understood, is that specification of the truth-role is just a 'job description' and that the normative truism is 'part of the core folk theory that individuates the truth-role'. The functionalist needs not, according to Lynch, be more specific than that. In particular, she needs not explain *why* truth is a worthy goal of inquiry and why it is a norm of belief. Can alethic functionalism account for this part of the truth-role, and can it incorporate it among the truisms about truth? I would like to argue that it does so at the price of misunderstanding the substantive nature of the norm of truth.

I shall first rehearse the reasons that we have for claiming, against deflationism, that the truism that truth is the correctness condition for belief has to be understood in the objective sense. The norm of truth for belief is actually a norm of knowledge. I shall then argue that this puts a strong constraint upon alethic functionalism, which threatens the claim that the truism can be realized in different domains. A consequence of alethic functionalism, which it shares with alethic pluralism in general, is that there should be different norms of truth for belief in different domains. But there are, I shall try to argue, good reasons to think that the norm of truth has to be interpreted uniformly across domains. The functionalist picture is thus threatened.

2. Can the norm of truth be deflated?

The origins of the present discussion about the normativity of truth are probably in Dummett's (1959) classical article, where the role of truth is compared to the role of winning in a game. Dummett argued against the then-called 'redundantist' conception of truth that it cannot account for the 'point' of the concept of truth. But the more proximate origins are in Wright's (1992) discussion of deflationism. Deflationism—the view that truth is not a genuine property and that all there to truth is the equivalence schema (ES)—is wrong, according to Wright, because it is not able to account for the difference between truth and assertibility and for the normative character of truth. Truth registers a different norm than warranted assertibility. In essentials, the argument is the following. Warrant and truth are intimately related in our assertoric practice: whenever I believe I am warranted in asserting some proposition, I also believe that it is true, and whenever I believe some proposition is true, I also believe that I have warrant for it. So truth and warrant coincide in positive normative force. Now according to deflationism, the equivalence schema (ES) has an equivalent for negation

> (*NE*) It is true that not-p iff it is not true that p.

But the corresponding instance of (NE) is wrong if we substitute 'warranted' in for 'true'. For any proposition that is for us neither warranted nor unwarranted (such as, say, that the Loch Ness monster does not exist) there is a conditional,

> It is warrantedly assertible that not-p if it is not warrantedly assertible that p.

So truth is a norm of correctness *distinct* from warranted assertibility: they diverge in extension (Wright 1992: 18, 2001: 756).

Truth is normative, in the sense that it is 'a property the possession or lack of which determines which assertions are acceptable and which are not' (Wright 2001: 775). Truth is a species of correctness, the correctness condition for assertions, and, more fundamentally, for beliefs. In other words, if one were to describe the assertoric practices of a population without mentioning that truth is what these assertoric practices are *for*, and that it is what makes them *correct*, one would have failed to describe these practices. We could not *explain* these practices if we took truth and warranted assertibility to coincide in extension.

Wright's discussion of the normative import of truth is led in terms of the norm governing assertion. But, although assertion and belief are distinct, the correctness condition for assertion can easily be transposed to belief: truth is what it is correct to believe.

Deflationists can deny that truth has any normative load in relation to assertion or to belief. They can argue that the so-called normativity that attaches to belief does not amount to more than the fact that beliefs have a mind-to-world direction of fit such that they are either true or false.[1] But most deflationists about truth accept the idea that there is a normative dimension in belief and in assertion and that insofar as belief and assertion have correctness conditions, this dimension belongs to our concept of truth as well. But they deny that this normativity is an *essential* feature of truth. So the deflationist (Horwich 1990/1998, 2001; Dodd 1999) can perfectly accept the idea that truth carries with it a normative load, and he can say that his account does take care of the norms

(i) One should assert (believe) only what is true.

or

(ii) Truth is what it is (good) valuable to assert (believe).

He denies, however, that this comes down to more than

(iii) One should (it is good to) believe that p iff p,

from which in turn one can derive a (potentially infinite) disjunction of sentences of the form

(iv) One should assert that snow is white only if snow is white; one should assert that grass is green only if grass is green, etc.

or

(v) It is good/valuable to assert that snow is white only if snow is white; it is good/valuable to assert that grass is green only if grass is green, etc

Indeed (i) or (ii) allow us to generalize over the conjunctions of claims (iv) and (v), but that does not mean that there is a general norm of truth for assertion independently of subject matter and of the particular assertions listed, and truth is neither mentioned in (iii) nor in conjunctions like (iv) and (v) (Horwich 1990/1998; Dodd 1999: 297). So the deflationist can claim that Wright's argument does not show that truth is normative in any robust sense.

Moreover, the deflationist claims that one can explain the value that is attached to truth in instrumentalist terms, on the basis of the familiar idea that true beliefs conjoined with desires lead to actions: for any action A resulting in

---

[1] See for instance Dretske: 'I agree that beliefs are necessarily true or false. If I didn't understand what it was to *be* true or false, I could hardly understand what it was to be a belief. But I do not see that I need go further than this. This seems like enough to distinguish beliefs from other mental states like wishes, desires, hopes, doubts, and pains [. . .]. Why, in order to understand what a belief is, do I also have to think of a belief as something that is *supposed to be* true? If I deliberately deceive you, is the resulting belief supposed to be true?' (2001: 248).

reaching a goal G, there are beliefs of the form 'If I do A I shall get G' that are true. Hence the truth of these beliefs is explained in instrumentalist terms. If one objects that truth is not simply instrumentally valuable but that it is also intrinsically valuable, the deflationist can also grant this and claim that the intrinsic value of truth does not amount to more than an infinite list of the form (iv) or (v) (Horwich 1999: 256–8, 2006).

But this reply is certainly unsatisfactory. First, because, as Wright points out, one cannot accept that what it is to satisfy the norm of truth for belief or assertion amounts to nothing more than knowing series of conjunctions like (iv) and (v) unless one *already* understands the difference between the proposition that snow is white or that grass is green and the proposition that those propositions are warranted (2001, 757). In other words, the normative character of assertion or belief expressed by conjunctions like (iv) and (v) does not capture the generality of the norm or value of truth.[2] Moreover, it seems to lead us to a form of particularism about norms or values according to which there as many cognitive norms as there are particular true sentences that we could assert or beliefs that we could entertain about particular subject matters. On the deflationist reading of the norms of truth for assertion and belief, we can only acknowledge the existence of particular norms or values attached to each sentence or belief, not the existence of a general norm such as (NT) (Lynch 2004: 512–3, 2008). In the second place, the deflationist dissolution of the normative character of truth does not capture the distinction between a *subjective* or *prima facie* reason to assert or to believe something:

(a) Believing that p is true is a prima facie reason for asserting that p

and an *objective* reason

(b) The fact that p is true provides a good reason to assert it.

Wright's inflationary argument involves this distinction between merely having a *prima facie reason* to assert (believe) that p and having a *warranted reason* to assert (believe that p). The difference is clearly brought out by Huw Price's (1998) distinction between three norms of assertibility:

  (I) *Subjective*: it is prima facie correct to assert that p if one believes that p
      or: one is incorrect to assert that p if one does not believe that p.

 (II) *Objective*: p is objectively assertible if S's belief that p is justified
      or: one is incorrect to assert that p if though one believes that p one does not have adequate grounds for believing that p.

(III) *Hyper-objective*: if p is true one should assert that p
      or: one is incorrect to assert that p if in fact it is not the case that p.

---

[2] See also Engel (2008b) for a similar criticism.

In order to sort these out, Price invites us to imagine a tribe, the 'Merely Opinionated Asserters' (MOA), who criticize assertions for flouting the principles of subjective assertibility and objective assertibility but not for flouting that of hyper-objective assertibility. These speakers 'express their beliefs—that is, the kind of behavioral dispositions that we would characterize as beliefs—by means of a speech act we might call *merely opinionated assertion*'. They criticize one another for making insincere or inadequately justified assertions, but not for asserting what's false. We can also imagine these speakers being fully competent in using a disquotational truth predicate, and so in applying the deflationist truth concept. They fully understand the deflationist truth concept, but not the concept of truth. Thus, the former cannot be the same as the latter.

The MOA's concept of truth is limited to the deflationist one and to the warranted-assertibility one. But they became extinct because they lack the capacity to express genuine disagreements. They can only express faultless disagreements. They would be relativists of sorts.[3]

Price's distinction between the three norms of assertibility is a useful one. But it does not settle the debate unless one answers the question: which of the three norms is the one that corresponds to our actual conception of truth? The deflationist will deny that we have any reason to think that (III), the hyper-objective norm, expresses the notion of truth, and he will argue that it expresses a stronger concept, which it not truth. Price himself claims that a community that, like the MOAs, would not have the resources to express objective disagreements in the sense of the hyper-objective norm would lack the resources to improve their assertions and their beliefs, but he denies that one needs to interpret the hyper-objective norm as expressing a substantive concept of truth: he agrees with the deflationist that truth has no hidden essence, but that the MOA behave *as if* they had the substantial concept:

> Suppose there is no substantial, objective, property of this kind, which the Mo'ans' belief-like behavioral dispositions either have or lack. Nevertheless, it might turn out to be very much to the Mo'ans' advantage to behave as if there were such a property. As it turns out, it isn't difficult to adopt this pretence. The practice Mo'ans need to adopt is exactly the same as that required by the previous alternative. They simply need to ensure that when they believe that p, they be prepared not only to assert (in the old MOA sense) that p, but also to ascribe fault to anyone who asserts not-p, independently of any grounds for thinking that that person fails one of the first two norms of assertibility. (Price 1998: 251)

According to Price, it is not unconceivable that the MOA, had they mimicked the hyper-objective norm instead of actually accepting it, would have

---

[3] And in a sense, they would be close to what is advocated by Kölbel (2008), MacFarlane (2005), and other contemporary versions of relativism about truth.

successfully survived. So it need not be associated with a realist conception of truth and is compatible with an ideal notion of warranted assertibility, such as the one that Wright calls superassertibility (that is, being warranted to assert or to believe in the ordinary sense and remaining warranted no matter how our information is expanded or improved).[4]

Price's diagnosis concurs in part with what Wright calls 'minimalism'. For Wright, we have to distinguish two levels: on the one hand our *concept* of truth, which is identifiable through the set of platitudes that are a priori associated with it (syntactic discipline, correspondence, objectivity, etc.), and on the other hand, the *property* of truth, which realizes the concept (Wright 2001: 752). The former is stable and invariant over all discourses that are truth-apt, whereas the second can vary from discourse to discourse. Minimalism in Wright's sense resembles deflationism in that it admits that there is a unique concept of truth, which is characterized by a set of *relatively* 'lightweight' features (this qualification will be explained below). But minimalism diverges from deflationism in that the later denies that truth corresponds to any property, whereas the former is compatible with truth being 'realized' or 'constituted'[5] differently from domain to domain. So it 'incorporates a potential *pluralism*' (ibid.) about truth, which allows that the metaphysical commitments that one can undertake about the property of truth may vary depending upon whether one deals with mathematics, ethics, physical objects, or other domains. Thus for physical objects, the truth property can be correspondence, for ethics it can be coherence, for mathematics superassertibility, and so on. The pluralism in question is 'potential' because it does not entail that there is no truth property shared by all true propositions. A view according to which the truth property would have to be distinctive in each domain would be a form of strong pluralism, which is not Wright's view.[6] Neither is Wright's minimalism a form of *conceptual* pluralism about truth. It is not the view that there are several concepts of truth or that the concept of truth is ambiguous.[7] On the contrary, it claims that there is a common core of the concept of truth that is uniform across various domains of discourse. This core is constituted by the platitudes that Wright (2001: 760) lists thus:

- *Transparency*: to assert (believe) that p is to present p as true;
- *Epistemic opacity*: some truths may not be known or be unknowable;
- *Embedding*: truth aptness is preserved under various syntactic operations;
- *Correspondence*: for a proposition to be true is to correspond to reality;

---

[4] Superassertibility is named 'superwarrant' by Lynch (2009).
[5] Wright uses the first vocabulary in his (2001) paper and the second vocabulary in his (1996: 926) response to commentators.
[6] I agree here with Pedersen & Wright (2013, fn. 6).
[7] Although Wright (1992) is sometimes unclear on this, Wright (1996: 924) is not. The idea that there might be a plurality of concepts of truth is what Lynch calls 'simple alethic pluralism' (2009: 54–9).

- *Contrast*: a proposition may be true without being justified and vice versa;
- *Stability*: if a proposition is ever true, then it is always true;
- *Absoluteness*: truth is absolute, there are no degrees of truth.

What is striking here is that the normativity of truth—truth is the correctness condition of belief—does not figure in this list of platitudes, whereas other pluralist views, in particular Lynch's, include it in the list. There are two possible reasons. One is that the normativity of truth—that truth is a norm of assertion—is implicit in the other platitudes. In particular, if one agrees that assertion is regulated by the norm of truth, this is implicit in the *transparency* feature. And if we agree that the norm is stronger than warranted assertibility, one could consider that this is implicit in the *contrast* feature. But given that the normativity of truth is taken to indicate a *substantive* feature, this means that the platitudes that are a priori associated with our concept of truth are not—at least for this feature—'lightweight'. This is in tension with the idea that our concept of truth involves non-substantive features that are uniform across truth-apt discourses. The other reason for normativity's absence is that for Wright, the normativity of truth is not simply a truism among the others. It is the sign of the divergence of extension between the *property* of truth and the *property* of warranted assertibility.[8] The difference does not lie at the concept level but at the realizer or property level. This means that *whatever* property realizes the concept of truth in a particular domain has to register the normativity of truth as a substantive feature. This seems plausible for the domains where truth seems to consist in some objective notion of correspondence or for which superassertibility is the appropriate model—such as discourse about physical objects or about numbers—but this is much less plausible for domains where the objectivity of truth is in question—such as ethics, law, or humor. But for the latter discourse, at least, it is unlikely that truth can outstrip warranted assertibility (it would correspond at most to the subjective norm in Price's sense).

So pluralism about truth à la Wright seems unstable: either the normativity of truth is a mere platitude associated to its *concept*, which means it cannot be said to be a substantive feature (and thus we come close to the deflationist view according to which normativity is trivial) or it is a substantive feature of the *property* of truth, but then this means that the scope of pluralism becomes limited, and we come closer to monism. This instability, which is proper to the normative feature of truth, is related to the one that has been said to threaten alethic pluralism in general (Pedersen 2010; Wright 2012). The second disjunct will be examined in §4 below. The first disjunct—incorporating the truth norm among

---

[8] This answer seems to be the one that Wright (2001: 754–5) himself adopts, since he explicitly formulates his inflationary argument in terms of the difference between the *property* of truth as warranted assertibility and the *property* of being normative.

the truisms about truth—is the one taken by Lynch's version of pluralism: alethic functionalism. But can it account for the force of the norm of truth?

3. Alethic functionalism and the norm of truth

Lynch's alethic functionalism does not identify truth with the properties that, in their respective domains, satisfy the truth platitudes. On the first version of his view (Lynch 2001), truth is the second-order functional property of having a property that plays the truth-role, according to the analogy with functional properties in the philosophy of mind (thus pain is the second-order property of having the properties that characterize the role of pain, and it is realized differently in various organisms). The truth-role is specified by a list of truisms that differs from Wright's list mainly in that it includes the *Norm of belief* (*NT*) and the *End of inquiry* (*EI*). The property of being true is the property that plays the truth-role, relative to a given domain. These properties are thus the realizer properties. But we cannot identify truth with the realizer properties, because, given that these are by definition distinct, what is common to them would be lost, just as the common explanatory power of truth would itself be lost. Indeed, if truth is in one domain correspondence, in another superassertiblity, and in yet another one coherence, it become unclear what common property these realize (Lynch 2009: 66). This is why Lynch prefers to say that truth is the property that has the truish features essentially or that plays the truth-role *as such* (74) and that truth is not realized but *manifested* in the various properties (correspondence, superassertibility, etc.):

> Truth is, as it were, *immanent* in ontologically distinct properties. Let us say that where property F is immanent in or *manifested by* property M, it is *a priori* that F's essential features are a subset of M's features [. . .] Propositions about different subjects can be made true by distinct properties each of which plays the truth-role. Thus (atomic) propositions about the antics of the ordinary objects and properties of our daily life may be true because they represent those objects and properties. For propositions of that kind, correct representation plays the truth-role and it is *a priori* that if a proposition represents correctly it will be true. For propositions of another sort, perhaps moral propositions, superwarrant may be what plays the truth-role, or manifests truth. (2009: 74, 77)

This, Lynch tells us, allows us to see how truth can be both many and one: many because different properties may manifest truth in distinct domains of

> [i]nquiry, one because there is a single property so manifested: it is the unique property that is, necessarily, objective, had by beliefs at the end of inquiry and which makes a proposition correct to believe. (ibid.)

But if one pauses for a moment to consider what alethic functionalism implies, the question arises: will the truish features that are essential to the property of truth be the same in all domains? In other words, and to limit ourselves to the norm of truth, will it be the *same* norm of truth that is manifested in, say, the domain of the ordinary antics of the objects of our daily life and the moral domain? Suppose that correspondence manifests truth in the first domain and superassertiblity in the second. If so, the norm of truth will be a distinct norm in each domain. In some domains, for instance for aesthetic or comic truths, it might be manifested differently, since the correctness norm in these latter domains may—if one grants that the aesthetic and comic domains are truth-apt—be presumably attached to a weaker notion of truth than that which holds for, say, mathematics or physics:

> According to our definition of manifestation, a property manifests truth only if it has the 'truish' features in some particular way. Consequently, depending on what property manifests truth for a particular proposition, we can say that what makes it correct to believe *that* proposition is that it has the property of superwarrant, or correspondence. (Lynch 2009: 153–4)

But this is counterintuitive, for, as we saw, a large part of the argument that motivates alethic pluralism à la Wright and alethic functionalism à la Lynch is precisely that the norm of truth is a stronger norm than warranted assertibility, or, to use Price's classification, it is either objective or hyper-objective. The alternative consists of agreeing with the deflationist that the norm of truth for belief is but a shallow feature that carries no particular weight.[9] So it seems that on Lynch's functionalist picture, if truth is a normative feature that is part of truth-role, it cannot be a substantive property. He writes:

> According to functionalism, both normative truisms about truth are integral to what truth is. They are part of the core folk theory of truth that individuates the truth-role. Consequently, any property that manifests truth must satisfy these normative platitudes. So for example, any property that plays the truth-role for propositions of a particular domain must be such

---

[9] A similar remark is made by Edwards:

> At most, the property of superassertibility can manifest a restricted truth property (perhaps moral truth, in this case). But this is not the result Lynch needs; he needs superassertibility—and all the domain specific properties—to manifest the *generic* truth property. That is, he needs them to contain the features of the *domain-free* truth property as a proper part. The generic truth property, however, is composed of the *unrestricted* readings of the truth platitudes; thus, to manifest truth, a property must contain *these* features as a proper part. But, it seems, this cannot be done: at most, they can manifest a property composed of *restricted* readings of these platitudes, which, as we saw above, may constitute a notion *closely related* to truth but, unfortunately, not truth itself. The problem for Lynch's view, then, is that the claim that truth is *manifested* in the domain-specific properties ends up in tension with the claim that truth is a property independent of any domain-specific annexing. (2011: 38–9)

that it is correct to believe propositions that have that property. Crucially, however, *this needn't be because of any intrinsic normative facts about the manifesting property itself*. Such properties considered independently of their role in manifesting truth, may be fully 'descriptive'. That is, correspondence qua correspondence may have no normative features. It may only be that correspondence qua manifestation of truth has such features. (2009: 154–5)

This is odd, because the alethic functionalist intends, like the alethic pluralist à la Wright, to differentiate his view from deflationism. If *Normativity of Truth* and the *End of Inquiry* are but platitudes, how can they register a robust property of truth? Indeed, Lynch argues that they do not belong to the essence or the nature of truth, but only to its nominal essence, or to its concept. As Lynch notes, that they are truisms does not imply that there is no more to be said about them and that there is no theory to be given of them. They are implicit in our understanding of the concept of truth, but they can be explained further. It is consistent with alethic functionalism that these are not recognized as such as truisms. They may be recognized only tacitly (Lynch 2005, 2009: 16–7). This is in line with the commitment of alethic functionalism to be able to explain the concept of truth and in this sense to consider it has being that is, at least potentially, substantial. But for the view to be both pluralistic and coherent, the norm of truth must exhibit different degrees of substantiality depending on the domains. Hence there must be distinct norms of truth and not one only.

One solution to this problem might be to abandon the assumption of uniformity of the property of truth that goes with the functionalist version of truth pluralism, to come back to a version of what has been called 'alethic disjunctivism'—the view that the generic property of truth is a disjunctive one, in the sense that a proposition is generically true just in case it possesses the truth property relative to a domain *or* relative to another—and to try to explain in what sense the properties of truth within a domain is more basic.[10] Alternatively one might abandon the characterization of truth through its constitutive platitudes altogether.[11] I shall not here explore these options and shall argue that one must not give up the uniformity of the concept of truth, because one must not give up the uniformity of the norm of truth for belief, which is, in my view stronger and more substantial than alethic functionalism allows.

4. The norm of truth is substantive

Is the norm of truth for belief a mere 'truism'? According to Lynch, that a belief is correct if and only if it is true and that truth is a worthy goal of inquiry are

---

[10] Pedersen (2010) proposes an adaptation of this view in terms of a distinction between pluralism about predicates and pluralism about properties. See also Edwards (2012) and Pedersen & Wright (2013).
[11] See C. D. Wright (2010).

truisms. This why Lynch uses formulations (*NT*) and (*EI*), which are meant to be neutral with respect to various interpretations. Let us for the moment restrict ourselves to (NT). A formulation of (*NT*) that is indeed neutral and truistic is for instance Gibbard's:

> [f]or belief, correctness is truth. Correct belief is true belief. My belief that snow is white is correct just in case the belief is true, just in cases snow is white. Correctness, now, seems normative [. . .]. The correct belief, if all this is right, seems to be the one [a subject] ought, in this sense, to have. (2005, 338–9)

But as soon as we try to cash out the notion of correctness, we encounter various formulations of the general norm of truth:

(*CT*) For any p a belief that p is correct iff p is true.

There at least two main interpretations of (*CT*). One uses explicity deontic notions such as *ought, must,* or *should*:

(*OT*) One ought to believe that p if and only if p is true.

Another one reads correctness along with such value or axiological notions as *good, bad, valuable,* or *disvaluable*. On the latter view, the correctness condition for belief expresses literally the fact that belief is an aim or goal that is prima facie—and perhaps *ultima facie*—good, and the correctness condition (*CT*) has to interpreted in a teleological way:

(*TT*) A belief that p is correct if and only if p

because

only true beliefs achieve the aim involved in believing.

(*OT*) and (*TT*) are clearly different in several respects. First, although they can both be understood as ways of cashing out the notion of reason for belief, they refer to two interpretations of the reason for believing: on the one hand, the normative version says there is a norm for belief, which grounds our reasons for believing, and such that the reasons always derive from this norm; and on the other hand, the teleological version says there is a value (intrinsic or instrumental) that grounds our reasons for believing, which derive from this value.

In the second place, they presuppose different ontologies: on the one hand, the normative account rests upon an ontology of norms, whether or not one conceives these norms as being based on facts (along cognitivist lines) or not (along expressivist lines); on the other hand, the teleological account presupposes an ontology of values (good, evaluations) which can here too be understood cognitivistically or expressivistically.

In the third place, the two views rest upon two kinds of conceptions of epistemic norms. Consider what is often considered as the evidential norm for belief: one ought to believe that P only on the basis of sufficient evidence. On the normative formulation (*OT*), the epistemic norms are categorically related to the norm (they flow from it), deriving their normative status from the basic norm of truth. On the value formulation they are instrumental, getting their normative status from their ability to guide us to achieve our aims. This difference has an important consequence: if our reasons for beliefs and our adhesion to epistemic norms are explained through an aim—truth—we should be able to weight this aim against other aims or values. But we typically do not balance the aim of truth against other aims. The teleological account, on the contrary, seems to allow the possibility, at least in principle, of comparing the aim of having true beliefs with other aims (for instance practical ones).

In the fourth place, normative requirements upon beliefs are typically categorical, whereas aims are typically hypothetical. This seems to imply different conceptions of epistemic rationality, a categorical one and an instrumental one (Kelly 2003). They do not involve the same kind of semantics for normative terms, the same kind of ontology, and the same kind of guidance or regulation. In particular, the normative regulation that seems to be attached to (*OT*) seems to involve categorical prescriptions to the effect that a believer ought to have true beliefs and avoid false one.

Moreover, formulations like (*OT*) have led to numerous objections about the feasibility of the normative regulation: does it entail that one ought to believe *any* truth whatsoever and that it prescribes one to believe only truths? Many doubts have been expressed about how prescriptions like (OT) can actually regulate belief formation and thus can be able to have a genuine normative force.[12] A formulation like (*TT*), which implies that truth is an aim or goal for belief, seems by contrast to provide us with clear normative guidance: a goal can be aimed at intentionally, and so the correctness condition can be understood in this sense: '[t]o believe that p is to have the aim of regarding that proposition as true only if it in fact *is* true' (Velleman 2000). But this reading too raises a number of problems, which I am not going to detail here.[13]

Lynch himself favors an axiological reading of (*NT*): it is prima facie good, to believe that p if and only if p. (*EI*), which saw that truth is a worthy goal of inquiry, is supposed to be a distinct platitude from (*NT*). But if one interprets the latter in the teleological sense (*TT*), one comes close to the idea that truth is a goal of inquiry. Lynch (2008), however, distinguishes the two and talks regularly about (*NT*) as the norm for belief. Clearly, he intends to formulate it so that it remains neutral over the kinds of interpretations that we have just considered. Alethic functionalism allows, as we saw, various interpretations of (*NT*). One way to interpret alethic functionalism and

---

[12] For doubts of this sort see, Bykvist & Hattiangadi (2007) and Glüer & Wikforss (2009).
[13] See Engel (2005, 2007) and Shah (2003).

the part of the truth-role played by (*NT*) among the truish features would be to suggest that the norm of truth for belief could be interpreted differently depending on the domain: in value terms, in deontic terms, in ontological terms, in expressivist terms (e.g. the meta-ethical domain), or in cognitive terms. But this move is hardly coherent, for two reasons. The first is that the norm of truth for belief, on Lynch's own view, *has* to be understood in cognitive or realist terms, for an expressivist reading of it is unstable: it oscillates between an 'engaged' ethical standpoint, from which one employs the evaluative language just as the realist does, and a 'disengaged' meta-ethical standpoint, from which ascriptions of correctness are neither true nor false (Lynch 2008). The second has already been indicated in the previous paragraph: the norm of truth would lose the uniformity that is needed if functionalism about truth is to work. So, on alethic functionalist's own terms, the norm of truth for belief cannot be a feature that would be manifested in different ways. It has to be univocal and the same *everywhere*. Lynch cannot renounce this commitment of his view without running the risk of bringing it dangerously close to deflationism.

There is a further, and in my view more important, reason to defend the uniformity and the substantive character of the norm of truth. The reason has to do with the plausibility of the view that not only truth, but *knowledge* is the norm of assertion and of belief. I cannot deal here with the reasons for defending the much-discussed claim that knowledge is the norm of assertion.[14] Since Lynch actually formulates (*NT*) in terms of a norm for belief, I shall limit my suggestion to the latter.

The difficulty that many writers have expressed about the standard of correctness (*OT*) for belief is expressed by Wedgwood: '[i]t seems implausible that this fundamental epistemic norm can explain the norms of rational belief, for after all, according to this principle, any belief in a true proposition is correct—even if the belief in question is grossly irrational; so how can this principle explain the norms of rational belief?' (2002: 270). The obvious suggestion, here, is that our main reasons to believe have to do not with the truth of the beliefs that we consider, but with the *evidence* or *justification* that we have for them. In this sense the norm of *evidence*—that one ought to believe only on the basis of sufficient evidence—seems much more effective than the truth-norm. It seems, in this sense, that evidence has a much more important role in the formation, the maintenance, and the revision or rejection of beliefs than truth itself. We can understand it as the requirement that a belief be *justified* or based on appropriate *reasons* and that it be revised or rejected if it not based on such reasons. And if justified believing is knowledge, why not say that the fundamental epistemic norm is the norm of *knowledge*? (*OT*), and (*NT*) as well, fail to explain the sense in which it is defective to believe a proposition

---

[14] See Williamson (2000) and the vast literature that it has engendered.

when one is not in a position to *know* that it is true. So why not simply accept that the constitutive norm for belief is rather:

> (*NK*) It is the *norm* of belief that one ought to believe that p if and only if one knows that p?[15]

This proposal has the advantage of explaining why we can say that 'Belief aims at knowledge' in Williamson's sense:

> Knowing sets the standard of appropriateness for belief [. . .] Knowing is in that sense the best kind of believing. Mere believing is a kind of botched knowing. In short, belief aims at knowledge (not just truth). (2000: 47)

Given that knowledge is factive and implies truth, it seems easy to derive the norm (NT) from this one. It also can explain why the norm of evidence is in place, for evidence, as much as truth, leads to knowledge.[16]

Much more would be needed here if one were to give an argument to the effect that knowledge rather than truth is the primary candidate for the truth norm. But given that knowledge involves a stronger commitment than truth, it entails that the norm governing belief is much more substantive than alethic pluralism, and indeed alethic functionalism, allows.

If this is correct, does it really threaten the alethic functionalist picture? Can't there be different norms of knowledge, depending upon whether truth is realized or manifested, in one domain as correspondence, as superassertiblity or as coherence, and with varying strengths of knowledge? Contextualists about knowledge ascriptions, after all, accept that knowledge is the norm of assertion, while claiming that the strength of knowledge is a matter of contextual sensitivity.[17] If the concept of knowledge lacks the kind of unity that the norm of belief is supposed to have, the pluralist's stance seems to be still available to us. But that would not do. That ascriptions of knowledge are contextual does not mean that the norm of knowledge is manifested differently in different domains. On the contrary, the norm involves a unity that truth does not, prima facie, have.

Another direction that alethic functionalism could take would be to reject (*NT*) and (*NI*) as truisms characterizing our common sense concept of truth. Lynch, unlike Wright, associates specific theses to the platitudes that constitute the truth-role, because he considers that the truisms are as much about truth as they are about belief:

> [i]t seems reasonable to think that if (*TN*) tells us something about belief, then it also tells us something about truth—namely that truth just is, in

---

[15] This view has been suggested, in various forms, by Peacocke (1999: 34), Williamson (2000: 47), Engel (2002, 2005), Smythies (2012), and McHugh (forthcoming).

[16] Even more so, when one holds, as Williamson (2000) does, that evidence *is* knowledge, but one need not defend this strong version in order to accept (NK).

[17] See for instance DeRose (2002).

part, a basic norm of correctness for belief. Truth and belief are clearly interrelated. And so it seems that if (*TN*) is a constitutive fact about belief, then it is also a constitutive fact about truth. Here Dummett's old analogy of truth and winning is on the mark: the fact that the aim of a game is to win is not just a fact about games; it is also a fact about winning. Similarly, the fact that the 'aim' of belief is truth is not just a fact about belief; it is a fact about truth. (Lynch 2008: 236)

But it is not clear that (*NT*), or any other norm of truth, 'tells something about truth' and is constitutive of *truth*. The fact that truth is the correctness condition of belief is a fact about belief but not a fact about truth. The normativity that attaches to (*NT*) is a normativity about belief (or about our concept of belief) as an attitude, not a normativity that attaches to truth itself. In particular, (*NT*) is perfectly compatible with the view that truth itself is not a normative notion. This conclusion will be welcomed by the deflationist, who continuously suspects that in the discussions about the norm of truth one slides too easily from the idea that truth is the norm of belief to the idea that truth is a normative property. But then we would move away as much from the pluralist perspective.

5. Conclusion

Where does this leave us? The initial motivation of Wright's version of alethic pluralism was the need to inflate the notion of truth that deflationism had reduced to the minimal equivalence schema in (*ES*). The extra element that was to distinguish Wright's view from deflationism was the normative nature of assertion and of belief, conceived as a 'robust' and resilient feature of our concept of truth. Alethic functionalism includes this robust feature within the platitudes that make the functional role of truth. But it does so either at the expense of an implausible pluralization of the norm of truth or at the expense of emptying it of its substance. I have tried to argue that the norm of truth is actually much more substantive that what deflationism and functionalism about truth allow. Does that necessarily lead us to monism about truth, the view that there is but one truth property that is possessed by all true propositions? Not necessarily, but it leads us to the view that even if truth is not the same in all domains (pluralism), the norm of truth for belief has to be uniform. Hence it leads us to a monism about the norm of truth, whereas the functionalist picture leads us to a pluralism about the norm of truth. So probably truth functionalism has to abandon the latter picture.[18]

---

[18] I thank in the first place Cory Wright for his extensive comments and help, and both editors for their patience. I then too thank Michael Lynch and Cory Wright and those who discussed this paper at Storrs in May 2009. I have had the occasion to present various versions on other occasions, and thank for their comments and invitations Dora Achouriotti, Timothy Chan, Jaakko Hintikka, Sebastiano Morruzzi, and Annalisa Coliva.

References

Bykvist, K., & Hattiangadi, A. (2007). Does thought implies ought? *Analysis* 67: 277–285.
DeRose, K. (2002). Assertion, knowledge, and context. *Philosophical Review* 11: 167–203.
Dodd, J. (1999). There is no norm of truth, a minimalist reply to Wright. *Analysis* 59: 291–299.
Dretske, F. (2001). Norms, history, and the constitution of the mental. In his *Perception, Knowledge and Belief* (242–258). Cambridge: Cambridge University Press.
Dummett, M. (1959). Truth. *Proceedings of the Aristotelian Society* 59: 141–162.
Edwards, D. (2011). Simplifying alethic pluralism. *Southern Journal of Philosophy* 49: 28–48.
Edwards, D. (2012). On alethic disjunctivism. *Dialectica* 66: 200–214.
Engel, P. (2002). *Truth*. Montreal: McGill-Queen's University Press.
Engel, P. (2005). Truth and the aim of belief. In D. Gillies (ed.), *Models in Sciences* (77–97). London: King's College Publications.
Engel, P. (2007). Belief and normativity. *Disputatio* 23: 153–177.
Engel, P. (2008a). Pragmatic encroachment and epistemic value. In A. Haddock, A. Millar, & D. Pritchard (eds.), *Epistemic Value* (183–203). Oxford: Oxford University Press.
Engel, P. (2008b). Truth is one. *Philosophia Scientiæ* 13, 1: 1–13.
Gibbard, A. (2005). Truth and correct belief. *Philosophical Issues* 15: 338–351.
Glüer, K. & Wikforss, A. (2009). Against content normativity. *Mind* 118: 31–68.
Horwich, P. (1990/1998). *Truth*. Oxford: Oxford University Press.
Horwich, P. (1999). The minimalist conception of truth. In S. Blackburn & K. Simmons (eds.), *Truth* (239–263). Oxford: Oxford University Press.
Horwich, P. (2001). Norms of truth and meaning. In R. Schantz (ed.), *What Is Truth?* (133–145). Berlin: de Gruyter.
Horwich, P. (2006). The value of truth. *Noûs* 40: 347–360.
Kelly, T. (2003). Epistemic rationality and instrumental rationality: a critique. *Philosophy and Phenomenological Research* 66: 612–640.
Kölbel M. (2008). 'True' as ambiguous. *Philosophy and Phenomenological Research* 77: 359–384.
Lynch, M. P. (2001). A functionalist theory of truth. In M. P. Lynch (ed.), *The Nature of Truth* (723–749). Cambridge, MA: MIT Press.
Lynch, M. (2004). Minimalism and the Value of Truth'. *Philosophical Quarterly* 54: 500–517.
Lynch, M. (2005). Functionalism and our folk theory of truth: reply to Cory Wright. *Synthese* 145: 29–43.
Lynch, M. P. (2009). *Truth as Many and One*. Oxford: Oxford University Press.
Lynch, M. P. (2008). The values of truth and the truth of values. In A. Hadddock, A. Millar, & D. Pritchard (eds.), *Epistemic Value* (225–242). Oxford: Oxford University Press.
MacFarlane, J. (2005). Making sense of relative truth. *Proceedings of the Aristotelian Society* 105: 321–339.
McHugh, C. (2011). What do we aim at when we believe? *Dialectica*, 65: 369–392.
Peacocke, C. (1999). *Being Known*. Oxford, Oxford University Press.
Pedersen N. J. L. L. (2010). Stabilizing alethic pluralism. *Philosophical Quarterly* 60: 92–108.
Pedersen, N. J. L. L. & C. D. Wright. (2013). Pluralism about truth as alethic disjunctivism. In N. J. L. L. Pedersen & C. D. Wright (eds.): *Truth and Pluralism: Current Debates* (87–112). New York: Oxford University Press.
Price, H. (1998). Three norms of assertibility. *Philosophical Perspectives* 12: 41–54.

Shah, N. (2003). How truth governs belief. *Philosophical Review* 112: 447–482.
Smythies, D. (2012). The normative role of knowledge. *Noûs* 46: 265–288.
Velleman, D. (2000). On the aim of belief. In his *The Possibility of Practical Reason* (244–281). Oxford: Oxford University Press.
Wedgwood, R. (2002). The aim of belief. *Philosophical Perspectives* 16: 267–297.
Williamson, T. (2000). *Knowledge and Its Limits*. Oxford: Oxford University Press.
Wright, C. D. (2010). Truth, Ramsification, and the pluralist's revenge. *Australasian Journal of Philosophy* 88: 265–283.
Wright, C. D. (2012). Is pluralism about truth inherently unstable? *Philosophical Studies* 159: 89–105.
Wright, C. J. G. (1992). *Truth and Objectivity*. Cambridge, MA: Harvard University Press.
Wright, C. J. G. (1996). Response to commentators. *Philosophy and Phenomenological Research* 56: 911–941.
Wright, C. J. G. (2001). Minimalism, deflationism, pragmatism, pluralism. In M. P. Lynch (ed.), *The Nature of Truth* (751–789). Cambridge, MA: MIT Press.

{ 5 }

Pluralism about Truth as Alethic Disjunctivism

Nikolaj J. L. L. Pedersen & Cory D. Wright

1. Monism versus pluralism

Traditional views on truth have often combined two theses, *monism about truth* and *substantivism about truth*. According to monism, there is exactly one way of being true. According to substantivism, truth is a property with a substantial nature or underlying essence. In combining them, traditionalists have supposed that the property of being true is reducible to some other alethic property, such as identity or correspondence; and it is in terms of this property that truth is to be accounted for across all truth-apt discourse.[1] Hence, early correspondence theories had it that truth always consists in correspondence to fact, whether in mathematical discourse (e.g., '$2^3 + 5^2 = 33$'), physical discourse (e.g., 'electrons have negative charge'), or moral discourse (e.g., 'burning heretics at the stake is wrong'). Other traditional theories exhibit roughly the same structure, merely exchanging the analysans for something deemed more plausible—coherence, superassertability, agreement at the end of inquiry, concordance, and so forth.[2]

Traditionalists meet opposition from two camps: deflationists and pluralists. Both camps construe the combination of monism and substantivism as

---

[1] Note that monism does not entail that all discourse is truth-apt, but rather that any and all discourse, when truth-apt, must be so in the same way. Thus, monists are not committed, by their theory of truth, to the truth-aptitude of any or all particular kinds of discourse—they can happily grant the denial of truth-aptness to propositions in normative ethics and moral theory, for example.

[2] C. J. G. Wright posited superassertability as an epistemically constrained property of truth, thereby improving upon similar posits advocated by Putnam and Peirce: 'a [proposition] is superassertable if, and only if, it is, or can be, warranted and some warrant for it would survive arbitrarily close scrutiny of its pedigree and arbitrarily extensive increments to or other forms of improvement of our information' (1992: 48). Lynch presents concordance as a candidate for truth in the moral domain: 'p is concordant if, and only if, p supercoheres with a moral framework and that framework's morally-relevant non-moral judgments are true' (2009: 175 ff).

being fundamentally misguided, but differ as to which of these two theses instigates the problem.[3] According to deflationists, truth does not have a deep underlying essence or substantive nature that can be subjected to rigorous analysis and that could go beyond our concept of it. Rather, all there is to say about truth is captured by the disquotational schema (*DS*), equivalence schema (*ES*), or operator schema (*OS*):

(*DS*) 'p' is true if, and only if, p.
(*ES*) ⟨p⟩ is true if, and only if, p.
(*OS*) it is true that p if, and only if, p.

Based on these or related schemas, deflationary analyses of predicative and attributive uses of 'true' suggest that truth is a merely expressive or logical device—one that is unlikely to participate in the explanation of other phenomena such as rationality, intentionality, meaning, or cognition. According to pluralists, however, the traditionalist's mistake is not that she takes correspondence, coherence, agreement at the end of inquiry, or other such properties to be legitimate objects of study in reductively analyzing the nature of truth. Rather, the mistake lies in assuming that studying one of these properties will exhaust what there is to say about truth. While specific properties may be plausible candidates in certain domains, each of them falters in others, and so no single property can cover all there is to say about truth-apt discourse. For example, truths about concrete objects can plausibly be accounted for in terms of correspondence to fact, although correspondence appears much less plausible when it comes to accounting for truths in topology or business advertising. Thus, the explanatory scope of correspondence theories is not wide enough; and mutatis mutandis for other traditional views.[4]

Viewed at this simplistic level of description, the relationship between these three camps can thus be understood as an inconsistent triad.

As figure 5.1 depicts, the traditionalist's conjunction of monism and substantivism is inconsistent with both the deflationist's rejection of substantivism and the pluralist's rejection of monism; the deflationist's conjunction of monism and insubstantivism is inconsistent with both the traditionalist's acceptance of substantivism and the pluralist's rejection of monism; and the pluralists's conjunction of substantivism and the rejection of monism is inconsistent with

---

[3] For more detail and context, see Pedersen & Wright (2012). See Beall (2013) for an example of a deflationary pluralist, however; see also Lynch (2009: 65), who argues that C. J. G. Wright's version of discourse pluralism is—contrary to appearances—quite deflationary.

[4] This consideration against traditional monistic theories was expressed by O'Connor (1975: 13), among others, and has been called the oscillation of 'modesty and presumptuousness' (Wright 1992: 1–2), the 'problem of the common denominator' (Sher 1998: 133–134; C. D. Wright 2005: 1–4), and the 'scope problem' (Lynch 2004: 385; 2009: 49–52). For an argument that the significance attributed to this consideration is overblown and so fails to give pluralism any leverage over deflationism, see Dodd (2013).

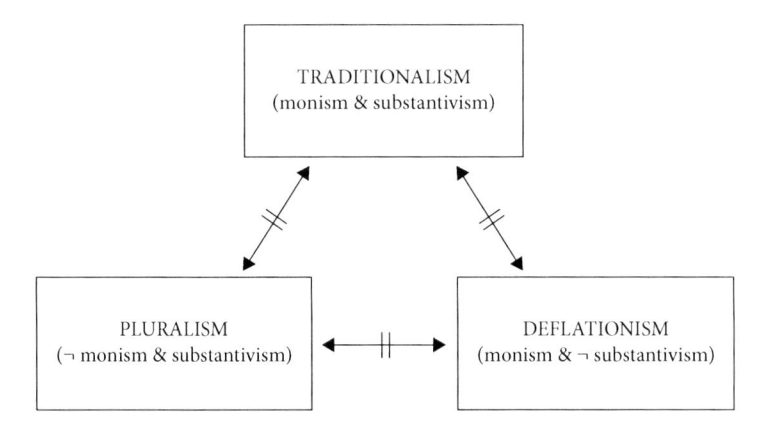

FIGURE 5.1. *Pluralism, deflationism, and traditionalism.*

both the deflationist's acceptance of insubstantivism and the traditionalist's acceptance of monism.

Although both monists and pluralists are united in taking inflationism to be the appropriate approach to truth, the relationship between their respective theories is more nuanced.[5] Turning first to monism, let us distinguish between weaker and stronger versions:

(SM) There is exactly one truth property, which is possessed by all true propositions. (*strong monism*)
(MM) There is a truth property, which is possessed by all true propositions. (*moderate monism*)

In parallel, we can distinguish between two versions of pluralism:

(SP) There is more than one truth property, and no truth property is possessed by all true propositions. (*strong pluralism*)
(MP) There is more than one truth property. (*moderate pluralism*)

Strong monism entails a commitment to its moderate counterpart, but not vice versa. It is also incompatible with both versions of pluralism: if there is exactly one truth property, then obviously there cannot be more than one, as both strong and moderate pluralists contend. Likewise, strong pluralism entails a commitment to its moderate counterpart, but not vice versa.[6] And it

---

[5] See, e.g., Lynch (2000; 2001), Sher (2004), C. D. Wright (2005), Pedersen (2006; 2010), Edwards (2008), and Wright & Pedersen (2010) for alternative construals of the strong/weak distinction.

[6] What has been labeled 'strong alethic pluralism' here should not be conflated with what Lynch refers to as 'simple alethic pluralism' (2006: §2; 2009: 54–5). According to Lynch, simple alethic pluralism is the view that there is a plurality of concepts of truth (as opposed to properties). Theorists attracted to pluralism about truth concepts include, among others, Max Kölbel (2008; 2013); monists about truth predicates who are attracted to pluralism about truth concepts include, among others, C. D. Wright (2005; 2012). Some critics of C. J. G. Wright also seemed to read him as a truth-concept

too is incompatible with both versions of monism: if there is no truth property shared by all true propositions—a generic truth property—then there can be no truth property that all true propositions possess, as both strong and moderate monists contend. Strong alethic pluralism is thus noteworthy for being what we will call a 'pure' pluralist view. It rejects the thesis that there is any truth property shared by every proposition that has one of the domain-specific truth properties. What specific truth property a proposition has, if true, depends on what domain of discourse it belongs to.[7]

Matters are different when we turn to the moderate versions of the two views. While moderate monism is incompatible with strong pluralism and moderate pluralism with strong monism, the two moderate theses are themselves compatible. The explanation is that the generic truth property to which the moderate monist is committed could be one among the several truth properties to which the moderate pluralist is committed.

2. Three kinds of moderate pluralism

In this section we present alethic disjunctivism, second-order functionalism, and manifestation functionalism—three 'mixed' or impure pluralist views that exemplify the compatibility of moderate pluralism and moderate monism about truth. We start by reviewing an approach to conceptual analysis that serves as common ground between many pluralists.

2.1 CONCEPT DELINEATION VIA CORE PRINCIPLES

The predominant approach to the conceptual analysis of truth has utilized collections of principles—or 'platitudes' or 'truisms', as they are sometimes called (Wright 1992; Lynch 2005c; 2009).[8] We use the label *core principles*. Our reason for doing so is that this label suggests that the principles are important as far as characterizing truth goes, but, unlike 'platitudes' and 'truisms', it does not suggest that the principles are immediate or obvious in any way, or even certain or infallible.

---

pluralist (see, e.g., Pettit, 1996; Sainsbury, 1996). However, we agree with Lynch's interpretation that Wright, who explicitly says as much (1996: 924), is not a simple alethic pluralist so defined. Rather, he is pretty clearly a moderate pluralist in the sense of *(MP)*, although some have interpreted him as a strong pluralist, too (see Wright, 1992: 141–3; 2001: 752–3). However, *(SP)* can be attributed to Wright only if he rejects the existence of a generic truth property. While Lynch (2006; see also 2009: 59–62) attributes such a rejection to him on the basis of his earlier work, it is unclear—in our view—whether this work includes enough detail to render such a verdict one way or the other. See Wright (2013) for his most recent take on pluralism.

[7] As C. J. G. Wright observed, it might not be transparent what truth consists in for certain domains. Figuring out could be a matter of further conceptual reflection, argumentation, or testing (2001: 753).

[8] Unfortunately, no philosopher has yet developed a sufficiently rich account of what it means to say that some p is a truism or a platitude. For criticism of the appeal to platitudes and truisms, see Sher (1998; 2004; 2005) and C. D. Wright (2005; 2010).

Pluralists take the core principles jointly to characterize the truth concept by connecting it to other concepts. For example, Lynch's three favored core principles are:

(O) For every proposition p, p is true if, and only if, were p to be believed, things would be believed to be as they are. (*Objectivity*)

(NB) For every proposition p, it is prima facie correct to believe p if, and only if, p is true. (*Norm of belief*)

(EI) For every proposition p, other things being equal, believing p is a worthy goal of inquiry if p is true. (*End of inquiry*)[9]

According to Lynch, Objectivity, Norm of Belief, and End of Inquiry are non-negotiable in the sense that if anything is to be a theory of truth—as opposed to a theory of something else—then it must include these three principles (2009: 17).

Many pluralists seem to be in broad agreement about at least some of the core principles. For example, two of Lynch's truisms share some similarity with two of the three principles that jointly comprise Sher's so-called *immanence thesis* (2004).[10] And some of their three principles share some similarity with one of Wright's two 'parent platitudes' (1992). However, there is no agreement among pluralists as to what the full list of core principles should look like. Furthermore, some pluralists (like Lynch, 2001) allow for changes over time, meaning that principles may be dropped from the list or that new ones may be included. These observations point to the need for proper criteria for inclusion in and exclusion from the list of core principles. C. D. Wright (2005; 2010) has argued that this methodological approach gives rise to a criteria problem: differences between concepts of truth are determined by the identity and individuation conditions of the conjunctions (lists, etc.) of core principles, and as the conjuncts (items, etc.) change so too do the concepts.

In the absence of criteria for respectively inclusion in and exclusion from the list of core principles, it is thus questionable whether pluralists are entitled to monism about the concept of truth.[11] In this chapter we set aside the criteria

---

[9] See Lynch (2009: 8, 10, 12). It should be noted that Lynch states (O) and (EI) in terms of beliefs, while (NB) is put in terms of propositions (which he takes to be the proper and primary truth-bearer (2009: 129–32)). Also noteworthy is that, as stated by Lynch, (O) and (NB) are schemas, while (EI) has the form of a universal generalization. Here, we adopt the regimented formulation provided by David (2013).

[10] For further explication, see Sher & Wright's (2007) reconstruction of the immanence thesis using lessons from Kant and Frege, as well as Rattan's (2010) analysis of the concept of truth in terms of its cognitive value for critical reflective thinking.

[11] Lynch (2005a) and Wright (2005) agree that such changes need not amount to a conceptual sea-change. But they do lead to polysemy in the semantic structure of truth predication, and the degree to which polysemy gains a foothold is the degree to which the monist thesis about the concept of truth is impercipient. With respect to Lynch's (2009) three core principles in particular, it is possible to endorse them as being necessary for fixing upon the concept of truth. Yet, since they are not jointly sufficient, we are not entitled to the claim that they determinately characterize the concept of truth itself. Again, this makes monism about the concept of truth just another open question—one that is not settled by merely adding ellipses to the list of core principles.

problem, however, and discuss a number of other issues pertaining to pluralism in §§3–5.

2.2 ALETHIC DISJUNCTIVISM

We now turn to alethic disjunctivism, the first moderate pluralist view that combines moderate pluralism and moderate monism about truth.[12] Qua pluralism, alethic disjunctivism postulates several domain-specific truth properties $T_1, \ldots, T_n$; yet, with monism, the view also postulates a generic truth property T_G, characterized as follows:

(T_G) $(\forall p)[T_G(p) \leftrightarrow ((T_1(p) \wedge \text{domain}_1(p)), \vee \ldots, \vee (T_n(p) \wedge \text{domain}_n(p)))]$

According to (T_G), a proposition p is generically true just in case either it possesses the truth property of domain$_1$ and belongs to domain$_1$, or possesses the truth property of domain$_2$ and belongs to domain$_2$, ..., or it possesses the truth property of domain$_n$ and belongs to domain$_n$.

A few further remarks are in place. First, if we utilize the aforementioned methodological approach to conceptual analysis, then what makes the domain-specific properties $T_1, \ldots, T_n$ truth properties is their satisfaction of some set of core principles relative to their respective domains in tandem with some further set of principles connecting properties and concepts. Second, mentioning 'domains' in the right-hand side of the biconditional is essential to capturing one of the core thoughts behind pluralism; that is, truth properties are truth properties relative to a domain (the generic, disjunctive property being the only exception—it applies across the board). Thus, it is not enough for the truth of a given proposition (whether generic or domain-specific) that it have a property that is the truth property of some domain. Rather, it needs to be the truth property of the particular domain to which the proposition belongs. To illustrate, suppose that corresponding with reality is the truth property for domain$_1$, and that superassertibility is so for domain$_2$. Consider now a proposition p that belongs to domain$_1$ and is superassertible, but does not correspond. Is p true? No. It does not have the truth property of domain$_1$ (i.e., correspondence), and so it is neither domain-specifically true nor generically true.[13]

Alethic disjunctivism faces competition from other kinds of views that incorporate moderate monism and so are likewise mixed or impure; these include second-order functionalism (e.g., Lynch 2000; 2001; 2004), manifestation functionalism (e.g., Lynch 2009; 2013), and correspondence pluralism

---

[12] For more on alethic disjunctivism, see Pedersen (2006; 2010; 2012) and Edwards (2013). For another sympathizer, see Cotnoir (2009: 478).

[13] Now, precisely because talk of domains is strictly needed, we will often allow ourselves to leave it implicit. For example, we often allow ourselves to talk about a proposition's being generically true in virtue of, e.g., corresponding to fact without tediously adding that correspondence is the truth property for the domain to which the proposition belongs.

Pluralism about Truth as Alethic Disjunctivism

(e.g., Sher 2005; 2013; Horgan & Potrč 2000; Barnard & Horgan 2006; 2013). In §6, we argue that it is difficult for adherents of other moderate pluralist views to reject the viability of some form of alethic disjunctivism. By this we mean that, by the lights of each of these other views, there is a disjunctive truth property T_G that ought to qualify as a legitimate truth property. In what follows, we give special attention to two functionalist views.

2.3 SECOND-ORDER FUNCTIONALISM

According to functionalists, the concept of truth is best characterized by looking at the role that it plays in our cognitive economy. That is, we look for widely—although perhaps tacitly—endorsed principles that connect truth to other concepts (Lynch 2001; 2004; 2009). By reference to these core principles, we can specify what it means for a property to play the truth-role relative to a given domain:

> (*TR*) For any property F, F plays the truth-role relative to domain$_i$ if, and only if, for every proposition p in domain$_p$, F satisfies the core principles for p.

In turn, (*TR*) positions one to provide a functionalist characterization of the conditions under which a proposition is true (Lynch 2001; 2004—but with some significant differences; see fns. 14–15):

> (F^{TC}) For every proposition p, p is true if, and only if, p has the property that plays the truth-role for the domain to which p belongs.

According to the second-order functionalist, (F^{TC}) points us directly to what truth—considered as a property—is. It is a certain second-order property, the role-property (Lynch 2001; 2004; 2005a):

> (T^{2O}) The property of being true is the property of having the (domain-relevant) property that plays the truth-role.

This characterization of second-order functionalism is schematic in one very crucial respect: it does not include a specification of what the salient principles are. For the sake of illustration (but not endorsement), let us just restrict ourselves to Lynch's three truisms—Objectivity, Norm of Belief, and End of Inquiry—as the individually necessary and jointly sufficient principles that delineate the truth concept exactly. Combined with (*TR*), this yields the following characterization of a property's playing the truth-role:

> (*TR**) For any property F, F plays the truth-role relative to domain$_i$ if, and only if, for every proposition p in domain$_p$, (i) p is F if, and only if, were p to be believed, things would be believed to be as they are, (ii) it is prima facie correct to believe p if, and only if, p is F, and

(iii) other things being equal, if p is F, then believing p is a worthy goal of inquiry.

Whatever specific set of principles the second-order functionalist endorses, she will say that the properties that play the truth-role are first-order realizer properties—in the jargon familiar from the philosophy of mind—while truth itself is a second-order multiply realizable property. (We will occasionally use 'T²ᴼꟳ'.) T²ᴼꟳ is a second-order property because a proposition's having it is always grounded in the possession of a property in the set of realizer properties—in other words, a property that plays the truth-role for the domain to which the proposition belongs.[14] T²ᴼꟳ is a multiply realizable property because different properties (correspondence, supercoherence, etc.) play the truth-role for different domains, and so truth can be realized in different ways across domains.

Like alethic disjunctivism, second-order alethic functionalism combines moderate pluralism and monism about truth. The view is moderately pluralist in the sense that there are several properties in virtue of which propositions can be true. This is because truth is multiply realizable. Yet, truth's multiple realizability concomitantly underwrites the moderate monism of second-order functionalism: the second-order, multiply realizable property T²ᴼꟳ is had by all true propositions.[15]

2.4 MANIFESTATION FUNCTIONALISM

We now turn to a different version of functionalism—what we will refer to as *manifestation functionalism*. This view substantially overlaps with second-order functionalism. Like the second-order functionalist, the manifestation functionalist seeks to map the nature of truth by looking at the truth-role. She endorses (*TR*) and (*F*^*TC*) as specifications of what it is for a property to play the truth-role, and the conditions under which a proposition is true, respectively (Lynch 2009: 70–3). In endorsing manifestation functionalism, Lynch adds

---

[14] Lynch does not himself relativize the truth-role to domains, as we have done in the presentation of second-order functionalism. Presumably, this needs to be done. The intended realizer properties do not play the truth-role for all propositions, for if they did, it would be difficult to maintain the idea that correspondence and the other realizer properties are alethically potent only *locally*. Indeed, if they did, why shouldn't they be capable of making propositions true, whatever their (truth-apt) domain might be? Here, we draw on David's contribution to this volume (§4), which discusses Lynch's versions of manifestation functionalism. David urges Lynch to relativize the truth-role to domains, but the point also seems apt for any functionalist theory.

[15] We have attributed second-order functionalism to Lynch (2000; 2001; 2004; 2005a; 2005b; 2005c; 2006). O'Connor (1975: 24) also 'suggests that [truth] is a second-order relational property'. Note that in these articles, Lynch explicitly formulates the view by relying on Ramsification in order to produce the requisite implicit definition and does so by appealing to a different list of principles than the one we have just used for illustration. However, the appeal to this technique faces a problem of epistemic circularity (C. D. Wright 2010). As Lynch (2013, fn. 12) observes, the problem also generalizes to other theories of truth besides second-order functionalism. In part because of such results, we have tried to describe second-order functionalism in abstraction away from both Ramsification and from any particular collection of principles. However, as mentioned earlier, doing so reopens the question of the empirical adequacy of monism about the concept of truth.

detail to (TR) by adopting (TR^*): that is, he adopts Objectivity, Norm of Belief, and End of Inquiry as delineating the truth-role. However, when it comes to a characterization of the functionalist truth property, the second-order functionalist's principle (T^{2O}) has been replaced by the following:

(T^M) The property of being true is the property that has the truish features essentially or which plays the truth-role *as such*. (Lynch, 2009: 74)

—also formulated as follows:

(T^{MN}) The property of being true is the property that is, necessarily, had by believed contents just when things are as they are believed to be; had by propositions believed at the end of inquiry and which makes propositions correct to believe. (Lynch, 2013: 55)

(T^M) and (T^{MN}) make no reference to the realizer properties that feature so prominently in the characterization provided by the second-order functionalist. Instead, Lynch characterizes truth as being the property that possesses the truish features essentially. In light of this, one might wonder what relationship the would-be realizer properties, like correspondence or superwarrant, bear to the truth property characterized by (T^M) or (T^{MN})?[16] To shed light on this matter, we need to look at what Lynch calls *manifestation* and *immanence*.

Manifestation, like realizability, is a metaphysical grounding relation. If a property M manifests a property I, something's being I is grounded in its being M. More precisely, Lynch (2009: 74–5) holds that:

(M) Property M manifests property I just in case it is a priori that the set of I's conceptually essential features is a subset of M's features. (*manifestation*)

(I) Property M manifests a property I just in case I is immanent in M. (*immanence*)

From (M) it follows immediately that the manifestation relation is reflexive, because any set is a subset of itself. Conceptually essential features of a given property F are thought to (i) be part of the nominal essence of F, (ii) hold of F with conceptual necessity, and (iii) serve to distinguish F from other properties.

(M) and (I) are presented as capturing a new kind of metaphysical grounding relation—one that is distinct from the determinable/determinate, type/token, and genus/species distinctions, among others.[17] Let us turn to the case where the immanent property is truth. The thought is that alethic properties

---

[16] At least one of the authors finds the assumption of uniqueness in (T^M) problematic. For now, we will grant the idea that (T^M) characterizes a unique truth property. For further discussion, see §6 and Pedersen (2012).

[17] See Lynch (2009: 67, 75). For a different conception of immanence, see Sher (2004) and Sher & Wright (2007).

like correspondence are truth-manifesting properties, that is, properties that manifest truth or in which truth is immanent. This is the relationship that truth, as characterized by (T^M) and (T^{MN}), bears to the other properties of interest on the manifestation functionalist view. Following Lynch, one can intuitively think of manifestation and immanence along the following lines: if M manifests I (or I is immanent in M), part of being M is being I (Lynch, 2009: 75). With this idea in hand, we can think of being true as part of corresponding with reality, and mutatis mutandis for other truth-manifesting properties.

Lynch now relativizes manifestation to propositions.[18] What specific property manifests truth for a given proposition depends on its subject matter and its logical structure. Let us turn first to atomic propositions. Consider the following thesis stating a necessary and sufficient condition for the truth of atomics where manifestation is understood as above.

(T^{CA}) For any atomic proposition p, p is true if, and only if, p has the property M that manifests truth for p and is distinct from truth.

As noted, truth always manifests itself, because manifestation is reflexive. However, (T^{CA}) tells us that what matters for atomic propositions is that there is some further truth-manifesting alethic property that p has. In such cases, we will say that the truth of p is strongly grounded. (T^{CA}) tells us is that atomic truths are exactly the strongly grounded—or, as Lynch would say, 'unplain'—truths.

The manifestation functionalist does not hold (T^{CA}) in full generality. Shapiro (2011) argues that there are atomic, plain truths—in other words, truths that are atomic but not strongly grounded—and Lynch (2013) agrees. In particular, truth-attributions such as 'it is true that grass is green' are atomic and yet plainly true. Hence, they are not true in virtue of possessing some truth-manifesting property other than truth. For this reason, there is no exact match between the atomic truths and the unplain truths. Still, Lynch seems sympathetic to the idea that even atomic, plain truths somehow depend on unplain ones. Thus, he takes the truth-value of 'it is true that grass is green' to depend on the truth-value of 'grass is green', an atomic unplain truth.

What about compound or complex propositions? According to the manifestation functionalist, these propositions are plainly true, where this is to be understood as follows:

(T^P) A proposition p is plainly true just in case it is true and does not have any property distinct from truth that manifests truth for it. (*plain truth*)

To take an example, consider the conjunctive proposition 'Earth is spherical and two plus two equals four'. This proposition is true. Suppose that

---

[18] Previously, Lynch (2009: 76–7) relativized manifestation to domains. The switch from relativization to domains to relativization to propositions has been suggested by David (2013), among others.

correspondence is the truth-manifesting property for the first conjunct and coherence for the second one. The truth of both conjuncts is strongly grounded: they each have a property distinct from truth in virtue of which they are true. However, neither correspondence nor coherence manifests truth for the conjunction. Instead the conjunction is plainly true. The conjunction is true, and truth self-manifests, but the conjunction possesses no further truth-manifesting property.

3. Levels and grounding

3.1 ALETHIC DISJUNCTIVISM AND SECOND-ORDER FUNCTIONALISM

We will return to plain and unplain truths in §4. Here, notice that strong alethic pluralism is a *one-level view*, in the sense that the extant truth properties posited by the view have no special status with respect to their applicability. They are all alethic properties within which truth consists relative to particular domains. On the other hand, alethic disjunctivism, second-order functionalism, and manifestation functionalism can be regarded as *two-level views*. At least one of the properties among the manifold of other ways of being true has an exalted status. For instance, according to alethic disjunctivism, above the disjunct properties there is a unique, generic disjunctive truth property, T_G. For second-order functionalism, above the realizer properties at the lower order, there is the second-order truth property, T_{2OF}. Finally, according to manifestation functionalism, the manifesting properties have a status that is distinct from immanent truth, T_I.

With respect to two-level views, it is an interesting issue how properties that have this special or exalted status relate to those that do not. Lynch (2009) and Pedersen (2010) suggest that the metaphysical link between them is a grounding relation, although they differ over the details. Let us dwell on the idea of metaphysical grounding for a bit.[19] First, we will take grounding to be (strongly) asymmetric, that is,

(SA) For all x, if F(x) grounds G(x), then it is not the case that G(x) grounds F(x). (*S-asymmetry*)

Second, we will also take grounding to be irreflexive, that is,

(IR) For all x, it is not the case that F(x) grounds F(x). (*irreflexitivity*)

We take these two features to underwrite certain explanatory claims. If F(a) grounds G(a), then G(a) obtains because F(a) does. Also, when F(a) grounds

---

[19] Just to be clear on terminology: 'F(x) grounds G(x)' and 'G(x) in virtue of F(x)' will be used interchangeably.

G(a) and (by asymmetry) we get that G(a) does not ground F(a), and we likewise get the explanatory claim that it is not the case that F(a) obtains because G(a) does.

Now, let us consider grounding in the context of alethic disjunctivism and second-order functionalism. On the alethic disjunctivist view, a proposition p's having a disjunct property grounds its having the generic disjunctive truth property, that is,

($G_\vee$) For all p, $T_i(p)$ grounds $T_G(p)$. (*ground$_\vee$*)

($G_\vee$) suggests that $T_G(p)$ obtains because $T_i(p)$ does. And by asymmetry, we also know that it is not the case that $T_G(p)$ grounds $T_i(p)$, in which case $T_i(p)$ does not obtain because of $T_G(p)$. So, when reading the biconditional in (TG)—namely, $(\forall p)(T_G(p) \leftrightarrow ((T_1(p) \wedge domain_1(p)) \vee \ldots \vee (T_n(p) \wedge domain_n(p))))$—one should do so with priority from left to right. For second-order functionalism we get something completely analogous: a proposition p's having a realizer property grounds its having the second-order functional property, that is,

(G_{2OF}) For all p, $T_i(p)$ grounds $T_{2OF}(p)$. (*ground$_{2OF}$*)

(G_{2OF}) suggests that $T_{2OF}(p)$ obtains, because $T_i(p)$ plays the truth-role of domain$_i$. Again, by asymmetry, we know that it is not the case that $T_{2OF}(p)$ grounds $T_i(p)$—and that is not the case that $T_i(p)$ obtains, because $T_{2OF}(p)$ does. So, the biconditional in (F^{TC}) should be read with priority from left to right. (Thus, (F^{TC}): for every proposition p, p is true if and only if p has the property that plays the truth-role for the domain to which p belongs.)

We conclude from the above considerations that lower-level truth grounds higher-level truth on the alethic disjunctivist and second-order functionalist views. Whenever a proposition has the disjunctive truth property, it is because it has the disjunct truth property of the domain to which it belongs, and not vice versa; likewise for the second-order functionalist's role and realizer properties, mutatis mutandis. Does the same hold of Lynch's manifestation functionalism? The answer to this question is not straightforward.

3.2 MANIFESTATION FUNCTIONALISM

There may seem to be a tension between our presentation of grounding and Lynch's talk of manifestation—which, as indicated, he considers to be a kind of grounding relation. The seeming tension is this: we have taken grounding relations to be irreflexive, while Lynch explicitly says that manifestation is reflexive. Every property manifests itself, because for any property it is a priori that the set of its essential features is a subset of the set of its essential features.

Pluralism about Truth as Alethic Disjunctivism

For a certain class of propositions, the tension is only apparent. The reflexivity of manifestation (as applied to properties) is compatible with the grounding of truth (as applied to propositions) being irreflexive. Consider, for example, the class of atomic unplain truths. Atomic, unplain truths are (immanence) true, T_I, and also have a further distinct truth-manifesting property M_i. Now, truth manifests itself for propositions that are unplainly true, as does any other property possessed by these propositions. But the fact that truth self-manifests for any proposition p that is atomic and unplainly true does not make it the case that $T_I(p)$ grounds $T_I(p)$. Rather, we must look to the further, distinct truth-manifesting property M_i for grounding:

(i) $M_i(p)$ grounds $T_I(p)$.

Indeed, for any atomic unplain truth p, the manifestation functionalist will say the following:

(ii) If $M_i(p)$ grounds $T_I(p)$, then it is not the case that $T_I(p)$ grounds $M_i(p)$.
(iii^{Mi}) It is not the case that $M_i(p)$ grounds $M_i(p)$.
(iii^{TI}) It is not the case that $T_I(p)$ grounds $T_I(p)$.

In other words, the grounding of atomic, unplain truth for propositions is asymmetric and irreflexive according to manifestation functionalists. But this should be distinguished from—and is compatible with—the manifestation relation being reflexive on properties.

This leaves open the question of what to say about the grounding of the truth of compounds and atomic, plain truths according to the manifestation functionalist. As seen, all compounds are plainly true, so we can focus our discussion by considering plain truth. Things get a little tricky here—indeed, in our view, they ultimately do so in a way that leads to an unfortunate bifurcation in the metaphysics of manifestation functionalism. Where q is a plain truth—whether atomic or compound—Lynch explicitly denies that q has some truth-manifesting property M_i distinct from truth, T_I. He takes q to be just T_I, that is, immanence true. This might be taken to suggest that

(iv^{TI}) $T_I(q)$ grounds $T_I(q)$,

in other words, that q's truth grounds itself. But it is not clear that the manifestation functionalist would want to commit to (iv^{TI}), if 'grounds' is to be read as involving a commitment to a self-sufficiency claim—that q's being true is what makes q true, or that q depends only on itself for its truth.

One way of avoiding a self-sufficiency claim would be to take plain truth to be asymmetrically dependent or supervenient on unplain truth:

(*PT*^{S}) Plain truth supervenes on unplain truth: a plain truth cannot change its truth-value without there being a change in the truth-value of some true atomic proposition whose truth is strongly grounded (i.e., due to the possession of some truth-manifesting property distinct from truth).

If (PT^S) holds good on the manifestation functionalist picture, plain truth can be regarded as being *weakly grounded* on unplain truth. Plain truths are not directly or strongly grounded in the possession of some truth-manifesting property distinct from truth. Yet they depend or supervene on truths that are grounded.[20] In particular, one can say that the plain truth of the truth attribution 'it is true that grass is green' supervenes on the unplain truth of 'grass is green' (as does Lynch). Similarly, one can say that the truth of 'Earth is spherical and two plus two equals four' supervenes on the unplain truth of respectively 'Earth is spherical' and 'two plus two equals four'.

Now, Lynch does seem to think that some propositions are plainly true and do not depend for their truth on any unplain truth. Suppose, for instance, 'there is milk in the fridge' is true. Then we are dealing with an atomic truth. It is also a contingent, unplain truth. Things could have been otherwise, and the truth of the proposition is grounded in its correspondence with reality, that is, in the possession of some truth-manifesting property distinct from truth. Now consider 'if there is milk in Bob's fridge, then there is milk in Bob's fridge'. This is a compound truth. As such it is plainly true, following Lynch. But it does not seem to depend for its truth on any unplain truth. Whatever p might be, any compound of the form 'If p, then p' is true, and necessarily so (see Lynch, 2013). It is true purely as a matter of logical form, irrespective of how the world is vis-à-vis p. The same applies to other logical truths.[21]

It seems pretty clear that Lynch takes logical truths, a certain type of plain truths, to be independent of any unplain truth. Presumably, though, Lynch would not take logical truths to undermine the supervenience thesis (PT^S). The reason for this is simple: necessary truths supervene on everything, because they hold true regardless of what the world is like. Thus, trivially, logical truth—classified as plain truth—supervenes on unplain truth. Many other plain truths, of course, supervene non-trivially on unplain truth: for example, the plain truth of 'Liverpool's home colors are red, and the speeding limit in

---

[20] Lynch endorses the following supervenience thesis for compound truth, which he labels the *weak grounding principle*: 'There can be no change in the truth-value of a compound proposition without change in the truth-value of *some* atomic propositions' (2009: 90). Our use of 'weak grounding' is consonant with Lynch's usage. However, the supervenience relata differ as we have formulated (PT^S) in terms of plain and unplain truths rather than compound and atomic truths.

[21] This last statement should be qualified. If logical pluralism can be regarded as a natural companion of alethic pluralism (see Lynch, 2009: ch. 5; Pedersen, forthcoming), whether a compound Φ qualifies as a logical truth might not merely be a function of its logical form, but also of the subject matter to which its constituents pertain. For example, anything of the form 'p ∨ ¬p' will qualify as a logical truth provided that p belongs to a domain that conforms to classical logic, while this is not generally so for domains over which intuitionistic logic holds sway (and that include propositions that are not effectively decidable).

Danish cities is 50 km/hr' supervenes on the unplain truth of the two ingredient conjuncts. The supervenience is nontrivial, because the conjunction is not true regardless of how the world is. In sum, we take it that Lynch can maintain that plain truth supervenes on unplain truth, that he can endorse (PT^S).

Where does this leave the manifestation functionalist? Supervenience, like grounding, is a kind of metaphysical dependence relation. Thus, the manifestation functionalist can say that all truths—whether plain or unplain—depend for their truth on lower-level truth-manifesting properties distinct from (immanence) truth. However, it should be emphasized that the manifestation functionalist's dependence relation is subject to a significant bifurcation. As we have seen, unplain truths depend for their truth on lower-level truth-manifesting properties in a very direct way. Their truth is strongly grounded in the possession of some lower-level truth-manifesting property. Unplain truths qualify as truths in virtue of possessing a truth-manifesting property distinct from truth itself. Plain truths are a radically different story. Their distinctive feature is precisely that they are not true in virtue of possessing some lower-level truth-manifesting property. The only truth-manifesting property they possess is truth itself. Now, if the manifestation functionalist wants to avoid accepting the alethic self-sufficiency of plain truths, she must commit to their depending for their truth on unplain truths—but in a way that is different from strong grounding. Supervenience is an option, as we have seen. However, by itself the idea that plain truth supervenes on unplain truth does not tell us too much. At most it tells us that plain truth somehow depends on unplain truth.

Dependence-as-supervenience strikes us as unclear compared to dependence-as-strong-grounding. In other words, in our view, one half of the manifestation functionalist's bifurcated metaphysics is somewhat obscure.[22]

4. The priority of pluralism: the many grounding the one

Apart from strong alethic pluralism, the other views we have considered are impure or mixed: they incorporate both moderate pluralism and moderate monism. This raises an interesting question: are these views more pluralist than monist, or more monist than pluralist? Or perhaps equally so? Here, we argue that mixed pluralist views (of the kind considered) are distinctively more pluralist than monist. The previous section has provided a rationale for thinking so.[23] We first turn to alethic disjunctivism and second-order functionalism, then to manifestation functionalism.

---

[22] Another very interesting proposal concerning alethic pluralism and grounding is that of Edwards (2013). See C. J. G. Wright (2013) for discussion of Edwards' proposal.

[23] The argument to be given is an extension of the kind of argument presented in Pedersen (2010), where the focus is specifically on alethic disjunctivism rather than mixed pluralist views more generally.

Recall that alethic disjunctivism incorporates the thesis that there is a generic, disjunctive truth property (T_G) that applies to all true propositions. Recall also that the view commits to the existence of a plurality of truth properties $T_1, \ldots, T_n$. As seen in the preceding section, for any proposition p, $T_G(p)$ is always strongly grounded in $T_i(p)$ for some T_i ($1 \leq i \leq n$). That is, generic truth is always strongly grounded in domain-specific truth. A proposition is generically true because it has the truth property of the domain to which it belongs. These relations are not reversible. It is not the case that $T_i(p)$ is grounded in $T_G(p)$, and it is not the case that $T_i(p)$ obtains because $T_G(p)$. So, although $T_G(p)$ and $T_i(p)$ are biconditionally related, there is an asymmetry: $T_i(p)$ is metaphysically prior to $T_G(p)$. In other words, the domain-specific properties are more fundamental than the disjunctive property. In light of this result, we conclude that alethic disjunctivism is distinctively more pluralist than monist.

What we have said just about alethic disjunctivism equally applies to second-order functionalism. The reasoning is similar, with the possession of the realizer property of the relevant domain serving to ground strongly the possession of the second-order functional truth property. As before, the lower-order properties are thus metaphysically more fundamental than the higher-order property. Hence, second-order functionalism is distinctively more pluralist than monist.

How about manifestion functionalism, the third mixed view? From a metaphysical perspective, it too is more pluralist than monist. Yet, the possession of the higher-order truth property is not generally as strongly grounded in lower-level truth properties as on the two other mixed views. Recall that the only truth property plain truths have is the immanent truth property, T_I. However, as also seen, plain truth supervenes on unplain truth—that is, on some truth that is directly grounded in the possession of some truth-manifesting property distinct from (immanent) truth. In this sense, unplain truth and the truth-manifesting properties are more metaphysically fundamental than the higher-level truth property.

In sum, for all three mixed views considered, the pluralist aspect of these views is more fundamental than its monism. The many ground the one.

5. On the viability of alethic disjunctivism

In this section, we support the claim made at the outset of the chapter—namely, that some form of alethic disjunctivism is viable by the lights of each of the other three pluralist views considered above. It is so in the sense that it is hard for these other kinds of pluralists to deny the legitimacy of a disjunctive truth property. We make our case for this claim against the background assumption that the truth concept is characterized by a collection of core principles. As seen, this is an assumption shared by many pluralists.

5.1 ALETHIC DISJUNCTIVISM AND STRONG ALETHIC PLURALISM

Recall that the strong pluralist accepts the existence of a range of domain-specific truth properties $T_1, \ldots, T_n$. Some authors have argued that the strong pluralist can reject the legitimacy of a generic disjunctive truth property—one that takes $T_1, \ldots, T_n$ as disjuncts—on metaphysical grounds.[24] The basic idea behind this strategy is that the strong pluralist can think of truth properties as sparse rather than abundant properties. Here, we suggest that this is not a viable strategy.

According to the abundant conception, for any set of things, there is a property possessed by exactly the members of that set.[25] Thus, in particular, the following holds:

($A_\vee$) If there is a range of m-place properties $F_1, \ldots, F_n$ of the same order, then there is an m-place property $F_\vee$ such that $F_\vee(a_1, \ldots, a_m)$ if, and only if, $F_1(a_1, \ldots, a_m)$, or $\ldots$, or $F_n(a_1, \ldots, a_m)$. (*abundance*)

Instantiating ($A_\vee$) with truth properties $T_1, \ldots, T_n$ immediately delivers a disjunctive property that applies precisely to the things that possess one of $T_1, \ldots, T_n$.

Here it might seem natural to think that viewing truth properties in a conservative manner—as being sparse rather than abundant—can be of help to the strong pluralist who wants to reject the existence of this disjunctive property.

According to the sparse conception of properties, objects need to be *qualitatively similar* in order to share a property. In particular, the propositions that are supposed to possess the disjunctive truth property must be unified by a qualitative similarity. The sparse conception is thus more restrictive or conservative than the abundant conception. For this reason, if truth properties are regarded as sparse properties, the generic disjunctive property has to satisfy a substantive constraint in order to qualify as legitimate from a metaphysical perspective. As such, provided that the strong pluralist can show that the propositions that possess some domain-specific truth property fail to be unified by the requisite qualitative similarity, she will have a principled metaphysical reason to reject the generic disjunctive truth property.

Unfortunately, this line of reasoning does not look plausible given the assumptions that the concept of truth is characterized by a collection of core

---

[24] One such author is Pedersen (2006), who defends strong pluralism by arguing along the lines presented below.

[25] The set {Anthony Soprano, $\aleph_0$, California's Lost Coast, the rise of Manicheanism} is populated with arbitrarily collected and unrelated elements spanning a wide range of metaphysical categories (e.g., fictitious persons, numbers, locations, events, etc.), and could be repopulated to include many others (e.g., tropes, moral facts, possible worlds, etc.). Subsequently, it may be that abundant theorists should restrict the scope of allowable sets; otherwise, it would appear that the only property that members of abundantly construed sets share is (mere) set membership. Set membership is not an alethic property, however; and so neither is having the property of being a member of $\{T_1, \ldots, T_n\}$.

principles (to be supplemented with principles connecting concepts with properties) and that $T_1, \ldots, T_n$ qualify as truth properties in virtue of satisfying these principles. For if the assumption holds, then satisfying the core principles is sufficient to satisfy this constraint of qualitative similarity that the generic disjunctive property has to satisfy in order to qualify as metaphysically legitimate. In light of this, it seems hard to deny the metaphysical viability of some form of alethic disjunctivism, even by the lights of the strong pluralist. The satisfaction of the core principles would appear to deliver precisely the kind of qualitative similarity that is required to make a disjunctive property like T_G metaphysically viable according to the sparse conception.

Thus, the increased degree of conservativeness that goes with this conception looks unhelpful to the strong pluralist. It does not put her in a position to rule out the legitimacy of the disjunctive truth property on metaphysical grounds.[26]

If the strong pluralist has no means of resisting commitment to T_G, her view collapses into alethic disjunctivism. Since strong pluralism is the only pure form of pluralism, a further conclusion suggests itself: pure pluralist positions cannot be upheld by appealing to metaphysical considerations of the sort just presented. In turn, unless other defensive maneuvers are available to fend off the challenge from alethic disjunctivism, this means that the only tenable positions in the pluralist landscape are of a mixed character—ones that incorporate both moderate pluralism and moderate monism (the former because of the domain-specific truth properties $T_1, \ldots, T_n$, the latter because of the generic disjunctive property T_G). This is a significant conclusion, as it decreases the territory that can be tenably held by the pluralist.

5.2 ALETHIC DISJUNCTIVISM AND SECOND-ORDER FUNCTIONALISM

It is difficult for the second-order functionalist to deny the legitimacy of some form of alethic disjunctivism. The second-order functional truth property, T_{2OF}, and the disjunctive truth property, T_G, are sufficiently similar that it would be quite odd for the second-order functionalist to endorse the existence of the former while rejecting the existence of the latter. They are sufficiently similar in the sense of being necessarily co-extensional.

---

[26] The line of argument just presented contravenes Pedersen (2006), which presents a form of strong pluralism and tries to resist the generic, disjunctive truth property by appealing to the sparse conception of properties. Pedersen (2010) leaves the issue open. Conversations with Edwards and Lynch have convinced one author—Pedersen—that the disjunctive truth property cannot be ruled out by appealing to the sparse conception, for just these reasons. The other author—Wright—is not yet convinced that the presented line of reasoning is compelling; see C. D. Wright (2012) for further details.

Let us start by considering the claim that T_{2OF} and T_G are co-extensional, turning afterwards to the necessity claim. Let $R_1, \ldots, R_n$ be the properties that the second-order functionalist takes to play the truth-role for $domain_1, \ldots, domain_n$. Let T_G be the property of being either R_1 (and belonging to $domain_1$), or $\ldots$, or R_n (and belonging to $domain_n$). Recall that the second-order functionalist's favored property is T_{2OF}, the property of having a property that plays the truth-role (for the relevant domain). Consider now the properties T_{2OF} and T_G. These properties are co-extensional:

(EQV) For all p, $p \in ext(T_G)$ if, and only if, $p \in ext(T_{2OF})$.

⇒ Suppose that $p \in ext(T_G)$. Then, by the characterization of T_G, $R_i(p)$ and $domain_i(p)$ for some R_i among $R_1, \ldots, R_n$. But R_i plays the truth-role for $domain_i$ to which p belongs. So, p has the property of having a property that plays the truth-role for its domain. Hence, $p \in ext(T_{2OF})$.

⇐ Suppose that $p \in ext(T_{2OF})$. Then p has the property R_i that plays the truth-role for $domain_i$ to which p belongs. By the characterization of T_G, p is T_G—i.e., $p \in ext(T_G)$.

Further, note that the disjunct-disjunction relationship between, on the one hand, $R_1, \ldots, R_n$ and T_G on the other holds of necessity since being T_G is simply defined as being either R_1 (and belonging to $domain_1$), or $\ldots$, or being R_n (and belonging to $domain_n$). Similarly, propositions belong to domains necessarily and each of the domain-specific properties $R_1, \ldots, R_n$ plays the truth-role relative to their respective domains necessarily. Given these necessary connections, we can strengthen the conclusion that T_{2OF} and T_G are co-extensional to the conclusion that they are co-extensional necessarily. For familiar reasons owing to Kripke, necessary co-extension seems to be required for identity between properties. Presumably, however, it falls short of being sufficient.[27] Yet, it does make them similar enough to suggest that it is odd to think that only T_{2OF} exists. What is needed reasonably to suppose that this is so is an independent reason for thinking that T_{2OF} exists, whereas T_G does not. Is such a reason available? We think that an independent reason that supports the opposite conclusion is available. Both T_{2OF} and T_G apply to propositions that have a property satisfying the truisms or platitudes delineating the truth concept, assuming with the second-order functionalist that the platitude-based strategy is adopted. As such, T_{2OF} and T_G apply to things that are qualitatively similar. This, in turn, makes it difficult to see why they should not both be ontologically admissible, even from the point of view of someone who occupies a conservative stance with respect to property ontology. But notice that

---

[27] Think of the property of being an odd number divisible by 2 with 0 remainder and the property of being an integer solution to the equation $x = \sqrt{2}$. In all possible worlds these two properties have nothing in their extension, and so, they are necessarily co-extensional. Yet, they are not identical.

the two properties are on a par in this regard, and so, that it would be quite odd to suppose that only one of them exists.

The above argument suggests that second-order functionalism and some form of alethic disjunctivism are notational variants, or at the very least that they are similar to some significant degree. There is convergence in two important respects. First, recall that we have proceeded on the assumption that pluralists—including alethic disjunctivists—take domain-specific truth properties to be properties that satisfy a set of core principles. But for a property to satisfy these principles relative to a given domain is for that property to play the truth-role relative to that domain, in other words, for it to have precisely the feature that the second-order functionalist takes to be distinctive of domain-specific truth properties. Second, although the disjunctive property of being R_1 (and belonging to domain$_1$), or . . . , or being R_n (and belonging to domain$_n$) is intensionally different from the property of having a property satisfying the truth-role, we have just seen that there is a strong connection between these properties from an extensional perspective: they are necessarily co-extensional. Putting these two points together supports the conclusion that there is a high degree of similarity between alethic disjunctivism and second-order functionalism. Given this high degree of similarity, we submit that it would be odd for the second-order functionalist to maintain that her view is viable while at the same time rejecting the viability of alethic disjunctivism.[28]

5.3 ALETHIC DISJUNCTIVISM AND MANIFESTATION FUNCTIONALISM

We now turn to manifestation functionalism. Below it is argued that the manifestation functionalist cannot deny the legitimacy of the generic disjunctive truth property.

According to the manifestation functionalist, truth is the property that has the truish features as a matter of necessity—that is, 'the property that is, necessarily, had by believed contents just when things are as they are believed to be; had by propositions believed at the end of inquiry and which makes propositions correct to believe' (Lynch 2013: 55). As seen earlier, according to Lynch, a property must have the truish features in order to qualify as a truth property. We will now argue that the disjunctive truth property, T_G, has the truish features necessarily and so is just like the truth property envisioned by the manifestation functionalist.

---

[28] Again, we have assumed that the alethic disjunctivist we are considering embraces the idea that the core principles play a crucial concept-delineating role. However, there is nothing in principle that excludes the possibility of a form of alethic disjunctivism that does not incorporate this assumption. This kind of alethic disjunctivism would quite different from second-order functionalism, and not just because there is disagreement as to the role of the core principles.

Pluralism about Truth as Alethic Disjunctivism

To show: T_G has the truish features necessarily:

(O) For all p, p is T_G if, and only if, if p is believed, things are believed to be as they are. (*Objectivity*)

(NB) For all p, it is prima facie correct to believe p is T_G if, and only if, it is correct to believe p. (*Norm of belief*)

(EI) For all p, other things being equal, if p is T_G, then believing p is a worthy goal of inquiry. (*End of inquiry*)

Now recall that T_G is characterized as follows:

(TG) $(\forall p)[T_G(p) \leftrightarrow T_1(p) \vee \ldots \vee T_n(p)]$

and that

(SAT) The domain-specific truth properties $T_1, \ldots, T_n$ satisfy the truisms.

We are entitled to assume (*SAT*) because the manifestation functionalist takes domain-specific truth properties like correspondence and superwarrant to qualify as truth properties in virtue of satisfying the truisms.

Let us now turn to *Objectivity*. We break our argument into two parts, one for each direction of the biconditional:

$\Rightarrow$

(1) $T_G(p)$ — Assumption
(2) If $T_G(p)$, then $T_i(p)$ (for some T_i) — (TG)
(3) $T_i(p)$ — (1), (2)
(4) $T_i(p)$ if, and only if, if p is believed, things are believed to be as they are. — (SAT)
(5) If p is believed, things are believed to be as they are. — (3), (4)
(6) If $T_G(p)$, then if p is believed, things are believed to be as they are. — (1), (5)

$\Leftarrow$

(1) If p is believed, things are believed to be as they are. — Assumption
(2) $T_i(p)$ if and only if, if p is believed, things are believed to be as they are. — (SAT)
(3) $T_i(p)$ — (1), (2)
(4) $T_G(p)$ — (TG)
(5) If things are believed to be as they are if p is believed, then $T_G(p)$. — (1), (4)

Since p was arbitrary, we get the desired result by combining $\Rightarrow$ and $\Leftarrow$. That is, for all p, p is T_G if, and only if, things are believed to be as they are if p is believed.

The arguments for Norm of Belief and End of Inquiry are similar, and included in Appendix A. We get that, necessarily, T_G has the truish features (or necessarily satisfies the truisms), because we have relied only on the characterization of T_G, (SAT), and basic logical reasoning. The disjunct-disjunction relationship between $T_1, \ldots, T_n$ holds as a matter of conceptual necessity since the characterization of T_G simply says that to be T_G is to be either T_1 (and belong to domain$_1$), or . . . , or be T_n (and belong to domain$_n$). (*SAT*) also holds of necessity because propositions belong to domains necessarily and each of the domain-specific properties $T_1, \ldots, T_n$ plays the truth-role relative to their respective domains necessarily. These things combined imply that there is no way that T_G can fail to have the truish features.

The argument just presented shows that the disjunctive truth property T_G has the characteristic that defines truth on the manifestation functionalist view, namely, necessary possession of the truish features. As such, the manifestation functionalist should recognize the disjunctive truth property as a legitimate truth property. It would be quite odd for her to reject the property as being illegitimate—or not a proper candidate for truth—when it passes muster by her own lights.[29]

6. Conclusion

We have pursued and executed a number of tasks in this chapter. First, we have provided a survey of much of the pluralist landscape. We take it that the distinctions between moderate and strong versions of monism and pluralism, respectively, exhaust logical space. However, we also take it that the four specific varieties of pluralism discussed here do not exhaust the pluralist part of that space; conspicuously absent, for example, are the views of Sher, Horgan and colleagues, and other correspondence pluralists. Still, the four varieties surveyed should be of particular interest in that they are prominent in the pluralist literature. Second, we hope to have illuminated the three mixed pluralist views—alethic disjunctivism, second-order functionalism, and manifestation functionalism—by discussing the idea of metaphysical grounding that is an integral part of each of them. Although they all incorporate a monist thesis, as the discussion made clear, they are distinctively more pluralist than monist from a metaphysical point of view. Again, to use a slogan: the many ground the one. We also hope to have made a case for thinking that alethic disjunctivism

---

[29] Three things deserve to be mentioned. First, the conclusion that T_G satisfies the truisms and does so necessarily puts pressure on Lynch's use of the definite article in the characterization of manifestation functionalist truth. At least it does so given his rejection of the idea that T_G is a viable candidate for functionalist truth. For a more elaborate argument against Lynch on this point, see Pedersen (2012). Second, the argument just given can be modified so it applies in the case of the second-order functional truth property, too. See Appendix B for details, as well as David (2013) for the same kind of argument. This point is highly relevant to Lynch (2009), because one of Lynch's main reasons for moving away from second-order functionalism and adopting manifestation functionalism instead is his contention that T_{2O} fails to have the truish features. Third, the argument just given can be used to account for the unity of truth on the alethic disjunctivist view. One might reasonably wonder what unifies the domain-specific—or disjunct—truth properties $T_1, \ldots, T_n$. For instance, just like Lynch worries whether the second-order functionalist property has the truish features, one might wonder whether T_G really has these features. We take ourselves to have shown that T_G does indeed have these features. This puts the alethic disjunctivist in a position to answer the question of unity: truths have something substantial in common. They all have a property that, necessarily, has the truish features.

is relatively compelling—that the three other kinds of pluralists will find it hard to reject the viability of the view. For the strong pluralist, the generic disjunctive truth property suggests itself, because it should be admitted into the ontology even by conservative standards with respect to property ontology.[30] It will be difficult for the second-order functionalist to resist alethic disjunctivism, because her favored truth property and the disjunctive truth property turn out to be quite similar. Lastly, the disjunctive truth property has the truish features as a matter of necessity—which on the manifestation functionalist view is the key characteristic of truth.

Appendix A: T_G satisfies Norm of Belief and End of Inquiry

Norm of Belief

$\Rightarrow$

(1)	$T_G(p)$	Assumption
(2)	If $T_G(p)$, then $T_i(p)$ (for some T_i).	(TG)
(3)	$T_i(p)$	(1), (2)
(4)	$T_i(p)$ if and only if it is correct to believe that p.	(SAT)
(5)	It is correct to believe that p.	(3), (4)
(6)	If $T_G(p)$, then it is correct to believe that p.	(1), (5)

$\Leftarrow$

(1)	It is correct to believe that p.	Assumption
(2)	$T_i(p)$ if and only if it is correct to believe that p.	(SAT)
(3)	$T_i(p)$	(1), (2)
(4)	$T_G(p)$	(TG)
(5)	If it is correct to believe that p, then $T_G(p)$.	(1), (4)

Proposition p was arbitrary. Thus, putting together $\Rightarrow$ and $\Leftarrow$, we get that T_G satisfies Norm of Belief: for all p, p is T_G if and only if it is correct to believe p.

End of Inquiry

(1)	$T_G(p)$	Assumption
(2)	If $T_G(p)$, then $T_i(p)$ (for some T_i).	(TG)
(3)	$T_i(p)$	(1), (2)
(4)	If $T_i(p)$, then believing p is a worthy goal of inquiry.	(SAT)
(5)	Believing p is a worthy goal of inquiry.	(3), (4)
(6)	If $T_G(p)$, then believing p is a worthy goal of inquiry.	(1), (5)

---

[30] These considerations leave other arguments for strong pluralism untouched, however. See, e.g., Wright (2010; 2012) and Cotnoir (forthcoming).

Proposition p was arbitrary. Therefore, for all p, if $T_G(p)$, then believing p is a worthy goal of inquiry.

Appendix B: T_{2O} satisfies the truisms

The truth property of second-order functionalism, T_{2O}, is characterized as follows:

> (T^{2O}) The property of being true (T_{2O}) is the property of having a property that plays the truth-role (relative to the relevant domain),

Furthermore, it is an integral part of the view that

> (SAT^{2O}) A property plays the truth-role for domain$_i$ if it has the truish features for every proposition belonging to that domain.

Given (T^{2O}) and (SAT^{2O}), we can straightforwardly modify the argument provided in the case of T_G to show that T_{2O} satisfies *Objectivity*:

$\Rightarrow$

(1) $T_{2O}(p)$ — Assumption
(2) If $T_{2O}(p)$, then $T_i(p)$ (for some T_i). — (T^{2O})
(3) $T_i(p)$ — (1), (2)
(4) $T_i(p)$ if and only if (if p is believed, things are believed to be as they are). — (SAT^{2O})
(5) If p is believed, things are believed to be as they are. — (3), (4)
(6) If $T_{2O}(p)$, then (if p is believed, things are believed to be as they are). — (1), (5)

$\Leftarrow$

(1) If p is believed, things are believed to be as they are. — Assumption
(2) $T_i(p)$ if and only if, if p is believed, things are believed to be as they are. — (SAT^{2O})
(3) $T_i(p)$ — (1), (2)
(4) $T_{2O}(p)$ — (TG)
(5) If (if p is believed, things are believed to be as they are), then $T_{2O}(p)$. — (1), (4)

Proposition p was arbitrary. So, by combining $\Rightarrow$ and $\Leftarrow$ we get the desired result: for all p, p is T_{2O} if and only if (if p is believed, things are believed to be as they are). The arguments for *Norm of Belief* and *End of Inquiry* can likewise be obtained by straightforwardly modifying the arguments provided for T_G.

One of Lynch's main reasons for moving away from second-order functionalism and adopting manifestation functionalism instead is that he takes T_{2O} not to have the truish features (2009: 64–6). As such, in his view, it fails to be a truth property properly so-called. The argument we have just provided suggests that Lynch has concluded too swiftly that the truth property of second-order functionalism fails in this respect (even if it fails in others—see Wright, 2010).

References

Barnard, R. & Horgan, T. (2006). Truth as mediated correspondence. *Monist* 89: 31–50.

Barnard, R. & Horgan, T. (2013). The synthetic unity of truth. In N. J. L. L. Pedersen & C. D. Wright (eds.), *Truth and Pluralism: Current Debates* (180–196). New York: Oxford University Press.

Cotnoir, A. (2009). Generic truth and mixed conjunctions: some alternatives. *Analysis* 69: 473–479.

Cotnoir, A. (forthcoming). Validity for strong pluralists. *Philosophy and Phenomenological Research*.

David, M. (2013). Lynch's functionalist theory of truth. In N. J. L. L. Pedersen & C. D. Wright (eds.), *Truth and Pluralism: Current Debates* (42–68). New York: Oxford University Press.

Dodd, J. (2013). Deflationism trumps pluralism! In N. J. L. L. Pedersen & C. D. Wright (eds.), *Truth and Pluralism: Current Debates* (298–322). New York: Oxford University Press.

Edwards, D. (2008). How to solve the problem of mixed conjunctions. *Analysis* 68: 143–149.

Edwards, D. (2012). On alethic disjunctivism. *Dialectica* 66: 200–214.

Edwards, D. (2013). Truth, winning, and simple determination pluralism. In N. J. L. L. Pedersen & C. D. Wright (eds.), *Truth and Pluralism: Current Debates* (113–122). New York: Oxford University Press.

Horgan, T, & M. Potrč. (2000). Blobjectivism and indirect correspondence. *Facta Philosophica* 2: 249–270.

Kölbel, M. (2008). 'True' as ambiguous. *Philosophy and Phenomenological Research* 77: 359–384.

Kölbel, M. (2013). Should we be pluralists about truth? In N. J. L. L. Pedersen & C. D. Wright (eds.), *Truth and Pluralism: Current Debates* (278–297). New York: Oxford University Press.

Lynch, M. P. (2000). Alethic pluralism and the functionalist theory of truth. *Acta Analytica* 15: 195–214.

Lynch, M. P. (2001). A functionalist theory of truth. In his (ed.), *The Nature of Truth* (723–749). Cambridge, MA: MIT Press.

Lynch, M. P. (2004). Truth and multiple realizability. *Australasian Journal of Philosophy* 82: 384–408.

Lynch, M. P. (2005a). Functionalism and our folk theory of truth: reply to Cory Wright. *Synthese* 145: 29–43.

Lynch, M. P. (2005b). Précis of *True to Life* and response to commentators. *Philosophical Books* 46: 289–291, 331–342.

Lynch, M. P. (2005c). Truisms about truth. In H. Battaly & M. P. Lynch (eds.), *Perspectives on the Philosophy of William P. Alston* (255–274). Lanham: Roman & Littlefield Press.

Lynch, M. P. (2006). ReWrighting pluralism. *Monist* 89: 63–84.

Lynch, M. P. (2009). *Truth as Many and One*. Oxford: Oxford University Press.

Lynch, M. P. (2013). Three questions about truth pluralism. In N. J. L. L. Pedersen & C. D. Wright (eds.), *Truth and Pluralism: Current Debates* (21–41). New York: Oxford University Press.

O'Connor, D. J. (1975). *The Correspondence Theory of Truth*. London: Hutchinson.

Pedersen, N. J. L. L. (2006). What can the problem of mixed inferences teach us about alethic pluralism? *Monist* 89: 113–117.
Pedersen, N. J. L. L. (2010). Stabilizing alethic pluralism. *Philosophical Quarterly* 60: 92–108.
Pedersen, N. J. L. L. (2012). True alethic functionalism? *International Journal of Philosophical Studies* 20: 125–133.
Pedersen, N. J. L. L. (forthcoming). Pluralism × 3: truth, logic, metaphysics. *Erkenntnis*.
Pedersen, N. J. L. L. & D. Edwards. (2011). Truth as one(s) and many: on Lynch's alethic functionalism. *Analytic Philosophy* 52: 213–230.
Pedersen, N. J. L. L. & C. D. Wright. (2012). Pluralist theories of truth. *Stanford Encyclopedia of Philosophy*. Fixed URL = http://plato.stanford.edu/entries/truth-pluralist/.
Pettit, P. (1996). Realism and truth: a comment on Crispin Wright's *Truth and Objectivity*. *Philosophy and Phenomenological Research* 56: 883–889.
Rattan, G. (2010). Metarepresentation and the cognitive value of the concept of truth. In C. D. Wright & N. J. L. L. Pedersen (eds.), *New Waves in Truth* (139–156). New York: Palgrave Macmillan.
Sainsbury, M. (1996). Crispin Wright: *Truth and Objectivity*. *Philosophy and Phenomenological Research* 56: 899–904.
Shapiro, S. (2011). Truth, function, and paradox. *Analysis* 71: 38–44.
Sher, G. (1998). On the possibility of a substantive theory of truth. *Synthese* 117: 133–172.
Sher, G. (2004). In search of a substantive theory of truth. *Journal of Philosophy* 101: 5–36.
Sher, G. (2005). Functionalist pluralism. *Philosophical Books* 46: 311–330.
Sher, G. (2013). Forms of correspondence: the intricate route from thought to reality. In N. J. L. L. Pedersen & C. D. Wright (eds.), *Truth and Pluralism: Current Debates* (157–179). New York: Oxford University Press.
Sher, G. & C. D. Wright. (2007). Truth as a normative modality of cognitive acts. In G. Siegwart & D. Griemann (eds.), *Truth and Speech Acts: Studies in the Philosophy of Language* (525–574). New York: Routledge.
Wright, C. D. (2005). On the functionalization of pluralist approaches to truth. *Synthese* 145: 1–28.
Wright, C. D. (2010). Truth, Ramsification, and the pluralist's revenge. *Australasian Journal of Philosophy* 88: 265–283.
Wright, C. D. (2012). Is pluralism inherently unstable? *Philosophical Studies* 159: 89–105.
Wright, C. D. & N. J. L. L. Pedersen. (2010). Truth, pluralism, monism, correspondence. In C. D. Wright & N. J. L. L. Pedersen (eds.), *New Waves in Truth* (205–217). New York: Palgrave Macmillan.
Wright, C. J. G. (1992). *Truth and Objectivity*. Cambridge, MA: Harvard University Press.
Wright, C. J. G. (1996). Précis to *Truth and Objectivity* and response to commentators. *Philosophy and Phenomenological Research* 56: 863–868, 911–941.
Wright, C. J. G. (2001). Minimalism, deflationism, pragmatism, pluralism. In M. P. Lynch (ed.), *The Nature of Truth: Classical and Contemporary Readings* (751–787). Cambridge, MA: MIT Press.
Wright, C. J. G. (2013). A plurality of pluralisms? In N. J. L. L. Pedersen & C. D. Wright (eds.), *Truth and Pluralism: Current Debates* (123–153). New York: Oxford University Press.

{ 6 }

Truth, Winning, and Simple Determination Pluralism

Douglas Edwards

There is good reason to think that there is a useful analogy between truth and winning.[1] When playing a game, the object of that game is to win, and this tells us something important about the practice of playing games. Likewise, when believing or asserting, the object is to believe or speak truly, and this tells us something important about the practice of believing or asserting.[2] It also, of course, tells us something important about truth, just as the observation about games tells us something about winning. In this chapter, I want to explore this analogy to demonstrate one way that we can arrive at an attractive formulation of *pluralism* about truth, which I call 'simple determination pluralism'.

1. Winning and truth, unity and plurality

Where winning is typically the goal of playing a game, truth is typically the goal of asserting or believing. In a particular game, the players will typically be trying to win that game, and in asserting or believing, an assertor or believer typically aims to hit the truth.

Given the clear multiplicity of games, there is a strong sense of *pluralism* about winning: *what it takes to win* will change from one game to the next. It is also plausible to think that we have an understanding of winning that is *not* tied to any *particular* game, expressed by the thoughts that winning is the

---

[1] The classic statement of this idea is due to Dummett (1959). The analogy is also discussed in Glanzberg (2004) and briefly discussed in relation to alethic pluralism in Edwards (2011).

[2] This is not to say that the aiming need be conscious in each case. Also, for the purposes of this chapter, I will bracket the issue of where other forms of cognitive achievement, such as justification and knowledge, fit as norms of assertion and belief.

general aim when playing any game and that winning is desirable. These might be said to be general features of winning that transcend any particular features regarding what it takes to win any particular game. We also often ascribe a general property of winning, such as when we say on Sports Day 'these are the winners' when gesturing toward the children holding sweets in their hands. There is a sense in which we would want to say that they share a property in common—*being winners*—which is distinct from the various ways in which they have become winners.

There is also a strong sense of *unity* with truth: truth is what all assertions and beliefs aim at and is the property that all true propositions have. Truth is a distinctive and unified norm of assertion or belief formation in the way that winning is a distinctive and unified norm of certain kinds of activity.[3] Moreover, if one takes seriously the project under discussion in this book—alethic pluralism—then there is also a strong sense of *plurality* to truth: even if we take it that truth is a single property, there may be very different things to say about how different kinds of propositions get to be true. This thought is supported by the idea that what there is to say about the truth of, say, mathematical propositions may be very different from what there is to say about the truth of propositions about the material world, which in turn is different from what there is to say about moral truths.

2. Winning: a proposal

With these thoughts in mind, suppose we were to try to give a theory of winning. To satisfy the twin constraints of unity and plurality, I suggest that we need to make sense of the idea that that there is a single property of winning, and that that there are a number of different ways to get to have this property. I contend that the best way to think of this structure is to hold that, for each game, there will be a *winning-determining* property, the possession of which by a player will determine possession of the general winning property.

First of all, what can we say about the nature of the general winning property? We need not look far to answer this question as we can begin by describing winning as the property that one aims to achieve when playing a game. There may also be other features we can use to describe winning, such as that if one has the property of winning the game is over; the property of winning is a desirable property; if one has the property of winning, one has been engaged in some form of competitive activity; and winning is a form of success.

A full list of features like these should give us a complete specification of the *property* of winning: they are used as descriptions that characterize the nature

---

[3] For an argument for this claim, see Lynch (2006).

Truth, Winning, and Simple Determination Pluralism 115

of the winning property and are intended to do so exhaustively. Consequently, there will be no *reductive* account of the property of winning that attempts to identify winning with any other property or properties.

To establish what the *winning-determining* property is for a game, the natural place to look is at the rules of the game in question. For the kinds of games we are interested in, there must be some move that one makes or some achievement in the context of the game, which determines that one has won that game. For a game to have this kind of structure, it is imperative that rules of the game are specified, which establish the permissible and impermissible moves, numbers of players permitted, and, of course, the specifications for winning that game. When we have done this, we will find that a conditional can be constructed of the form:

(*Cx*)   When playing game *x*: if one possesses property F then one has won (has the property of winning).

Specific examples of conditionals of this form for chess and tennis, respectively, are plausibly:

(*Cc*)   When playing chess: if one has the property of having checkmated one's opponent's king, then one has won.

(*Ct*)   When playing tennis: if one has the property of amassing a majority of the allotted sets, then one has won.

The rules of each game thus specify a property the possession of which determines possession of the property of winning. On this view, we treat the game-specific property as the property that determines the possession of the separate property of winning, and the nature of the game-specific property will be established by the rules of the game in question. The key distinction, then, is between winning and *what it takes to win*, or between the property of winning and the properties that determine winning.

This account explains both the unity and the plurality involved in winning. We have a single property of winning, which is shared by all winners and is the property that one aims to achieve when playing a game. We also have an explanation of how this property is attained, which fits nicely with the intuitive thought that it is the *rules* of the game in question that establish the property that determines winning.

3. Truth: simple determination pluralism

If one takes truth pluralism seriously, then truth, like winning, has claims to both unity and plurality. We can now consider how a pluralist theory of truth analogous to our account of winning might look, which I call 'simple determination pluralism' about truth.

First, we would start by collecting a list of truth features, or truth 'platitudes', and rewrite them so that they make reference to a property. What we would end up with would be a list of claims like the following:[4]

Truth is the property that is the goal of inquiry.[5]
Truth is a property that is distinct from justification.
Truth is a property that is distinct from warranted assertibility.
The proposition that p has the property of being true if and only if p.[6]
To have the property of being true is to tell it like it is.
To assert p is to present p as possessing the property of truth.

A full list of platitudes, or features, like this would give us a complete description of the nature of truth. There will be no reductive account of truth available: unlike some views (e.g., Wright 1992, 2003), the platitudes are not to be used to find another property that exhibits the truth features that will then be identified with truth.[7] All true propositions, then, will possess this 'simple' truth property. *This* property is truth, and this ensures that the generality constraint is met: there is *one* property that is truth, and this property is possessed by all true propositions.[8]

We now need to address the question of how propositions get to have this truth property. To explain this, we are going to need to say some more about domains of discourse.

Take it that a domain of discourse is like a game in that there is a goal for those participating in that discourse: to hit the truth. The idea is that truth is attained in virtue of the possession of a *distinct* property that, in accordance with the nature of the domain, *determines* truth in that domain. To establish which property determines truth in a domain, we need to examine carefully the domain in question. What we will need to do is to examine the rules of a domain to generate conditionals analogous to (*Cx*). To do this, I suggest we will need to carefully examine at least the following two features.[9]

---

[4] This list of platitudes takes inspiration from the list of C. J. G. Wright (2003: 271–2).

[5] Sub-versions of this platitude would include aforementioned claims of the form approximating 'truth is the property that is the goal of assertion' and 'truth is the property that is the goal of belief'.

[6] For ease of use, I will use propositions as the chosen bearers of truth, with an assertion or belief being true insofar as *what* is asserted or believed (a proposition) is true.

[7] This view of the truth property is similar to that advanced by Lynch (2009). The similarities and differences between simple determination pluralism and Lynch's view are discussed briefly below and in more detail in Edwards (2011).

[8] This allows simple determination pluralism to respond to problems for views that do not allow for a single truth property. The problem of mixed inferences (Tappolet 1997; Pedersen 2006) can be solved as there is a single truth property preserved across valid inference. The problem of mixed compounds (Tappolet 2000) is more complex, but I have outlined a solution elsewhere (Edwards 2008, 2009) that is available to the simple determination pluralist; see also Cotnoir (2009) and Cook (2011) for discussion.

[9] This issue is also discussed, approached in a slightly different way, in Edwards (2011).

First, we will need to examine the nature of the domain itself and the nature of the subject-matter of that domain. The main purpose of this exercise is to establish what kind of content is in play, in particular, whether that domain can be said to deal in what we might call 'genuinely representational' content. One way that we can do this is to develop a set of criteria by which to judge whether a domain deals in genuinely representational content. This is a project undertaken by Wright (1992) and developed by Fine (2001). I will not develop the precise criteria that we should use here, as it is clearly worthy of careful study independently, but I suggest that the establishment of the kind of content operational in a domain is the first step to establishing the required conditionals.

Once the first task has been completed—namely, when we have a grasp on how to establish in general the kind content in a domain, and when we have established of a particular domain what kind of content it deals in—we then need to look at the practices of assertion and belief-formation in that domain. In particular, we need to look at what *kind* of property would be required to determine truth in that domain, and whether this property is a property that is properly described in terms of a relation between linguistic and nonlinguistic entities (such as a correspondence property, for example), or a relation between linguistic entities (such as a coherence property), or a construction out of justification or warrant (such as superassertibility). Part of this job will have been done by the establishment of the content of a domain, in that if a domain is deemed to deal in genuinely representational content, it is likely that a property like correspondence will be the truth-determining property for that domain. However, the issue is not fully decided until we look at the standards for assertion and belief formation, and at whether the property in question is able to play the required role in those practices.[10]

Of course, these two tasks are big tasks, and any pluralist view should take seriously the size of the project ahead when it comes to establishing what the relevant properties are in individual domains of discourse. However, as we are dealing with framework issues in this chapter, we can bracket these concerns for the moment and finish the explanation of the structure of simple determination pluralism.

Suppose, then, that the two tasks I have outlined have been accomplished to a reasonable standard. If so, we should get conditionals of the form:

(*Cdx*) In domain of discourse *x*: if ⟨p⟩ has property F, then ⟨p⟩ is true (has the property of truth).[11]

---

[10] For example, even in a genuinely representational discourse, there might still be issues about correspondence as a truth property if it could be shown—perhaps through arguments akin to Dummett's (1959) concerns—that such a property could have no governing impact on the practice of assertion or belief formation.

[11] '⟨p⟩' abbreviates the words 'the proposition that p'.

Some examples of these might be:

> (*Cmw*) In material world discourse: if ⟨p⟩ corresponds to the facts, then ⟨p⟩ is true.
>
> (*Ca*) In arithmetical discourse: if ⟨p⟩ coheres with basic axioms, then ⟨p⟩ is true.
>
> (*Cmo*) In moral discourse: if ⟨p⟩ is superassertible, then ⟨p⟩ is true.

On the supposition that that there is only one truth-determining property in a domain, these will form one direction of *biconditionals* of the form:[12]

> (*Bdx*) In domain of discourse *x*: ⟨p⟩ is true (has the property of truth) iff ⟨p⟩ has property F.[13]

Using our examples, we can construct the following:

> (*Bmw*) In material world discourse: ⟨p⟩ is true iff ⟨p⟩ corresponds to the facts.
>
> (*Ba*) In arithmetical discourse: ⟨p⟩ is true iff ⟨p⟩ coheres with basic axioms.
>
> (*Bmo*) In moral discourse: ⟨p⟩ is true iff ⟨p⟩ is superassertible.

It is important to note that there will be an *order of determination* on these biconditionals from right to left that reflects the explanatory primacy of the original conditionals. In the material world domain, for example, it is *because* ⟨p⟩ corresponds to the facts that ⟨p⟩ is true, whereas it is not *because* ⟨p⟩ is true that ⟨p⟩ corresponds to the facts. The nature of each domain will thus specify a property the possession of which *determines* the possession of the separate truth property.

The structure of simple determination pluralism is thus as follows. Truth is given as the property that is exhaustively described by the truth platitudes. This property is the property possessed by all true propositions, regardless of domain. For each domain there will be a property that determines possession of the truth property, and these properties are held fully distinct from the truth property itself. The relationship between the truth-determining properties and truth is underwritten by the conditionals of the form (*Cdx*) above, which in turn ground the order of determination on the biconditionals of the form (*Bdx*).

4. Advantages of simple determination pluralism

I have noted that the view presented accounts for the unity of truth by holding that there is a single property shared by all true propositions. While this

---

[12] Without thus supposition, there is a risk of contradiction, as, within a domain, one proposition may possess one truth-determining property and lack another.

[13] Analogous biconditionals are more complicated in the games case due to circumstances like forfeiture.

feature alone may give the view an advantage over some pluralist theories, there are other positions that allow for a single truth property.[14] In the remaining space, I will briefly consider how simple determination pluralism measures up to these views.

4.1 SECOND-ORDER FUNCTIONALISM AND DISJUNCTIVISM

One proposal about the general truth property is given in the 'second-order functionalist' proposal of Lynch (2001, 2006) and discussed by C. D. Wright (2010). On this view, the truth platitudes carve out a functional role, and different properties (such as correspondence, coherence, and superassertibility) realize this role in different domains of discourse. Truth is then identified with the second-order property of having *one of* the domain-specific realizers. All true propositions thus share a property in common—the property of having one of the domain-specific realizers—even though they may not share *the same* domain-specific realizer.

A similar proposal is the 'disjunctivist' view discussed by Pedersen (2010) and Pedersen & Wright (2013). On this view, the single truth property is again formed using the domain-specific realizer properties, but the property is not formed by existential generalization, but through disjunction: the disjunctivist holds that truth is the disjunctive property of either corresponding or cohering or being superassertible. Again, all true propositions from all domains will possess this property, even though they may not all share the *same* disjunct.

Both of these views give us generality, but they both suffer from the same kind of concern. As Lynch (2009: 66–7) notes, it is part of the methodology of both of these kinds of views that a theory of truth is designed to give us a property that satisfies the truth platitudes: the platitudes describe *essential* features of truth, and any property that does not satisfy those platitudes cannot be identified with truth. The worry is that both of the properties identified by the second-order functionalist and the disjunctivist may fail to meet this constraint. Here is Lynch on second-order functionalism:

> suppose the color red is a second-order property: being red is having the property of having a property with certain features, such as reflective variance. Does the property of having a property with a given reflective variance itself have that reflective variance? Not obviously; indeed, obviously not. (2009: 66)[15]

Carrying the argument over to the second-order truth property, we can ask: given that truth is the property of having a property with certain features, such

---

[14] See, for example, C. J. G. Wright (1992, 2003).
[15] See also Kim (1998) and Horton & Poston (2012) for similar concerns about second-order properties.

as being the goal of inquiry, is the property of having a property that is the goal of inquiry the goal of inquiry? Answer (according to Lynch): No.[16]

The point, if good, would also seem to carry over to the disjunctive proposal: the individual disjuncts are identified by their ability to realize the truth role, which means that they must each exhibit the truth features, such as being the goal of inquiry. But is the disjunctive property of having either property 1 that is the goal of inquiry or property 2 that is the goal of inquiry or property 3 that is the goal of inquiry *itself* the goal of inquiry? Again, it seems not.

I do not wish to claim that these considerations are conclusive, but they do point to some problems for these approaches that are not shared by simple determination pluralism.[17] Because simple determination pluralism holds that truth is the property that is described entirely by the truth platitudes, there can be no question that this property will fail to exhibit any of the features laid out in those platitudes. These kinds of concerns about the veracity of the truth property on offer will thus not apply to simple determination pluralism, which is to its advantage.

4.2 MANIFESTATION FUNCTIONALISM

The other main competitor in this area is 'manifestation functionalism' (Lynch 2009, 2013).[18] On this view, truth is identified with the property that exhibits the truth features essentially, and this property is immanent in, or manifested by, the domain-specific properties by virtue of those properties possessing the essential features of the truth property as a proper part. There is kinship between manifestation functionalism and simple determination pluralism in that both have a very similar account of the general truth property, which enables both views to avoid the concern raised above about second-order functionalism and disjunctivism.

However, there are also important differences. One is that manifestation functionalism wants to maintain an intimate connection between truth and the domain-specific properties by holding that truth is a *part of* these properties. Simple determination pluralism, on the other hand, holds that truth is entirely separate from the truth-determining properties, which get their status as truth-determining properties from facts gleaned about the nature of the domains in question.

---

[16] This is not because of the exclusivity of 'the' in '*the* goal of inquiry'—the argument would also run with '*a* goal of inquiry'. I used the former to fit with the platitudes as stated above.

[17] See C. J. G. Wright (2013) for some trepidation about the force of the concerns in the second-order case, and Pedersen & Wright (2013), Pedersen & Edwards (2011) and Edwards (2012) for some thoughts on the disjunctivist's response to this problem.

[18] Lynch calls the view 'alethic functionalism', but I use 'manifestation functionalism' to clearly distinguish the view from second-order functionalism.

Again, it is not my aim here to offer conclusive reasons to favor simple determination pluralism over manifestation functionalism, just to note some plausible advantages. For manifestation functionalism to succeed, it is crucial that the complex metaphysics of manifestation works. However, this is very questionable: Lynch's notion of manifestation is a new and controversial notion, and it has some serious problems.[19]

Simple determination pluralism, on the other hand, requires no complex and controversial metaphysics. It offers the same benefits as manifestation functionalism just through the establishment of the relevant biconditionals in each domain, which nail down the determination of truth in each domain. Thus, simple determination pluralism has an advantage over manifestation functionalism because it requires no complex metaphysics, and it has the added bonus of not being hostage to the success of the controversial manifestation relation.

5. Conclusion

Simple determination pluralism is thus worth taking seriously as a form of alethic pluralism. It meets the twin constraints of unity and plurality by holding that there is a single truth property with a plurality of truth-determining properties, and there are prima facie reasons to think that the view is structured in such a way that avoids some of the problems with other pluralist views on the table. By taking the analogy between truth and winning seriously, it also highlights the *normative* aspect of truth, namely that it is the goal of assertion or belief. Finally, it is worth noting that it presents a framework that has the potential to have application beyond truth to pluralist projects in general, offering a way of capturing unity and plurality that is different from the standard functionalist approaches.[20]

References

Cook, R. T. (2011). Alethic pluralism, generic truth, and mixed conjunctions. *Philosophical Quarterly* 61: 624–629.

Cotnoir, A. J. (2009). Generic truth and mixed conjunctions: some alternatives. *Analysis* 69: 473–479.

---

[19] See, for example, Edwards (2011) and C. J. G. Wright (2013).

[20] I would like to thank Nikolaj Pedersen and Cory Wright for inviting me to contribute to this volume, and Aaron Cotnoir, Michael Lynch, Aidan McGlynn, and Crispin Wright for helpful discussion and comments. This paper was written with the support of a postdoctoral award from the Irish Research Council for the Humanities and Social Sciences and a visiting research fellowship from the Northern Institute of Philosophy, Aberdeen, both of which I gratefully acknowledge. This research was supported by a Marie Curie Intra European Fellowship within the 7th European Community Framework Programme.

Dummett, M. (1959). Truth. *Proceedings of the Aristotelian Society* 59: 141–162.
Edwards, D. (2008). How to solve the problem of mixed conjunctions. *Analysis* 68: 143–149.
Edwards, D. (2009). Truth-conditions and the nature of truth. *Analysis* 69: 684–688.
Edwards, D. (2011). Simplifying alethic pluralism. *Southern Journal of Philosophy* 49: 28–48.
Edwards, D. (2012). On alethic disjunctivism. *Dialectica* 66: 200–214.
Fine, K. (2001). The question of realism. *Philosophers' Imprint* 1: 1–30.
Glanzberg, M. (2004). Against truth-value gaps. In JC Beall (ed.), *Liars and Heaps: New Essays on Paradox* (151–194). Oxford: Oxford University Press.
Horton, M. & T. Poston. (2012). Functionalism about truth and the metaphysics of reduction. *Acta Analytica* 27: 13–27.
Kim, J. (1998). *Mind in a Physical World: An Essay on the Mind-Body Problem and Mental Causation*. Cambridge, MA: MIT Press.
Lynch, M. P. (2001). A functionalist theory of truth. In his (ed.) *The Nature of Truth* (723–749). Cambridge, MA: MIT Press.
Lynch, M. P. (2006). ReWrighting pluralism. *Monist* 89: 63–84.
Lynch, M. P. (2013). Three questions about truth. In N. J. L. L. Pedersen & C. D. Wright (eds.): *Truth and Pluralism: Current Debates* (21–41). New York: Oxford University Press.
Lynch, M. P. (2009). *Truth as One and Many*. Oxford: Oxford University Press.
Pedersen, N. J. L. L. (2006). What can the problem of mixed inferences teach us about alethic pluralism? *Monist* 89: 102–117.
Pedersen, N. J. L. L. (2010). Stabilizing alethic pluralism. *Philosophical Quarterly* 60: 92–108.
Pedersen, N. J. L. L. & C. D. Wright. (2013). Pluralism about truth as alethic disjunctivism. In N. J. L. L. Pedersen & C. D. Wright (eds.): *Truth and Pluralism: Current Debates* (87–112). New York: Oxford University Press.
Pedersen, N. J. L. L. & D. Edwards. (2011). Truth as one(s) and many: on Lynch's alethic functionalism. *Analytic Philosophy* 52: 213–230.
Tappolet, C. (1997). Mixed inferences: a problem for pluralism about truth predicates. *Analysis* 57: 209–210.
Tappolet, C. (2000). Truth, pluralism, and many-valued logics. *Philosophical Quarterly* 50: 382–383.
Wright, C. D. (2010). Truth, Ramsification, and the pluralist's revenge. *Australasian Journal of Philosophy* 88: 265–283.
Wright, C. J. G. (1992). *Truth and Objectivity*. Cambridge, MA: Harvard University Press.
Wright, C. J. G. (2003). Truth: a traditional debate reviewed. In his *Saving the Differences: Essays on Themes from Truth and Objectivity* (241–287). Cambridge, MA: Harvard University Press.
Wright, C. J. G. (2013). A plurality of pluralisms? In N. J. L. L. Pedersen & C. D. Wright (eds.), *Truth and Pluralism: Current Debates* (123–153). New York: Oxford University Press.

{7}

A Plurality of Pluralisms
Crispin Wright

1. Background

I have only recently come back to this debate. I left it for about ten years and more or less stopped thinking about the issues, so it's been a great pleasure to find that others have been running on with it in the meantime and saying very creative and interesting things of, I think, considerable potential significance across wide areas of philosophy.

First a bit of autobiography. I got interested in thinking about truth in a very general pluralistic way—you know: maybe truth doesn't always consist in the same kind of thing; nothing more specific than that—for two broad reasons. One was because it looked as though making some sense of different *kinds* of truth might help to explain why the traditional debate about truth turned out to be sterile and incomplete. Maybe the reason why the correspondence theorists, the coherence theorists, and the pragmatists couldn't get anywhere was because they were all over-generalizing. Of course, there were other problems with their proposals. Correspondence, for instance, notoriously had explanatory difficulties actually making out some interesting notion of correspondence and explaining what the terms of the correspondence relation were. But the general idea of truth being determined by *fit*, by accuracy of some sort, doesn't go away just because when you press, you find it's hard to explain its parameters. It's more resilient than that. What really seems wrong with correspondence is that it seems a tendentious way to think about mathematics, for instance, and a bad way to think about the comic: one doesn't want to be saddled with some metaphysics of 'out there' comedic facts to which one's impressions about comedy may correspond just by being willing to apply 'true' to ordinary ascriptions of 'funny'. The 'out there' view is doubtless a possible view—it's something someone *could* think (and Someone, in Oxford, probably does). But it doesn't seem that it sits well with our ordinary conceptions of truth and comedic discourse; one wants to think differently about the import of 'true' in such a discourse.

So that was one thought: that maybe the right thing to say about the traditional debate is that it couldn't get anywhere because actually all the protagonists were saying locally plausible things, thinking about different paradigms, thinking about different areas of truth, and their mistake was one of overextension. This idea connected with my desire to resist *deflationary* accounts of truth, which of course originally drew a large part of their credibility, for those who found them credible, from the failure of the traditional debate. In general, I distrust philosophical accounts of anything that say, 'There's not much here, it's not as interesting as you think it is.' I don't want to be told that something isn't interesting. I want to be told, 'It is *more* interesting than you think'—because one has missed certain ramifications and nuances, for example. So, perhaps just as a matter of temperament, I wanted to find a way of avoiding the collapse into deflation, and I saw that collapse as primarily motivated by the sterility of the original debate and a different diagnosis of it: that the truth debate was bad because the antagonists weren't talking *about* anything, because 'the nature of truth' is not an authentic subject. That's not the right account of the matter, in my view.

That was one motivation. The other was my long-standing interest in the debates about realism and objectivity, Dummett and Wittgenstein, and all that. Dummett had given us a model of those debates, or some of those debates, where what's at stake are differing conceptions of the form that statement-meaning takes in the region of discourse in question. And I thought that he was right, up to a point, because if you are a correspondence theorist about truth, you are thinking of meaning as consisting in, so to speak, correspondence conditions. And if you are not a correspondence theorist, you may still say, 'I am thinking of meaning as truth-conditional', but you are not thinking of truth-conditions in the same way. So it does look as though there would be implicitly differing conceptions of meaning in play if you conceived of the different disputes in that way. But that was not exactly what Dummett had in mind. Rather, his anti-realist *rejected* truth-conditional semantics—presumably because no way of thinking about truth was in view except correspondence—proposing an assertibility-conditional model instead. And here, I thought, Dummett got into trouble trying to sustain the meaning-theoretic model of the disputes, because he couldn't actually construct any assertibility-conditional accounts of meaning. Indeed, Timothy Williamson is still complaining, forty years later, that Dummett never gave us a proper theory of meaning.[1] Well, it's true, he didn't. And he didn't because you *can't*, and you can't because assertibility conditions, except in the area of mathematics, which Dummett was focusing

---

[1] Here is a characteristically acerbic expression: 'Dummett's requirement that assertibility be decidable forces assertibility-conditional semantics to take a radically different form from that of truth-conditional semantics. Anti-realists have simply failed to develop natural language semantics in that form, or even to provide serious evidence that they could so develop it if they wanted to. They proceed as if Imre Lakatos had never developed the concept of a degenerating research programme.' (Williamson, 2006: 181)

on, aren't recursively characterizable, since—for the most part—all kinds of Quinean holisms and empirically grounded conceptions of evidence enter into one's notion of the assertibility-conditions of an arbitrary empirical statement. Generally speaking, the assertibility-conditions of a statement are not purely *recursively semantically* determined, so of course a proper semantic theory can't fully characterize assertibility-conditions.[2] So my thought was just that if we've got differing notions of truth, or differing conceptions of what truth consists in—and I wasn't yet thinking about distinctions between the range of different ways of capturing the pluralist idea—then you didn't need to engage any of that. You could just allow that truth-conditions are fine across the board; that disquotational—Davidson-style—semantics is fine across the board (as far as it goes, whatever it's supposed to illuminate exactly). What's really varying is the way in which the various discourses engage with reality, the kind of truth that applies. So, if disquotational semantics is an adequate basic semantics, then the realist/anti-realist debate is not a semantic debate in the end.

So, that was me reacting against my inspirational teacher and wanting to say something that addressed the same concerns and removed some of the wrinkles.

2. Three modes of pluralism

If you are starting from an interest in the above two issues, it's obvious that there must be lots and lots of different ways of fleshing out the basic idea. What are these different 'kinds' of truth—what does the claim mean exactly? There is a big space, here, of ways of trying to explicate the alleged plurality. But it does seem to me that there is a basic constraint on any plausible proposal in this direction, which drives my reservations concerning some of the 'disjunctivist' things that Pedersen has proposed (see Pedersen 2010; 2012; Pedersen & Edwards, 2011; Pedersen & Wright 2013). I think we have to take seriously the *appearance* that generated the traditional debate. It wasn't just a clumsy mistake to look for an analysis of truth *per se*, to try to say what truth consists in. There is a strong intuition (I hate to call it that—contemporary philosophers are radically confusing themselves by their use of the term 'intuition', but the term is entrenched) of some kind of unity, or univocality if you are thinking at a semantic level. That has to be reckoned with by any plausible account. So, as Michael Lynch puts it in *Truth as One and Many* (2009)—and I think this is spot on—the first problem for any kind of pluralism is to save the *unity* alongside the plurality; you have got to have a robust account of why these are all forms of *truth* or all species of *truth*, of why we use the same word, why we

---

[2] I take an opportunity to discuss these issues further in Wright (2012).

seem to talk in terms of a single concept. If you haven't got an answer to that, you have lost the subject matter.

So I want to impose that constraint, and then my interest in what follows is just the large variety of prima facie possible ways to address it. I think there are even more possible answers than the ones to be reviewed. It's important to keep that in mind, as well as the apparent strengths and weaknesses of these answers. The issues here are open. But I am also going to suggest—of course, you would be disappointed if I didn't!—that with minor adjustments and developments, the proposal in *Truth and Objectivity* (1992) is still roadworthy. I don't say it cannot be improved on! Indeed, we'll review a proposal that I think, if it can be stabilized, will improve on it in certain respects. But I do think that a version of the proposal made in *Truth and Objectivity* still runs. Maybe you will be able to persuade me otherwise.

I think it's helpful to think in terms of four basic *modes* of pluralism, as I am going to call them. And then there are sub-types under those modes. Here are the first three modes:

Mode A. There is a mode of *Simple Alethic Pluralism*, or as Lynch (2004) called it, *SAP*. This is the thought that 'true' has no single meaning, so it's a thesis at the level of *concept*, or of *sense*.

In order to give *SAP* a chance, it's not going to be the thesis that 'true' is like 'bank', or 'rent', or 'spare'. It's going to be the thesis that 'true' is like: 'fixing', or 'dispensing', or 'poor', as in

> Fixing dinner, fixing a race, fixing the car;
> Dispensing a prescription, dispensing justice, dispensing sweeties to the class;
> Poor relation, poor performance, poor wee thing.

These aren't ambiguities exactly. You don't have to learn each type of use separately. They are witness to a phenomenon that we haven't studied enough, which is center-stage in a very interesting but neglected book by the late James Ross called *Portraying Analogy* (1982). It's a feature of linguistic competence that it is creative in the following way (this is not Chomskyan 'creativity' or anything like it): it's creative in the sense that it's acceptable and commonplace to *stretch*. If you are skilled at using language, you will use words in new contexts, in stretchy ways that don't amount to metaphor. When someone stretches, it's not that he uses words so bizarrely that we think, 'What's he doing? That's absurd . . . Oh, I see, what he is suggesting is the following comparison.' A metaphorical meaning, as it were, pops up as a creature of linguistic incongruity. (Though in saying that, I don't mean to propose any particular conception of what happens when a metaphor is coined, or when it's entrenched for that matter.) But to have recourse to stretching is not to coin a metaphor. It is to exploit a degree of elasticity of meaning, contrasting with ordinary borderline vagueness. It's not a question of, as it were, pulling away from the core cases, in the way you may stretch the concept *red* as you run down from the paradigms into the borderline areas; that's not the

Plurality of Pluralisms

kind of stretching concerned. No, you just pick a word that isn't ordinarily used in a certain kind of case and you use it in a different kind of case; and doing so is fine because there are relevant similarities that let the word be understandable in the new kind of context; there is elasticity of an intelligibly exploitable kind.

So, someone who wanted to argue for *SAP*, it seems to me, would do well to do some work on Ross's book, which is chock full of interesting data, and see whether a case could not be made that 'true' has the relevant kind of elasticity, and indeed whether we are not exploiting that in using it to talk about propositions about comedy and religion and chemistry and whatever else. *SAP* should be the thesis that there is a relevant species of semantic elasticity in the truth-predicate, and that it's manifest in its various applications when you look carefully.

I haven't done that work; I don't have a developed view about what the outcome would be. But I am, I confess, skeptical that an interesting alethic pluralism might eventuate. (But let's not just discount the proposal; it should be on the table and thought about.)

Mode B. Analogy of meaning needs to be distinguished from Wittgensteinian *family resemblance*s, insofar as we know what the latter were intended to be. Anyway, we have Wittgenstein's own prototype of 'game' to go on. It does seem, on the face of it, that 'game' is a very interesting concept for something like the reasons he gives and that maybe there are lots of concepts that turn out to be in a similar case when you look at them carefully. On the usual account, the *concept* of game is univocal: 'game' doesn't stretch its meaning as you apply it to croquet and to war games and to mind-games, and so on. It's not that there is analogy in the Ross sense. It's rather that there's semantically relevant analogy at the level of *reference*. A family resemblance concept is associated with a multiplicity of marks that are canonically relevant to its application. You can argue about the application of a family resemblance concept and the argument will consist in adducing and weighing the presence of the relevant marks. There is some scope for discretion; you can judge what weight to give to the marks and how many of them you need to be present. But all of that is at the level of semantic value and reference and is not so to speak in the concept. Chess and tennis are not games in different senses of the word, and it is not a stretch to apply the same word to both. But GAME, though univocal, has no necessary and sufficient conditions of application, only canonically relevant marks.

Surely, that's a possible shape for a concept to have. Whether it is what the historical Wittgenstein had in mind or not, I don't know. (But if you are teaching the *Investigations*, you will probably outline something like that notion.) In any case, family resemblance, so conceived, is a possible mode of pluralism that contrasts with *SAP*, as I am thinking of *SAP*. And again someone drawn to pluralism about truth might be tempted by the idea that maybe the right way to think about the variety in the notion is that certain *marks* of truth in different areas present this kind of Wittgensteinian pattern of a network, crisscrossing, overlapping, but not amounting to necessary conditions, nor sufficient conditions.

However, this looks to me an unpromising way to regard truth. The postulated 'marks' of truth don't come to mind in the same way that they do with games. 'Let's look at truth as applied in physics and compare it with truth as applied in comedy. Which marks of truth do we find in common in those two areas and which go missing? Which are found in only one?' The question falls a bit dead. I don't know what a 'mark' of truth is in the intended sense. There are different kinds of reasons in the two areas for thinking something true, but that difference is not to the point.

Now, when I wrote *Truth and Objectivity*, what I had by way of a template for an alethic pluralism were basically just those two models: analogy of meaning and family resemblance. I had read and talked to Jim Ross, I had read Wittgenstein, and I wondered, what could a competitive alethic pluralism be? Neither of those two models seemed to promise terribly well, so the question that exercised me was: how else might one elaborate the thesis in such a way as to address the two overarching issues that I was interested in?

What I eventually came up with in *Truth and Objectivity* prefigured what I later said rather better, namely, the account in 'Truth: A Traditional Debate Reviewed' (1999). That paper proposed that the way to think about the unity and the plurality in truth is this: there is a single *concept* of truth, and the *property* it presents can vary from area of discourse to area of discourse. This is a bit like how Lynch (2009: 60–62) interprets my view when he invokes the parallel of a flexible definite description, allowing that there is some uniform content associated with the concept, but that the content is not 'rigid'—it's variably satisfiable. However I don't really think that I was thinking of 'true' as having a complex descriptive sense; I wanted to say that the concept is also unanalyzable, so there would be no question of producing a definite description providing a paraphrase of it.

This thought was intended to be consistent with another idea I found attractive. I was drawn to the kind of thing that Michael Smith (1994) and Frank Jackson (1998), following suggestions of David Lewis (1970), were saying about one form of conceptual analysis, what I called a *network analysis*. Specifically, I was approaching the view that the right thing to think about the quest for an analysis of the concept of truth might very well be that what the philosopher should do is to give a sensitive description of its *constitutive connections with other concepts*, which, when done sufficiently well and in a properly elaborated way, will identify that concept, or capture its conceptual essence, in an essentially relational or 'networking' way. The nature of the fit between the concept so characterized and the property presented would then be that the property realizes, or *models*, what goes into the network analysis.

I also thought that when you are going to attempt a network analysis, you better start with stuff about the concept that we are likely to agree about.

Otherwise there is no obvious beginning point. But I don't think I ever thought that one should start with *incontestable* platitudinous a priori first principles—there is going to be some discussion of what goes into the list; there needs to be a process of ordinary philosophical critical reflection. Anyway, that was the general set-up: we were going to try and do a network analysis of the concept of truth. The program would consist in trying to tabulate some plausible initial, suitable-looking claims, looking for counterexamples, refining them in the light of those (or junking them altogether) and thereby trying to build up a picture of what seem to be the essential interrelationships between the concept of truth and others that feature in the resulting network of principles.

I think that activity characterized like that actually fits a great deal of what passes for philosophical 'analysis'. We hardly ever sit down and try to generate an explicit analytical equivalence, X is F iff, ... We repeatedly got burned trying to do that; we hardly ever said anything interesting or correct, or anyway both interesting *and* correct. But we do say interesting and correct things, I think, sometimes, when we do it well, when we are trying to 'network', trying to explore mutually identifying connections between concepts. That seems a better direction in which to start, and a more fruitful way to proceed.

The major difference between this form of pluralism and family resemblance pluralism thus emerges as the following: that we are going to say, if we are following this program, that to be a truth-property requires satisfying *everything* in a stable, complete, and correct network of truth-specific principles. There is no flexibility about how many principles need to be satisfied, no weighting of the relevant principles against each other. Whereas to be a game is to satisfy perhaps most, perhaps enough of the more significant, of the characteristics that will feature in a compendious description of the marks that we treat as game-relevant. GAME thus has a kind of vagueness, or a discretionary aspect to its applications, which a concept that allows of the kind of network analysis proposed for truth does not. That's the big difference, I think, with the family resemblance proposal: the network of truth-involving principles constitutes a set of interrelated, exceptionless conditions. There is no analogue of the idea of relevant but neither necessary nor sufficient marks as in the case of GAME.

That's **Mode C** pluralism: one concept, variably satisfiable in domain-specific ways. One concept, many properties. It's about as far as I got in my earlier work.

3. Predicates and properties

Thinking again about all this, I have become uneasy about the best construal, for the pluralist purpose, of the relation between concept and property. I was thinking of it then in what I take to be broadly Fregean terms, so that concepts are taken as senses of predicates, or open sentences, which are thought of as presenting a property in much the way that a Fregean term will express a singular concept associated with it as its sense and thereby present that object, as its reference, which uniquely falls under that concept. So a concept would be a mode of presentation of a property in just the way the sense of a Fregean singular term is a mode of presentation of the object to which the term refers. But reflecting on it now, it doesn't seem that's at all a happy way to conceive the matter, although it has been implicit in the discussion we have been having today at various points. It's a bad fit if we want to take into account certain of the intuitive differences between predicates and terms and what it is respectively to understand them.

Predicates don't denote properties as terms denote objects—at least not if the sense of a predicate is a *satisfaction-condition*; and that the sense should be the satisfaction-condition seems imposed if, crudely, to understand a predicate is to know how something has to be if the predicate is to apply to it. But, of course, in general many things may meet that satisfaction-condition. To understand a singular term on the Fregean model, on the other hand, is to know how an object has to be if it is to qualify as *the* referent to the term: the sense is a satisfaction-condition but with an inbuilt constraint of uniqueness. Now, if that's the model, we should think of a predicate as presenting, not an associated property but the *plurality* of things that satisfy it. That's what happens when you run the comparison straight through. The referent of a singular term is the thing that satisfies the condition that constitutes its sense; so the referent of a predicate should be the *things*—the plurality (though perhaps just a plurality of one, or zero!)—that satisfy the condition that constitutes *its* sense.

Someone may reply, 'Very well. An extension, or set, will represent the plurality determined in that way, so we may as well conceive of the reference of a predicate as a set, the extension'. But that's a further, noncompulsory step, and we will then have 'Concept HORSE'–type difficulties describing the relations between the predicate and a singular term standing for the relevant set. So while we can, at a cost, conceive of predicate reference as to sets, the closest analogy, if you follow the Fregean singular-term model through, is one of divided reference among the satisfiers.[3] In either case, though—the set or the satisfiers—the predicate does not refer to the property; the property is what its satisfiers have in common. In sum: we should think of the sense of a predicate, conceived on the Fregean model, not as presenting the relevant property, but rather as presenting the plurality—the satisfying things; and the relation of the sense, or concept, to the property is that it's *by having* that property that the

---

[3] Whether *this* conception can avoid 'Concept HORSE' problems will depend on whether 'divided' reference can be explained as a mode of reference contrasting with that of 'The things of which "F" is true.'

relevant things are able to satisfy the sense, to meet the satisfaction-condition. So we need to think of the relation between concept and property rather differently to the way that I, and perhaps others, have generally been thinking about it in this context.

So, what is the relation between the predicate, 'is a horse' and the property of being a horse? The model I am suggesting we drop says that the property is what the mode of presentation—the sense, or satisfaction-condition—presents, as the sense of a definite description presents the object the definite description stands for. What I suggest we replace it with is the generic idea that the property concerned is that property possession of which, necessarily, fits an object to meet the satisfaction-condition of the predicate. This idea allows for both 'sparse' and 'abundant' realization. If, in a spirit of abundance, we count *being such as to satisfy F* as itself a property, then it is a property possession of which, necessarily, fits an object to satisfy F. But we may equally well regard being composed of H_2O as that property that, necessarily, fits a sample to satisfy the sense of 'is water', however exactly the latter should be specified. When we go for abundance, the nature of the associated property will be transparent in the sense of the predicate; when we approach matters in the metaphysically sparser spirit, it may not be at all obvious, or even a priori assessable at all, what property fits something to satisfy the predicate concerned.

Mode C pluralism says: one concept, many properties. But the train of thought we just ran through suggests that the pluralist does best not to think of 'true', as used in different regions of discourse, as presenting, or referring to these various properties. The domain-specific truth properties should rather enter the fray as those properties possession of which somehow *fits* a proposition to satisfy the truth-predicate for the domain of discourse to which it belongs. And the nature of these properties, although not presumably a posteriori, should not be expected to be immediately explicit in the sense of the predicate 'true', but will take reflective analysis and philosophical argument to disclose.

I don't say this changes very much, at least for the purposes of a Mode C view. But it does bring out, what perhaps was obvious anyway, that a properly developed alethic pluralism is going to have to include a substantial investment in the metaphysics of properties and, associatedly, the semantics of predication.

4. Lynch's objections

Let's go back to Mode A pluralism (*SAP*): the idea that 'true' varies in meaning. In his 2009 book, Lynch lays down four objections to *SAP* that I think are good to rehearse, so that we can consider which of these objections lapse under other modes, and which, if any, remain.

The first objection is originally due to Christine Tappolet (1997). If 'true' varies in its meaning, what does validity of argument consist in? It seems that all that can be said is that a valid argument is one where necessarily if you start off with propositions to which 'true' applies in one or another sense and you reason via the argument concerned, you will wind up with conclusions to which 'true' applies in some sense. As an account, that sounds objectionably metalinguistic. However, if you say instead that there should be some *property* preserved by valid inference—but bear in mind now that, according to *SAP*, we have a truth-predicate that has some kind of semantic elasticity about it- what is that preserved property? So it appears a significant problem to explain what valid inference is for an *SAP* view.

Tappolet (2000) has also raised the 'compound statements' objection (as have others; see Williamson 1994). If predications of 'true' are regarded as having a variable meaning in some way, and now we take, for example, a conjunction where one conjunct is correctly described as 'true' in one meaning of 'true' and the other is correctly described as 'true' in another meaning of 'true', and we say on that basis that the conjunction is true, on what meaning of 'true' is *that* true? If for example, 'true' means *superassertible* as applied to p and *corresponds to the facts* as applied to q, what does it mean as applied to p & q? It looks like a good question.

Lynch's third objection reflects that a different question applies to generalizations. Suppose Socrates says lots of things: he talks about comedy, he talks about cosmology, he talks about the weather, he talks about the color of Xanthippe's eyes. And we remark that everything he said is true. One question is what it takes for our generalization to be correctly described as 'true'—what sense of 'true' is that? That's a counterpart of the question about conjunction. But another question is in what sense we are using 'true' when we report that everything he said is *true*. What is the sense of 'true' as it occurs in our report? That seems to be a separate (though related) problem.

Lynch's fourth objection is that the general *normativity* of truth becomes unaccountable on any *SAP* story. Why? Of course, not all agree that truth *is* normative. But those who agree that truth is normative think it is so not because it just so happens that all the variable meanings of 'true' share a kind of normative implicature. That would be remarkable. Could it be better than a coincidence that the elasticity that we have allegedly exploited in using this same word in different areas always retains a normative aspect? That would be very puzzling. It could be so; it could happen. But maybe one should smell a rat.

A defender of *SAP* may of course have various responses to these objections. But my question here is, how many of them carry over to apply to Mode C (that is, the *Truth and Objectivity* proposal): one concept, many properties? Lynch thinks: all of them. I think: none of them! You may think, some do, and some don't. Here are my reasons for saying that none of them do.

The validity objection will apply if there is independent reason for thinking that validity has to be preservation of a single property, or if that's somehow a given. If validity has to be so conceived, then reasoning in a way that crosses domains, using bridging premises, may very well generate what we regard as valid inferences that don't preserve a single property, because the conclusion is, if true at all, true in virtue of having a truth-property that none of the premises have. So we will not have preserved any single property, although there is still an intuitively valid inference. But to run this objection, you first need to ground the idea that validity has to be preservation of a single property. And so far as I can see, there is no independent motivation for that.

Jc Beall (2000), in the first round of discussion of the issue, gave a logician's answer to the objection in terminology, which I think is distracting, but whose point is substantially correct. Beall said what's important is preservation of a *designated* property. There can be several designated properties: superassertibility, coherence, correspondence—these can all be designated with respect to different domains. And as long as a mixed—domain-crossing—inference preserves designation, that's good enough for validity.

Lynch replied to Beall, 'Who on Earth cares about *designation*?'[4] But the underlying point, I take it, Beall was making, which is the one I am now making, is that truth-preservation can be agreed on all hands to be preservation of *falling under the concept of truth*. The apparatus of different designated values gives us a useable model for a system in which there are different ways of doing that. What makes the propositions that fall under the concept of truth interesting is that they fall under the concept of truth: that's what is important to us. It's quite enough for the interest and point of the notion of validity that valid argument ensures conclusions that fall under the concept of truth when the premises do. That there are different ways of falling under that concept is no obstacle to this.

So I am inclined simply to deny that there is any good motivation for the thought that validity has to consist in preservation of a single *property*. Our interest is in the concept of truth, and hence in any property that realizes the concept. Another way of putting the matter: As long as we preserve the *abundant property* of falling under the concept of truth, we have a notion of validity that is perfectly good and intelligibly of interest to us.[5]

What about the additional part of the third objection, the bit that goes beyond the mixed-compounds objection? The question was, what are we saying when we say that everything Socrates says is true? What's the meaning of the token of 'true' in that assertion? The answer should be: we are saying that everything Socrates said falls under the concept of truth.

---

[4] Lynch (2004: 388–389).
[5] Lynch (2009: 66–67) briefly considers a similar suggestion.

Does Mode C incorporate some kind of threat to the normativity of truth? No, it doesn't—because we will surely have built it in to our network analysis that truth has whatever normative features should properly be included.[6] Platitudes about normativity will surely be in there, if—as I agree—they are part of the concept. So Mode C is certain to have resources to accommodate the normativity of truth.

It seems to me that the objection of Lynch's four against *SAP* that maybe survives—and that is anyway the most interesting—is the compound-statements objection. How does that look in a Mode C setting? How does the objection go now? The question will not now be, for instance, what's the meaning of 'true' as applied to a conjunction? Rather it will be, what property does a conjunction have, when, for example, one of the conjuncts (say, an ethical statement) is superassertible in a domain where superassertibility is the truth property and the other (say a mathematical statement) is coherent in a domain where coherence is the truth property? There is, on any natural understanding of the notion, no domain of discourse to which the subject matter of such a conjunction belongs. What property—superassertibility, or coherence, or neither—is the truth-property for the conjunction? What can we say?

I think this is a good—in other words, a prima facie awkward!—question, but I think it's a version of a very old question: one that is not a question that is triggered by pluralism but was already there for monism. Insofar as I see an objection here, I think it's simply a version of the objection that people made to the logical atomists about compound statements generally. Atomic propositions are true by dint of correspondence to atomic facts. So when a conjunction of such propositions is true, to what fact does the conjunction correspond? If you reply, 'The fact, obviously, that p and that q', that's question begging, because you just helped yourself to a conjunctive expression to denote a fact. And the concern was: what in a world of atomic facts *is* a conjunctive fact?

In a lecture at Harvard, considering the corresponding problem about negation, Russell once suggested that there were negative facts and apparently he almost caused a riot![7] And understandably so, because there aren't any negative facts, one wants to say—or at least I want to say.[8] And you might want to say, in the same spirit, that there aren't conjunctive facts either. There can be the fact that p and that fact that q, but there isn't any extra thing: the conjunctive fact to which their conjunction corresponds.

---

[6] I here record that Douglas Edwards, Michael Lynch, and Nikolaj Pedersen, who each listed putative truth-platitudes at various points in the discussions at the Dublin workshop where this paper was first presented, all included a couple that are normative: for instance, *It is bad if you miss the truth*, *truth is the end of enquiry*, and so on.

[7] See Russell (1956: 211–212).

[8] I am tempted to agree with Peter Simons (in the Dublin workshop discussion) that there are *lacks*; but lacks are not facts.

So we have the precedent of that old discussion. How do we make sense of the truth-values of conjunctions, given that we have so far got nothing further than an account of what confers truth on their conjuncts? We don't want to invoke a special category of conjunctive facts—the truth-makers for the individual conjuncts should somehow be enough. That is why conjunction is a truth-*function*. Settle the truth-values of the conjuncts and you have already settled that of their conjunction. But how can they be enough? They are not enough *on their own*. But how can we harness their conjunctive—as it were, their collaborative—force without postulating an extra conjunctive fact?

It's an old and teasing issue. But whatever the solution, it is going to be something that lets us say the right thing. And the right thing to say is that what makes the conjunction true is that the first conjunct is true AND the second conjunct is true! That's the right answer. We have to be allowed to *use* conjunction (or negation, or any other truth-functional operator) in characterizing the truth-conferrer. If you are not allowed to do that, you are lost. And now, whatever the nature of the license to use conjunction in explaining the truth-conferrer for a conjunction, whatever we need to say to demystify that response, the Mode C theorist can say the same, in response to the compound-statements objection. The difference is only that the Mode C pluralist's account will appeal to different truth properties on the two sides: the conjunction is true, for instance, because the first conjunct is superassertible under ideal ethical reflection AND the second coherent with the iterative conception of set.

Just now, I did my best to convey the impression of a problem. Actually, I don't *really* think there is a problem here at all, but there is a perspective in which it seems that there is a problem: a dilemma, that only a conjunctive fact is up to the task of making for the truth of a conjunction, but that there are no conjunctive facts—there are only 'atomic' or otherwise basic facts. But let it be that I am wrong and that there is something very hard to reconcile here. Then it seems to me that this is a problem whether we are monist about truth or pluralist. Let it be a good problem. If there is a solution, there is no reason to think that solution won't be available to the pluralist.

So I am not moved by the objections that Lynch highlighted for *SAP* and then sustained against the *Truth and Objectivity* account, at least not before further discussion.

5. Modeling the platitudes—Edwards's dilemma

A distinct objection is due to Douglas Edwards (2011). Roughly speaking, the objection is as follows: I am proposing that to qualify as a truth property is to satisfy the axioms in the network analysis (or the 'platitudes', as I shall usually continue to say). But the problem is that if you formulate those platitudes *without domain restriction*, then the various proposed candidates—other than, perhaps correspondence—don't seem to satisfy them. If I just lay down the platitudes unrestrictedly and affirm that superassertibility, say, provides a model of them, I'll be wrong. Any good case for saying that superassertibility models the platitudes will be subject to special assumptions about the relevant domain. Such a case, when we can make it, will, admittedly, be an a priori case; it will be made by reflection and reasoning, not empirical science. But the a priori case will be made under the hypothesis, itself presumably a priori if correct at all, that the domain has certain relevant features. And of paramount importance for superassertibility in particular is the circumstance that the domain in question be *epistemically constrained*.

I guess that is obvious, but I'll spell it out. Superassertibility is a property with this feature: that if a proposition is superassertible then, given time and world enough, you can get evidence for its truth. This is so because for a proposition to be superassertible is for there to be a state of information which a subject can access and on the basis of which he can then believe or assert that proposition in an epistemically appropriate way—where epistemic appropriateness is then stable under improvements to his state of information. That's the intuitive idea. So clearly he must be able to get into the initial state of information—as it were, the superassertibility base—and if he does, he will then be in a position to assert the proposition in question.

So a superassertible proposition has to be one for which evidence is available, at least in principle. But that's not true of truth in general, at least according to our folk-philosophical ideas. We, most of us, want to say that there are areas where we may hit on the truth as it were serendipitously, without being able to find out or even get weak evidence that we have. It's in the nature of truth, we tend to think, that that should be a possibility, at least in some areas of enquiry. So if we formulate the truth-platitudes unrestrictedly, then as soon as someone says: superassertibility models these, the reply will come, 'Not so fast; it depends on what you are talking about'.

The modeling claim is thus subject to special provisos about the domain that we are considering. Indeed, that is the whole point: it is because domains of discourse have special variable features—epistemic constraint, lack of epistemic constraint, the presence of a core conception of the nature of the domain (as maybe provided by the iterative conception of set) coherence with which will do for truth, or the lack of any such core conception—it is because these features vary, that what it takes for a property to behave like the truth property will vary. So there won't be any unrestricted satisfiers of the platitudes other than truth itself, in general.[9]

---

[9] It may be suggested that correspondence is an exception, but I actually take exception to that claim. I think if you understand correspondence in a substantial way, it may very well be that there are regions of discourse where it doesn't actually deliver what we want. I think you have to deflate it in a certain way before it seems obvious that correspondence to fact behaves in the ways mandated by a good network analysis.

So, the first horn of Edwards's dilemma says: if the platitudes are formulated unrestrictedly, we don't have a plurality of satisfiers of the platitudes. The second horn then charges simply that if we *restrict* the platitudes—if we formulate them in such a way as to speak of a specific domain—they stop being platitudes and become substantial, controvertible claims.

I am inclined to think the force of the second horn is illusory and may depend upon conflating two different notions of 'restriction' of the platitudes. So far as I can see, it will not compromise the platitudinous status of what we say if, rather than saying, for example, that truth is one thing, justification another, or that to assert is to present as true, we affirm instead that in ethics, truth is one thing, justification another, or that when discussing comedy, to assert is to present as true. I therefore wonder if the idea that explicitly domain-restricting the platitudes has the effect of, as it were, controversializing them and does not depend on considering instead domain-restricted versions in which mention of a *candidate modeling property* is made in place of 'true', so that what we get is, for instance, that in discussion of comedy, to assert is to present as superassertible; or that in ethics, justification is one thing, superassertibility another. These are indeed controversial claims. But why are they the relevant kind of restriction?

So I am a little uncertain about how the second horn of Edwards' dilemma is exactly supposed to go. But what I wish to say in response is in any case that I want nothing to do with either horn. More accurately, I do want to formulate the platitudes purely generally and to affirm that truth properties satisfy them as generally formulated. But I want to allow the scope of the quantifiers in these general formulations to vary. In each case, there will be an implicit 'For all p' quantifier. And what we vary in order to construct the various models of 'true' is the range of that quantifier. So we don't mention domains in the way we formulate the platitudes; we don't say, 'In ethics. . . .' That truth in ethics is under consideration is, so to speak, behind the scenes. We simply let the quantifiers vary over different domains of discourse, and we find—so claims the pluralist—models that will vary depending on that varying range.

That was the intended proposal. So, whatever exactly are the problems on the second horn of Edwards's dilemma, I believe we should be able to avoid them. Whether the proposal escapes other problems is for discussion. But if Edwards's objection depended on my being forced to pick one of those two horns, well, as far as I can see, I am not so forced. I propose to slip between them in the way I have just outlined.

So, my interim conclusion is: none of the objections to the *Truth and Objectivity* account that have so far proved influential should move a proponent of that account. (Probably, there is only one such proponent!) That's not of course to say that other approaches may not prove superior in other respects.

6. Mode D and the conferral relation

Now we come to the fourth pluralist mode. The first three were: analogy of meaning, family resemblance, and one concept/many properties. **Mode D**, the fourth mode is: one *property*/many properties.

In this mode, we bring the issue of pluralism down to the level of reference, semantic value, or however we now want to think about predicate-semantics and properties. The mode of the pluralism is, broadly, of the kind that Michael Lynch has been defending in all his work on this topic: there is a to be single property of truth, and there are many *other* satellite properties hanging around in its vicinity which are somehow of interest, are somehow doing something to service the application of the truth-property. So we have got the One property, Truth, and the Many properties—I'll call them the B-list—including correspondence, coherence, superassertibility, assertibility at the end of enquiry, fully deflated truth[10] . . . and there might be others: some theorists may very well want to include (one or more) relativistic properties in the B-list.

The attractions of this approach are obvious. If we go for Mode D, we get certain advantages straight off the bat. There is no special problem for the Mode D pluralist with valid inference. If you thought there was a problem before, there certainly isn't one now because valid inference can simply be truth-preservation—(unless, of course, *that* account is problematic). Anyway, there is no *special* problem. And there is no special problem with compound statements—unless it's the old problem we touched on above, whatever exactly that problem is. There is no problem with normativity, assuming it goes with the very concept of truth that it's normative in the ways that people think. In effect, we restore all the advantages of monism and lose all the objections, good or not, that the other modes of pluralism were felt to trigger.

The downside is that now we have to take on a new issue. We have got to say, now, how the truth property relates to the B-list properties. And it's a constraint on saying something useful that we explain how having a B-list property can, in the right circumstances, *confer* truth on a proposition. So all the action now has to do with the conferral relation. How are we to understand conferral? We have these many properties that are somehow truth-relevant, and we want to say that having one of those properties can, in the right circumstances, confer truth on a target proposition. How does that happen?

Here are some of the proposals about conferral that are worth consideration.

(i) *Simple existential generalization.* To be true is to have some property that gets on the B-list. There will be conditions for entry onto the B-list. Certain

---

[10] I mean the property of truth that Horwich, e.g., grudgingly admits when he allows that truth can be a property in a sufficiently thin sense by saying 'every term that functions logically as a predicate stands for a property' (1998: 141–142).

Plurality of Pluralisms 139

properties meet them. To be true is simply to have such a property: truth is just a generalization of the B-list in that way.[11]

Lynch (2009: 66) and Edwards[12] have objected that this property—the property of *having some B-list property*—doesn't itself satisfy the platitudes. This is not obvious to me. If the B-list properties have, one and all, been selected so as to satisfy the platitudes so that each of them, for example, is potentially extensionally divergent from justification, then won't the property of having some B-list property likewise be potentially extensionally divergent from justification? The issue needs detail. But I think we are owed a clear counterexample by those who doubt it.[13]

Notice that on this account, the conferral relation is in any case very straightforward: it is simply *entailment*. The way in which a B-list property confers truth is by witnessing the existential generalization. What could be simpler than that? It would be nice, if—assuming the Simple Existential generalization proposal does indeed fail—we might preserve this feature some other way.

(ii) *Proto-functionalism*. Now some more intellectual autobiography. When Lynch first started talking in functionalist terms, suggesting that my real thesis—or what at any rate I *should* be saying—is that truth is a *functional* property, I had an ambivalent reaction. I had a vague sense of unease—of a risk of perhaps unnecessarily encumbering the pluralist thesis with hostages. But it also seemed harmless if the suggestion was merely that we could see the platitudes as defining a 'role' and the B-list properties as playing it. It was only much later that it dawned on me that there is a bad confusion here. Let me run that past you.

The proto-functionalist says: truth is a functional property—a *role property*—with the B-list properties as *realizers*. So compare truth with *kidney*: surely an archetype of a functional property. Kidney is a functional property in the sense that to be a kidney is to play a certain characteristic functional role, namely, to filter the blood. That's what kidneys do 'by definition', as we are wont to say. It is why it is possible for there to be such a thing as an *artificial* kidney: anything will be a kidney that discharges the characteristic role or purpose of kidneys, even a machine. But notice that it is the *instances* of the property of being a kidney that discharge the function; it's *the kidneys* that discharge the function. And it's something they do in virtue of having other non-functional properties: there will be an analogue of the B-list—a list of characteristics that enable an object to perform that role, perhaps by giving it a certain kind of microstructure. There are no conceptual limits on the design of an artificial kidney; all you have to do is come up with something that does that job. But

---

[11] This is Lynch's former view. See Lynch (2004).
[12] In earlier drafts of Edwards (2011); see also Lynch (2008; 2009: 66).
[13] For an argument to the effect that the property favored by the simple existential generalization approach satisfies the truisms of Lynch (2009), see David (2013) and Pedersen and Wright (2013).

when you have done that, it will be the relevant properties designed into it that qualify it, that enable it to discharge the functional role.

But here is the disanalogy: we don't want to say that a proposition's being true is *the proposition's* playing a certain functional role. That's what we should say if we thought that truth is a functional property in the way that *kidney* is. Functional properties are properties that objects possess that have a certain function. If truth were a functional property, it would be a property whose possession marked its bearers—propositions, beliefs, or whatever—as things that fulfill, or are apt to fulfill, a certain function. But it doesn't. To call a proposition 'true' is not to ascribe a function to it.

That level—the level of the bearers—is not where the putative functionality of truth is. The functionality is at second-order. It is intended to be the *truth properties* that play a certain functional role. So there is a property connected with truth that is functional, in an extended sense of 'functional' maybe. But it is the B-list properties that have this property—that perform the function—and the bearers of the B-list properties that have the property of truth. So there is simply no relevant model of conferral to be elicited from the tie between realizer and role properties. Truth is not a role property.

This is a decisive objection to what I am calling proto-functionalism. Again, the functional property in the vicinity simply isn't a candidate for the interpretation of the predicate 'true' as applied to the usual bearers of truth. The functionality, if there at all, is to be found one order up, as a characteristic of the *properties* that are available to interpret the truth predicate. So, I don't think proto-functionalism—that is, the initial functional thought—is a starter; I think there is a muddle there. But I don't want to make too much of this; it's only the 'proto' version of the view.

(iii) A third proposal for the conferral relationship is that between *determinate and determinable* properties. This is entailment, once again, but this time, in contrast with proposal (i), without generalization; there is no implicit existential quantifier. You shouldn't say that being red is having some property in the list: crimson, vermilion, scarlet, ... We don't know how to enumerate the list. Being red is a property in its own right. Of course, it's true that if something is red, then necessarily it will have some property in a certain range of shades; there will be a determinate of red, where red is determinable, some specific shade of red that it has. But that's not the right thing to say about the logical structure of the property of redness. Redness doesn't have a quantifier in it, so to speak.

It would be nice if we could fruitfully model the conferral relation on the relation between a determinate property and the determinable property of which it is a determinate; that would again be pleasingly simple. Of course, it would not be the end of the game. We would need to say something about the metaphysics of the relation. But at least we could take ourselves to be on

Plurality of Pluralisms

relatively safe ground; we know that there is a robust conferral relation associated with determinate-determinable that we can appeal to.

But there is a major problem with this suggestion. When you really do have an instance of the determinate-determinable relation, the different determinates under the same determinable *compete in the same conceptual space*: they exclude each other. An object cannot be both crimson and vermilion; the determinates are alternative modes of the determinable: they crowd each other out.[14] Of course, we—pluralists—want to say that about, for instance, superassertibility and correspondence too. These are essentially different ways of being true within the domains of application where they are respectively relevant. But the difficulty is that, in a region of thought where, for example, correspondence is our favored conception of truth, there will still be such a thing as superassertibility, and a proposition's being superassertible need not compete with its corresponding. There is no exclusion of the kind we would expect with distinct determinates under a common determinable. In short: being crimson and being vermilion are always incompatible, and always ensure being red. But being superassertible and corresponding are not incompatible, and where one is a way of being true, the other is not.

So whatever the relationship between the B-list properties, it's not the same as the relation between determinates under a given determinable. We need to look again.

(iv) A fourth proposal for the conferral relation is Lynch's newly introduced notion of *manifestation*. The B-list properties, he avers, *manifest* truth.

Lynch's treatment (2009) gives a firm impression that the way to understand his proposal is something along the following lines. Lynch likes the idea of the kind of conferral that runs from determinate to determinable, but he thinks that determinate-determinable is only a special case of a *more general* conferral relationship. The manifestation relation that he introduces is intended as something that encompasses the relation between determinate and determinable as a special case, but also covers other kinds of conferral, in such a way as to take us past the problems associated with taking determinate-determinable as the prototype.[15]

---

[14] Lynch (2009: 86, fn. 4) makes the same point.

[15] For example, Lynch writes: "The manifestation relation is similar to the determinable/determinate relation. It is *a priori* that the essential features of redness, whatever they are, are a subset of the features of being scarlet. Consequently, if one understands that something is scarlet, one has all one needs to understand that it is red. But according to the traditional distinction, determinables cannot determine themselves, so the relations are distinct." The claim about redness and scarlet is false, for reasons about to be noted in the main text. Lynch goes on to draw further distinctions between the relations: determinates, but not manifesting properties, are subject to linear ordering; and determinates, but not manifesting properties, are mutually exclusionary: nothing that is scarlet at a single point and time can also be crimson at the same point and time (2009: 75). These points are well taken but, as it seems to me, simply emphasize the difficulties in the suggestion that manifestation can, as it were, borrow conferral-powers from the determinate-determinable relationship.

Let us first consider Lynch's original formulation of manifestation. In essentials, I take it to be the following: for one property to manifest another is for it to be the case that every feature that the latter property, the *manifested* property, has *a priori essentially*, is possessed by the manifesting property, though not necessarily possessed essentially. In other words, if all the a priori essential properties of F are also properties of G, then G manifests F (Lynch 2009: 74–75). But wait: that's not actually true of determinates and their determinables. So if the idea was to be that manifestation can give us a generalized form of the kind of conferral that operates in the determinate-determinable case, which carries over to cases that aren't determinate-determinable, then the problem is that the generalization misgeneralizes the base case. It is easy to think of a priori essential features of redness, for example, that crimson doesn't have. There are any number of essential features of redness that its determinates do not have—and moreover any number of a priori essential such features, features that anyone who grasps the notion will recognize as essential to it but which one or more of its determinates may lack. These are features, broadly, that belong to its relative generality. Red is more general than crimson; that's an essential feature of red. And from it follow a large class of features—you can elaborate them at leisure—that crimson won't share. So there is a structural difficulty with the attempted generalization: determinates do not, in general, *manifest* their determinables in Lynch's sense.

Let me not overstate the significance of this. The point speaks only to what seems to be the motivation for the notion of manifestation as Lynch introduces it in *Truth as One and Many*. It could still be true that manifestation in that sense gets us a form of conferral. But it won't get us conferral in the way that determinate-determinable does, because it doesn't generalize that relationship. The reason why it gets us conferral, if there is one, has to be something independent. So a proof is needed. What is the argument for thinking that this relation ensures a kind of conferral or sufficiency? Why can't it happen that F manifests G, according to the letter of the definition, even though there are possibly Fs that are not G?

I think that is a fair question. But there is a distinct objection that is actually lethal to the proposal of *Truth as One and Many*. I'll present the objection and then discuss whether the revised proposal newly offered by Lynch is able to block it.

The objection is that it is, near enough, *self-refuting* to suppose that the alethic B-list properties all manifest truth. Why so? Well if they do, it will presumably be an a priori essential feature of truth that it is so variably manifested. It will be in the *nature* of truth to be capable of variable manifestation, and this aspect of its nature will be accessible to reflective philosophy, so presumably a priori. More, it will be an a priori essential feature of truth that it is manifested by the B-list properties that do manifest it. But it's not even a feature, let alone an a priori essential feature, of the B-list properties that they

Plurality of Pluralisms 143

manifest *each other*. (The need for this additional observation is what makes the self-refutation 'near enough', rather than strict.) So, right there, we find an essential feature of truth that the B-list properties don't have, namely being capable of variable manifestation by the B-list properties. According to the letter of the *Truth as One and Many* characterization, truth itself is *not* manifested by the B-list properties!

Does Lynch's new proposal[16] walk free of this problem? The reformulated proposal has it that we need to restrict attention within the class of features of the manifested property not just to those that are a priori essential but to those that are elicitable from the *nominal* essence, purely on the basis of conceptual reflection. G manifests F if G has every feature that belongs, a priori, to F's *nominal* essence.

Does this help? Well, obviously enough, only if the case is not merely that it doesn't belong to the nominal essence of truth that it is capable of variable manifestation, but that it cannot be elicited just by *conceptual reflection on the nominal essence* that is capable of variable manifestation. So what constitutes the 'nominal essence' here? If the nominal essence is given by the pluralist's initial network analysis, and the network is such that necessarily, on reflection, it is capable of variable realizations by different models, the objection will stand.

Lynch might respond by denying that variable manifestability is part of the nominal essence of truth, on the grounds that this feature is not evident purely in virtue of grasping the truth concept.[17] I think that's a difficult position to take, but let's explore the issue.

Let's distinguish three proposals that Lynch might make. They are, respectively, that G manifests F just in case:

I   Every feature that is included in the nominal essence of F is possessed by G; or
II Every feature that is, in some sense, transparent in the nominal essence of F is possessed by G; or
III Every feature that is elicitable by conceptual reflection on the nominal essence of F is possessed by G.

Now, provided the nominal essence includes all the principles that feature in the network analysis, proposal III is exactly what is needed to set up the objection. So Lynch needs to support one of the other two. One problem we have here is that it is not clear what Lynch is proposing to take as included in the 'nominal essence'. But I think there are foreseeable difficulties whatever is said about that.

---

[16] First made in his presentation at the Dublin workshop. See Lynch (2013).
[17] Lynch made this suggestion in discussion at the Dublin workshop.

Lynch faces a dilemma: does the nominal essence embrace all the network platitudes that he wishes to countenance or is it narrower? If it is narrower, well then, by what principle is its extent to be determined and which of the platitudes do we properly exclude? But if it embraces all the platitudes, then proposals I and II won't help with the objection unless 'included in' or 'in some sense, transparent in' are not closed under deduction and reflective analysis. So we will be limiting the range of features of truth that are relevant to its manifestability by other properties to what is available via a certain kind of *relatively straightforward* reflection. And we mustn't idealize this notion or we risk inflation into proposal III and the reentry of the objection. For again, Lynch's view has to be, presumably, that the fact is out there to be accessed by conceptual—philosophical—reflection that truth is variably manifestable! Take the nominal essence (as characterized by the platitudes), think about it clearly, reason in the appropriate way, and you will figure out that, Yes indeed, this has to be a variably manifestable property. So Lynch will have to cut that process off somewhere, and the cutting off has to be something that involves refusing to idealize, but insisting that the features of F that are relevant to the issue of its manifestation by G go no further than those that, limited as we are, with intelligence quotients below a certain threshold, and so on, we can recognize as belonging to F's nominal essence. The question is then this: how can any distinction drawn in those terms—terms that make essential play with our logical and imaginative limitations—be of any *metaphysical* significance? How can manifestation, so characterized, be a metaphysical relation?

In summary, my concern is this. The basic idea of manifestation is that manifesting properties must possess all those features that belong to a certain special class of the features of the manifested property. The crucial issue is what that special class is and how it is to be characterized. And remember that we are looking for a relationship between two properties such that when it obtains, if something has the one (manifesting) property, it *must* have the other (manifested) property: we want *conferral* here, guaranteed as a matter of metaphysics. It seems to me that once you start putting constraints on the sought-after special class of features that have to do with our *concepts* of the manifested properties concerned, and especially constraints that somehow exploit the potentially *limited* nature of those concepts—the extent to which we don't think things through all that far, or our concepts themselves may be superficial, and so on—once you start doing that, you risk putting the kind of metaphysical guarantee that conferral should consist in, and which we do have with the prototype of determinate-determinable, out of range. My worry is that anything in the direction of the revised proposal offered by Lynch as a response to the original self-refutation objection is very likely to run into this kind of snag. We don't want a bar that turns on our conceptual limitations when what we actually want to arrive at is a guarantee, at the level of the nature

Plurality of Pluralisms

of the properties concerned, that when the one applies, it brings it about that the other applies.

So, in sum: as far as proposal (iv) is concerned, I am stuck on the issue of manifestation and how to characterize that relation in such a way as to get the right results. I think that we have not yet been shown how to do that, and in particular that Lynch's new suggestion (2013) remains problematic for the purpose.

7. How better to think of conferral

(v) *Edwards's proposal*. There is a beautifully simple Mode D suggestion due to Douglas Edwards (2011, 2013). Familiarly, many philosophers have found it helpful, in a variety of ways, to compare truth and *winning*. When we play chess, we are normally, or should be, aiming to win. When we play the language game, we are normally, or should be, aiming to say true things. The broad comparison is to be found in Michael Dummett and earlier in Wittgenstein. Lots of people have used it. Truth is an end of thought and talk, it is suggested, in the way that winning is an end of game-play.

I want to recommend at least an aspect of this analogy. Winning, for its part, seems to wear a kind of pluralism on its sleeve. It is obvious that different things amount to winning in different games. Depending on what game you are playing, it suffices to accomplish different things in order to win. If you are playing chess, you had better checkmate your opponent; if you are playing draughts, you had better take all his pieces; if you are playing football, you and your team had better score more goals than the opposition within the period of the game; if you are playing croquet, you need to peg-out. Winning is variably realizable. But it's not a family-resemblance concept—there is no network of overlapping and crisscrossing features that tie together what it is to win in the four mentioned games; the different winning positions have in common only and purely that they are winning positions. Nor is 'winning' ambiguous or, in these uses, elastic. There are not shades of difference in meaning as 'winning' is transferred from chess to draughts to football to croquet. There is just one concept being applied here and, it is very tempting to say, there is just one property. It is the property you have whenever, in a game, you have done the appropriate thing for winning in that game.

So, the proposal will be—no doubt it will need refinement—that just as conditionals like the following are true in games:

If you are playing chess, then if you checkmate your opponent's king, you have won.

If you are playing draughts, then if you take all your opponent's pieces, you have won,

. . . .

so conditionals like these (I'll call them *Edwards conditionals*) are true in different regions of discourse:

> If you are talking morals, then if you say something superassertible, you say something true.
> If you are talking set theory, then if you say something coherent with the iterative conception of set, then you say something true.
> If you are talking Big Bang cosmology, then if you say something that actually corresponds to what went on back then, then you have said something true.
> . . . .

The essential thought is that, in a very intuitive sense, just as winning consists in doing different things in different areas, so saying something true consists in doing different things in different areas. And these constitutive relationships are *necessities*: they surface in the (conceptual) necessity of the kind of compound conditionals illustrated. Thus conferral is, so to speak, entailment within the scope of a hypothesis. It is entailment within the scope of a master antecedent: if you are talking ethics, if you are playing chess, ... that is the idea. The embedded conditional holds in all worlds in which the master antecedent is true.

This seems to me to be the best proposal about conferral so far made—and hence the best of all Mode D accounts. It gives the shape of the view that we (alethic pluralists) should strive to make out if we are going for Mode D. And the advantages of Mode D were explained above. But there is a problem. In the case of winning, the correctness of the conditionals leaps at you, if you understand them. It is not at all controversial that if you are playing chess, and you checkmate your opponent's king, you have won. If someone thinks that is controversial, they don't know what chess is. But if I were to affirm that in moral discourse, if you were to say something superassertible, you would have said something true, that will doubtless start a philosophical discussion—and one in which it will not be a good move to allege that to dispute the conditional is to show that you do not understand what moral discourse is! Maybe the superassertibilist can prevail in the discussion; maybe she can at least successfully maintain the thesis against all comers. But her claim does not seem to stand comparison with the obvious and uncontroversial correctness of the corresponding conditional about chess. Indeed, it doesn't present as a *conceptually* necessary truth at all.

A possible first thought by way of response is that this can just be a case of the Open Question point, to which it can therefore be simply replied that conceptual necessities can be unobvious. I say, 'Do you know that the following formula has no solution in the positive integers: $x^n + y^n = z^n$?' That it doesn't have a solution is, I think, a conceptual necessity; it's Fermat's only recently established 'Last Theorem'. But it has never been obvious to anyone.

It may be doubted, though, whether a parallel with Fermat's Theorem makes for a convincing reply. Of course, conceptual necessities can be intricate and involve remote consequence relations. The difficulty here, though, is that it won't do just to say, 'This claim about moral discourse and the notion of superassertibility, although conceptually necessary, is one of these unobvious cases, so it needs a bit of discussion'. The trouble is that we don't have a model of the *kind* of discussion of which this might in principle be the conclusion, so that we could announce: 'We have finally learned that truth in ethics is superassertibility!' That is because philosophy is not mathematics. We did all along know what it would be to determine that Fermat's Last Theorem is conceptually necessary (if indeed that is the right reading of the purport of the theorem. Let us for present purposes assume that the truths of pure number theory are conceptual necessities). It would be to construct a fully explicit mathematical demonstration, and Andrew Wiles did that, eventually. But there are no salient, accepted first principles about morality and truth, such that a fully developed theory based upon them might yield an ingenious deduction of the moral Edwards conditional.

Even to one sympathetic to it, the moral Edwards conditional doesn't feel like the recognition, or conjecture, of a remote-consequential conceptual necessity in the kind of way needed to sustain an analogy with Fermat. If it were conceived as that, we should want much better—certainly a different style of—argument for it than we have been hearing! No; it feels much more like a *proposal*. It's a case of—as so often in philosophy—'Look at [some targeted notion] like this. If you look at it like this, you can explain, simplify, and clarify lots of issues'. If the mark of conceptual necessity is analyticity, it may be felt, then either there should be some procedure that proves the Edwards conditional, or it should be among a certain basic set of principles that all who grasp the concepts involved are disposed to accept. But it doesn't impress as either.

But let's go carefully. There are examples of claims that might be conceptually necessarily true—I mean: which *are*, if true, conceptually necessarily so—for which we can get no conclusive proof and that are not basic either. So there is *scope* for something like this kind of proposal in the arena of conceptual necessity. Think, for example, of Church's Thesis, that every effectively calculable arithmetical function is general recursive. Church put his thesis forward as part of the enterprise of trying to say what the intuitive notion of an effectively calculable function comes to, of giving a mathematically exact characterization of it. You probably know the history: we had all these different, independently arrived at proposals—general recursiveness, Turing computability, Markov algorithms, and so on, and so forth—and these all proved to be coextensive. So a lot of mathematicians thinking about the intuitive notion and trying to give it a mathematically exact account converged in different ways on the same extension. In the nature of the case, there can be no proof of Church's Thesis, because the thesis is a proposal to bring the notion of effective calculability under a certain kind of formal or technical discipline which it otherwise doesn't have yet;

it's an intuitive, informal notion. A proof of the thesis could only work with formally disciplined notions, so there is a sense in which Church's Thesis is *beneath* proof. The theorists who analyzed it and converged with each other were doing the best that could be done with an intuitive notion, and their proposals were essentially conjectural, although the fact that they converged strongly suggests at least that they had the same notion in mind and hence—though this is a nice point—that their conjectures are all correct.

So there is an example of a (possible) conceptual necessity which is neither an obvious first principle nor derivable from such. It seems a reasonable view that if Church's Thesis is true, that it is so is attributable solely to the nature of the concept of effective calculability, the intuitive notion, and the nature of the concept of general recursiveness, the exact notion characterized mathematically. If Church's Thesis is true, it is conceptually necessarily true: the notions of effective calculability and general recursiveness have, of conceptual necessity, the same extension. That's the plausible upshot. But there is and can be no proof of it, in the way that Fermat's Last Theorem, or indeed any less arcane theorem of number theory, is provable. But nor is it epistemologically basic and part of ordinary conceptual competence to know.

So, is that a better precedent for the pluralist's discourse-specific conditionals about truth—the Edwards conditionals? Maybe the suggestion should be that the Edwards conditionals connecting truth in different discourses with various of the B-list properties are in the same kind of case as Church's Thesis, and have, if true, that same kind of grounding in the concepts concerned. They are, if correct, in the same camp as the game-winning conditionals, but the grounds for so regarding them, as in the case of Church's Thesis, are necessarily conjectural and inconclusive. Should we take up this suggestion?

Well, I already mentioned what is, I think, reason for discomfort with this parallel, too. The Edwards conditionals seem *essentially controversial* in a sense that exceeds anything entrained just by the point that, as with Church's Thesis, we have no conclusive demonstration of their truth. That there is and can be no conclusive demonstration of Church's Thesis means that someone who wishes is free to doubt it. But such a person is not free to regard their doubt as *justified*: all the evidence, though not conclusive, speaks for the thesis. Whereas if I assert a moral Edwards conditional, 'If you say something superassertible in morals, you thereby eo ipso say something true', some consequentialist will spring out of the cupboard and reply, 'That's the most absurd notion I have ever heard. You have completely misunderstood the nature of morality if you think that'. Such a theorist does not suspect that there may be counterexamples. He regards the Edwards conditional as mistaken across the board, and the idea of moral truth as conferred by superassertibility as embodying a profound philosophical mistake. And he seems, in some sense, to be *at liberty* to do so. There seems no option of a similar stance with respect to Church's Thesis. The identification of general recursiveness with effective calculability

Plurality of Pluralisms

might—just might—prove extensionally mistaken. But everyone appreciates the arguments for it and no one is at liberty to think that it is utterly (philosophically) misguided.

So: if we want to regard Edwards conditionals as candidates for conceptual necessity, we need to do something to reconcile that view of them not merely with the seemingly inescapable lack of conclusive grounds on their behalf but with their philosophical *controversiality*. The account of conferral that the parallel between the game-winning conditionals and the Edwards conditionals facilitates is highly attractive: but to earn the right to it, we need to say something to explain how someone who grasps all the relevant concepts is somehow left at liberty to regard the conditionals not merely as at best inconclusively argued for but as involving some kind of systematic mistake. What can be said to address this obligation? I shall conclude by outlining, very speculatively, one possible approach.

The first thing to do is to develop a template for argument *in support of* an Edwards conditional. We want to explain how it might best be argued that in the right domains—perhaps ethics, perhaps comedy—superassertibility, for instance, should confer truth: that it should hold, locally, as a matter of conceptual necessity that when a statement is superassertible, it is true and that its truth is grounded in its superassertibility. And to be clear, because we are working under the aegis of Mode D pluralism here—one property, many properties—the necessity we seek to argue for is that *the property* of truth applies when and because a statement of the domain in question is superassertible. We can assume that we already have the result—call this the Modeling Assumption—that superassertibility locally satisfies a correct network analysis of the concept of truth, modulo the inclusion perhaps of certain a priori certifiable principles that are specific to the domain in question. (We better be able to make that assumption or there is no case for superassertibility as a local truth-conferrer in the first place.)

To fix ideas, consider the case where a participant in the discourse concerned understands the word 'true' actually to *mean*: superassertible. Then the Modeling Assumption should entail that this will make no difference: that there need be nothing to distinguish the agent's use of 'true' in that discourse from that of another agent, of matching competence and opinions, who by 'true' just means philosophically unconsidered *truth*. The profiles of the uses of 'true' by the two agents are going to match. And, since we can idealize the agents—suppose them perfectly rational, humane, empathetic, and whatever else may seem relevant—that is as much as to say that the profiles of the concepts of superassertibility and truth will locally match.

So the Modeling Assumption, the suggestion is, entails that, in the region of discourse concerned, there is no operational distinction between fully competent exercise of the concept of the modeling property—superassertibility—and fully competent exercise of the concept of truth; and hence that the application of the former concept ensures the application of the latter. Since the superassertibility of a statement ensures that it will fall under the concept of superassertibility, it will follow that this conditional holds: that if a statement in the discourse in question is superassertible, it will fall under the concept of truth.

We are not quite there. To complete the case for the Edwards conditional, what is needed now is an argument from concept to property—an argument for the transition from falling under the concept of truth to having the property of truth. *Argument* is needed because on certain conceptions of concepts and properties this is not a trivial transition. It is not a trivial transition on any conception whereby the concept of a property—equivalently, if you will, the sense of a predicate that putatively attributes the property—can imperfectly reflect what it takes to possess the property in question. In that case, there may be scope for overextension: scope for cases ('Fools' cases) that fall under the concept but lack the property it imperfectly presents. But it *is* a trivial transition when our metaphysics of properties is suitably *abundant*: when properties are essentially tied to well-determined satisfaction-conditions of predicates and their natures fully manifest in those senses. (Call this metaphysical assumption Abundance.) If the property of truth is linked in that way to the sense of 'true', the transition we need is assured. An abundant metaphysics of properties will give us that the application of the concept ensures the application of *the property* of truth. To have the property of truth, so conceived, *is* to fall under the concept, as characterized by the network analysis. That's all there is to it.

The Modeling Assumption coupled with Abundance thus gives the result that superassertibility suffices for truth in the domain of discourse in question; and that is tantamount to the result that the Edwards conditional holds. It's a very simple argument in outline: for any statement s in the region of discourse in question,

(i) If s is superassertible, s falls under the concept of superassertibility.
(ii) If s falls under the concept of superassertibility, s falls under a concept whose competent exercise is operationally indistinguishable from that of the concept of truth (by the Modeling Assumption.)
(iii) If s falls under a concept whose competent exercise is operationally indistinguishable from that of the concept of truth, s falls under the concept of truth.
(iv) If s falls under the concept of truth, s has the property of truth (by Abundance).

What next? Well, for someone who regards this argument—or a more explicit, rigorous development of it—as cogent, the epistemological situation of an Edwards conditional, so supported, is clearly unlike that of Church's Thesis. We are not restricted to quasi-inductive or indirect evidence. A fully explicit, rigorous version of the line of argument sketched will deliver a philosophical proof, of sorts. But I say 'of sorts' because any argument of this character is surely going to be open to challenge. You would imagine that our consequentialist of a few paragraphs back might be inclined to try to make trouble for the Modeling Assumption on the foreseeable grounds that truth for claims about the maximization of satisfaction, for instance, will not stand interpretation in terms of superassertibility. But the more significant point is that argument for an Edwards conditional, if it is to be to the intended purpose, needs to do more than establish the conditional: it needs to show that the conditional stands interpretation as a claim about *conferral*. It is not just that when superassertible, a statement of the relevant domain is true—as if by extensional coincidence. The intended thesis is that superassertibility is there the *ground* of truth. How does that result fall within the compass of the outlined template? How is it supposed to be shown?

It is at this point, I think, that the controversiality is accommodated that I said we needed to address. For the obvious and reasonable move is to appeal to a version of the principle of inference to the best explanation. To possess the abundant property of truth is to fall under the concept of truth; and until more is said, the best explanation of a statement's falling under the concept of truth is that it has the only substantial property that has been shown to model the postulated network analysis of the concept. It is only if a second such substantial property is shown to do that that the issue of mere extensional coincidence arises. And naturally—provided of course that it is granted that superassertibility does meet the Modeling Assumption—the consequentialist will hold that there *is* a second such property: that of correspondence to the facts about maximization of satisfaction. So there is the nub of the controversy, located exactly where it ought to be, at the issue whether consequentialism can indeed provide an adequate model of moral truth.

So much for controversiality. But what about conceptual necessity? Even if superassertibility proves to have the field to itself, the point remains that the argument for conferral rests upon the good standing of an abundant conception of properties—or at least that of an abundant conception of the property of truth—and Abundance is a philosophical *proposal*: a recommendation about how best, at least locally, to think about the idea of a property, which will be supportable, or not, by characteristically inconclusive considerations of conceptual cost-benefit profile, intuitive satisfaction, explanatory fruitfulness, and so on. The case for such proposals in philosophy will still be reflective and a priori. But it seems a stretch to insist that, if acceptable, a principle of this character should be regarded as holding of conceptual necessity, just in virtue of the nature of the concepts involved. The credentials, even when impressive, seem to be of a different character.

Obviously, we are here on the cusp of some very profound and difficult issues about the nature of good philosophical theory and the standing of its theses. Anything I say within the space remaining to me here is going to be superficial. But one proposal that seems to me broadly faithful to the phenomenology, as it were, of good philosophical argument and negotiation, is that we should see a thesis like Abundance not as a description of the Platonic metaphysical nature of properties, nor as embodying a partial analysis of the notion of property that we actually have, but as a motivated *recommendation*: a recommendation that we build into the concept of a property the intimate relation that Abundance involves with predicate-satisfaction—that so to do addresses central purposes, connected with the logical, semantical, and metaphysical roles of the notion. If the recommendation is accepted, the crucial final step in the argument-template for the Edwards conditionals *will* be grounded purely conceptually. And if the other assumptions of the argument—the Modeling Assumption, and the coextensiveness of concepts with the same operational profile (step (iii))—may in the best cases be regarded similarly, the relevant Edwards conditionals will be conceptual necessities.

That, then, is one strategy for upholding the analogy with the game-winning conditionals and so availing ourselves of the mode of conferral which the latter illustrate, consistently with acknowledgment of the controversiality of the Edwards conditionals. The issues are clearly very open, but here I can do no more than end on this suggestive note.[18]

References

Beall, Jc. (2000). On mixed inferences and pluralism about truth predicates. *Philosophical Quarterly*, 50: 380–382.

David, M. (2013). Lynch's Functionalist Theory of Truth. In N. J. L. L. Pedersen & C. D. Wright (eds.), *Truth and Pluralism: Current Debates* (42–68). New York: Oxford University Press.

Edwards, D. (2011). Simplifying alethic pluralism. *Southern Journal of Philosophy*, 49: 28–48.

Edwards, D. (2013). Truth, winning, and simple determination pluralism. In N. J. L. L. Pedersen & C. D. Wright (eds.), *Truth and Pluralism: Current Debates* (113–122). New York: Oxford University Press.

Horwich, P. (1998). *Truth*. 2nd ed. Oxford: Clarendon Press.

Jackson, F. (1998). *From Metaphysics to Ethics: A Defence of Conceptual Analysis*. Oxford: Oxford University Press.

Lewis, D. (1970). How to define theoretical terms. *Journal of Philosophy*, 67: 427–446.

Lynch, M. (2004). Truth and multiple realizability. *Australasian Journal of Philosophy*, 82: 384–408.

---

[18] This paper, as its style will betray, is a lightly edited transcript of a talk, given at *Truth: Concept and Property*, a workshop held at University College, Dublin on October 9, 2010. Warm thanks for helpful critical feedback to Douglas Edwards, Michael Lynch, Nikolaj Pedersen and other participants in the workshop, and also to participants in the discussion of a presentation of these ideas at the SIUCC SEFA 'Workshop with Crispin Wright' held at the University in Barcelona in March 2011. Also, thanks to Sharon Coull for typing from the recording, to Marguerite Nesling for proof correction, and to Nikolaj Pedersen for assistance with editing.

Lynch, M. (2008). Three forms of truth pluralism. *Philosophia Scienciæ*, 12: 109–124.
Lynch, M. (2009). *Truth as One and Many*. Oxford: Oxford University Press.
Lynch, M. (2013). Three questions for truth pluralism. In N. J. L. L. Pedersen & C. D. Wright (eds.), *Truth and Pluralism: Current Debates* (21–41). New York: Oxford University Press.
Pedersen, N. J. (2010). Stabilizing alethic pluralism. *Philosophical Quarterly*, 60: 92–108.
Pedersen, N. J. L. L. (2012). Truth alethic functionalism? *International Journal of Philosophical Studies*, 20: 125–133.
Pedersen, N. J. L. L. & C. D. Wright. (2013). Pluralism about truth as alethic disjunctivism. In N. J. L. L. Pedersen & C. D. Wright (eds.), *Truth and Pluralism: Current Debates* (87–112). New York: Oxford University Press.
Pedersen, N. J. L. L. & D. Edwards. (2011). Truth as one(s) and many: on Lynch's alethic functionalism. *Analytic Philosophy*, 52: 213–230.
Ross, J. F. (1982). *Portraying Analogy*, Cambridge: Cambridge University Press.
Russell, B. (1956). *Logic and Knowledge: Essays 1901–50*, edited by R. Marsh. New York: Macmillan.
Smith, M. (1994). *The Moral Problem*. Oxford: Blackwell.
Tappolet, C. (1997). Mixed inferences: a problem for pluralism about truth predicates. *Analysis*, 57: 209–210.
Tappolet, C. (2000). Truth pluralism and many-valued logics: a reply to Beall. *Philosophical Quarterly*, 50: 382–385.
Williamson, T. (1994). Critical Study of *Truth and Objectivity*. *International Journal of Philosophical Studies*, 2: 130–144.
Williamson, T. (2006). Must do better. In P. Greenough and M. Lynch (eds.), *Truth and Realism* (177–187). Oxford: Clarendon Press.
Wright, C. (1992). *Truth and Objectivity*. Cambridge, MA: Harvard University Press.
Wright, C. (1999). Truth: A traditional debate reviewed. In S. Blackburn & K. Simmons (eds.), *Truth* (203–238). Oxford: Oxford University Press.
Wright, C. (2012). Meaning and assertibility: some reflections on Paolo Casalegno's 'The Problem of Non-conclusiveness'. *Dialectica* 66: 249–266.

{ PART II }

Pluralism, Correspondence, and Descriptions

{ 8 }

Forms of Correspondence: The Intricate Route from Thought to Reality

Gila Sher

1. How to maximize the substantiveness of truth without minimizing its unity

My starting point is the observation that truth is a substantive and complex subject matter, playing an important role in many areas of human life and the object of multiple human interests. As such, it is unreasonable to expect that it could be adequately accounted for by a single and simple definition, definition schema, or necessary-and-sufficient conditions. But many philosophers do equate the possibility of a substantive theory of truth with that of a substantive definition. It is not surprising, therefore, that the prevalent attitude toward truth is deflationist, one which supposes that truth is not a substantive subject matter since it resists a substantive definition.

Truth, however, is not the only substantive subject matter to resist a substantive definition, and the rational response, in most cases, is not to forego substantive theorizing. Theorists of truth, in my view, should learn from their colleagues in science and mathematics. Instead of insisting on one substantive comprehensive principle, they should be open to the possibility of a complex network of such principles. The task is to unravel the structure of this network, identify its general and special principles, and formulate a theory that fruitfully balances its attention to unity and diversity.[1]

Among the first to connect the substantiveness of truth with its plurality in a systematic manner was Wright in *Truth and Objectivity* (1992). Wright

---

[1] This is a 'substantivist' approach to truth, one that regards truth as a substantive subject matter and requires the theory of truth to provide a substantive account of this subject matter. By 'truth is a substantive subject matter' I mean that truth has a rich, complex, and intricate nature or structure (of some kind). By 'the theory of truth is a substantive theory' I mean that it provides a theoretical, informative, systematic, and explanatory account of the nature and structure of truth.

suggests that the substantiveness of truth lies in the variety of ways the (one) predicate of truth is instantiated in diverse areas. Accordingly, he divides the theory of truth into two parts: a part that deals with the common features of truths and a part that deals with the specific principles underlying truth in particular areas. His underlying assumption is that the principles governing all truths are thin, obvious, and often trivial; hence, their account is minimalist. In contrast, the principles underlying the specific types of truth are thick, non-obvious, and nontrivial; hence they require substantive theorizing. The general principles of truth are captured by one-line *platitudes* (Wright 1992: 34):

> to assert is to present as true;
> any truth-apt content has a significant negation, which is likewise truth-apt;
> to be true is to correspond to the facts;
> a statement may be justified without being true, and vice versa; . . .

In contrast, the special principles of truth in different areas of discourse are those elaborated by the different substantive theories of truth we are familiar with: correspondence, coherence, superwarrant, and so on.[2]

Wright's approach has been further developed by Lynch (2001; 2004a; 2004b; 2009). Lynch turns Wright's pluralist theory of truth into a *functionalist* theory, modeled after functionalist theories in the philosophy of mind. This approach enables him to sharpen the pluralist analysis of truth: truth is a single, high-level concept, defined by its functional role.[3] This role may be fulfilled by different properties in different domains. Truth supervenes on these properties but is not reducible to them. We may say that in different domains truth is differently realized or has different natures. Following Wright, the general role of truth is accounted for by a list of platitudes, its specific realizations by the substantive yet radically diverse principles of correspondence, coherence, superwarrant, and so on.

The differences between the correspondence, coherence, and superwarrant conceptions of truth are, however, so radical as to result in a highly *disunified* theory—a theory in which what it is for, say, a physical statement to be true is altogether different from what it is for, say, a mathematical statement to be true. One aspect of this disunity is the problem, raised by Tappolet (1997), of mixed sentences and inferences. Consider a conjunction of, say, a correspondence truth and a coherence truth. Such a conjunction is true. But what kind of truth is it? Or consider a logically valid inference with true premises, some

---

[2] As I understand him, C. J. G. Wright treats the platitude of correspondence as a nonsubstantive statement, but treats theories of correspondence for specific fields (e.g., a theory of physical correspondence) as substantive theories.

[3] Lynch (2009) no longer characterizes truth as a high-level concept, but he continues to characterize it as a single concept defined by its functional role.

of the essential premises of which are merely superwarranted, and a conclusion whose truth is based on full-fledged correspondence. How can such an inference guarantee the correspondence-truth of the conclusion based on the mere superwarrant of essential premises?

Another problem with Wright's and Lynch's respective views concerns their claim that the universal principles of truth are platitudinous. Methodologically, the most problematic aspect of this claim is the presumption that with respect to these principles there is no room for further study, let alone a deep, thorough, and comprehensive investigation. But this presumption, as far as I can see, has never been justified. Recognizing the *plurality* of truth means recognizing the *partiality* of its commonalities, that is, recognizing that the common principles of truth can provide only *partial* knowledge of truth. But partiality does not imply nonsubstantiveness: some partial principles are substantive (and some substantive principles are partial).[4]

The solution to these problems lies, in my view, in the realization that, on the one hand, diversity comes in degrees, and, on the other hand, substantiveness is compatible with partiality. Recognizing the diversity of truth, therefore, need not involve commitment to a radically disunified theory of truth, and recognizing the partiality of the universal principles of truth need not involve commitment to their triviality. If, instead of viewing truth as based on correspondence principles in one area and on coherence principles in another, we view it as based on correspondence principles in all areas, yet some of these principles as possibly varying from area to area, we will achieve a better balance between unity and diversity in our conception of truth. And if, instead of viewing truth as based on *trivial global* principles and *substantive local* principles, we view it as being based on a network of *substantive* principles, some more global, others more local, we will not sacrifice the substantiveness of truth by acknowledging its diversity. That is the solution I offer in this chapter: truth is *correspondence* throughout, but correspondence is a *family* of substantive and interconnected principles rather than a single, monolithic, deflationary principle.[5]

What is meant by 'correspondence'? By the view that truth is correspondence, I understand something like the following:

(COR) Truth is a matter of substantive and systematic connections between language and the world. These connections hold in a particular case if, and only if (iff), that aspect of reality that a given sentence or theory is about is, directly or indirectly, and

---

[4] For critical yet sympathetic discussions of platitude-based strategies among current pluralist approaches to truth, see C. D. Wright (2005; 2007; 2010, 2012).

[5] See Sher (1998; 2004) for earlier renditions of this approach. To avoid repetition, I will not discuss here many of the issues raised in those papers.

based on some pertinent principles (according to the type of case), as the sentence or theory says it is.[6]

This is not intended as a *definition* of correspondence. Instead, it is intended as an informal characterization, one that can be used as a guideline for an elaborate, substantive, and multifaceted theory of truth as correspondence.

Why correspondence? In Sher (2004) I argued that truth emerges at the intersection of three features of, or conditions on, human thought: *immanence*, *transcendence*, and *normativity*. By 'immanence' I understand the cognitive stance we take when we think or speak from *within* a theory (in the sense of a body of knowledge)—that is, the stance of thinking directly about the world, about some facet of the world, or about something in the world. To be immanent, in this sense, is to be directed at something factual, usually external[7]—to place no barrier between us and our subject matter, perceived as part of reality. Bearers of truth, according to this account, are *immanent* thoughts of some type (statements, beliefs, theories, or similar entities).

Immanent thoughts by themselves, however, are not sufficient for truth. To focus directly on the world is not yet to see it through the prism of *truth*. Truth requires a *transcendent* perspective, a perspective from which we can view both our immanent thought and the world, or rather those facets of the world it is directed at. It is only at this level, a level in which we observe an immanent thought from outside it, that truth, as a property of, or more precisely a standard for, such a thought can arise. It is important to note, however, that 'transcendence' here is not something mysterious or superhuman. Rather, it is something quite simple and humanly commonplace, something on the order of *ascending to a meta-language* or *moving sideways to a background theory*— in other words, taking a perspective external to the immanent thought we are examining, a perspective from which we can ask questions and say things about various aspects of this immanent thought, including its object.

Immanence and transcendence by themselves, however, are still not sufficient for truth. By ascending to a higher level of discourse we can ask many kinds of questions about immanent thoughts, not just questions of truth. We can even ask many questions about their relation to the world that are not questions of truth. For example, we can ask whether a given sentence expressing an immanent thought names a certain object by a word whose sound imitates that object's sound (onomatopoeia), whether a given sentence describes

---

[6] (i) 'World' and 'reality' are used as synonyms in this paper. (ii) The idea of indirect correspondence was earlier suggested by Horgan (2001) and Barnard & Horgan (2006). See also 'The Syntactic Unity of Truth' (this volume). My view is similar to theirs in some ways, different in others. For example, as readers shall see, my account of logical and mathematical truth is very different from Horgan's.

[7] 'External' here implies '*significantly* independent of the mind' but not '*completely* independent of the mind'. The idea is that x can be significantly independent of y in some pertinent respects and significantly dependent on it in others; see §2.

a given situation briefly or at length, whether two sentences describing the same situation are synonymous, whether the objects a given theory is about are animate or inanimate, observable or unobservable, and so on. *Truth* arises when we ask a *normative* question about immanent thoughts, and not just any normative question but a specific normative question, namely, the question whether things are or the world is as a given immanent thought says they are (it is). In other words, truth emerges when we ask whether a given immanent thought (statement, theory, etc.) 'measures up' to reality. I will call this 'the question of *truth*'.[8] At issue is whether a given statement or theory is systematically connected to reality in a way that justifies a positive answer to the question of truth. Truth, on this conception, is a *standard* for a positive answer to this question, a standard satisfied by some immanent thoughts but not others. When a given immanent thought satisfies this standard we say that it is *true*, or that it has the property of truth.[9]

This brief account of the basic conditions for the emergence of truth is far from complete. Indeed, it is partly in elaborating and extending this account, attending to the issues it raises, and connecting it to parallel accounts of the emergence of language and knowledge, that the challenge (and opportunity) of a substantive account of truth, including a substantive theory of the universal principles of truth, lies. Now, it is clear that if this conception of the basic conditions of truth points in the right direction, truth is *correspondence with reality* (in the sense of *COR* above), rather than coherence or super-warrant. It is for that reason that my proposed solution to the tension between the unity and diversity of truth lies in *correspondence*. The solution lies in realizing, first, that truth is based on *correspondence* principles (*unity*), and second, that it is based on a *network* of correspondence principles (*diversity*).

2. Pluralism within the bounds of correspondence

One remarkable thing about truth is its enormous scope. Every declarative statement, it seems, is a candidate for a truth value, regardless of its content or the field of discourse it belongs to. The account of truth given in the last section explains why this is so. The question of truth, indeed correspondence truth, arises with respect to every immanent thought, and the domain of immanent thoughts encompasses all fields of knowledge and others besides. Given the immense scope of immanent thoughts and our unlimited ability to

---

[8] I am here talking about 'the' question of truth, but could alternatively talk about a 'cluster' of questions of truth—questions that raise, in one way or another, the issue noted above.

[9] This tripartite structure of truth is one of the distinctive characteristics of the present correspondence theory. Transcendence, for example, may not be required by other conceptions of correspondence. It is required, however, by Tarski's (1933/1983) theory, where truth is essentially a metatheoretic notion.

transcend them and raise the question of correspondence truth with respect to them, there is a sense in which we cannot get away from correspondence truth altogether no matter where we go.

Suppose you and I stand in meta-arithmetic, or in meta-meta-arithmetic, and you say: 'the truth of arithmetical statements is purely conventional'. That is, you look at the totality of arithmetic statements and deny that their truth value is based on correspondence. Now, this itself is an immanent claim, a direct factual claim about some subject matter, and I am free to ascend to the next level in the meta-theoretical hierarchy and raise the critical question: 'is arithmetic truth in fact conventional?' with respect to it. Of course, you are free to refuse to answer my question (as you are free to refuse to answer any question), but the question all the same arises. Suppose you say: 'it is more convenient (simple, efficient, fruitful) to think of arithmetic as conventional than as true based on correspondence'. This gives rise to the truth question: 'Is it in fact simpler, more efficient, more fruitful, to think of arithmetic truth in this way?', and so on. So long as you make an immanent statement, the question of truth arises with respect to your statement. The ubiquity of truth is, thus, the result of the ubiquity of immanent thought together with our freedom to transcend any immanent thought and raise the critical question of whether it measures up to reality (or to that aspect of reality it is directed at). Transcendent claims, too, are for the most part immanent; in particular, truth claims are immanent and as such subject to the question of truth. We may say that whatever level of immanent thought we reside in at a given time, truth-as-correspondence arises at the next level of thought, a level that we are always free, and able, to ascend to.

This said, the question still arises whether the same correspondence principles are at work in all areas of truth. Are the standards of measuring up to reality the same for all truths? Are all true sentences connected to reality in the same way? Do they all correspond to the same 'level' of reality? Are the routes or patterns of correspondence the same in all fields? At question is not whether all true sentences correspond to the same thing. Clearly, different sentences (up to synonymy) say different things about reality and therefore different things have to hold for different sentences to be true. That much is trivial. At issue is the nontrivial question whether the *principles* underlying correspondence in one area are systematically different from those in other areas. Suppose that in physics, reference (an important constituent of correspondence) is largely based on a direct *causal* relation between physical expressions and objects in the world. Must reference in mathematics be based on a direct causal relation between mathematical language and the world? Suppose the existence of physical individuals is necessary for the truth of physical statements. Is the existence of mathematical individuals necessary for the truth of mathematical statements? These questions, I believe, cannot be answered by platitudes. We cannot decide in advance how truths in various areas are connected to reality or what facets of reality they are connected to. Investigating these issues requires

Forms of Correspondence

looking deeply, thoroughly, and critically into the matter. This investigation, however, is not a task for the theory of truth alone: to understand how truth is connected to reality in a particular area we need to understand the area in question. But it is not a matter for the specialist in this area to investigate alone either. Answering these questions requires an understanding both of truth and of the area we are interested in, and it is out of this joint understanding that the pattern of correspondence in that area will become known.

There is much more to say about the general conception of a theory of truth delineated above, but space constraints limit me in doing so. Therefore, I will limit myself to listing a few of the distinctive features of this conception:

1. It does not require either that truth be *exclusively* a matter of how the world is or that the world's contribution to truth be *completely independent* of that of the mind. Instead, it requires that truth be *significantly* a matter of how the world is, and the world *significantly* independent of the mind.[10]
2. It does not determine in advance what the correspondence connection between truths and reality is, but takes this as an open question, the target of an open-ended investigation. In particular, it is not committed to any of the existent conceptions of truth as correspondence: the picture theory of correspondence, the museum metaphor of correspondence, the isomorphism view of correspondence, and so on.
3. While it allows the correspondence connection between truths and reality to differ from one field to another, to be direct in some fields and indirect in others, to be affected more or less by context (purpose, interest, perspective, etc.), it leaves it an open question how it is in particular fields and particular contexts.
4. It admits units of truth of various sizes, from single statements to full theories and even clusters of theories.
5. It does not take a definite stand in the controversy on the bearers of truth (aside from the point indicated in (4)).
6. It is a holistic conception. It is holistic not in the sense of taking our language or body of knowledge as a whole to be the smallest unit of semantic or epistemic significance. It is holistic in acknowledging the existence, in principle, of a broad and diverse network of semantically and epistemically significant connections between language/

---

[10] In this respect, the present theory, at least initially, is compatible with several views of 'world', i.e., several metaphysical outlooks. My method is to start from more general and open-ended views and proceed to more definite views, so a reader can agree with the former but disagree with the latter. In this chapter I will go as far as saying that there is just one reality and it has both physical and formal features, or more generally, both material and abstract features. This implies that neither extreme empiricism nor extreme Platonism (the view that there are two separate realities, material and abstract) is compatible with the present theory in its more definite form.

mind/theory/knowledge and reality (including connections involving nonvicious circularity). We may say that it is a *relational holistic conception*.[11]

7. It demands systematic connections between true statements (theories) and reality in all genuine fields of *knowledge*. This implies, among other things, that it rejects the traditional tie between holism and coherentism, and that it extends the correspondence approach to fields like logic and mathematics (to the extent that they are genuine fields of knowledge).

Elsewhere, I have investigated the applicability of correspondence to logic (see Sher 1999, 2004, 2008). My conclusion has been that logical truth and consequence are grounded in the formal structure of reality, a structure studied in detail in mathematics. In §4 I will investigate correspondence in mathematics; in §3, I will show how the pluralist approach developed in this chapter avoids a challenge (involving logic) that threatens other pluralistic approaches.

3. The problem of mixed truths and inferences

In two articles, Tappolet (1997, 2000) raised two related challenges to C. J. G. Wright's (1992) early version of discourse pluralism about truth: the challenge of 'mixed' truths and the challenge of 'mixed' inferences. Her analysis of the relevant features of Wright's theory proceeds as follows:

> Truth pluralism, as defended by Crispin Wright, is the view that there are different truth predicates corresponding to different sorts of sentences. Briefly, whereas descriptive sentences are claimed to be assessable in terms of 'heavyweight' truth, which involves realism about the corresponding entities, allegedly nondescriptive sentences, such as sentences about the moral or the comical, are supposed only to be assessable in terms of 'lightweight' truth, a kind of truth that does not involve realism. (2000: 382–3)

Her first challenge concerns 'mixed' inferences:

> [T]here is a simple and . . . powerful objection to the claim that there is a plurality of truth predicates. Consider the following inference:
>
> 1. Cruel cats are hungry.
> 2. This cat is cruel.
> 3. Therefore, this cat is hungry.
>
> The validity of an inference requires that the truth of the premises necessitates the truth of the conclusion. But how can this inference be valid if we are to

---

[11] For more on the holistic nature of this conception, see §5.

Forms of Correspondence

> suppose with Crispin Wright that two different kinds of truth predicates are involved in these premises? For the conclusion to hold, some unique truth predicate must apply to all three sentences. But what truth predicate is that? And if there is such a truth predicate, why isn't it the only one we need? (Tappolet 1997: 209–10, 2000: 383)[12]

Her second challenge concerns 'mixed' sentences:

> There is a further problem for the claim that there is a plurality of truth predicates, thrown up by mixed sentences and, more particularly, mixed conjunctions. The sentence 'This cat is wet and it is funny' can obviously be true. But what sort of truth predicates would apply to it? This is a tough question for truth pluralism. On this view, the first conjunct is supposed to be T_1, if true at all, and the second T_2, if true at all. Given this, it would be extremely odd to say that the conjunction itself is assessable in terms of either T_1 or T_2. Suppose that T_1 is a matter of correspondence to natural facts, whereas T_2 is the result of a social agreement. The problem is that conjunctions involving the two kinds of truth predicates will be neither a matter of correspondence to natural facts nor a result of social agreement. (2000: 384)

Leaving it for Wright to defend his own version of pluralism, let us see which parts of Tappolet's challenge apply to our theory. Clearly, there is no duality of 'lightweight' and 'heavyweight' truth predicates in our theory, nor, indeed any plurality of truth predicates. There is just one truth predicate: a 'heavyweight', correspondence, truth predicate. This truth predicate has all bearers of truth in its scope, though to avoid paradox it may be technically construed as a hierarchy of truth predicates. This truth predicate attributes the same property—correspondence with reality—to every true truth bearer, and it is this property that is transmitted from premises to conclusion in a valid argument. Still, Tappolet might argue, this single truth predicate sets varied truth (correspondence) conditions on truth bearers in different fields. Does this not create a problem for mixed truths and inferences?

Before setting out to respond to this challenge, let me deepen and expand it. Tappolet presents the challenge as one of dealing with a specific 'mixture' of truths, that is to say, a mixture due to *logical* composition of sentences, and indeed to logical composition of *independent* sentences. But there is an important sense in which most sentences and inferences we use, including sentences that are logically simple (atomic) and sentences involving logical composition of proper parts of sentences rather than whole, independent sentences, are

---

[12] In this citation I replace Tappolet's original example of a mixed inference by a later example she gave, which is simpler to discuss since it contains truth-bearers of types that we are more familiar with than those appearing in the original example.

mixed in the sense of having constituents with different kinds of reference, satisfaction, and fulfillment conditions. Consider 'causing pain is bad'. This sentence combines physical, mental, and moral expressions, and these may very well have different reference and satisfaction (hence truth) conditions. Lynch (2005) regards mixed atomic sentences as belonging to a single domain (for example, the above sentence, according to him, belongs to the moral domain.) But the present theory offers a different approach, one that is far more general, works for sentences of any complexity, and does not depend on our ability to determine a single domain.

In a sense, the present theory approaches the challenge of mixed sentences in the same way that an engineer approaches a multifaceted engineering challenge. Take, for example, the challenge of building a bridge over a large body of water in a big city during an economic downturn. In designing such a bridge the engineer has to combine principles belonging to multiple fields of knowledge: mathematics, various branches of physics, economics, sociology, aesthetics, and so on—fields governed by principles that are significantly different in kind from each other. There is no specific field of knowledge that consists of this particular combination of principles, but in each case the engineer creates a combination that fits the specific project he/she is engaged in. The situation faced by our correspondence-truth theorist is similar. Having figured out (with the help of specialists) the general principles involved in physical, mathematical, psychological, biological, and moral truth, our truth theorist combines these principles together in determining the correspondence truth-conditions of each mixed sentence. When the sentence includes logical vocabulary, the correspondence theorist has to take into account the reference-, satisfaction/extension-, and fulfillment/value-conditions of logical expressions as well. The fact that the truth and reference conditions of linguistic expressions with diverse components are often compositional is helpful in managing this task.

Dealing with sentences involving logical constants, as in Tappolet's example, let me first note without explanation that, on the present account, truth in logic is correspondence with the formal structure of reality, or more precisely, with certain laws governing its formal structure (laws studied in mathematics, as I mentioned above).[13]

Thus, take the mixed sentence:

(1) The cat is wet and it is happy.[14]

Reading this sentence as a first-order sentence, it has the logical form:

(2) W(c) & H(c).

---

[13] This has been extensively discussed in Sher (1998; 2004; 2008).
[14] I prefer this variant of Tappolet's example since it is less controversial that there are facts concerning happiness than that there are facts concerning 'funniness'.

On my correspondence account of truth in logic, '&' is a denoting expression, whose denotation (in contexts of the above form) is *intersection*. Therefore, the truth-condition of (1) is captured by,

(3) 'The cat is wet and it is happy' is true
iff
The referent of 'the cat' is in the *intersection* the properties denoted (or indicated) by 'is wet' and 'is happy'.

On this account, the truth value of (1) depends (i) on the referents of 'the cat', 'is wet', 'is happy', and 'and', and (ii) on whether they are related in the requisite way in the world (i.e., on whether the referent of 'the cat' is in the *intersection* of the properties denoted by 'is wet' and 'is happy').[15] Now, the expressions 'the cat', 'is wet', 'is happy', and 'and' are biological, physical, mental, and logical, respectively, and this might affect their reference and satisfaction conditions on our account. But due to certain features of the referents involved, this is not problematic. Since a biological object (like a cat) can have properties of various kinds (including physical and mental properties) and since intersection, being a formal operation (see next section), can apply to properties of various kinds (including physical and mental properties), the truth of (1) is a mixed truth whose constituents mesh together seamlessly in spite of their diversity.

Proceeding to mixed logical inferences, consider Tappolet's

(4) (i) Cruel cats are hungry
 (ii) This cat is cruel
 (iii) This cat is hungry.

Since (4) is a *logical* inference, its validity depends only on the formal portion of the truth-conditions of its premises and conclusion. These are: (i) the intersection of two sets, call them 'A' and 'B', is included in a third set, call it 'C'; (ii) an object, call it 'a', is in the intersection of A and B; and (iii) a is in C.[16] The inference is logically valid in virtue of a certain formal law governing the world, namely: whenever an object is in an intersection included in a given set, it is also in that set. Or, in terms of properties: Whenever an object has an intersective property included in another property, it has the latter property. This is a formal law governing the behavior of objects and properties in the world, and (4) is grounded in reality through this law.[17]

How, then, does (4) guarantee the unmixed (physical) truth of (iii) based on the mixed truth of (i) and (ii) (whose mixed nature is reflected in the mixed

---

[15] More precisely, on whether it is in the intersection of the extensions of the properties denoted by 'is wet' and 'is happy'.

[16] The explanation could also be formulated in terms of having a property (instead of being in a set).

[17] This may involve some circularity, but circularity of this kind is permitted by our holistic methodology (see previous sections). The discussion of mixed inferences offered here expands an earlier discussion of the same issue in Sher (2005).

vocabularies of these sentences—physical, moral, and logical in the case of (i) and physical and moral in the case of (ii))? Our answer is that the truth conditions of all three sentences have a common element, namely, *formal* parameters, and the relations between their respective formal parameters are sufficient to guarantee the truth of the third sentence based on those of the other two. (Here is a partial analogy: how does the sale of John's home guarantee his ability to buy, say, a yacht, given that selling a home and buying a yacht are two different things? The answer is: money. The fact that his *home's sale* gives John a large sum of *money* guarantees that he can do any number of things that have nothing to do with selling and homes, e.g., *buying* a *yacht*.) The law relating the formal constituents of the situations said to hold by the premises and conclusion of (4) is sufficient to guarantee that the conclusion-situation holds given that the premise-situations hold, in spite of their dissimilarities.

Since, as mentioned above, I have already explained the correspondence conditions of logical truths and consequence in great detail elsewhere, I will not deal with them here. Instead, I will expand the earlier work by investigating the correspondence conditions of mathematical truths.

4. Mathematical correspondence[18]

In this section, I will propose a tentative account of mathematical truth as based on *indirect correspondence*.[19] I will proceed in two steps: First, I will argue that reality has formal features and mathematics offers theories of the

---

[18] To avoid unnecessary confusion, let me explain my use of the terms 'property', 'feature', 'object', 'individual', 'formal', and 'mathematical' in this section:

(a) Property: often, when I talk about properties I mean 'properties and/or relations' and sometimes 'properties, relations, and/or functions'. The reader will be able to figure out from the context which usage is appropriate.
(b) Feature: I use 'feature' as a general term. In the present context it usually means property (in the sense indicated in (a)). Often, 'feature' is used for properties of level 2 (i.e., properties of first-level properties), but more generally it is used for properties of any level, including first-level properties (i.e., properties of individuals).
(c) Object versus individual: 'object' is a general term, used for individuals, properties, relations, functions, etc. 'Individual' is used for an *atomic* object, an object of level 0, one that does not have (or is treated, in a given context, as not having) an internal structure (constituents, arguments, etc.).
(d) Formal versus mathematical: 'formal is usually used to characterize a feature or law of objects, properties, or reality more generally; 'mathematical' is usually used to characterize linguistic expressions, theories, and laws on the linguistic level. These expressions, however, can be used interchangeably, since we can characterize a formal object as having the kind of properties that are indicated by mathematical expressions (or as being the kind of object that is denoted by mathematical expressions), and similarly we can characterize a mathematical expression as denoting (indicating) a formal object.

[19] The idea of indirect correspondence, as I have mentioned above, appears earlier in Horgan (2001) and Barnard & Horgan (2006). Neither author, however, conceives of mathematical truth as based on indirect correspondence.

Forms of Correspondence

laws governing its formal features. Next, I will develop a tentative account of truth for mathematical theories of formal structure, based on indirect correspondence.

Mathematics as a theory of the formal structure of reality. My starting point is the observation that objects in the world have, in addition to physical, biological, psychological, and other properties, also formal properties. Elsewhere[20] I have extensively discussed the notion of 'formality', and I will not repeat these discussions here. But in a nutshell, a *formal property* or relation is one that takes into account only the *pattern* delineated by its arguments in a given domain and *not the identity of the individuals* involved. Using model-theoretic terminology, we may say that a formal property *does not distinguish between isomorphic arguments* or argument-structures, or is *invariant under isomorphisms*.[21] Under this characterization, the first-level relation of identity is formal because it does not distinguish between isomorphic structures of the type <A, b, c>, where A is a non-empty set (domain or universe of individuals), and b and b′ are members of A. That it to say, if <A′, b′, c′> is the image of <A, b, c> under some isomorphism, then $b = c$ iff $b' = c'$. In contrast, the first-level relation of having a greater mass than is not formal since it is not preserved under all isomorphisms: if <A, b, c> is a structure of physical individuals such that b has a greater mass than c, there is an isomorphic structure <A′, b′, c′> in which this does not hold. (Let b′ and c′ be abstract individuals, e.g., numbers, thoughts, ideas, political institutions, etc.). Likewise, all the second-level cardinality properties are formal, because they do not distinguish between isomorphic argument-structures of the type <A, B>, where A is as above and B is a subset of A. But the second-level property of being a property of humans is not formal, because whenever <A, B> is such that B is a set of humans (an extension in A of a first-level property that holds of some, and only, humans in A), there is an isomorphic structure

---

[20] See Sher (1991, 1996, 1999, 2001, 2002, 2008).

[21] (i) A *structure* S is an n-tuple <A, $\beta_1, \ldots, \beta_n$>, where A is a nonempty domain (universe, set) of individuals, and for $1 \leq i \leq n$, β_i is a member of A, or a subset of A, or a relation on A, etc.

(ii) Structures S = <A, $\beta_1, \ldots, \beta_n$> and S′= <A′, $\beta'_1, \ldots, \beta'_n$> are *isomorphic* iff there is a 1–1 and onto function f from A to A′ such that for $1 \leq i \leq n$, β'_i is the image of β_i under f.

(iii) An *argument-structure* of a property P or a relation R is a structure representing an argument of P or R extensionally. An argument-structure for P is of the type <A, β>. If P is a first-level property, β is a member of A; if P is a second-level property, β a subset of A. An argument-structure for an n-place R is of the type <A, $\beta_1, \ldots, \beta_n$>, where <$\beta_1, \ldots, \beta_n$> represents an argument of R in A. An argument-structure of an individual a is of the same type as a structure for a first-level property P, namely, a structure <A, β>, where β is a member of A.

(iv) P is *invariant* under isomorphisms (does not distinguish between isomorphic argument-structures, or is preserved under isomorphisms) iff for all isomorphic argument-structures for P, <A, β> and <A′, β'>, β has the property P in A iff β' has the property P in A′. R is invariant under isomorphisms iff for all isomorphic argument-structures for R, <A, $\beta_1, \ldots, \beta_n$> and <A′, $\beta'_1, \ldots, \beta'_n$>, $\beta_1, \ldots, \beta_n$ (in that order) stand in the relation R in A iff $\beta'_1, \ldots, \beta'_n$ (in that order) stand in the relation R in A′. a is invariant under isomorphisms iff for all isomorphic argument-structures for a, <A, β> and <A′, β'>, $\beta = a$ iff $\beta' = a$.

<A′, B′> for which B′ is not a property of humans (i.e., not the extension of a property that holds of some and only humans in A′).

Now, to see that objects in the world have formal properties, let us consider objects that are accepted both by nominalists and by antinominalists; say, the students in my current graduate seminar ('Truth in Kant', UC San Diego, Fall 2010, 17 students). Clearly each student has the formal properties of being identical to himself/herself and being (numerically) different from me; the property of being a student in the class has various formal properties, for instance, the second-level cardinality property we may call 'SEVENTEEN'; the properties of being a philosophy professor and being a woman can be combined by formal operations like union and intersection; students stand to other students in relations that have formal properties, for example, the relation of studying in the same class as, which has the formal properties of being reflexive, symmetric, and nontransitive; and so on.

But if objects, properties, and relations in the world have formal or mathematical features, these features potentially exhibit regularities or are governed by laws. And these regularities or laws, like many other regularities and laws, have a certain modal force, a modal force that goes beyond their application to objects that actually exist (or are instantiated) in the world.

Next, to see that mathematics, through some of its theories, studies these formal laws, note how absurd or strange it would be if otherwise. For example, it would be very strange if properties of things in the world had cardinality features, these features were governed by laws, mathematicians knew about these features and knew they were governed by laws, yet they studied the laws governing other, *unreal* (so-called) cardinalities, cardinalities governed by laws that had nothing to do with those governing the cardinalities of real properties of real objects in the world. It would not do to say that only *applied* mathematics has something to do with reality. To give a general and precise account of the *laws* governing formal features of objects in the world (e.g., the laws of cardinality) we need highly general and abstract theories of cardinality—in other words, something on the order of 'pure' mathematical theories.

But if mathematical theories (or some mathematical theories) are theories of the laws governing formal features of objects in the world, then they are true or false in the sense of *COR*. If, and to the extent that, the laws of our current arithmetic theory do govern the relations between finite cardinalities in the world, there is a systematic connection between the laws described by arithmetic theorems and the laws governing finite cardinalities in the world. Our next task is to figure out what this systematic connection is like.

Mathematical correspondence. In trying to figure out this connection, an apparent incongruity presents itself. Our analysis suggests that the level at which cardinalities arise in reality is the level of properties of properties, but modern arithmetic considers cardinalities to be individuals. This creates a puzzle: if cardinalities are in fact second-level properties, how can first-order arithmetic get things right? How can an arithmetic theory which treats cardinalities as individuals be said to *correspond* to reality? From the opposite perspective the puzzle is this: if, in the world, there are no cardinal individuals but only second-level cardinal properties, why do mathematicians construct their theories of cardinalities as theories of individuals? Why do they treat cardinalities as individuals if in fact they are properties of properties?[22]

To understand why mathematicians construe cardinalities as (numerical) individuals, we have to take into account the fact that *mathematics is a discipline created by and for humans*. As such, it may take a form that is advantageous for humans even if circuitous from the point of view of correspondence. Thus, it is possible that the most natural or effective way for humans to make discoveries and/or develop theories of any subject matter (or of formal subject matters or of certain formal subject matters) is to do so on the first level. In other words, humans may be better at discovering formal regularities and constructing a systematic theory of such regularities when they think of them as concerning individuals rather than higher-level properties. Their—our—cognitive resources may work better in a first-level setting than in a higher-level setting. And if reality does not supply such a setting, we create one for ourselves by constructing a first-level model of reality, or those parts/aspects of reality we wish to study. Arithmetic, in that case, gives an indirect account of some facets of reality. It describes the laws governing cardinalities by describing the laws governing their first-level numerical correlates (in a model constructed by and for humans). First-order arithmetic (if correct) thus corresponds to reality in an indirect manner, but that does not render its correspondence to reality insignificant or nonsystematic. First-order mathematical laws may not be true of reality in exactly the same way that laws of physics (the discipline) are true of reality, but they are true of reality just as much (in their own way). Rephrasing the title of Cartwright (1983), we may say that once you know how to read them, 'the laws of arithmetic do not lie'.[23]

---

[22] Note that even if there are mathematical individuals in the world, properties of individuals do often have cardinality features, so that cardinalities as second-level properties still emerge in the world and must be taken into account in studying cardinalities.

[23] Two notes. First, for my present purpose, it does not matter whether mathematicians always prefer first-order theories to higher-order theories. It is sufficient that such a preference is possible. My task is to explain how this possibility is compatible with the correspondence approach. Similarly, for the present purpose there is no need to show that the conjectural explanation of people's preference for first-order theories offered above is empirically correct; it is sufficient to show that it is possible to explain this preference in a way that is compatible with our approach. Second, someone might construe my view as saying that second-order mathematics is 'worldly mathematics' and first-order mathematics is 'human mathematics'. This might be useful in some contexts, but it would be misleading in others. The reason it would be misleading is that the very terminology of individuals, first- and second-level properties, etc., is human terminology, and this means that worldly mathematics, on my view, is also human mathematics. Likewise, human mathematics has systematic connections with reality, and as such it is also worldly mathematics.

An indirect correspondence relation. What form does the indirect correspondence of mathematics with reality take? Let us first compare two renditions of the truth conditions of the same mathematical sentence, the one direct, the other indirect. Consider

(5) α + β = γ,

where 'α', 'β', and 'γ' are numerical singular-terms, '+' is a first-order function, and '=' is the first-order identity relation. A direct rendition of the truth (correspondence) condition of (5) will give us a *single-layer* condition:

(6) True 'α + β = γ' iff $n_\alpha +_n n_\beta \approx n_\gamma$,

where n_α, n_β, and n_γ are the individual numbers denoted by 'α', 'β', and 'γ', respectively, '$+_n$' is the first-level function denoted (or indicated) by '+', and '$\approx$' is the first-level identity relation denoted (or indicated) by '='. In contrast, an indirect rendition of the truth (correspondence) condition of (5) along the lines delineated above will give us a condition that, using familiar logical and set-theoretical terminology, can be formulated by:

(7) $(\forall P_1)(\forall P_2)[(\alpha(P_1) \& \beta(P_2) \& P_1 \cap P_2 = \emptyset) \supset \gamma(P_1 \cup P_2)]$,

where **α**, **β**, **γ** are the second-level properties indirectly referred to by 'α', 'β', and 'γ', respectively. This, of course, is not the traditional correspondence condition of (5). But traditional correspondence theories disregard the diversity of the patterns connecting immanent thoughts to reality and therefore are limited to a single, monolithic pattern of correspondence.

To see how a complex pattern of correspondence might work and how it is related to the simple pattern, let us assume that everyday physical truths follow a simple route of correspondence, and let us compare physical and mathematical truths of the same syntactic form. First, consider the true (everyday) physical sentence

(8) Barack Obama is a male.

We can express its truth condition as:

(9) 'Barack Obama is a male' is true
iff
The individual denoted by the singular term 'Barack Obama' satisfies the first-level predicate 'is a male', i.e.,
iff
The individual Barack Obama has the first-level property of being a male.[24]

---

[24] To simplify the comparison, I chose a very simple, essentially deflationist, formulation of the truth condition of (8), rather than a more elaborate, substantive formulation. The same applies to the other examples in this paper. For examples of more substantive formulations of truth conditions see Sher (1998; 2004).

Forms of Correspondence

Skipping the intermediate condition, we have a *single-layered* definition of truth:

(10) 'Barack Obama is a male' is true
iff
The individual Barack Obama has the first-level property of being a male.

Next consider a mathematical sentence of the same syntactic form, say:

(11) 'Four is even'.

In contrast to (8), the truth-condition of (11) is t*wo-layered*:

(12) 'Four is even' is true
iff
The individual four has the first-level property of being even,
iff
The second-level property of holding of exactly four individuals has the third-level property of being even.

Using the subscripts 0, 1, 2, and 3 to distinguish types of linguistic and ontological elements (0: individual terms/objects; 1–3: first-, second-, and third-order/level predicates/properties), we can represent the difference between direct and indirect correspondence in terms of simple versus complex or composite reference[25]:

(13) **Simple Reference**　　　　　　　　**Complex Reference**

Language: Sing.Terms$_0$　Predicates$_1$　　**Language:** Sing.Terms$_0$　Predicates$_1$
　　　　　　　↓　　　　　↓　　　　　　　　　　　　　⇓　　　　　⇓
World:　　Individuals$_0$　Properties$_1$　　**World:**　　Properties$_2$　Properties$_3$

But this representation is still insufficient to *explain* the complexity of mathematical correspondence compared with (simple) physical correspondence. What the mathematician is actually doing is *positing* a new level of reality, a level containing mathematical individuals and first-level properties (relations, functions) of such individuals. These *represent* the second- and third-level properties that (first-order) arithmetic objects are anchored in.

---

[25] Terminology: I use 'refers' and 'denotes' (synonymously) for singular terms and 'refers', 'denotes', and 'indicates' (synonymously) for predicates. I talk about the 'satisfaction' and 'extension' of predicates (and by analogy, properties) and the 'fulfillment' and 'value' of functional expressions (and functions).

Figuratively, we can distinguish direct and indirect correspondence (in terms of reference) by a finer diagram:

(14) **Simple Reference**   **Composite Reference**

Language: Sing.Terms$_0$ Predicates$_1$ **Language:** Sing.Terms$_0$ Predicates$_1$
                                                                      ⇓   ⇓

                ↓   ↓   **Posit:**   Individuals$_0$ Properties$_1$

                                                                      ⇓   ⇓

World: Individuals$_0$ Properties$_1$ **World:**   Properties$_2$ Properties$_3$

It is important to note that the level of posits need not be *fully* reducible to the level of reality. In a sense, it has a life of its own. Once the adequacy of the first-level mathematical representation of the higher-level formal features of reality is established, we can proceed *as if* mathematical truth were based on straight (direct) correspondence. (Explaining the exact standing of this posited level is another job for a substantive correspondence theory of truth.)

There are some similarities between this analysis of mathematical truth and the fictionalist's analysis (e.g., Field 1980, 1989), but there are also significant differences. For the fictionalist, (11) is false in the correspondence-with-reality sense; for the composite-correspondence theorist, (11) is true in that sense. For the fictionalist, physical applications of (11) are reducible to *physical* statements; for the composite-correspondence theorist, they are reducible to higher-order statements with both *formal* and *physical* constituents. For the fictionalist, reality has no irreducibly formal features; for the composite-correspondence theorist, it does. And so on. The fictionalist may be right in claiming that mathematical individuals are fictional posits, but he/she is wrong in thinking that mathematical theorems about these fictions are false, or that applied mathematical theorems are conservative extensions of physical truths.

5. An intricate mind—an intricate route from thought to reality

Let us conclude with a few underlying principles and a few philosophical consequences of the present approach to truth.

Truth, on the present analysis, is a standard for immanent thoughts of all forms, in all areas, and of all sizes, from the atomic to the logically complex, from the physical to the moral and mathematical, and from the single statement to the single theory and up to our system of knowledge as a whole. It is a standard for a positive answer to the critical transcendent question: is it so as a given statement, theory, or system of knowledge says it is? Are the things it talks about the way it says they are? Is the world as it says it is? Truth, on this conception, is a correspondence standard throughout, and when an immanent thought satisfies this standard, it is said to be true, or have the property of truth.

Thoughts, however, are creations of our mind, and the more intricate our mind, the more intricate the route from thought to reality. In a sense, it is because of the mind's ability to create or engage in thoughts that go beyond direct perceptual (sensory and/or rational) contacts with the world that a standard of truth is so critical.[26] The mind's propensity to transcend direct perception is not an obstacle, however; it is our greatest asset in seeking knowledge of reality. Given the meagerness of the information provided by direct perception, we have no choice but to forge intricate, circuitous, and at times messy (though ideally systematic) routes to reality. The greater our desire to know the world, the greater our need to experiment with new cognitive routes; and the more we experiment with new routes to reality, the greater our need for a standard of truth. We thus vacillate between venturing further and further in exploring reality and setting tighter and tighter restraints on our creative, adventurous minds.

In seeking to fathom reality, we use a wide variety of mental capacities. The availability of many of these capacities is, to a considerable degree, beyond our control. Partly, this is a matter of biology, partly of culture, history, and chance. Either way, we have no choice but to cognize the world through the prism of our present cognitive machinery, some of which is less than ideal for the task. But our cognitive resources are not completely beyond our control. The development of new areas of knowledge, new theories, and new ideas is always accompanied by the development of new concepts, new methods of proof and experimentation, new perspectives—in short, new cognitive tools of a variety of kinds.[27] All this means that the route from thought to reality is dynamic, intricate, complex, and multifaceted, a route that takes multiple forms and is constantly evolving.

In conceiving of truth as a standard for immanent thought having to do with its connection to reality, the present theory takes a holistic approach. By this we mean that it allows a multitude of patterns of such connections (including patterns involving nonvicious circularity), and in dealing with these connections it permits the (judicious) use of all our cognitive resources. This applies both to physical and to mathematical truth, and, indeed, knowledge. It means, among other things, that physical and mathematical knowledge may be attained by multiple combinations of (multiple) routes, spanning the whole

---

[26] Direct rational contact with the world (rational perception or intuition) is advocated by, e.g., Gödel (1947/1964/1990, 1953–9/1990).

[27] In the case of mathematics, the development of a first-order logical framework for the construction of theories is one example of a new cognitive tool.

spectrum of faculties, from sensory perception to conceptualization, categorization, abstraction, generalization, rational intuition, reflection, combinatorics, analysis, model building, experiment design, and others. And all these act in tandem to gain us access to different parts and aspects of reality: physical, formal, and so on.[28]

This holistic approach to truth and knowledge has the philosophical advantage of avoiding the minefields of both Platonism and empiricism. In allowing rational reflection to play a crucial role in mathematical knowledge, we eschew the problems of empiricism; in drawing a bridge between reason and experience we avoid the problems of Platonism. On the one hand, mathematics (or its veridical part) is genuinely grounded in the formal structure of reality; on the other hand, the reality in whose formal structure mathematics is grounded is the same reality that physics and other branches of science are grounded in. Mathematical truth is correspondence with the formal facets of reality, but these facets belong to the same reality that physical truth corresponds to (or to whose physical facets physical truth corresponds).

In eschewing mathematical Platonism, we avoid some of the most pressing problems of contemporary philosophy of mathematics, including Benacerraf's problems of *cognitive access* (1973) and *identity* (1965).

The problem of cognitive access is the problem of accessing those aspects of reality that are associated with the truth conditions of mathematical statements. The epistemology and semantics of mathematics must be closely connected, according to Benacerraf, so that (i) our knowledge of mathematical statements is knowledge of their truth, and (ii) the truth of mathematical statements is (in the case of knowable truths/falsehoods) a matter of conditions that are accessible to knowers. Now, Benacerraf rightly believes that neither empiricism nor Platonism can satisfy this requirement. But the outlook developed here has the potential of satisfying it. The problem of access can be solved by the combination of (i) a holistic methodology and (ii) the idea of indirect, composite, correspondence. This is achieved as follows: First, our outlook rejects the dualistic conception of reality characteristic of Platonism, so the problem of reaching mathematical reality from another, physical, reality, does not arise. Second, we do not require the existence of mathematical individuals, so the problem reduces to that of cognitive access to formal *features* of reality. Third, we show how the standard truth-conditions of first-order mathematics can be connected to higher-level formal facts. And fourth, we allow new cognitive routes to reality, for example, routes generated by a combination of rational and sensory capacities, hence new avenues for accessing

---

[28] This conception of cognitive access, I should emphasize, is holistic but not coherentist. Contact with reality is mandatory for truth, though it may take an abundance of routes and a great variety of interconnections. See also Horgan (2001) for good examples of indirect routes of empirical cognition.

Forms of Correspondence 177

the formal features of reality. (An extended discussion and examples must be left for another essay.)

Benacerraf's identity problem is the problem of the identity of mathematical individuals. There are many distinct, yet isomorphic (standard) models of first-order arithmetic, including models in which the same numerals are assigned different referents. For example, in Zermelo's model, the numeral '2' is assigned one object—the set {{Ø}}—while in von Neumann's model it is assigned a different object—the set {Ø, {Ø}}.[29] Which object is the real number two? Our (tentative) account of mathematical truth above shows how one can think of mathematical truth so this problem does not arise. Both Zermelo's and von Neumann's numerals are posits representing the second-level property TWO, and since being TWO is a formal property, all isomorphic systems of posits for it are equally good. In other words, Zermelo's 2 represents a second-level property, TWO, just as well as von Neumann's 2 (in their respective systems). In constructing, say, numerical posits, we have to give them a definite identity, but what identity we give them is immaterial, so long as the result is a systematic representation of cardinality properties.

Should we say, then, that the real 2 is the second-level property being TWO? From the point of view of our tentative account of mathematical truth above, the answer is: yes. But the tentative status of our account suggests that this is still an open question. Another way to put this is that from an *immanent* perspective (the perspective of the proposed account) the answer is positive, but from a *transcendent* perspective, a perspective from which we acknowledge the possibility of alternative accounts of mathematical truth, the question is open.

Allowing a posited layer of mathematical individuals enables us to deal with another thorny ontological problem: the problem of the immense ontology of contemporary mathematics. So long as this 'immense ontology' is a collection of posited objects, its size, by itself, poses no (genuine) ontological problem. If, and to the extent that, a large layer of posited entities is required, or even instrumental, for a precise, informative theory of the formal structure of reality (i.e., of the laws governing the formal features of objects in the world), then positing such a large layer is warranted.

Another advantage of the present approach is its ability to clarify the relation between the truth of statements and the truth of theories. One natural way to deal with the truth of theories is to say that a theory is true iff all its sentences are true. This view, however, is too simplistic. Suppose you have two theories, T_1 and T_2, such that for some sentence S, $S \in T_1$ and $\sim S \in T_2$, yet T_1 and T_2 both correspond to reality. For example, let T_1 be Zermelo arithmetic, let T_2 be von Neumann arithmetic, and let S be 'Successor {Ø} = {{Ø}}'. Then S is true in T_1 and false in T_2; hence, according to the above solution, T_1 and T_2 cannot be both true. Yet T_1 and T_2 are both accurate arithmetic theories, so if one of

---

[29] Here 'Ø' names the empty set, and '{x,y}' names the set of x and y.

them is true, so must the other be. Our analysis offers a simple solution to this conundrum: T_1 and T_2 represent the system of laws governing the behavior of cardinalities in two different ways. This is not different from the decimal and binary systems representing the same mathematical operations in different ways. The fact that 'Successor {Ø} = {{Ø}}' is true in Zermelo arithmetic and false in von Neumann arithmetic is no more problematic than the fact that '10 + 10 = 100' is true in binary arithmetic and false in decimal arithmetic. This phenomenon reminds us that truth, even correspondence truth, is a matter not just of the world but also of the mind.

Let me end with a general methodological point. It is important to realize that the task of a substantive correspondence theory of truth is not to give an algorithm for figuring out the route of correspondence in each and every case or for each and every true sentence in our language. That task is not only unachievable but also pointless. We have already introduced the analogy between the task of figuring out the truth conditions of mixed sentences and the task of carrying out an engineering project based on a compendium of (pure) scientific principles. In the same way that it is absurd to demand that the scientist or even the engineer develops a single algorithm describing all possible applications of all possible combinations of all 'pure' scientific laws, so it is absurd to demand that the theorist of truth develops such an algorithm for the truth (correspondence) conditions of all possible or even existent immanent thoughts. The task of a substantive correspondence theory of truth is a challenging task, but it is not an impossible task. The task is to identify and explain the central principles of correspondence, show how they are connected in principle, demonstrate their adequacy by well-chosen examples, and respond to pertinent objections. The task is not to construct an algorithm that tells what the (full) truth conditions of each and every sentence are and how all their particular elements intertwine.[30]

References

Barnard, R. & Horgan, T. (2006). Truth as mediated correspondence. *Monist* 89: 31–50.
Barnard, R. & Horgan, T. (2013). The synthetic unity of truth. In N. J. L. L. Pedersen & C. D. Wright (eds.), *Truth and Pluralism: Current Debates* (180–196). New York: Oxford University Press.
Benacerraf, P. (1965). What numbers could not be. *Philosophical Review* 74: 47–73.
Benacerraf, P. (1973). Mathematical truth. *Journal of Philosophy* 70: 661–680.

---

[30] I would like to thank the audiences at the conference on pluralism and deflationism about truth at the University of Connecticut, the 2010 Southern California Philosophy conference, participants of the philosophy colloquium at UC Irvine, and the 2010 annual meeting of the Israeli Philosophical Association (where this paper was presented as a keynote address) for thoughtful and stimulating comments. Special thanks are due to Cory Wright and Michael Lynch for helpful discussions following the pluralism conference, and to Nikolaj Pedersen for written comments that considerably improved the paper.

Cartwright, N. (1983). *How the Laws of Physics Lie.* Oxford: Oxford University Press.
Field, H. (1980). *Science without Numbers: A Defense of Nominalism.* Princeton, NJ: Princeton University Press.
Field, H. (1989). *Realism, Mathematics, and Modality.* Oxford: Basil Blackwell.
Gödel, K. (1947/1964/1990). What is Cantor's continuum problem? In Feferman, S., J. W. Dawson Jr., S. C. Kleene, G. H. Moore, R. M. Solovay, & J. van Heijenoort (eds.), *Collected Works of Kurt Gödel Vol. II: 1938–1974* (254–270). New York: Oxford University Press.
Gödel, K. (1953-9/1990). Is mathematics syntax of language? In Feferman, S., J. W. Dawson Jr., S. C. Kleene, G. H. Moore, R. M. Solovay, & J. van Heijenoort (eds.), *Collected Works of Kurt Gödel Vol. II: 1938–1974* (334–362). New York: Oxford University Press.
Horgan, T. (2001). Contextual semantics and metaphysical realism: truth as indirect correspondence. In M. P. Lynch (ed.), *The Nature of Truth* (67–95). Cambridge, MA: MIT Press.
Lynch, M. P. (2001). A functionalist theory of truth. In his (ed.), *The Nature of Truth* (723–749). Cambridge, MA: MIT Press.
Lynch, M. P. (2004a). *True to Life: Why Truth Matters.* Cambridge, MA: MIT Press.
Lynch, M. P. (2004b). Truth and multiple realizability. *Australasian Journal of Philosophy* 82: 384–408.
Lynch, M. P. (2005). Replies to critics. *Philosophical Books* 46: 331–342.
Lynch, M. P. (2009). *Truth as One and Many.* Oxford: Oxford University Press.
Sher, G. (1991). *The Bounds of Logic: A Generalized Viewpoint.* Cambridge, MA: MIT Press.
Sher, G. (1996). Did Tarski commit 'Tarski's fallacy'? *Journal of Symbolic Logic* 61: 653–686.
Sher, G. (1998). On the possibility of a substantive theory of truth. *Synthese* 117: 133–172.
Sher, G. (1999). Is logic a theory of the obvious? *European Review of Philosophy* 4: 207–238.
Sher, G. (2001). The formal-structural view of logical consequence. *Philosophical Review* 110: 241–261.
Sher, G. (2002). Logical consequence: an epistemic outlook. *Monist* 85: 555–579.
Sher, G. (2004). In search of a substantive theory of truth. *Journal of Philosophy* 101: 5–36.
Sher, G. (2008). Tarski's thesis. In D. Patterson (ed.), *New Essays on Tarski and Philosophy* (300–339). Oxford: Oxford University Press.
Tappolet, C. (1997). Mixed inferences: a problem for pluralism about truth predicates. *Analysis* 57: 209–210.
Tappolet, C. (2000). Truth pluralism and many-valued logics: a reply to Beall. *Philosophical Quarterly* 50: 382–385.
Tarski, A. (1933/1983). The concept of truth in formalized languages. In his *Logic, Semantics, Metamathematics* (152–278), ed. J. Corcoran. Indianapolis: Hackett.
Wright, C. D. (2005). Remarks on the functionalization of pluralist approaches to truth. *Synthese* 145: 1–28.
Wright, C. D. (2007). *Truth & Cognition.* Doctoral dissertation, University of California, San Diego.
Wright, C. D. (2010). Truth, Ramsification, and the pluralist's revenge. *Australasian Journal of Philosophy* 88: 265–283.
Wright, C. D. (2012). Is pluralism about truth inherently unstable? *Philosophical Studies* 159: 89–105.
Wright, C. J. G. (1992). *Truth and Objectivity.* Cambridge, MA: Harvard University Press.

{ 9 }

The Synthetic Unity of Truth
Robert Barnard & Terence Horgan

1. Introduction

Long philosophical tradition has come to recognize that assertoric language comes in many varieties, as do the forms of thought expressed by such language. What ties these forms together and at the same time sets them apart is their concern for truth. From the outside, this genuine concern for truth unifies them; they all seek to state and assert what is true. But seen from within, the supposed unity of truth across discourses appears to be replaced by irreconcilable difference and distance between various discourses. How statements and assertions come to be called true can appear to be very different. All forms of assertoric discourse, and all thoughts expressible by such discourse, claim to be concerned with truth; all claim to have something to say about how truth works; most seem to disagree.[1]

This same philosophical tradition long held that truth was a kind of agreement between thoughts or statements and the world: the so-called correspondence theory. But this unitary conception of truth has also been fractured. The tensions between and among metaphysics and epistemology and theories of language have twisted apart this intuitive view, replacing it with theories that preserve agreement but throw out the world, theories that place successful action before accurate representation, theories that deny that truth is a property (or at least a substantive property), theories that treat truth ascriptions as redundant reformulations of first-order assertions, and even theories that offer noncognitive expressivist accounts. Truth has been framed in formal terms by some, and by others as whatever satisfies collections of simple platitudes.

---

[1] Hereafter, in order to simplify exposition, we will usually focus explicitly only on assertoric discourse itself, rather than on both assertions and the thoughts they express. But our discussion will also be applicable, mutatis mutandis, to thoughts.

For many, the demand that truth respect the diversity and divisions within language and thought has become the demand that truth itself be divided and diverse, that truth be plural. This pluralist vision finds articulation in many ways—for example, by multiplying predicates or properties or by rethinking what a truth predicate or a truth property does.

Our view is that truth is still correspondence and that this claim can be maintained in the face of the differences and diversity one finds within language. We maintain that even as truth looks and feels different from within various discourses, it remains correspondence. Truth is plural, except that under the broader heading of correspondence, it isn't.

This paper will articulate a version of correspondence theory that holds that truth is always correspondence, but that respects the divisions and distinctions in thought and language that drive many to embrace pluralism about truth.[2] By separating questions about the nature of truth from questions about the correct ontology, we occupy a metaphysically neutral position. When assertoric language is deployed in such a way that its singular terms and unnegated existential quantifications carry ontological commitment to particulars that putatively belong to the right ontology, and its predicates carry ontological commitment to properties and relations that putatively belong to the right ontology, then correspondence functions in what we call a *direct* way. But when language is truth apt, but does not purport to be directly aligned with the objects, properties, and relations in the right ontological story, then correspondence functions in an *indirect* way. We hold that truth is always correspondence but is rarely direct correspondence. Thus, we shall argue that propositions native to radically different discourses can all be literally true, and true via correspondence, although very often their truth will constitute an indirect kind of correspondence that does not require the right ontology to include objects, properties, or relations answering to the proposition's singular, predicative, or existential-quantificational constituents.

2. Preliminary assumptions

We want to begin by making explicit three meta-metaphysical assumptions that we think function as a sort of common sense foundation to thinking about truth.

(1) There is a universe, and it has a definite nature.

---

[2] Our specific purpose here is to explicitly compare our favored version of the correspondence theory to alethic pluralism. For related discussions of the general approach to truth we describe here, see, e.g., Barnard & Horgan (2006), Horgan (2001), Horgan & Potrč (2008a).

This is a form of minimal metaphysical realism. It is hard for us to imagine how things might be otherwise, and theoretical interest in questions about the nature of truth seems to presuppose such a minimal realism.

(2) The universe must have a nature that is consistent with, and to a certain degree determinative of, the world appearing as it does in experience.[3]

This assumption functions as a negative, but very weak, constraint on how the world might be.[4]

(3) How the world appears in experience supervenes on how the world is. Thus, changes in appearance are accompanied by changes in the world.

We do not make assumptions about what changes in the world must be like, merely that there is some sense in which such changes are possible.

Thus, we assume that there is a world and that the world is a certain way. Since the world includes human beings and their activities, part of how the world is will be determined by what humans do, but human thought and action are part of the world without in any deep sense "constituting" it.[5] What does seem to follow here is that how things seem to be is constrained by how things are and that the world could not be any way that would yield appearances radically different from those one has every day. Among the apparent contributions of humans to the world are thoughts, statements, assertions, and propositions, the sorts of things that purport to make claims about how the world is. These, we assume, can get the world right or wrong. This is the core of the concept of truth, and also the impetus for the traditional picture of truth as correspondence.

3. Correspondence, ideology, and ideological mediation

On the traditional picture, a thought or proposition is true when it agrees with or corresponds to how things are or, in other words, agrees with how the world is, in whole or part. We have suggested that there may be more than one way

---

[3] It bears emphasis that this assumption does *not* require the appearances to be veridical, or by-and-large veridical. One way for the universe to be consistent with one's having the experiences one does is for one to be a lifelong envatted brain.

[4] This intuitive position is argued for at length by Tienson (1989).

[5] While there is a definite contribution made by human thought, language, and behavior to how the world is, we do not see this contribution as playing an overriding role in the constitution of how the world actually is. There is a special place in our theory of truth for the mediating influence of human thought and language, but there is no corresponding role with respect to the nature of the correct ontology.

in which correspondence works, but we hold that the various species of truth fall under a common genus.

Different kinds of discourse vary significantly in the uses to which they deploy singular terms, predicates, and idioms of existential quantification. We will call such linguistic expressions a discourse's *positing apparatus*; we will call the deployment of such expressions *positing*; and sometimes (using what Carnap called the 'material mode' of philosophical discourse) we will speak of the *posits* of a given discourse—the items the discourse talks about.[6] Various discourses deploy positing apparatus in different ways, and these differences constitute different forms of *ideology* (as we will call it). One kind of discourse posits items like tables, chairs, desks, and other 'middle-sized dry goods'; another posits items like corporations, nations, and universities; another posits items like electrons and quarks; another posits items like natural numbers, geometrical figures, and vector spaces; and so forth. Ideological differences among various discourses extend too to the kinds of *features* that they posit and attribute to the items they posit.

On the generic version of the correspondence conception of truth that we ourselves advocate, truth is an *ideologically mediated* relation between statements, on the one hand, and the world on the other hand. Such mediation is a matter of two correlative aspects of a given form of discourse, operating in tandem: first, the discourse's ideology itself (its range of posits), and second, the semantic norms that govern the correct assertoric use of statements deploying these posits. A statement corresponds to the world—in other words, is true—just in case the world is in fact one of the ways it would have to be, under the semantic norms operative in the given discourse, in order for the statement to be deploying the discourse's posits in an assertorically correct way.

Ideological posits, on this way of construing generic correspondence, are constructs of language and thought.[7] In general, in order for a statement deploying such constructs to be true, the statement's positing apparatus need not map directly onto objects and properties that belong to the correct ontology. Rather, the semantic standards governing mediated correspondence,

---

[6] Here and throughout, it is important to bear in mind that the approach to truth we are describing in this paper is applicable to philosophical discourse too, including the discourse in which the approach itself is being set forth. If (for example) in the course of philosophical discourse one makes the material-mode claim, 'Corporations are among the posits of much everyday discourse', one does not thereby incur ontological commitment to putative items in the correct ontology that would answer to the category 'corporation'.

[7] We speak freely of posits and ideology and discourses without telling a special story about such things, because the broader story about ideology applies even to the discourse of posits, ideologies, and discourses. If such things are part of the correct ontology, then using those terms in ontologically committed ways is harmless (and to be hoped for). If the correct ontology does not contain such bits, then they are just more posits—so that statements such as 'The statements in a discourse will posit objects, properties, and relations ideologically, but without genuine ontological commitment' will, if true, be true on the basis of ideologically mediated indirect correspondence to the world. For related discussion, see Horgan & Potrč (2008a, ch. 3).

within a given form of discourse, can perfectly well operate in such a way that (1) the world is as it would have to be, according to those standards, in order for the statement to be assertorically correct, and yet (2) the statement deploys a positing apparatus that does not pick out items in the correct ontology.

Ideological mediation of the correspondence relation can work in significantly different ways across different forms of discourse—a fact that gives this conception of correspondence the flexibility to smoothly accommodate much of the motivation for alethic pluralism (about which more below). But one important coarse-grained distinction is between *indirect* and *direct* mediation. In cases of indirect mediation, a statement counts as assertorically correct under the operative semantic standards (i.e., it counts as true) even if its positing apparatus does not pick out items in the correct ontology. In cases of direct mediation, on the other hand, the operative semantic standards work in such a way that the statement's positing apparatus is being deployed in an *ontologically committal* way; thus (to speak in the material mode), the statement is true only if its posits are items in the correct ontology.

It bears emphasizing that there is a way of construing truth conditions that is both very familiar and also entirely consistent with the claim that truth often consists of indirectly mediated correspondence to the world—namely, the construal of a proposition's truth conditions as comprising a set of *possible worlds*—or perhaps a set of 'centered' possible worlds, with centers corresponding to the actual spatiotemporal location of the person affirming the proposition at a specific place and time. (Possible worlds themselves can be construed in various ways—for instance, as maximal properties instantiable by the whole cosmos, 'ways the world might be'.) This possible-worlds approach to truth conditions does not by itself impose, as a requirement for the truth of a given proposition, that there are objects in the correct ontology answering to all the proposition's singular or existential-quantificational constituents, or that there are properties and relations in the correct ontology answering to all the proposition's predicative constituents.

We contend that cases where one employs discourse in a manner that purports to describe how things are in the correct ontology are rare, whatever the correct ontology might be. In our view, the fact that the ideological commitments incurred by various discourses diverge sufficiently to make alethic pluralism plausible constitutes evidence that most actual talk is governed by indirectly mediated correspondence standards rather than by directly mediated correspondence standards. So we maintain that the semantic standards operative in most forms of discourse are indirect-mediation standards (henceforth, IM standards) rather than direct-mediation standards (DM standards). To mention just one plausible example, among many that could be chosen, consider this statement:

(EU) The European Union has 27 member nations.

This statement is unproblematically true (in June 2011), even if (as seems plausible) the right ontology does not include items answering to posits like nation and the European Union. As another potential example, consider this:

(EP) Two is the only even prime number.

Again, statement (EP) is certainly true even if the right ontology does not contain numbers or properties like even-ness or prime-ness in its inventory.[8]

4. Correspondence and metaphysical neutrality

The traditional correspondence picture often turns on substantive metaphysical assumptions that we claim are dispensable. The first is the assumption that the correspondence relation only comes in one version. The second metaphysical assumption is manifested in cases when a statement is true. There, a common presupposition has been that there is a unique 'truth maker' for the statement, involving items in the correct ontology that answer directly to the posits deployed in the statement. Thus, despite its intuitive appeal, the acceptability of the correspondence conception of truth has often turned on whether or not one was willing to countenance certain classes of entities and truth makers.[9] For example, in many cases if a materialist desired to speak of numbers, then correspondence mathematical truth was presumptively ruled out because it seemed to require numbers and number-involving states of affairs in the correct ontology. Likewise, in metaethics, correspondence accounts of moral truth are usually ruled out for metaphysical reasons. Similar dilemmas confront a variety of other discourses.

Our contention is that this is approach is upside down. We maintain that correspondence is properly seen as ontologically neutral among any substantive metaphysical view that is consistent with assumption (1) above. To make things plain, we hold that truth is correspondence regardless of whether the correct ontology is Parmenidean monist, or materialist, or Platonist, or Cartesian dualist, or whatever. Moreover, numerous claims that ordinarily are regarded as unproblematically true—claims within many different forms of discourse—really *are* true, regardless whether the right ontology is Parmenidean monist,

---

[8] To be fair, if the correct ontology did contain, e.g. numbers and properties like being-even and being-prime, then although (EP) would still be true under everyday IM semantic standards, it also would be true under DM semantic standards. Thus, although it is plausible that ordinary mathematical discourse does not require there to be mathematical objects and properties in the right ontology, it is also plausible that the ordinary mathematical discourse does not preclude this possibility either.

[9] This is seen clearly in, e.g., Benacerraf (1973). There, Benacerraf argues that despite its intuitive plausibility in many discourses, correspondence truth does not seem plausible for mathematical discourse because it appears to be committed to Platonic entities and nonempirical modes of knowing them. Thus, the decision about how to think about truth is made on the basis of certain presuppositions about the correct ontology and about human epistemic capacities.

materialist, et cetera. These claims are true because they really do correspond to the world, even if (as is typically the case) their positing apparatus does not map directly onto objects, properties, and relations that belong to the correct ontology. On our view, a metaphysically neutral account of truth is a transcendental condition for the possibility of a correct metaphysical theory; statements regarded as unproblematically true, from various different forms of discourse, must turn out to be capable of corresponding to the world (regardless of what the correct ontology actually is). Truth, in this sense, comes first.[10]

Once one acknowledges that conceptual mediation takes place at all, worries about how to distinguish the 'degree' of mediation of one discourse context from another become secondary. That competent speakers of a language can navigate such shifts in degree of mediation or from one discourse context to another is not at the heart of any dispute. Rather, an objector might insist that the question of determining whether a statement is true would require that one be able to determine and specify the context and degree of mediation. To this we reply that in practice people communicate quite well without being able to articulate such specifications, so competent conformity to the contextually operative standards does not turn upon the capacity to make such standards explicit.[11] Furthermore, it has always been the case that explaining the nature of truth is a distinct project from explaining when particular statements are true and is also a distinct project from explaining the cognitive processes that constitute competent assertoric behavior within various different forms of discourse. Here we are only addressing the question of truth's nature.

According to the picture we have just sketched, truth is always correspondence. Apparent differences in how truth works in different discourses or ontological worries about truthmaking are finessed by strictly adhering to a stance of ontological neutrality. We do assume there is a world and that how the world appears is a function of how the world is, but we have nothing substantive to say here about the character of the world's actual ontological makeup.[12] Metaphysical theorizing about the correct ontology of the world is a difficult and methodologically subtle business—so much so that some might even conclude that well-warranted beliefs about this matter cannot be had.

---

[10] One way to formulate this transcendental neutrality requirement is as follows. It is a very strong—albeit defeasible—constraint on theorizing about truth that regardless what ontology one embraces, most statements that are ordinarily regarded as unproblematically true should turn out to be both *capable* (given that ontology) of being true and also *in fact* true. Although, in principle, abductive considerations governing theory construction could end up evidentially favoring a semantical-cum-ontological theory according to which most statements ordinarily regarded as unproblematically true would turn out to be incapable of being true, there is an enormously strong default presumption against any such semantics-cum-ontological theory.

[11] For elaboration of this theme, see Horgan & Potrč, (2008a: ch. 6; 2008b)

[12] It is fair to say that if we did discuss substantive ontology here the authors would disagree about several things. Nevertheless, in the face of such disagreement, we two can agree about the nature of truth. The issues are separate.

Synthetic Unity of Truth 187

But, whatever the right story might be about matters of ontology and about whether such matters are epistemologically tractable, truth is abundant. Truth is *ideologically mediated* correspondence, and in general it can be expected to be some form of *indirectly* mediated correspondence.

Moreover, one can be confident that *knowledge* of what is true is often possible, for everyday standards for what counts as epistemically warranted assertability, in a given form of discourse, can be expected to be closely linked to the *semantic* standards operative in such discourse. This is an insight well worth retaining from the verificationism of logical positivism and from pragmatist and neo-pragmatist attempts to construe truth epistemically—even though we contend that semantically correct affirmability (i.e., truth) cannot be reduced to some form of epistemically warranted affirmability.[13]

5. More on mediated correspondence

There are four issues that deserve mention in connection with mediated correspondence and ideological mediation. First, with respect to vagueness, depending upon the form of discourse in play, many of the objects, properties, and relations that are ideological posits of that discourse are vague—for example, vague with respect to synchronic composition and/or diachronic boundaries (in the case of objects) and vague with respect to range of instantiation (in the case of properties and relations).[14] We maintain, but will not argue here, that whatever the actual correct ontology is, it does not contain vague objects, properties, or relations.[15] This means that, where vague posits are concerned, the operative kind of truth-constituting correspondence is always IM correspondence.

Second, it is essential to recognize that IM correspondence is the default stance one must take toward the truth of a statement in any discourse. If one embraces the intuitively plausible idea that truth is some sort of agreement between a statement and the world, then the central question one must confront is how to characterize this relation of agreement. Correspondence is the natural way to do this. But when this intuitive idea is combined with the working assumption that a theory of truth should be ontologically neutral, then the most plausible way to proceed is to let the default construal of truth be what we have called indirectly mediated correspondence.

---

[13] This theme is developed most recently in Horgan & Potrč (2008a: 104–106), and in related writings of Horgan's cited there.

[14] By our lights, this is a material-mode statement that is being asserted within a form of philosophical discourse that is itself governed by IC semantic standards. Thus, it is only ideologically committed to vague objects and properties, not ontologically committed to such items. Cf. note 6 above.

[15] For a recent defense of this claim, see Horgan & Potrč (2008a: 20–28), plus writings by Horgan and by Horgan & Potrč cited there.

Third, given a mediated-correspondence approach, the semantic standards that emerge will probably include a place for some statements whose truth turns on the meanings of the terms in use. Such statements would be analytic truths and would be limit cases of indirectly mediated correspondence—limit cases in which the semantic norms by themselves render correctly affirmable the relevant statements deploying the posits in question, quite apart from how the world is. Indirect ideological mediation does all the truth-guaranteeing work by itself, so to speak, so that there is nothing that world itself needs to contribute. (For example, a plausible candidate is the statement 'there exists a natural number that is not even'. It is plausible that indirect ideological mediation, despite here deploying such posits as natural numbers and non-evenness, guarantees the truth of this statement, regardless of how the world is.)[16] Analytic truth, construed as a limit case of indirectly mediated correspondence in which the semantic standards governing the discourse-posits guarantee truth all by themselves, resides at one end of a spectrum of instances of mediated correspondence; at the other end are cases of directly mediated correspondence, in which a statement's posits constitute outright ontological commitments.[17]

Fourth and more centrally, mediation is not a mysterious or especially complicated notion. In any case, where a statement is true, that statement is articulated in a particular language against a particular conceptual framework. This fact, together with how the world is and the usual issues of tensing, indexicality, and so on, contextually frame the statement within its discourse. Consider this simple illustrative case of how directly mediated correspondence and indirectly mediated correspondence might be related. With apologies to those with a taste for desert landscapes, let us suppose that among the things in the ultimate ontology are trees. In fact, let us imagine a toy-world, a domain containing many trees. This is a simple domain and so its ontology contains just trees. So statements of the form 'this is a tree' or 'some tree exists' would be the sort of thing that would count as true in a direct-mediation way. Some claims about how

---

[16] Analytic truths are a possible theoretical consequence of our view. Directly mediated correspondence is the minimal degree of ideological mediation. By hypothesis, there would need to be some degree of mediation that is maximal. This means analytic truths are possible, but still part of the mediated correspondence framework. In the particular case above, analytic truths with respect to mathematics would be unnecessary if the ultimate ontology were Platonist in the appropriate ways. If number objects and properties such as being-prime were part of the ultimate ontology, then mathematical claims would be true in a directly mediated way. If the ultimate ontology contained sets then there could be some ideologically mediated correspondence to constructions on sets.

[17] Suppose that statements deploying moral predicates operate semantically in accordance with some form of meta-ethical expressivism. If so, then another potential kind of limit case arises, one involving truth ascriptions to moral statements. Such truth ascriptions would express 'fused' semantic and moral appraisal and would be subject to expressivist treatment themselves. Likewise for meta-linguistic statements asserting, of specified moral statements, that they 'correspond to the world'. For development of this line of thought in a way that is congenial to the general approach to truth described in the present chapter, see Horgan & Timmons (2006).

many trees are found in the domain would also be true in a direct-mediation way, even when the right ontology (at least for this hypothetical toy-world) contains no numbers, for such claims can be rendered entirely in terms of the quantification plus identity plus the predicate 'is a tree'. For instance, 'exactly two trees exist' might be rendered thus: There exist x and y such that x is a tree and y is a tree and not $(x = y)$ and for every z, either $z = x$ or $z = y$.

Among the other features we might want to attribute to this arboreal domain might be forests, glades, clearings, and so on. But none of these are counted as elements of the world's ontology—only trees. Certainly claims like 'there exist forests' would be true. They would be made true by the nature of this world, the ontology of which contains trees; but they would not be true under the stricter standards of directly mediated correspondence. Instead, they are true under mediated-correspondence standards. Loosely, the concept of 'forest', as something like 'a fairly large and expansive bunch of trees', mediates the connection between the tree-filled world and the discourse of forests. Here the mediation is via *compositional* posits and is indirect because—by stipulation—this is a world in whose ontology there are only trees and not tree-composites. (Of course, in worlds more complex than this toy-world—e.g., our own actual world—there are vastly many potentially useful ways of introducing posits into language and thought and vastly many associated modes of indirect conceptual mediation whereby talk deploying such posits could exhibit indirectly mediated correspondence to the world.)

Epistemically, any evidence one has in favor of true tree-talk as applied to the envisioned toy-world will likewise license forest-talk as true. But even in hypothetical cases, absent specific evidence, we should be able to assert that if there were a region full of trees, we would be permitted to assert the truth of the proposition that the region is forested. This, in part, is how correct assertability can diverge from epistemic warrant. Metaphysically, to intentionally employ directly mediated correspondence standards involves making an explicit ancillary commitment about the nature of the world's ontology. To say, in a deliberately ontological mode of discourse, that the universe is made only of matter, is to suppose that directly mediated correspondence standards apply in matter-talk cases and that all the other truth-apt talk is not subject to directly mediated correspondence standards.

Now, because we are officially neutral regarding the metaphysics of the situation, we might invert the ontology here. Suppose (or stipulate) that the right ontology for this hypothetical world includes only forests (but not trees!). Our true-by-directly-mediated correspondence discourse will now contain propositions asserting that forests exist. Talk of trees will still be true (because to be a forest is to be a bunch of trees), but true under *indirectly* mediated correspondence standards. The proposition that there is tree here will be true, but not true because the ontology of this world includes a tree; instead, it is true because the world contains a forest (or forest-parts).

From this it is clear to see that indirectly mediated correspondence is very much about how the way the world is with respect to its ontology combined with the granularity of our descriptions of it. Indirectly mediated correspondence is what underwrites the fact that it is true that there is a university here, even though Gilbert Ryle's visitor only finds students and buildings and faculty and grounds and so on. In both cases, correspondence with the world makes the propositions in question true.

We have just been discussing simple cases of mediation. No doubt, some philosophically interesting cases are mediated to a greater degree, but not in a way that is any more mysterious than these cases. The degree of mediation, if you want to call it that, does not change the fact that the proposition is made true in virtue of its correspondence with how the world is. It is correspondence that counts, regardless of whether this correspondence is conceptually mediated in a direct manner or instead is conceptually mediated in one or another indirect manner.

This concludes our articulation of our positive view. Truth is always correspondence—ideologically mediated correspondence. Almost always, when one talks about a statement being true one is appealing to a relation of indirectly mediated—rather than directly mediated—correspondence between statement and world. Only when the semantic standards in a given discourse require a statement's positing apparatus to map directly onto items in the actual correct ontology is DM correspondence in play. Because we take truth to be independent of metaphysics, we accept that it is always a methodologically complex question whether DM correspondence semantic standards are in play. The default assumption for almost any discourse other than what goes on in the so-called 'ontology room' is that the discourse is governed by one or another kind of IM correspondence semantic standards.[18]

We have suggested that this approach to truth as ideologically mediated correspondence can respect the considerations that motivate a pluralist theory of truth while resisting pluralist urges at the same time. Let us turn now to the question of alethic pluralism.

6. Correspondence and pluralism

The alethic pluralist maintains both that truth has more than one form or nature and that this must be so in order to cover all the cases where one wants to employ truth-talk. The case for pluralism almost always turns

---

[18] This point, which is quite obvious from a standpoint of ontological neutrality, is obscured by the tradition of articulating correspondence accounts of truth by reading the actual ontology off of some set of preferred exemplary statements. The universe, we maintain, is not merely the domain of cats and their mats.

upon the inability to articulate how truth works in each specific discourse, given a particular theory of truth. Because truth-talk exceeds the bounds of the proposed theory of truth, a multiplication of theories is claimed to be necessary; this might involve the multiplication of properties or relations or kinds of truth.

We ourselves recognize the multiplication of discourses and contexts, but we remain unconvinced that this demands a real pluralism about truth. We maintain that there are many species of correspondence that fall under a single unified genus—namely, ideologically mediated correspondence, including its limit cases (e.g., directly mediated correspondence and analytic truth). Is our view a pluralist view about truth? Merely having more than one kind of semantic standard in play is insufficient for pluralism, since the different semantic standards could be tracking the same underlying property or relation.[19] We are committed to multiple, contextually determined, semantic standards, yes. But does our view require a multiplication of truth properties or truth relations?

From the perspective of the view itself, the query just posed is best regarded as posing two distinct questions rather than just one. First, there is the ontological question: on our view, does the correct ontology include more than one truth property or truth relation? Second, there is a question about the workings of the notion of truth within and across the variety of different forms of discourse: are different discourses, singly or jointly, theoretically committed to more than one truth property or truth relation? Let us address these questions one at a time.

Concerning the first question, one must appreciate that our construal of truth is applicable to much philosophical discourse and, indeed, is reflexively applicable to philosophical discourse about truth itself. So, since numerous uses of truth-talk work disquotationally in a manner that conforms to Tarski's schema (T), such applications of the truth predicate thereby inherit key semantic features of the first-order statements to which they are being applied. In particular, in a discourse context in which a first-order statement p is itself governed by IM semantic standards, governance by IM standards will carry over—via schema (T)—to the metalinguistic statement attributing truth to p. This means that the statement ascribing truth to p is only ideologically committed—not ontologically committed—to the posited attribute of truth.

Given this lack of ontological commitment, there are at least two reasons to deny that the correct ultimate ontology includes any relations of indirectly mediated correspondence. First, theoretical parsimony militates against such

---

[19] This point is familiar to anyone who has ever considered moral relativism at length. As Herodotus famously noted, one may eat or burn one's honored dead, but what is important is that relative to one's cultural context, one is committed to showing respect for the dead. Different behaviors reflect sameness of moral principle.

relations. Second, truth ascriptions governed by IM semantic standards are typically vague in a way that mirrors the vagueness of the first-order statements to which truth is ascribed. So, if the right ontology were to include relations of IM correspondence, presumably these would be ontologically vague. But we deny that the right ontology includes any vague objects of properties of relations.

Does the correct ontology include the relation of *directly* mediated correspondence? Our proposed treatment of truth is neutral on this matter, as far as we can tell. But even if the answer is yes, this would not amount to alethic pluralism at the level of ontology, since the correct ontology would contain only one kind of truth-relation, that is to say, DM correspondence. (IM correspondence would be a posit of semantic discourse without being part of the correct ontology—but would be none the worse for that.)

Turn now to the second question posed above: are different discourses, singly or jointly, theoretically committed to more than one truth property or truth relation? The pertinent kind of commitment being asked about is *ideological* commitment rather than ontological commitment. (This is one lesson of our remarks about the first question.) A key consideration here is the fact that various forms of discourse, despite their distinctive and ideologically diverse deployments of the positing apparatus of language, typically interpenetrate one another fairly smoothly, working together as an integrated whole. One reason why is that some uses of positing apparatus are shared in common across the different discourses—including, in particular, the fact that they all deploy the notion of truth. Given this commonality, the default answer to the second question is: no, the different discourses are all ideologically committed to one and the same property of truth.

Although this answer would be difficult to sustain if one were to insist that this common property is always *directly* mediated language-world correspondence, the answer fits smoothly with the contention that truth is the more generic feature of ideologically mediated correspondence. Ideological mediation takes many forms, depending on the contextually operative semantic standards governing the use of linguistic positing apparatus. Most of these are forms of indirectly mediated correspondence; directly mediated correspondence is really just a limit case of ideologically mediated correspondence—the most constrained and disciplined species, under this wider genus.

One significant advantage of our mediated-correspondence approach, as compared to alethic pluralism, is that ours provides a smooth and natural way to address the familiar problem of 'mixed inferences'—a problem that causes enormous trouble for alethic pluralism.[20] At root, the problem is that valid deductive inferences are truth preserving, but if one accepts that there

---

[20] It might be plausible to identify genuine pluralist theories of truth as those that suffer from mixed inference problems. For a fuller discussion of the problem and its significance for pluralism, see Tappolet (1997, 2000), Beall (2000), and Pedersen (2006, 2010).

Synthetic Unity of Truth

is more than one kind of truth, then, when an inference proceeds from premises that differ in the kinds of truth they possess, one must explain what sort of truth, if any, the conclusion has inherited from the premises. If a view asserts that there are multiple distinct truth-properties (as does genuine alethic pluralism), then ordinary deductive-inferential practices seem to be compromised.

We respect the variety of assertoric discourse-forms. We hold that different epistemic and semantic standards can be in play in different discourses. We deny, however, that this results in inferences that are pathologically mixed. Consider a simple conjunctive inference, where p is stipulated to be true under one set of mediated-correspondence standards and q is stipulated to be true under another set of mediated-correspondence standards:

(SC) p, q, therefore p & q.

The truth of p and q, respectively, is a matter of whether p corresponds to the world and whether q corresponds to the world. The truth of the conjunction is a matter of whether p & q corresponds to the world, where here the pertinent kind of ideological mediation is *logically complex*: it involves the applicability of one kind of ideological mediation to the first conjunct (the kind that governs p) and a different kind of ideological mediation to the second conjunct (the kind that governs q). The truth of the conjunction thus depends on whether p and q both correspond to the same world. On this approach, truth is correspondence always and everywhere in the inference, but the different degrees of ideological mediation vis-à-vis the respective conjuncts are preserved and with them the genuine incongruity between the epistemic, evidential, and even semantic standards for evaluating, p, q, and p & q individually. Bluntly, how one determines the presence of trees differs from how one determines the presence of a forest, but a world or state of affairs that makes it true that there is a forest also makes it true that there are trees. So, that world or state of affairs will make it true, as a matter of mediated correspondence that (a forest is present *and* trees are present).

Clearly, it is not difficult to find more complicated examples where the degrees of mediation governing different statements within the inference seem to be more substantially different than in the case of forest and trees. For instance, suppose one were to argue as follows:

[J] (P1) If there are exactly four public universities in Arizona, then Bob will dance a jig.
(P2) There are exactly four public universities in Arizona.
Therefore,
(C) Bob will dance a jig.

Statements (P1) and (C) are subject to significantly different degrees of ideological mediation. Be that as it may, the conditional premise (P1) nevertheless is subject to a form of ideological mediation that smoothly accommodates both (P2) and (C)—namely, a logically complex kind of truth-functional mediation according to which the whole statement is semantically correct (i.e., true) just in case either (P1) is false under the form of ideological mediation that governs (P1), or (C) is true under the form of ideological mediation that governs (C). The inference thereby preserves a univocal truth-property—namely, the generic property of *ideologically mediated correspondence*. The semantic standards governing the logically complex conditional premise (P1) are logically complex compared to the semantic standards governing the conclusion, but this does not change the underlying nature of truth.

To sum up: with respect to so-called mixed inference cases, we recognize that when the premises and conclusions can come from different discourses that operate under different semantic standards, the putative truth preservation of a valid inference may appear to be compromised. But since truth is always the univocal generic attribute of ideologically mediated correspondence, this allows a logically complex premise in a mixed inference to be subject to a logically complex form of ideological mediation—in other words, (in the case of the logical connectives of sentential logic) a form of mediation under which the way the whole premise would correspond to the world is a function of the ways that its respective constituents would correspond to the world. Our view is that the widely varying semantic standards governing various statements in the inference, no matter how diverse and (in the case of logically complex statements) no matter how logically complex, should always be understood as expressing different degrees of ideological mediation and not as reflecting genuinely diverse construals of the nature of truth.

With mediated correspondence, we aim to synthesize the plurality of truth and the unity of truth. We embrace pluralism: pluralism about discourses, pluralism about degrees of mediation, and pluralism of semantic standards; here, we think, everyone has always been and ought to be a pluralist. We do reject pluralism about the nature of truth, however. Here truth has always been and ought to be just correspondence.

7. The synthetic unity of truth

Alethic pluralism holds that respect for the diversity between and among different truth-apt discourses requires that one hold that truth has more than one fundamental form. We respect this intra-discourse and trans-discourse diversity, and we are willing to concede to the pluralist that truth can look different in different contexts. Nonetheless, we also maintain that taken together, the variety of ways in which truth can arise from a synthetic unity is rooted in the recognition that truth is always correspondence. The correspondence relation is always ideologically mediated and only in *some* (probably rare) contexts does this amount to direct correspondence. In other words, only rarely is one's discourse ontologically committed to its posits.

Understanding truth in terms of correspondence is not new, but many have found traditional versions of correspondence too limited to respect the wide variety of language forms and the diversity manifested by putatively truth-apt discourses. Our approach to articulating a correspondence account of truth diverges from this long tradition by emphasizing that the theory of truth should be independent of metaphysical theorizing and should remain neutral among the various accounts of fundamental ontology one might offer.

This neutrality about ontology entails that the familiar project of trying to cash out the truth conditions of a statement in terms of its ontological commitments is untenable. In place of this approach, we speak of appealing to the ideological commitments of a statement and to the multifarious ways that ideology can interact with ontology to generate ideologically mediated correspondence. The contextually framed semantic standards governing the discourse's positing apparatus determine how the world must be in order for a statement deploying this apparatus to be true. This is mediated correspondence. And it is within the framework of mediated correspondence that one discovers the contextually determined standards for semantically correct affirmability that function as criteria for truth.

The ultimate unity of truth on this view is found in two complementary observations. First and foremost, truth is always correspondence. No statement is true except insofar as it bears a relation of ideologically mediated correspondence to the world. Sometimes the correspondence is direct, but it is almost always indirect. Second, unless one antecedently knows the content of the actual correct ontology, one cannot—from within the situated use of various forms of discourse and merely by virtue of one's competence in conforming one's linguistic practice to the semantic standards governing the correct deployment of the discourse's positing apparatus—recognize statements that are true in virtue of *directly* mediated correspondence with the world. From the standpoint of a human being using language to state the truth, all truth is ideologically mediated, and there is no readily detectable or experientially salient distinction between those posits of human discourse to which the discourse is ontologically committed and those to which it is merely ideologically committed.

Is language diverse and does it contain many different kinds of talk that purport to be truth-apt? Yes. Does this mean that truth is in some sense different in these cases? Yes. Does this require that truth be plural, that it have more than one fundamental nature? No. Truth is indeed manifold; yet, when one comes to appreciate that correspondence is also manifold, one discovers that truth, understood as mediated correspondence, is ultimately one.

References

Barnard, R. & T. Horgan (2006). Truth as mediated correspondence. *Monist* 89: 31–50.

Beall, Jc. (2000). On mixed inferences and pluralism about truth predicates. *Philosophical Quarterly* 50: 380–382.

Benacerraf, P. (1973). Mathematical truth. *Journal of Philosophy* 70: 661–679.

Horgan, T. (2001). Contextual semantics and metaphysical realism: truth as indirect correspondence. In M. P. Lynch (ed.), *The Nature of Truth* (67–95). Cambridge, MA: MIT Press.

Horgan, T. & M. Potrč. (2008a). *Austere Realism: Contextual Semantics Meets Minimal Ontology.* Cambridge, MA: MIT Press.

Horgan, T. & M. Potrč. (2008b). Contextual semantics and particularist semantic normativity. In M. Lance, M. Potrč, & V. Strahovnik (eds.), *Challenging Moral Particularism* (123–139). London: Routledge.

Horgan, T. & M. Timmons (2006). Cognitivist expressivism. In their (eds.) *Metaethics after Moore* (255–298). Oxford: Oxford University Press.

Pedersen, N. J. L. L. (2006). What can the problem of mixed inferences teach us about alethic pluralism? *Monist* 89: 102–117.

Pedersen, N. J. L. L. (2010). Stabilizing alethic pluralism. *Philosophical Quarterly* 60: 92–108.

Tappolet, C. (1997). Mixed inferences: a problem for pluralism about truth predicates. *Analysis* 57: 209–210.

Tappolet, C. (2000). Truth pluralism and many-valued logics: a reply to Beall. *Philosophical Quarterly* 50: 382–385.

Tienson, J. (1989). A conception of metaphysics. *American Philosophical Quarterly* 26: 63–72.

{ 10 }

Alethic Pluralism and the Correspondence Theory of Truth

Richard Fumerton

1. Truth as correspondence

In this chapter I explore the ways in which a correspondence theory of truth can embrace both a kind of relativism about truth and a view that accommodates the appearance of a pluralism about truth. I will first argue that the correspondence theory and the realism it implies is perfectly compatible the idea that one can 'carve up' reality in any number of different ways. And this allows one to give some sense to the idea that truth is relative to a conceptual framework and, consequently, that one can express truths within one conceptual framework that one cannot express in another. I will also argue that the correspondence theorist has the resources to 'co-opt' whatever initial plausibility so-called pluralist conceptions of truth might have. The theory can allow for the intelligibility of alternative conceptions of 'truth', but "truth" is in scare quotes for a reason. These alternative conceptions of truth are best construed as 'faux' truths perfectly compatible with the correspondence theorist's conception of truth as correspondence to facts.

As I understand a correspondence theory of truth, the most fundamental commitment of the theory is that being true is a property. Correspondence theorists must come up with a view about what has the property of being true (an account of truth bearers) and what would make the truth bearers true (the truth makers). They also need to figure out what the critical relation of correspondence is between truth bearers and truth makers. Among the various candidates for truth bearers, it's likely that the correspondence theorist will make a distinction between primary and derivative truth bearers. So, for example, I would argue that a sentence token is an obvious candidate for being a truth bearer, but only derivatively. As I indicated, any defensible version of the correspondence theory of truth is going to require that there be truth makers.

I think that truth makers are facts, facts that are ontologically independent of their being represented by language or thought. My own view is that thoughts are the primary bearers of truth value and that thoughts are true when they stand in an unanalyzable relation of correspondence to facts. False thoughts fail to correspond to anything, even though they or their component parts have the capacity to correspond.[1] I take thoughts to be non-relational properties of mind. If properties can exist unexemplified, then thoughts can exist without minds. If they cannot, then thoughts (and truth) are held hostage to the existence of minds.

Having sketched the view this way, I want to acknowledge that this distinction between truth bearers and truth makers is itself potentially misleading (though in a way that is relatively harmless). If the correspondence theory of truth is correct, then there is a trivial sense in which something's being true is fundamentally a *relational* state of affairs. And relational states of affairs obtain only if the relata of the critical relation exist. So when the thought arises that p is true, strictly speaking, the truth maker for the thought is the relational state of affairs of the thought's corresponding to the fact. The representation-independent fact to which the thought corresponds does not *by itself* 'make' for truth, and it is for that reason misleading to suggest that it is by itself a truth maker. In the same sense, one cannot exemplify the property of being a son without one's standing in a relation to someone else. My being a son is a fundamentally relational state of affairs. But that doesn't mean that it isn't useful to distinguish the son from his parents. In the same way, one can recognize that truth is essentially relational but distinguish the representation-independent truth maker from the thought that it makes true as two distinct and crucial constituents of the complex relational state of affairs that creates truth.

Many of us who embrace a correspondence theory of truth are honestly bewildered that anyone rejects it. While we will acknowledge that there are all kinds of interesting variations within the theory, the basic idea seems so obviously right to us that we are often content to respond to objections. So, for example, we'll spend time disarming the so-called slingshot argument as a supposed weapon of mass destruction for use against correspondence theories. The slingshot relies on principles of substitutivity that should so obviously be rejected by any self-respecting correspondence theorist that one can only

---

[1] A thoroughgoing naturalist, who also embraces a correspondence conception of truth, will labor long and hard to naturalize the relation of correspondence. The best hope is to secure representational content through some sort of causal connection between thought and what it represents. But one must, of course, be very careful not to secure too tight a connection. One must allow for misrepresentation— even radical misrepresentation. Dretske's various efforts at naturalizing representation are some of the most thoughtful and sophisticated (see, e.g., 1995), but I remain very pessimistic that they can succeed. There are simply too many distinct links in the causal chain leading to a given brain state and resulting in reinforceable behavior to select that which is 'represented' by the relevant brain state.

wonder why the objection was ever taken seriously by anyone in the first place (see Fumerton 2002, ch. 3).

Still others spend a great deal of time fretting about the fact that one cannot identify language- or thought-independent facts without speaking or thinking of such facts. If one can't think of a fact that is unthought of, then how can one make sense of facts that are mind-independent? To state the argument clearly is to see what the problem is (Fumerton 2002, ch. 3). While it is a necessary truth that all of the facts that have been thought of have been thought of, it is not a necessary truth that someone has thought of all facts.

A somewhat related objection (perhaps most closely associated with Strawson (1950), but also suggested throughout the writings of Putnam (e.g. 1987) and even related to the forces driving deflationary theories of truth) rejects the very category of representation-independent fact upon which the correspondence theorist relies. The worry, crudely put, is that the world does not come *structured*. Indeed, the existence of structured facts, this critic argues, is a kind of illusion that results from projecting representations out into the world. The idea might get some initial footing from the observation that in ordinary language we probably do interchange such expressions as 'it is true that' and 'it is a fact that'. Indeed, one might suspect that we typically use 'it is a *fact* that' just to emphasize what we assert. If reference to the fact that p is just a way of emphatically asserting p, then it would be horribly misguided to appeal to our understanding of fact talk as part of our way of explicating the concept of truth.

A proper response to Strawsonian worries would take us deep into controversial metaphysical issues. The friend of truth makers does indeed think that the world contains the exemplification of properties and that those properties could exist quite independently of any representations of them. A fact just is the exemplification of properties. There are, as we shall see, many options open to the correspondence theorist when it comes to the details of this commitment to property exemplification. The basic idea is compatible, for example, with both realism and trope theory, with the idea that all properties are perfectly determinate, and with the idea that there are both determinate and determinable properties. But without a world differentiated by properties one will be hard pressed to make sense of any talk of thought representing reality. Even on thoroughly naturalistic accounts of representation, property exemplifications will be the most plausible candidates for the relata of the causal relations that ultimately are supposed to secure reference.

Rather than respond to objections focusing on the conceptual building blocks of a correspondence theory, in what follows I want to emphasize what a correspondence theory of truth can allow, particularly in connection with the idea that there are many different but equally true pictures of the world. I further want to emphasize the extraordinarily rich resources available to the correspondence theorists when it comes to incorporating into their theories so-called 'alternative conceptions' of truth (the idea behind pluralism about truth).

It should be obvious that the correspondence theorists are not committed *by their theory of truth* to various forms of metaphysical realism. One can be a correspondence theorist of truth and an idealist, for example. Berkeley was almost certainly a correspondence theorist (and, in a sense, a robust realist) about *truth*. To be sure, the only truth makers for Berkeley were facts about minds and ideas. For that matter, the only truth bearers for Berkeley were mental states. Truth, for Berkeley, would consist in one sort of idea corresponding to another sort of idea. Hume was, I believe, firmly committed to a correspondence theory of truth, and he thought that the only truth makers were perfectly determinate facts about perceptions. So there is an obvious sense in which a correspondence theorist of truth is not committed to truth makers being perceiver-independent. One can consistently embrace both the correspondence theory of truth and the view that all facts are mental facts. That should cause no confusion unless one confuses being mind-dependent with being representation-dependent. The view that all of reality is mind-dependent is intelligible. The view that all of reality is representation-dependent is not. The latter view entails that representations depend for their existence on meta-representations, which depend for their existence on meta-meta-representations, and so on, ad infinitum. The regress is vicious. We can never get our 'world-making' started.

There is another important sense in which the correspondence theorist might reject the idea that truth is mind-independent. We just noted that we might live in a world in which all truth makers depend for their existence on minds. It might also be the case that all truth bearers depend for their existence on minds. It seems to me entirely plausible to suppose that without conscious beings there would be no thought, no intentional states, and that without thought there would be no representations of the world to be true or false. Again, virtually all of the classical British empiricists held some version of the correspondence theory of truth and also thought that truth bearers were mental 'pictures' of reality—ideas in the mind. Without minds there would be no 'pictures' to correspond or fail to correspond to the world. Without minds there would be no truth.

To be sure, one must be careful here. There is a sense in which one can take thought to be the most fundamental truth bearer and also think that the world could contain truths without minds. *If* one embraces in one's ontology uninstantiated universals and thinks that my having a thought is my exemplifying a 'thought' universal, one would probably be well advised to take the *universal*, say thinking that p, to be that which corresponds or fails to correspond to the world. Such a view avoids at least one serious problem that faces the correspondence theorist who takes truth bearers to be instantiated thoughts and who wants to preserve traditional distinctions between contingent and necessary truths. Most philosophers want necessary truths to be true in all possible worlds. But there are possible worlds in which there are no thoughts. Such worlds will be worlds in which there are no truth bearers and thus no truths. One can revise one's account of necessary truth so that a necessary truth is conceived of only as one that is true in all possible worlds in which the truth bearer exists. But then if thoughts are the primary bearers of truth-value, one gets the awkward implication (perhaps one we can get used to) that it is a necessary truth that there are thoughts.

Just as a correspondence theorist can reject metaphysical realism about physical objects, so also a correspondence theorist can reject realism about universals. As we saw in connection with our brief discussion earlier, some dissatisfaction with the correspondence theory of truth is rooted in the conviction that the correspondence theorist is committed to a world neatly carved up into facts that can serve as truth makers. But again the radical empiricists, correspondence theorists all, were almost universally suspicious of the idea that there are abstract or generic properties in the world—most didn't want much to do with determinate universals, let alone determinable universals. While they did think that the world allows true mental representations of it, that world was more often than not thought of by them as a world of perfectly determinate properties, properties that not only can be, but must be, *organized* by conscious beings if we are to think about it. And just as we can organize books on our bookshelves in any number of different ways—by title, by author, by subject, by shape, by color, by interest, et cetera—so also thought can make sense of the bewildering array of perfectly determinate properties in radically different ways. It is, of course, bizarre to suppose that there is only one way of classifying the indefinitely many perfectly determinate color properties. There are many different similarities and differences of which we can take note. Determinate colors can be sorted by language and thought in different ways.

Interestingly, it seems to me that the correspondence theory of truth may have the best resources to make sense of all this talk of mind-structuring world. It is the capacity of a thought to correspond to the exemplification of many different perfectly determinate properties that, arguably, allows us to understand what numerically distinct determinate properties have in common in virtue of which they can all be viewed as instances of, say, blue. If we are searching for the source of abstraction, the most obvious place to look is in the mind that supplies truth bearers. The correspondence theory has the resources to allow for a robust role played by the mind in creating truth.

2. Alternative truth

Is the correspondence theorist committed to the views (often associated with it) that every thought is either true or false and that there is one and only one true complete description of the way the world is? I think not. Consider the first. Of all theories of truth, it has always seemed to me that the correspondence theory lends itself rather naturally to the idea that there might be gradations of truth. There is nothing to stop a correspondence theorist from thinking that the critical relation of correspondence between thought and fact admits of degrees. Consider the familiar metaphor of picturing reality so often invoked by correspondence theorists. Pictures can be better or worse representations of what they picture—they can vary in how 'true' they are to reality. So also, one might think that a given thought, say the thought of red, can vary in how exactly it corresponds to some particular color property. It can correspond well to a determinate color dab smack in the middle of what we might think of as the red spectrum, but not so well to some determinate color at the 'edge' of the red continuum. Wherever there is vagueness (and vagueness afflicts almost all ordinary concepts) we can find various continua where the items along the continua range from paradigmatic to problematic instances of the kind. And there is no reason the correspondence theorist cannot think of this in terms of differences in the level of correspondence between thought and the world.

If one concedes that correspondence can come in degrees, then there is a sense in which one will find harmless the pluralist's idea that there are different kinds of truth—something like clear, precise truth when the correspondence is paradigmatic, and less and less clear truths as one moves out from the paradigm. But the distinction is just that—a distinction in degree, not a distinction in kind. Nor does allowing these distinctions suggest that we should recant the claim that correspondence is unanalyzable. I am convinced that the concept of intense pain is unanalyzable, but one can at the same time recognize that some such pains are more intense than others. Moore (1903) thought that being intrinsically good is unanalyzable but also recognized that some things are intrinsically better than others. Whether correct or not, both views are surely perfectly intelligible.

Is there only one true complete description of the world? Well, there are many different ways of picturing one and the same reality. Think of paintings—realistic, impressionistic, and abstract—all of which picture one and the same person or scene. Or think of the radical difference between a painting and a statue, each of which succeeds in representing the same person. Is there not a perfectly clear sense in which different thoughts might succeed in picturing or representing one and the same reality? But would any of this bear on the question of whether there is a single true picture of the world?

In the final analysis, the answer to that question depends on what one has in mind by saying 'one true complete description of the world'. On anyone's view, to be complete a description of the world would have to be infinitely complex. And if actual instantiated thoughts are the primary bearers of truth value, there obviously won't be any actual truth that succeeds in describing everything there is to describe about our world. To have any plausibility, the one true picture idea should be thought of as a modal claim: it is in principle possible to have one true complete description of the world. With the claim understood as asserting only a possibility, it is not clear that the existence of alternative equally correct pictures of reality presents any difficulty for the idea that it is in principle possible for there to be one true picture of the world. Although there are radically different conceptual frameworks—different ways of organizing and structuring the world—there is nothing to prevent one from conjoining all these different pictures of reality into one gigantic representation of how things are.

The correspondence theorist *will* deny that there are can be equally correct but *incompatible* representations of the world, but then almost everyone backs down from that sort of claim when push comes to shove. And well they should. There is no way of making sense of the idea that there can be equally correct—that is, true—but *incompatible* descriptions of reality. To say of two claims that they are incompatible is just to say that they can't both be true. The idea that there can be two true claims that can't both be true is an idea with which you don't want to be associated! You can paint the Eiffel Tower and I can make a statue of the Eiffel tower. There are two quite different ways to represent the tower. But there is no sense in which the two different representations are incompatible.

3. More robust relativism

But aren't we missing the point of the realist's critics? To be sure, we can't say from within one conceptual framework that p and not-p are both true. But someone occupying one conceptual framework F_1 can say and think truly that p, while someone else occupying another, different conceptual framework F_2 can say and truly think that not-p. Furthermore, one might suggest there is no way of stepping outside the respective frameworks in such a way that one can successfully think both p and not-p. All this might sound vaguely suggestive, but can it survive any sort of detailed scrutiny? What precisely does all this talk about truth relativized to conceptual frameworks come to?

One might suppose that one could make sense of the idea by associating it with a kind of radical holism about meaning. As I understand holism, the rough idea is that individual statements don't have meaning outside of vast theories in which they are embedded. The meaning of a statement is a function of the logical and probabilistic relations in which it stands to other statements, and these connections are themselves theory relative, where theories are constructed by people.

Frankly, I have always found holism to be essentially unintelligible. Consider, for example, logical relations such as entailment. Logical relations are just that: relations. And they require relata. And logical relations are paradigms of what some call internal relations—relations that necessarily obtain between relata in virtue of the intrinsic character of the relata. So, for example, blood red is darker than pink, and that relation holds just in virtue of what blood red and pink are. There is no possible world in which blood red and pink exist but fail to stand in that relation. But precisely for this reason, it doesn't make sense to suppose that two propositions can be the propositions that they are while in one world they stand in a logical connection and in another world they fail to stand in that connection. The claim that p happens to entail q but it doesn't have to is literally unintelligible. But then the content of p doesn't depend on its entailing q (when it does). That's to get things backward. That the entailment exists depends on the contents of p and q.

The same is actually true of evidential connections, but it is much easier to get confused on this issue. It is tempting to think, for example, that litmus paper's turning red is evidence in this world for a liquid solution's being acid, but that there are other possible worlds in which that evidential connection wouldn't hold. But the fact is that litmus paper's turning red isn't evidence in this world or any other for a solution's being acid (see Fumerton 2004). The description of the evidence is enthymematic. The real evidence includes all of the background knowledge, which includes propositions describing correlations between the color of litmus paper and the nature of liquid solutions, and if that evidence makes probable a conclusion, it necessarily does.[2] Again, on such a view it wouldn't even make sense to suppose that the existence of evidential connections determines the content of the relata of such connections.

But suppose for a moment that we can understand all this talk about meaning being holistic. Suppose that I have an elaborate theory in which I assert the sentence 'p' and you have a quite different theory in which you assert the sentence 'not-p'. And again, assume for the sake of argument that our respective theories themselves somehow determine what evidential connections hold between our respective assertions, and that these in turn determine the meaning of our respective assertions. If we could make sense of all this talk, it obviously follows that 'p', said by you, doesn't mean the same thing as 'p' said by me. So we aren't contradicting each other when I say 'p' and you say 'not-p'. We don't have a case of different and incompatible truths.

Don't we still have, however, a case in which we might have different and *incommensurable* truths? Well, I don't know what would make them incommensurable. Am I supposed to be incapable of understanding your conceptual framework? Are you incapable of understanding mine? I suppose

---

[2] I'm engaging in a bit of rhetorical excess here. Everything I said is true but is hardly uncontroversial. It ultimately hinges on fundamental disputes between internalists and externalists in epistemology.

it might depend on the strength of the modal operator. If we are talking merely about causal possibility (relative to circumstances)—the sense in which it is causally impossible for me right now to do fifty pushups—then I suppose my being entrenched in one theory might make it causally impossible for me to grasp the concepts in terms of which someone else expresses another theory. But that is no more interesting than the observation that a really stupid person might not be able to grasp the concepts in terms of which perdurantism is expressed, or even that a blind person might not be able to grasp the concepts in terms of which truths about phenomenal color are expressed. It will still be metaphysically possible for me to grasp the various propositions that breathe holistic meaning into your assertions, and since the truth of my assertions are not threatened by the truth of yours, I can easily incorporate the truth of your assertions into one gigantic true world view.

If incommensurability is understood not in causal terms but in logical or metaphysical terms, it seems to me that the phenomenon of incommensurability does not and could not exist. There is no sense in which it could be logically or metaphysically impossible to understand another person's assertion. And anyone denying this is caught in a trap of self-refutation. Those who profess to understand talk of strong commensurability and who believe that they can think of examples that would underwrite it have just had the very thoughts that show that they can think from within more than one conceptual framework.

4. Truth and coherence

This brings us naturally to a theory of truth that might seem to hold the best hope of making sense of genuinely incompatible but equally true pictures of the world—the coherence theory of truth. Although it is quite distinct from the coherence theory of justification, the coherence theory of truth might be thought of as a natural outgrowth of the former. It has become fashionable for at least some epistemologists to replace the old veil of perception with an even more impenetrable curtain of belief that prevents us from gaining access to a representation-independent world. There is, the new slogan goes, no escaping the circle of beliefs. If we combine the view that we suffer such imprisonment with a commitment to some vestige of verificationism, we might be led to the idea that we had better define truth in terms of those beliefs that are the bars of our prison. We can make sense of a belief's being true only in terms of the way it 'fits' or 'coheres' with other beliefs.

There are all sorts of variations on the basic theme. In particular, one gets different versions of a coherence theory of truth depending on how one specifies the class of beliefs with which a given belief must cohere in order to be true. So, for example, one might assert that S's belief that p at t is true just when S's belief that p coheres with the rest of S's beliefs at t. Or one could hold that S's belief that p at t is true just when p coheres with the rest of the beliefs S would have were S to engage in systematic exploration of the world. Yet again, one might hold that S's belief that p at t is true just when p coheres with the propositions believed by the intellectual community to which S belongs. And again, one can distinguish that view from the view that defines truth to be coherence with those beliefs that the community would end up with as a result of some prolonged, idealized inquiry. None of these distinctions matter for what follows. What I say about one view will apply mutatis mutandis to the others. So let's stick with the simplest view—the idea that your belief is true just when it coheres with the rest of what you believe.

There are also all sorts of different ways that coherence theorists can try to make sense of the critical concept of coherence. One might suppose that the strongest sort of coherence exemplified by a belief system is one in which each proposition believed is entailed by the rest. Sometimes such a view is dismissed as requiring something far too strong. In fact, however, coherence understood this way is far too easy to come by. Because I have a background in logic, every time I believe p and believe q, I will believe (at least dispositionally) that p iff q. But, trivially, p and (p iff q) will entail p and q conjoined with (q iff p) will entail p. Achieving this sort of coherence is a snap. Ironically, perhaps, one gets stronger 'glue' holding beliefs together if one turns to probabilistic connections among beliefs. Again, however, none of these distinctions will matter for what follows.

I have argued (1994) against the intelligibility of coherence theories of both justification and truth claiming that both views face vicious regress. On the most natural way of thinking about a coherence theory of truth, one is building truth out of beliefs and relations between them. But what is all this talk of belief? Either there are such things as belief states (which would then be the obvious candidates for truth makers of propositions describing them), or we will have to 'build' truth about belief states (and the relations that hold between them) out of additional belief states (including, of course, the critical meta-belief state that we are in such-and-such belief states). And these meta-beliefs will either have a robust reality constituting the obvious truth makers for claims about them, or they in turn will need to be built out of relations of coherence holding between the meta-meta-belief that we have such a meta-belief and the coherence of that meta-meta-belief with the rest of what we believe, and so on ad infinitum. So the coherence theorist is either going to be committed to a world of beliefs that exist independently of the way in which they are represented or face an endless regress in which the building blocks of belief states are forever just out of reach. If one embraces the first horn of the dilemma, one will face the obvious absurdity of allowing into one's ontology belief states, but not viewing them as the truth makers for propositions about beliefs (the very conception of truth as correspondence the coherence theorist is rejecting). If one embraces the second horn and tries to build reality/truth out of ever higher levels of belief states, one will face a vicious regress.

5. Pluralism about truth

There is perhaps a response to the above objection to a coherence theory of truth. I have been arguing all along as if there is just one legitimate conception of truth, and that a philosopher will be committed to understanding all claims about truth from within the framework of a single theory defended by that philosopher. But some philosophers (Lynch 2004; Sher 1998, 2004; Wright 1992) have suggested that there might be alternative and equally legitimate conceptions of truth. On that view, some conceptions of truth are deployed in certain domains but not in others. So, for example, we could argue that claims about what we believe are made true by facts about what we believe in precisely the way envisaged by the correspondence theorist. At the same time, perhaps we might insist that mathematical truth should be understood in terms of what can or cannot be proved from within a given formal system. Perhaps, philosophical truths would be more plausible in terms of coherence. It is, after all, sometimes difficult to convince oneself that the debate between realists and nominalists is settled by some representation-independent truth maker involving such mysterious entities as universals, tropes, bare particulars, and substances.

In what follows, I want to argue that the correspondence theorist should not be seduced by the idea that there is more than one concept of truth at work in our thoughts about the world. Any apparent need for an alternative conception of truth in a given domain of discourse is a kind of illusion. Let me explain by thinking more about truth as coherence. Again, let's begin by noting again that if a coherence theory of truth were plausible, then we would *seem* to have a way of talking about the same proposition being both true and false. A belief that p can be true relative to S's belief system but false relative to R's belief system. More informally, and distressingly familiar to us through many of our students, we can even talk about p's being true for S while it is false for R.[3] When truth is relativized to the belief systems of communities, we can talk about p's being true relative to one community while it is false relative to another.

Again, I want to stress that such talk is philosophically problematic unless one's ontology includes belief states that are what *they* are independently of the way they are represented. These belief states are best understood as

---

[3] Though it is hardly so-called 'coherence truth' that the student typically has in mind. That 'true for'-talk can usually be translated simply into 'believed by'-talk.

facts that will serve as the truth makers for claims about them. But why can't we plausibly suppose that at least some *other* claims are best thought of as true or false as the coherence theorist understands truth and falsehood? We can, of course, understand all this talk of a proposition's cohering with other propositions believed. At least we had better be able to understand it if we are to make sense of the coherence theorist's view. And I suppose we can't stop a philosopher from trying to use the word 'true' to describe the fact that a given proposition stands in the relevant relations of coherence. Of course, it would be equally 'impolite' to forbid the rest of us from putting an asterisk beside the world 'true' just to remind everyone of just how the coherence theorist is using the word. *But note that we know precisely how to talk about all this truth* from within the framework of a classic correspondence theory.* With respect to p, we correspondence theorists will think that it is true (true without an asterisk) that p is true* relative to S's belief system while it is false* relative to R's belief system. I know what 'true*' means, and I know what makes it true that p is true* (relative to a given belief system). The coherence theorist has successfully located the representation-independent truth maker for the relativized truth* claims and all these relativized truth* claims can be included in the one true (without an asterisk) complete description of the world!

A couple of analogies might be helpful. Consider a very poor attempt at generating a paradox or puzzle. Jones is 6′ tall. Yesterday, I heard someone who seemed perfectly reliable describe Jones as 'tall'. But today I was listening to a basketball scout lamenting the fact that Jones is so short. Whom do I believe? Why did these people contradict each other? The puzzle is so lame, of course, because a clever child in grade school can figure out its solution. The expression 'tall' has an essentially relativized meaning. Put another way, 'S is tall' is always incomplete. It always means something like 'S is tall relative to the class of F's'. So the person who described Jones as 'tall' probably meant something like 'S is tall relative to the class of men' while the basketball scout probably meant something like 'S is not tall relative to the class of professional basketball players'. Both were saying something true, and the correspondence theorist trying to figure out which statements to include in the one true description of the world should, of course, include both.

While the treatment of 'tall' seems uncontroversial, I have heard even serious philosophers get very confused about truth and coherence in contexts that should be no more problematic. So in tort law, it seems plausible to claim that the law is at least partially defined by reference to the way in which a given prescription or prohibition coheres with past legal decisions (and possibly also ethical norms accepted by members of the society whose law is under discussion). The language used reminds some legal theorists of the coherence theory of truth, and they then decide that we need to embrace a coherence theory of truth, at least insofar as we are concerned with truths about what the law is![4] But all of this involves massive confusion. Correspondence theorists will, of course, recognize that the class of truths include truths about coherence. Such truths will involve a correspondence between a representation of various relations of coherence to the fact that the coherence relations obtain. That a claim about what the law is involves a claim about coherence presents no difficulties for a correspondence theorist trying to find the appropriate truth maker for the claim. And truths about the law in a given culture can be contained in the correspondence theorist's one true picture of the world.

Or consider the disputes interpreters of a literary work often have when considering the truth of various claims made about fictional characters in that work. Hamlet, someone argues, had a romantic interest in his mother. Someone else rejects that claim. What is the debate about? There is no real person named 'Hamlet' and, consequently, it is initially puzzling to think that one can make true or false claims about which characteristics Hamlet has. A philosopher might well try to dissolve the puzzle by suggesting, plausibly enough, that a statement attributing to Hamlet some property is best understood as a complicated claim about the various statements that comprise the text. As a crude first approximation, one might suggest that the statement that Hamlet is F is true when that statement coheres well with other statements explicitly made in various characterizations of Hamlet contained in the play. And again, because relations of coherence seem to be the truth maker of one's claims about Hamlet, one might be tempted to wonder if one shouldn't endorse something like a coherence theory of truth as the best way to understand the truth and falsehood of claims made about fictional characters and events.

But by now it should be clear that there is no reason whatsoever to abandon one's correspondence theory of truth because one finds attractive the claim that literary claims about fictional characters are best understood as claims about the work and evidential connections that obtain between statements that comprise the work and other statements. If the philosophical theory about how to understand the literary theorist's statements is correct, then we have located the representation-independent facts that are the truth makers for such claims. The truth makers just are facts about the relevant propositions cohering.

Claims about the coherence theorist's truth* are just like claims about the tort theorist's law and the literary theorist's fictional characters. Truths about truth* can be unproblematically handled from within the framework of a correspondence theorist. *Now to be sure, the truth maker for the claim that p is true* has become strangely divorced from what p asserts.* The meaning of p is what we have to think about when we discover all these logical

---

[4] See, for example, Raz (1992).

and probabilistic connections between p and other propositions we believe. It would be decidedly odd to suggest the proposition that p makes an *assertion* about all these coherence relations. And it is decidedly odd to suppose that the assertion that p is true, in any interesting sense of 'true', can be divorced from what p asserts. But that's the coherentist's problem. That's the price they pay for using the expression 'true' with the meaning of 'true*'. I'm merely pointing out that claims about what is true* have obvious truth makers in the sense to which correspondence theorists have appealed all along.

Now I have no doubt that the coherence theorist will balk at all this. You can't just take our relations of coherence holding between beliefs to be truth makers for claims about what is true* in the correspondence theorist's sense of truth makers. You would be begging the question against the coherentist's attempt to provide an alternative to the correspondence theorist's conception of truth. I think I can see how this objection might go, but only if the thrust of the complaint is that we can't think of the world as containing belief states that exist independently of their being represented (meta-represented) any more than we can think any other feature of reality existing independently of the way in which it is represented. But now the coherence theorist is firmly impaled on the second horn of the dilemma discussed above. We never will get a coherent story of truth from the coherence theorist. We will be led on an endless search for higher and higher level representations, all of which get constructed out of meta-representations forever receding beyond our grasp.

6. The strategy generalized

We saw above how a correspondence theorist has the resources to relegate the coherentist's conception of truth to a species of truth in the old and familiar sense of truth captured by the idea of correspondence to reality. And the strategy will work for any other suggestions concerning how to understand truth. So suppose a philosopher comes up with a so-called pragmatic conception of truth. Start with something as crude as the following: p is true if believing p would be pragmatically useful. There isn't a chance that such a view is capturing any interesting notion of truth, but if we get tired of arguing about it, we should simply give the pragmatist their use of 'true'. To keep track of that use of 'true' and distinguish it from the coherentist's use of 'true' we can add a double asterisk to the expression. As correspondence theorists we can humor the pragmatist and ask how all this pragmatic utility is to be understood. If we get an intelligible answer, we will have all that we need to identify the correspondence theorist's truth maker for the claim that p is true**. We'll know what the claim that p is true** means and we will know what fact would make it true that p is true**. Of course, as was true of the coherentist's term 'true*', we will probably think that the meaning of 'p is true**' doesn't have much to do with the meaning of p, but that's just a problem for the philosopher who claims that this theory captures some ordinary use of 'true'.

Or consider a Dummett-inspired antirealism about mathematical truth. Presupposing some version of verificationism, one might suppose that a highly theoretical mathematical claim becomes both meaningful and true only insofar as it can be successfully proved from within the framework of a theory of axioms and inference rules that defines the framework within which contemporary mathematicians argue. Again, we will, of course, need to be able to make sense of all this talk of provability. To the extent that we genuinely understand it, we will know what conditions constitute the satisfaction of this criterion for what is denoted by 'truth***' (as we shall call it to distinguish it from being true, true*, and true**). Since we have identified the relevant conditions that are supposed to make for the satisfaction of the concept of true***, we will also have a correspondence theorist's truth maker for the representation that a given mathematical proposition is true***. Once again, this conception of truth*** doesn't seem to me to have much to do with being true. And again one reason for this is that we have divorced the property of being true*** from the meaning of the mathematical proposition—at least we have if my earlier claim is correct and logical relations between propositions presuppose identity conditions for propositions that are independent of those relations.

So I can pretend to find unproblematic the meaning of these alternative truth predicates. Indeed, they can all be defined in a perfectly clear way that allows us to think clearly (from within the framework of a correspondence theory) about whether the predicates apply to various propositions. I don't think any of these predicate expressions have much to do with our ordinary conception of truth, and the best way of seeing that is to think about that recurring question of whether these alternative conceptions of truth have divorced that understanding of truth from what the proposition in question asserts. I want a claim about the truth of p to be parasitic upon what p asserts! The correspondence theorist of truth will give you that. The coherentist's theory of truth*, the pragmatist's theory of truth**, and the verificationist theory of truth*** won't. Nor will any other alternative to truth as correspondence that might be lurking in the background.

References

Dretske, F. (1995). *Naturalizing the Mind*. Cambridge, MA: MIT Press.
Fumerton, R. (1994). The incoherence of coherence theories. *Journal of Philosophical Research* 19: 89–102.
Fumerton, R. (2002). *Realism and the Correspondence Theory of Truth*. Lanham, MD: Rowman and Littlefield.

Fumerton, R. (2004). Epistemic probability. *Philosophical Issues* 14: 149–164.
Lynch, M. P. (2004). Truth and multiple realizability. *Australian Journal of Philosophy* 82: 384–408.
Moore, G. E. (1903). *Principia Ethica*. Cambridge University, Press.
Putnam, H. (1987). *The Many Faces of Realism*. LaSalle, IL: Open Court.
Raz, J. (1992). The relevance of coherence. *Boston University Law Review* 72: 273–321.
Sher, G. (1998). On the possibility of a substantive theory of truth. *Synthese* 117: 133–172.
Sher, G. (2004). In search of a substantive theory of truth. *Journal of Philosophy* 101: 5–36.
Strawson, P. F. (1950). Truth. *Proceedings of the Aristotelian Society* 24: 129–156.
Wright, C. J. G. (1992). *Truth and Objectivity*. Cambridge, MA: Harvard University Press.

{ 11 }

Naturalizing Pluralism about Truth
Wolfram Hinzen

1. Introduction

Philosophical naturalism has been in the background of much of the debate on the metaphysical nature of truth in the twentieth century. The nature of truth is thus assessed on the basis of a prior metaphysical commitment. Since naturalism may by now appear as a rather minimal philosophical commitment, this strategy may seem innocuous enough. Yet, it is not clear why we should constrain an inquiry into the nature of truth metaphysically. Especially if we pursue naturalism along more narrow (yet quite standard) physicalist lines, it may be more problematic to assume that a theory of truth needs to be consistent with such prior commitments.

In principle, the above priorities could be reversed. A naturalistic inquiry into the nature of human truth might show it to be of a certain nature. Therefore, we might then conclude, whatever metaphysics of truth we hold should be consistent with that nature or even derive from it. Puzzling as this reversal may seem at first, it is quite conceivable and in fact coherent. Similarly, empirical inquiry into the forces of nature can shake our confidence in a certain metaphysical conception of matter, and has done so, for example, in Newton's *Principia*, where such an inquiry served to bring down the 'mechanical philosophy' that had reigned before. That naturalistic inquiry into the structure of mind might constrain the metaphysics of mind in similar ways is a less familiar thought, yet I aim to illustrate its coherence here.

This possibility appears to have been rarely endorsed in twentieth-century philosophy of mind, and it has not affected the philosophy of truth. This is unsurprising given a long semantic and externalist tradition in which truth has been primarily understood as a relation to the world rather than a function of what kind of mind we possess. By and large, the philosophy of truth, despite the naturalism usually endorsed in it, has remained an enterprise in conceptual analysis, logic, and metaphysics—not in, say, tracing the evolutionary origins of truth (see Carstairs-McCarthy 1999) or the deduction of its nature from its naturalistic basis in the structure of the human mind.

A metaphysical naturalistic premise is paradigmatically exemplified in one of the formal constraints that Tarski (1936/1983: 406) imposed on any viable theory of truth: the elimination of semantic notions in favor of solely logical or physical ones, a requirement that itself followed from deeper concerns with the Unity of Science and the physicalism of the time. While the Unity of Science movement is less popular today, debate on the foundations of semantics (the 'naturalization of content') has remained premised by physicalist constraints. In the philosophy of truth, Lynch gives expression to a long-standing philosophical concern when he argues that moral properties just do not belong to 'the furniture of the physical world' (2009: 2), and that, therefore, moral truth, if there is such a thing, cannot consist in a 'correspondence' to this physical world.[1] Hence, the conclusion is, there might be different *ways* in which propositions can be true, depending on the domain of discourse in which they are put forward (moral, aesthetic, taste, etc.): the pluralist alternative in the philosophy of truth (Lynch 2009; Wright 1992).

Other conclusions have been drawn from this predicament as well, and they have equally left the basic physicalist premise unchallenged. Thus, the error theory questions whether there can be such a thing as moral truth at all. If truth is correspondence to a physical world, and moral properties are not a part of it, then any moral claim must be false. On the other hand, moral claims might be wrongly analyzed *as* claims that some proposition is true, in which case they cannot be false either—as the expressivist concludes, who in this way presumes himself to stay particularly closely within the confines of an approach to morality and the mind that is consistent with a scientific and naturalistic worldview. Finally, it has been suggested that truth may attach to propositions of all sorts, irrespective of their ontological domain, yet be a property so "thin" and metaphysically empty that there is no harm attaching it to moral propositions as well. This is the deflationist option: truth *poses* no mysteries, which a "metaphysics of truth" would have to resolve.

It is also commonly thought that the correspondence theory of truth (with correspondence usually understood as one to a physical world) is one way—though not the only way—in which truth itself (i.e., the *existence* of it) can be naturalized. Given that physicalism is a metaphysical premise in this debate, physicalism therefore *motivates* the correspondence view. A common way, more specifically, to proceed in this naturalization is via the notion of *belief,* in the standard sense of a propositional attitude directed toward getting the facts of the world right. More precisely, belief is first analyzed as a device of *representation*—a common assumption in the broadly functionalist tradition in the

---

[1] The problem has an enormous pedigree. See, e.g., Harman (1977) and Blackburn 1991.

philosophy of mind. Second, representation is defined in terms of *reference*, which then, third, is given a causal or teleological analysis (e.g., Jackson 2006). The existence of truth is now thought not to pose any problem any more for a naturalistic worldview. As Lynch (2009: 32) crisply puts it, "to think of truth as correspondence is no more or less spooky and no more or less trivial, than to think of the mind as a device for representation." The mystery that philosophers may have thought truth poses is thus gone; but metaphysics prevails, both through the metaphysical premise (physicalism) and through the claim on the nature of truth that the theory involves.

Finally, a naturalistic analysis of truth broadly on the lines above is a strategy for naturalizing closely related notions such as meaning (content) and intentionality as well. The leading intuition here is that the meaning of a sentence has an intrinsic relation to some external condition under which the sentence is true, thought of as a "fact" or "state of affairs." If truth, paradigmatically, is a relation between sentences and such external conditions, truth is the very relation that, presumably after being subjected to a causal or teleosemantic analysis, will naturalize meaning and intentionality.

This chapter offers a meta-analysis of this naturalistic component of the contemporary truth debate and outlines what I will call a naturalistic inquiry into the nature of truth. This inquiry adopts a *methodological* naturalism, weaker than the metaphysical naturalism usually maintained, and is arguably free of relevant metaphysical premises altogether. Like in other domains of naturalistic inquiry, no conceptual analysis of the object under study will be provided here. Instead, the object is isolated and described, its naturalistic dimensions are identified, and a possible inquiry into these is pursued.

Though aiming to be free of metaphysical *premises*, the inquiry suggests a number of metaphysical conclusions. Insofar as I will question the coherence of the physicalist metaphysics that underlies the motivation for pluralism above, pluralism will not be supported. On the other hand, I will point to aspects of truth-theoretic cognition supporting the intuitions that truth is not a unitary thing, and that there are different external properties that 'realize' the one functional role that the concept of truth plays in human cognition (Lynch 2009). In other respects, deflationism will be supported by the naturalistic perspective taken here. In these ways, naturalistic inquiry into the phenomenon of truth links up with different metaphysical paradigms in the philosophy of truth and may prove philosophically fruitful in naturalizing some aspects of the views involved.

In §2, I begin by outlining what I mean by studying truth naturalistically and argue that naturalistic inquiry into the origin of truth is appropriately directed toward the inherent structure of our (linguistic) minds. In §3, I argue that naturalistic inquiry allows no sense in which the physical is real and minds are not. Moral properties are a consequence of moral cognition, hence of having a certain kind of mind, and hence are as natural as these minds themselves. Truths about these properties are truths about the natural world, and one motivation for pluralism about truth therefore disappears. In §4, I nonetheless explore the possibility of a naturalistic interpretation of the pluralist intuition, namely as deriving from differences in the conceptual structure of domains of human knowledge; §5 points to apparently crucial *structural* aspects of truth, lending support to its linguistic nature and lack of rationale in external physical structures of the environment; §6 briefly contextualizes the approach in regards to deflationism; and §7 concludes.

2. Truth as a natural object

We may assume that linguistic behavior exhibits semantic properties—in addition to acoustic, electrophysiological, or phonological ones, say, from which the semantic ones are empirically distinguishable. I will here accept the existence of such properties as a matter of empirical observation and hypothesis, whatever their ultimate ontological status. What lends support to the assumption of their existence is the fact that we can fruitfully study them: they exhibit a systematic behavior and form a distinctive domain of inquiry with formal properties that are subject to theory.[2] Numerous ontological and metaphysical issues arise in this inquiry. But its success does not depend on addressing or prejudging them (and in practice, formal semantics in linguistics largely ignores them).

In the characterization of these properties, the human notion of truth naturally enters: speakers think of the sentences they hear as being put forward with assertoric force and as being true or false. It is the *truth* of something that we assert (not the probability, say, or its adaptive significance, or whatever other forms of semantic evaluation are conceivable in forms of communication that are unlike human language). Tarski's Convention T illustrates this: we tend to agree that snow is white if and only if 'snow is white' is *true*, and there is no other semantically evaluative predicate for which such equivalences are known to hold.[3] It makes sense, then, when studying truth as a natural

---

[2] For example, we find that, cross-linguistically, in the words of Huang, certain truth-theoretic aspects of sentences relating to the scope of quantifiers can 'to a large extent [be] seen to pattern on a par with matters of form' (1995: 131). This finding entails that linguistic form (syntax) and semantics align (in the respects in question). If so, this will be an interesting empirical finding, which we cannot justify in terms of metaphysical considerations, though it may well suggest certain metaphysical implications (see Hinzen & Uriagereka 2006).

[3] While assertions, therefore, necessarily involve some predication of truth (as opposed to another evaluative predicate), the predicate need not be expressed lexically. Thus, for example, the embedded clause in the sentence *She considered [that proposition true]* involves a predication of truth, but this clause does not occur asserted in that position. It is her considering the proposition in question true, which the speaker maintains is a fact. That is what he says is true. The difference lies in the fact that the main clause not only involves a (silent) predication of truth, but a finite Tense as well (the embedded clause, which is untensed, lacks this).

phenomenon, to study it as an aspect of our normal use of language and in terms of the semantic properties that such activity involves.

As inquiry into the naturalistic basis of our ordinary use of language has factually proceeded, it has been based on the rejection of a *physicalist methodology*: the attempt (Skinner 1957) to deduce properties of language from the physical features of the environments in which it is used. This methodology was motivated by a *metaphysical premise* (though perhaps not necessitated by it): Skinner endorsed a physicalist (more specifically eliminativist) metaphysics, according to which mental states do not exist. Hence, he concluded, explanations of linguistic facts must only appeal to physically identifiable variables. Crucially, Chomsky's well-known critique is *neutral* on this metaphysical premise: instead, it demonstrates that the physicalist methodology in question is too restrictive. The specific physicalist and externalist explanations offered for certain empirical linguistic phenomena shed no light on their nature and origin. *Internalist* determinants of linguistic behavior have to be taken into account, notably the existence of a *grammar* that lies behind human language use and powers its inherent generativity. Put differently, Chomsky endorses a *methodological* naturalism only, leaving metaphysics aside. That said, the inquiry driven by this methodological naturalism has at least prima facie mentalistic consequences: the physical aspects of the brain do not seem to illuminate the generative processes in question. These consequences may be consistent with a metaphysics of physicalism, but the enterprise does not depend on such a metaphysics and does not specifically support it, either. On some views, it directly *conflicts* with such a metaphysics, be it because physicalism is empty, unformulable, or in conflict with naturalistic inquiry (Chomsky 2000), or for other reasons (Hinzen 2006b, c; Hinzen & Uriagereka 2006).

The subject matter of naturalistic inquiry into human language has thus been the genesis—developmentally and evolutionarily—of a specific form of mental organization in creatures that have brains like us. This mentality matures in childhood on a biologically timed path (Stromswold 1999) reflecting a species-specific and unique way of organizing our experience: a biological a priori. Thus, babies reflexively categorize certain acoustic stimuli as 'linguistic' from their first days (Sebastián-Gallés 2009), imposing a richly constrained set of categories on them in subsequent months and years (syllable, word, noun, verb, etc.). This developmental path is stable cross-culturally as well as across a large range of sensory-motor deficits. Part of this process of maturation is the transition from imperative to declarative pointing, perhaps one of the first developmental signatures of a maturing notion of propositionality and truth (Terrace 2005). There is evidence that these two notions are inherently related to the evolution of human language. Thus there appear to be specific grammatical patterns on which judgments of truth depend (for further details, see §5), and there is developmental evidence that such specific forms of grammatical organization are instrumental in the development of the child's theory of (other) minds, to which the development of a concept of truth appears closely linked (de Villiers 2007). Arguably, a propositional mode of thought is part of the mental reorganization in the human lineage that made language possible and lies at the heart of the speciation of modern *Homo sapiens* itself (see Crow 2008).

The linguistic specificity of the phenomenon of truth is also supported by comparative considerations. Any animal has an adaptive system of cognition that can be used to represent its environment. Very few, and possibly only one species, however, exhibit productive and propositional forms of thought to which human notions of intentional reference and truth can be applied (Penn et al. 2008; Terrace 2005). Clearly, adaptive cognition does not *require* a propositional (as opposed to associative) mind. Ipso facto, generic notions of reference or representation do not illuminate what makes truth-theoretic cognition specific: the evolution of grammatical forms of organization must have added and possibly reformatted prelinguistic modes of thought. Nonhuman animal reference in particular is inherently functional, stimulus-bound, affective, largely non-compositional, and causally controlled (Hauser 2000). Human intentional reference as linked to the use of words and sentences appears to have precisely none of these properties, and indeed exhibits the opposite ones.

In what follows, I will thus assume that human truth is both connected to language and has a contingent evolutionary history behind it. It needs to be naturalistically explained. Any such explanation probably cannot hope to trace the origin of our *concept* of truth itself. But that concept might share this fate with most other human concepts (Fodor 1998), whose origins generally remain shrouded in mystery (and saying that they are 'innate' may be read as a way of conceding that). An inquiry into the process of cognitive maturation that underlies ordinary language use will often simply take for granted what concepts humans have and then discuss how these concepts are *mapped* to the overt verbal forms that a language has (see Gleitman et al. 2005; Gelman 2009). Particularly in the case of abstract concepts such as CAUSE, BELIEF, or OBJECT, it is unclear what the alternative could be.

A more likely object of inquiry, therefore, than the origin of such concepts, is how they are systematically *applied*, how they mature in childhood (Scholl 2007; Spelke 2003), and to what extent they are species-specific. Our judgments about when something is an 'object' or ceases to be the 'same' one—which exhibit a rich and systematic structure—in particular form part of a data set revealing implicit 'theories' of what objects (truth, causation, etc.) are. We may regard such theories as bringing out a particular 'metaphysics' that we intuitively hold (largely unaware of the principles that underlie it). That metaphysics will depend on available cognitive resources in a species and is thus partially species-specific (Mendes et al. 2008).

The process of cognitive growth involving concepts such as space, time, causation, or number has recently been described as involving 'foundational abstractions' (Gallistel 2009). They are 'foundational' in the broadly Kantian sense that experience is conditioned by them, indeed from early on in evolution and, in part, millions of years before humans arrived. They are 'abstract' in the sense that their contents are not given by low-level experiential data or stimuli. Truth, though not on Gallistel's list and less investigated in developmental psychology, appears to be a paradigmatic such foundational abstraction, as no learning, judging, or logical reasoning can do without such a notion. Without it, it seems that our metaphysics would be radically different, and in practical terms we would relate to the world in different ways. That we have a concept of truth is, therefore, part of the explanation of why we relate to the world in the way we do. It is *because* we have conceptual powers that other animals lack that we can mould our sense of reality differently. In particular, we can now make sense of the idea that the world might be a certain way even if it is not the way we think it is. A conception of 'objectivity' will form in our minds.

That we relate to the world in objective terms is not explained by standing in such a relation. Reference is not explained by positing a 'reference relation', and saying that truth is explained as a relation to The Truth is to trivialize the problem of the origin of truth. Even if there is a reference relation, we need a mind configured in the right way in order to position itself to the world in truth-theoretic terms: many, perhaps all, other animals fail to do so (they don't have science, don't explain, and don't think propositionally, though they approximate such forms of thought to varying degrees). Perhaps to say that a notion of truth arises because of how it relates us to the world is like saying, of a skeleton usable for walking, that walking caused the existence of this skeleton. Adaptation, generally, however, is not the cause of evolutionary novelty: it is its consequence (see Hinzen 2006d).

The notion of truth, then, I will take it, is an evolved aspect of a species-specific mode of cognition linked to the evolution of the faculty of language and one of a number of foundational abstractions that characterize our kind of mind. Having this mind will be the result of having had genetic accidents of an appropriate sort, leading to a reorganization of the brain allowing for language and the kind of thought that a language can encode (see Crow 2008 for a specific genetic proposal).[4] From a naturalistic point of view, a mind of this kind *may* be in a deep resonance with the world, and the truths it maintains may reflect the nature of this world. Even if so, this will not, for our naturalistic purposes, be the explanation of why this mind came to exist in evolution.

In summary, I have now outlined what I take the problem of the origin of truth to be and how we might tackle it empirically and naturalistically: as an aspect of how our kind of mind arose and what principles structure it,

---

[4] Genetic accidents of this sort are blind to their potential adaptive consequences.

grammatical ones in particular. Such inquiry proceeds on an internalist course and has a mentalistic ontology, though this leaves potential metaphysical conclusions open. Note that, from a naturalistic point of view, the *origin* of truth should clearly speak to its *nature*. Moreover, we have argued that what metaphysics we consider intuitively correct should reflect what kind of mind we happen to possess.

3. From metaphysical to methodological naturalism

Taking a step back from the above, why should we adopt the attitude of a methodological naturalism (Chomsky 2000) in the first place, and how does it affect the metaphysical premise from which truth-theoretic pluralism proceeds? Methodological naturalism consists in the stance that the methodological standards of naturalistic inquiry should and can be legitimately applied uniformly to any phenomenon of nature, regardless of its ontological status. Hence, a natural 'science' of the mind or of language is possible: its validation will simply lie in the standards of intelligibility applied, which need to be continuous with those of the core sciences, and it will depend on whether they can be fruitfully applied in the domains in question. Naturalism in this sense—which further pursues the early modern (seventeenth-century) goal of a 'Natural Philosophy'—involves no metaphysical claim: it doesn't say of which metaphysical nature anything ultimately is (e.g., whether it is something mental or physical). Metaphysical naturalism (Papineau 1993), by contrast, *does* involve such a claim: usually some form of (reductive or non-reductive) physicalism. Physicalism is the ontological view that everything that exists is physical (or supervenes on the physical, reduces to it, or is realized by it). It typically does *not* come with any specific methodological commitments.[5] Thus, for example, a physicalist would be unlikely to suggest, say, that economics should proceed using the tools of quantum physics. The claim is one about the ontology of economics as a science.

Problems for metaphysical naturalism arise when we see methodological naturalism to be in a certain tension with it and when a problem with its formulability arises. To start with the first problem, twentieth-century philosophy of mind appears to have largely arisen as a rejection of Cartesian dualism—not as the result of applying a naturalistic methodology to the study of mental properties or of particular results or milestones of such a study. Today the fight against Cartesian dualism continues on much the same grounds. Melnyk, in his *Physicalist Manifesto*, extensively argues that 'there *is* evidence that mental

---

[5] Where, in the past, metaphysical naturalism in the domains of language and the mind has involved a methodology, however, it has been that of behaviorism (Quine 1960) or the 'functional analysis of behavior' (Skinner 1957, ch.1; Lewis 1983). Such methodologies however are by and large abandoned.

phenomena are physical or physically realized' (2003: 281). Yet no empirical evidence is presented, and judging from the empirical study of mind today, it does not seem that dualism is any less supported by it empirically than physicalism. There neither were nor are particular empirical properties of brains that are explanatory for the structures of mental properties that we find across species, despite myriad interesting and curious *correlations* between mental processing and the physical activity of the brain that are studied in cognitive neuroscience today (Poeppel & Embick 2005). In short, it is unclear whether applying a naturalistic methodology to the study of mind actually supports the traditional and virtually axiomatic rejection of Cartesian dualism in the analytic philosophy of mind.[6]

Internalist inquiry in generative grammar, despite its mentalistic ontology (Chomsky 1957; Lenneberg 1967), is consistent with a trivial understanding of physicalism, where this doctrine consists in the contention that there is only one universe (or 'pluriverse'), which ('everything that exists') happens to be a physical one. Hence, everything is physical, including the mental objects whose structure modern linguistics aims to characterize. But a substantive doctrine of physicalism needs to have more in mind than this.

Where it is coupled with functionalism (Lycan 2003), a conflict with methodological naturalism directly arises. Functionalism stipulates that mind is function and is independent of species-specific forms of embodiment and any specific material basis involved. Yet, our mind is a species-specific endowment, the explanation of which appears to lie not least in the 'interfaces' that, say, the language system in the brain forms with extra-linguistic (e.g., perceptual, conceptual-intentional, emotional, etc.) systems (Chomsky 2008). Insight into the organization of language, in short, depends on its embodiment (see, e.g., Crow 2010).[7]

The functionalist notion that the mind consists of 'mental representations', too, where the latter are understood as symbols whose 'contents' are determined by relations to the external world, is also not consistent with the internal structures of mind as described in standard linguistics textbooks: theories characterizing the notion of a 'noun' or a /t/, say, do not make reference to any

---

[6] The conception of dualism that is criticized in this paradigm is, moreover, still largely the one inaugurated by Descartes. For some modern variants of dualism based on a different physics, and arguably supported by it, see Hinzen (2006c).

[7] Chomsky (2003) makes the stronger claim that functionalism *abandons* naturalism. Adopting a similarly functionalist attitude in the case of chemistry, say, he points out, would be like studying the laws of chemical combination "in general," irrespective of what specific physical universe we live in. Even where such levels of abstraction prove useful, as in Artificial Life research, they typically do not give rise to the *ontological* speculation that there are non-biological 'organism-types', on analogy with the functionalist's abstract 'mental state types' (Chomsky 2003: 261). These seem hardly the subject of naturalistic inquiry and do not seem to illuminate the principles organizing the mentality of particular organisms. The proposal to replace current paradigms in biolinguistics by the study of 'linguistic minds in general', irrespective of whether they are correlated with brains, robots, or angels, does not seem to be a naturalistic perspective to take either.

structure in the external environment that such notions pick out or 'refer' to. They reflect an aspect of our mental organization by means of which we organize our experience of acoustic stimuli, but they are not independently given physical aspects of the external world (for extensive discussion, see Rey 2003; Chomsky 2003).

Eliminative materialism in turn allows no naturalistic inquiry into the mind, as there is no mind, a metaphysical premise on this view. Supervenience theories in turn start from the premise of the priority of the 'physical', understood as something that axiomatically excludes the "mental." This doesn't invite a natural science of the mind either, and whether there is any sense of supervenience to the physical that illuminates mental properties of human and other natural beings is questionable in light of the fact that, arguably, physicalism, if defined as or involving an opposition to Cartesian dualism, became unformulable three hundred years ago. This argument is that Descartes' formulation of the mind-body problem depended on a notion of matter ('body', 'the physical') that science abandoned at the very end of the century in which dualism was born. Ever since then, there is no notion of 'body' any more from which 'mental' properties can be excluded (Chomsky 2000, ch. 4).

This argument needs to be answered by providing such a notion of body. Yet that cannot be Descartes' notion or an intuitive one, for both of these are based on a 'mechanical philosophy' now abandoned and on assumptions that natural science does not validate.[8] Natural science, however, offers no conceptually satisfactory replacement. With the acceptance of Newton's theory of gravitation, it became widely *accepted*—in philosophy notably by Hume and Locke—that even in the *physical* realm, causation is not in fact mechanical, and the mind-body problem is incoherent. If causation is not mechanical, there is no machine, but only a ghost. At the same time it was recognized that scientific theories—like Newton's—can be intelligible and explanatory, even if the world they describe is essentially not and remains mysterious to our understanding.[9] As Locke put it, there wasn't a conception of matter any more on which it could be ruled out that God might have superadded a faculty of thinking to it (Yolton 1983). With physical matter capable of thinking, materialism becomes incoherent, as do all reductionist, eliminativist, and supervenience theories, all of which presumably require for their basic coherence

---

[8] Shortly after Newton, the Jesuit Boscovich, in particular, conceptualized matter as essentially unextended (based on forces as the primitive ingredients of matter). Though particular proposals have of course been abandoned, by and large, this trend has continued: physical objects, as we intuitively think of them (heavy, solid, extended, localized, etc.), are not part of the 'furniture of the physical world' (thus current physicists speculate about the existence of 'massless mass', objects need not be localized in space, energy, which matter is, need not be extended, etc.).

[9] Thus Hume famously wrote that 'Newton seemed to draw off the veil from some of the mysteries of nature', but 'he shewed at the same time the imperfections of the mechanical philosophy; and thereby restored [Nature's] ultimate secrets to that obscurity in which they ever did and ever will remain' (Hume 1841: 341; see also Chomsky 2000: 110).

that matter (or whatever provides the reduction, realization, or supervenience base) doesn't think and has mental properties. Real matter out there, as Locke put it, is not *answerable* to our preconceptions of what it is like: 'our comprehension is no measure for the power of God' (quoted in Leibniz 1704/1996: 23; see also Hinzen 2006b: 7). It is simply subject to empirical and naturalistic inquiry instead, which has whatever ontological consequences it does and is subject to certain standards of intelligibility that the scientific community sets. The 'physical' is a catch-all term for what naturalistic inquiry will concoct: it imposes no constraints on ontology. Excluding properties from the physical that are now termed 'linguistic' would be like excluding properties termed 'chemical' in nineteenth-century chemistry—an unadvisable step now as much as then.

Minds are natural objects unproblematically, then, and as such objects of naturalistic inquiry. Some minds will associate acoustic patterns they perceive with more abstract phonological, syntactic, and semantic properties. If so, these reflect no properties that environments have irrespective of the minds in question that inhabit them. Talk about such properties is therefore not 'true or false' in a sense where truths depend on (or mirror) any nonlinguistic features of the external environment. A correspondence theory for truths about linguistic properties is therefore misconceived (as is a coherence theory). It is simply that minds, as natural objects, and because of their intrinsic structure, make environments exhibit such properties. The question, therefore, as to whether there 'really are' linguistic properties out there—realism about linguistic properties—is a wrong one, and similar remarks apply to moral and aesthetic properties, and for exactly the same reason.

Applying all of this to the problem of truth, there is no such thing as truth in the environment of a creature irrespective of what cognitive endowment it has. Propositional reasoning involves the ability to compose discrete and independent linguistic elements into more complex representations in systematic ways, giving rise to new properties recursively. This combinatorics is enacted in human brains alone and does not exist 'out there'. Objectivity and truth are a consequence of propositional minds (or the underlying brains), rather than their cause. We think objectively if we group our experiences into categories and these categories combine compositionally by specific and systematic laws. These laws are not found in experience. In this way, language, morality, and truth are in the mind of the beholder—the kind of mind that gives us propositional thoughts to think and can determine truth-values objectively. Relations between words or mental representations and the external physical world, if merely causal or functional, *don't* as such ground objective cognition. They are not *necessary* for it (as in the case of cognitive systems such as grammar, arithmetic, morality, or music), and they are not *sufficient* for it either: nonhuman animals might stand in the same causal relations to the external world or objects as independently characterized, yet they lack the ability to think objectively and make judgments about them.

As propositional minds work in the human case, this objectivity does indeed appear to affect the moral domain in ways it does the linguistic or folk-physical one. Morality is a domain of cognition to which abstract and systematic principles seem to apply, which do not vary arbitrarily with culture (Hauser et al. 2007; Mikhail 2007). Like in the case of language, where it is a matter of empirical discovery which linguistic representations of acoustic input our minds generate, it is a matter of empirical discovery which moral representations our minds generate for particular kinds of environmental triggers. The question can be studied experimentally and naturalistically and has been. Moral properties are therefore real, and the notion of the physical that requires us to expel them from the physical universe depends on the rejection of methodological naturalism in the study of the mental aspects of nature. It so happens that we have minds that impose linguistic (propositional), aesthetic, and moral structure on our experience, which will therefore exhibit such properties. Insofar as this is the case, truth-theoretic pluralism proceeds from a false problem: cleansing the physical of whatever doesn't fit our ontology is itself to reject the attitude of a methodological naturalism. No pluralism is called for to make sense of our judgments about moral, aesthetic, or linguistic properties, since 'correspondence to a physical world' fails for them. Judgments in these domains are of course empirically very different. Yet, as I will argue in the next section, this is not plausibly due to any polysemy in the concept of truth applied in them, or else its functional nature.

4. Response-dependence

According to the current 'core knowledge' hypothesis, human knowledge comes prestructured through a small number of cognitive domains such as number, morality, geometry, social relations, and object mechanics, none of which are specific to humans (Spelke 2003; Gelman 2009; Gallistel 2009). These systems—replacing the older view that the mind is comprised of a myriad of specialized and functionally dedicated 'modules'—internally direct the infant's active engagement with its environment and its appropriation to the infant's specific mode of cognition. As argued, they constitute a biological a priori. Hence every 'correspondence' with the world is mediated by this a priori. That said, depending on the core domain in question, there may be a higher or lower degree of *external control* of the properties of stimuli that the cognitive system represents (Fodor 2000). Thus, one can imagine that the evolution of a cognitive system interpreting motion through a system of principles determining object permanency and potential causes of motion is subject to greater external control from the physical environment than a core system determining grammatical or musical properties. In the latter case, the external physical conditions impose few demands on what such a system has to be like. The social environment will constrain externalizations of such grammatical configurations to be usable and communicable, but communication as such poses few constraints on which structures a communication system contains, as the large variety of communication systems in animal nature suggests. In the case of the former kind of cognitive system, however, no such system is likely to prevail if its principles do not cohere with what the physical world is actually like. Here we expect a relatively tight coupling and covariance between cognition and the environment, and we don't expect much variance in such judgments across human populations.

Now, as we noted, the pluralist grants the correspondence intuition for some instances of truth while seeing it as inappropriate for others. As Lynch thinks of the correspondence theory, it is plausible only where 'mental states with G-ish content are causally responsive to an external environment that contains Gs [. . .]. In a bumper sticker, *if we are to correspond, we must respond*' (2009: 32). In the context of the above, we might now say that the pluralist intuition arises from the fact that human knowledge happens not to be a unitary domain but a highly structured one, and that, in particular, there may be a higher or lower degree of *external control* for a given cognitive system. In none of the cases where there is less control should this convince us that the properties represented are therefore not real, however. In this sense, we can happily accept that the truth is plural, and its nature can be partially determined by the respective conceptual structures of the core knowledge domains in question.

In short, in some domains of cognition, mental structures are more responsive to the structure of an environment as independently characterized. Even in the most plausible cases where we may assume this, though, 'correspondence' now still cannot mean anything like the mirroring of an independently characterizable external structure. There appears to be no empirical evidence for this assumption, and the linguistic specificity of the structures that support a propositional mode of thought (see the following section) appear to provide contrary evidence: the relevant grammatical patterns do not appear to mirror any independently characterizable structures out there. Even where external control is manifestly exerted, the natural selection of a cognitive system that satisfies certain external and adaptive demands is arguably not a *causal* force (Hinzen 2006d). If so, we cannot assume, even in such cases, that the external structure of an environment brings internal cognitive systems into place, even though it can, at a population level, lead to *stabilizing* them within a given range of variants in the population.

There may be cases where the connection between the internal structures of an adaptive cognitive system and the structure of an environment is so close that it can be characterized through a kind of isomorphism. As Gallistel (1990) has documented, for example, insect navigation forms an example where cognitive systems are *representational* ones standing in a one-to-one correlation to selective aspects of an environment to which the computations involved optimally adapt the animal. However, even if we follow this characterization of the experimental evidence in question, there are no independently identifiable, selective aspects of an environment to which *language* uniquely adapts us: as Descartes (1637/1984) first stressed, it is a *universal* tool, which can be appropriately used in any circumstance or ontological domain.

A cautionary note is thus in place for validating the correspondence intuition, even in cognitive domains where it seems more appropriate due to a greater degree of external control: what is externally controlled, in this case, are linguistic acts that involve structures that lack, as far as we know, externalist origins. There is also another (and related) cautionary note. Despite differences in degrees of external control, *any* act of assertion involving the right structural configuration and the notion of truth comes with an element of objective force. As we ordinarily use language, the lack of connection between a judgment and the structure of the external physical world is no reason for us to qualify the alethic force with which we put utterances forward. Quite the contrary: we get as (or indeed more) passionate about the truth of religious and aesthetic matters as about physical ones. We may passionately agree or disagree with whether Mahler was a great composer and consider this a matter of objective fact (however difficult to assess). While doing so, we have no such qualms as what belongs to the furniture of the physical world or how 'physical' music is. Neither does it seem descriptively adequate to claim, of somebody who finds that torture is wrong, that what he is saying is not that it is true that torture is wrong, but that this fact merely 'coheres with his beliefs'. Such a person, particularly in a heated debate, could certainly find that torture is wrong, *period*—whatever other beliefs others might hold.

Truth, then, is a paradigmatically domain-general notion, in the same way that language is a domain-general device (Spelke 2003).[10] By cutting across domains, truth has a unitary character as opposed to a domain-specific one, which is a naturalistic argument against the pluralist conclusion. Overall, then, there are aspects to the claim that truth is a different property in different domains of discourse (Wright 1992) that can be naturalized, for what we

---

[10] Much of the point of the core knowledge hypothesis is that language and our ability to use it is paradigmatically domain-general and independent of ontology: with human language, a cognitive system has evolved for the first time that unlike core knowledge systems allows thinking *across* domain boundaries, as in the expression 'to the left of the green square, whenever you hear a noise', which combines systems of spatial orientation, color, acoustics, time, and geometry in one single complex property (Spelke 2003).

talk about in these domains is conceptually and ontologically different. Since numbers are abstract and material objects are not, human judgments in both domains will function differently. Domains are different if their ontology is and if core knowledge principles operative in one domain will not be applied in the other; but this does not affect the way we reason about them using language, if language is a paradigmatically domain-general device. If truth goes with language it is not plausible to conclude, from differences in core knowledge domains, that truth (or ways of being true) differs, too. Once language evolved in the human lineage, we can transcend the differences that core domains of knowledge encode: truth becomes unitary. Whether I talk about numbers or tables makes no difference to the way I predicate truth within certain grammatical patterns.[11]

5. Truth as structural

Human languages are combinatorial systems, containing rules or principles for combining primitive elements into more complex structures. This happens at multiple levels, with different rules and primitives involved in each case: in particular, it happens at phonological, syntactic, and semantic levels. As complex linguistic units arise, their combinatorial primitives come to stand in a small number of structural relations that have intrinsic semantic effects at the syntax-semantics interface. Thus, for example, as a verb combines with its first, or 'internal', nominal argument, that argument will stand in a specific thematic relation to the verb: it will play the roles of a Theme/Patient or Experiencer, as in the events denoted by the verbs (Vs) in (1) and (2):

(1) [$_{VP}$ kill [Bill]]
     THEME

(2) [$_{VP}$ frighten [me]]
     EXPERIENCER

As structure building continues beyond the bounds of the verbal phrase, a sentence will arise in which this verb phrase will stand in a relation of predication to the sentence's subject, which may be the verb's internal argument (as for example in passives; see (3) below) and is otherwise its external argument. If it is the internal, this argument is, in systematic ways, still interpreted as a Theme/Patient, as is in the nature of an internal argument (see again (3)). If it

---

[11] It is interesting that, as an abstract concept, TRUTH, like BEAUTY, does not allow for pluralization: (i) and (ii) are deviant (unless, in (i), the interpretation changes, and some personifications of beauty, say, are intended):
   (i) ??I saw three beauties
   (ii) ??All beauties are problematic

is the external, this argument is, again systematically, either interpreted as the Theme (if the internal argument is an Experiencer, as in (4)) or as the Agent (if it is not, as in (5)):

(3) [Bill [$_{VP}$ was [killed]]]
    THEME

(4) [That [$_{VP}$ frightens [me]]]
    THEME   EXPERIENCER

(5) [John [$_{VP}$ killed [Bill]]]
    AGENT   THEME

Moving beyond verbal phrases, if we generate a configuration in which there is a subject and a predicate, but a specification of finite Tense is missing, as in (6), we get a predicational structure, but not a truth-evaluable one: (6), whether standing alone or occurring in (7), is not evaluated as either true or false:

(6) [John stupid]

(7) I consider [John stupid]

Even where the subject-predicate configuration, unlike (6), can occur self-standingly, as in (8), the expression need not be evaluable for truth: clearly, (8) tends to have an emotional content that we don't find in ordinary propositional claims. That makes (8) not quite equivalent to (9):

(8) You idiot!

(9) You are an idiot.

Hence, it is clear that there is—as structural complexity builds up—a *progression* toward a properly truth-evaluable structure: nothing short of exactly the right kind of complexity will be grammatically evaluable as true or false. It isn't that a sentence is needed, for (8) presumably is a sentence, as is (10), and (6) is at least a clause. Yet none of these are either true or false:

(10) Who killed Bill?

Therefore, it is not that a sentence is needed, but rather, the right kind of underlying abstract configuration and its inherent structural relations—something that only a syntactic analysis reveals.

As we have seen, the first essential unit in this progression is that corresponding to a completed verbal phrase: having that, we have a representation of an *event*, with its intrinsic Agents, Patients, Experiencers, and so on assigned: to take a concrete case, suppose we have the root of an event, call it √DESTRUCT, which is not yet specified for either nominality or verbality, and an Agent and a Patient, say 'Caesar' and 'Syracuse', as in (11):

(11) Caesar √DESTRUCT Syracuse

Naturalizing Pluralism about Truth

Clearly, then, we have the basic elements of an event, and yet, (11) isn't yet either true or false. The root in question can now be further specified formally and get categorized. If the category is determined to be a nominal one (N), as in (12), we still have nothing that is either true or false:

(12) Caesar's [$_N$ √DESTRUCT-ion (of) Syracuse].

Truth therefore plainly depends on categorical specifications beyond the decision on eventive ingredients, which are all present in (11). Only (13) does the job of yielding a truth-evaluable object—at least as long as it remains unembedded as a clause, for if it enters another configuration and becomes subordinated, it ceases to be a truth-functional ingredient of the structure that embeds it (as in (14), where the truth of *John believes that Caesar destructed Syracuse* does not depend on whether or not Caesar did any such thing):

(13) [Caesar [$_V$ √DESTRUCT-ed Syracuse]]
(14) John believes that [Caesar [$_V$ √DESTRUCT-ed Syracuse]]

One thing is clear in this progression toward truth-theoretic complexity: (12) and (13) involve the exact same event. So an event representation is only a proper subset of the ingredients we need for a structure that is evaluable for truth, like (13). It is a *necessary* sub-part, though: it is the *thematic basis* on which a judgment of truth is inherently constructed. If (13) is uttered in discourse, the finite Tense specified on the verb will anchor the event specified in the verbal phrase at a time prior to the point of speech. The alethic force that such an assertion can at this point come with can now be conceded or rejected.

In sum, extensional and truth-theoretic forms of evaluation arise, not in the beginning of a derivation (words are not true or false), but only at its very end (neither verbal nor nominal phrases, nor embedded clauses, are evaluated as true or false). As complexity builds up toward this point, different ontologies arise on the way: in particular, an ontology of objects (associated to nominals) and of events (associated to verbal phrases). This ontology does not constrain what other ontology we adopt in physics (the world might consist all and only of waves, for that matter), and external control for this linguistic ontology from physics is presumably weak.

So far in this section we have talked about truth as involved in linguistic acts that are structurally constrained, compromising the sense in which such acts can be made sense of as mirroring an independently given structure of external environments. The nature and origin of truth in this sense relates to the nature and origin of the syntactic configurations that our minds need to generate in order to give rise to it: it is, inherently, a *structural* phenomenon. On the other hand, it of course also so happens that most or all human languages *lexicalize* a way of formally evaluating the use of linguistic expressions in discourse: they have *words* such as (in English) 'truth' and 'true', based on the same lexical root, √TRUE. Words are not configurations. Truth is thus both a structural/configurational and a lexical phenomenon.

√TRUE lexicalizes (gives lexical expression to) the phenomenon of alethic force. Retrieving lexical items involving this root from our mental dictionaries, we can now do things like commenting on what others have said without necessarily mentioning it ('What you say is true', 'John said that the earth moves; but that's not true', etc.). The use and distribution of this lexical root appears to tell us what we noted at the end of the previous section: it is applied uniformly across domains, and its use does not appear sensitive to considerations of which 'physical' properties are involved. It appears primarily sensitive to the right grammatical configurations, and it is interesting to see that, in languages across the world where the *source of evidence* for an assertion is obligatorily specified in the grammar of a sentence (Aikhenvald 2004), this does *not* affect the truth-value assigned. That, again, is evidence that our concept truth, as it functions when we engage in acts of assertion, is *not* sensitive to differences in domains relating to such things as how truths are established. Note this is a claim about truth-theoretic cognition, not a metaphysical claim about the nature of truth.

The function and content of the predicate 'is true' brings us finally to our last topic, the question of how close the present, non-metaphysical approach is to the metaphysics of truth that the deflationist proclaims.

6. Deflationism within bounds

Given the above one could, if one wanted, agree to the deflationist's claim that truth has no substantive nature: on the deflationist view, truth is wrongly characterized as involving anything like correspondence, and to whatever extent our concept of truth corresponds to a 'property', that property is only a shallow one that doesn't go beyond the concept we have of it. From a naturalistic point of view, talk of properties is questionable, too, and needs to be naturalized. It makes no sense, in particular, from the present point of view, to say that the lexical root √TRUE is a 'property'. Assuming that a property is something that we can *predicate* of something else, what comes closest to a property is the word 'true' used as part of a verbal phrase, 'be true'. The word 'truth' or the phrase 'the truth' are distinct from that. The latter in particular semantically depicts a thing, not a property. There is also 'being true', which presumably depicts an ongoing state of affairs. We thus see denotation and semantic intuitions changing with the grammatical construction used, and the question of what truth is, ontologically speaking, and whether it is a property makes little sense: we need a grammatical construction to assess this question. A natural explanation of why denotation changes is that 'the truth' is structuralized as a noun phrase, while 'something's being true' is a gerund (a nominalized verbal phrase), and 'be true' is a verbal phrase (which, when combined with a finite Tense (T), as in '(this) [$_T$ is true]', yields a sentential predicate). Again, there is no sense in which truth, intrinsically, is a property (or not): it can only be mapped to a property if it occurs in the right grammatical configuration.

If it does so occur, talk about a sentential predicate's being 'mapped to a property' (as opposed to a thing or state of affairs) need not be understood as a remark with metaphysical import: it can be taken as what Wittgenstein would have called a 'grammatical remark'. Evidence for this is that we lack independent evidence—evidence independent of the specific grammatical forms used—for when something is a property, or 'really exists' as a property. There is no empirical research program investigating 'properties', in general, any more than *which* 'properties', in general, exist. No search for properties outside of human heads will find truth as one of them.

Whether or not truth really is a property, outside of the head, in addition to being a human lexical concept grammaticalized in particular ways and predicated of certain kinds of subjects within sentential configurations, thus does not seem a well-defined question. It is, of course, not a property like 'being bald' or 'being soluble', as Horwich (1998) stresses. But this is not a metaphysical insight: it follows from the intrinsic content of the concept, which happens to be abstract. Yet, to say that truth, therefore, 'denotes an abstract property' (or not) is, as far as I can see, again to make a grammatical remark rather than an empirical claim.

Lynch (2006, §4), arguing against the particular pluralism of Wright (1992), suggests that truth is the *same* (functional) property across domains and that this property is more than the concept we have of it. Yet, we cannot know which property we are meant to think about here, unless we understand it as the property denoted by *that concept*. Understanding the concept is what allows the mapping to the 'property' in question. Again, an independent access to the property in question seems to be lacking. Lynch's argument for the need for a distinctive property of truth, realized by different properties (correspondence, coherence, etc.) in different domains, derives from the explanatory role of truth. It is widely maintained, for example, that the truth of a particular proposition explains why we should believe it.[12] Hence, Lynch reasons, it is also the case that when we reason across domains using an apparently univocal notion of truth, a single property of truth is needed to explain why I should draw the particular inferences in question or consider them sound. Now, it may indeed be the case that a prior grasp of the concept of truth is needed to explain why we draw certain inferences. But if a single, unified property of truth is needed to make such

---

[12] Though it seems uninformative to claim that when we wonder whether we should believe a particular proposition—i.e., whether the proposition in question is true—what decides over whether we should believe it or not is the proposition's truth. It is *always* the case that if we wonder whether A is B, A's being B is a reason for endorsing that A is B.

explanations work, the differences between different properties of truth that the pluralist argues for have to be precisely ignored again: having established diversity, unity is now called for. What, however, makes for this unitary 'property', and what allows us to grasp it or refer to it, if not the univocal *concept* that we have of it? If so, it is that concept that unifies the differences, not any unitary functional property of truth, realized by different properties in different domains.

Denouncing, with some deflationists, all such metaphysical talk of 'properties', one could agree that Caesar destructed Syracuse just in case it is true that he did. This assertion, on the above analysis, holds because the lexical item "true" as used in this equivalence is precisely what allows us to comment on what happens when we assert such things as that Caesar destructed Syracuse. It makes an alethic force formally explicit. For the same reason, however, the equivalence does not *illuminate* the notion of truth, in the way that the deflationist says it does. As I see it, the problem is this. *Either* the equivalence really is an intuitive equivalence. Then what it states is the equivalence between a sentence used with assertoric force and a sentence in which that assertoric force is made formally explicit. Nothing is therefore won, in terms of understanding what is involved in this alethic force (which *involves* a predication of truth, as noted in §2). *Or*, it is *not* an equivalence, and then it simply doesn't hold. That is so if, for example, its left-hand side ('Caesar destructed Syracuse') is understood as a mere proposition *without* specified alethic force. In short, either the equivalence tells us nothing, or it is not an equivalence. We cannot concur, therefore, that the basic explanatory tool of the deflationist, the equivalence we have just discussed, removes the mysteries that the human phenomenon of truth poses.

In fact these abound, speaking against the basic deflationist contention. While we have here tried to push the attitude of methodological naturalism to its extremes, substituting it for a metaphysical approach to its essential nature, we have won nothing in terms of the mystery that the notion of truth involves. As things stand, we are clueless as to how the structural relations evolved that enter into the configurational patterns depicted in §5. Although research on the evolution of language is well under way, it would be self-delusional to claim that we understand the evolution of just about any unit of linguistic organization—let alone the 'maximal' forms of complexity that a judgment of truth, as we have seen, depends on. It seems reasonably clear, by now, that animal calls and symbols are radically different from human lexical concepts both phonologically and semantically (Hauser et al. 2002: 1576; Hauser 2000). The evolution of even the simplest atomic lexical items in the human cognitive system confronts us with a mystery: 'lexicalization' is a name for a process about which we understand very little.

Experiments can be done that illuminate the problem, but they leave the basic mystery untouched: how we possess lexical concepts in the first place, which we map to language specific words when acquiring a language (Gleitman et al. 2005). As Gleitman shows, knowing about the syntactic frames in which words appear helps infants to solve this mapping problem—which says next to nothing about how the concepts are acquired to start with. A sentential complement for example makes us expect that the concept expressed by the verb taking it as its internal argument must be something like *believe*, *doubt*, or *wonder*. If we take this as an indication, it is not an unreasonable conjecture that understanding the structural configuration that judgments of truth require helps us in acquiring a word such as 'true' as well. For the *concept* of truth, again, this does not help.

It is useless to hold that truth has no metaphysical nature or that it finds a naturalistic explanation, if, in the naturalistic investigation of this phenomenon, mystery over mystery reappear. It is equally unhelpful to sound defeatist, for the evolution of language or our propositional mind can be, and is, investigated experimentally. Yet, with regard to human intentionality, reference, and truth, and even the conceptual understanding that is prior to these, it remains the case that there has been little progress.

In this context, the philosophies of language and mind have taken the route of illuminating the meanings of words and sentences through the notion of a relation of reference or representation to an external world. It is suggested that it is precisely here where the mystery of human concepts and meaning can be lifted. Yet, as noted in §2, to be told that there are words and that there are objects, and that the former 'refer' to the latter, is merely to restate the phenomenon to be explained. No doubt the word 'London' is used to refer to London. Yet how this happens, and why it happens in the specific ways it does, is precisely what we wanted to know.

As we begin to inquire into this phenomenon, the sense in which London is an external 'object' dissipates into thin air. One would like to know: *which* object, and be able to identify it somehow, independently of the word 'London' and our use of it (which would be circular). But as we quickly notice, we refer to London with and without regard to its location, as in the sentence (15):

(15) This city should be relocated elsewhere.

As Chomsky (2000: 37) has observed, London might be destroyed and rebuilt later, like Carthage, though on a different spot. People might consider it the 'same city' then, or perhaps even the 'same place', even if, through an additional tsunami, London ceases to be a city and only a small habitation is left. London might come to be covered entirely in a solid layer of rock due to a volcanic eruption, to be uncovered later and rising to its old grandeur. We might comment then that it—'the same city'—has become a much *happier* city, taking its mental aspects in view this time, rather than its location or physical structure. It might be less *polluted* also, then, though the mental aspects of its inhabitants wouldn't be, in this case.

These are some of the intrinsic properties of the referent of 'London': it has concrete and abstract, physical and mental features. There is one single thing, London, and it has all of these characteristics. It is to say nothing about the explanatory problems that the above acts of reference pose, if we say that there is an object out there, London, and there is a word 'London', and there is 'a reference relation' between them. Much the same remarks apply to the problem of truth thought of as a relation to the world.

Progress that has been made in semantics has almost entirely been in the domain of *internal* aspects of meaning (mental computations), such as the generation of hierarchical structures underlying sentences and the compositional semantic effects of these structures. Pursuing the internalist course of our inquiry, we note that it illuminates the phenomenon of reference, if we see, in the transition from the structural complexity of (11) to that of (12), that one of these expressions has reference (namely, (12)), while the other only provides a conceptualization (of an event) that enters into the reference encoded in (12). Hence we can analyze the difference between (11) and (12), which makes the former have a merely conceptual use, while the latter has an intentional one (Uriagereka 2002). The difference is one of the internal representations assigned to these strings by human speakers. We can also analyze what makes (12) different from (13), given that both have intentional and referential properties, but the one refers to an event, while the other refers to a time at which this event took place. Since (13) is true or false, while (12) is not, the problem of the nature and origin of truth would be significantly illuminated if we understood the difference between these two very expressions. Similarly, we need to understand the difference between an embedded or subordinated clause, which does not carry truth-values, and a root clause, which can.

Answers to these questions are sought in an internalist inquiry into the operative generative principles. The principles in question do not refer to the structure of the external environment but to the nature and derivation of the syntactic categories involved and their semantic reflexes. This is, then, to reiterate the claim that the origin of truth, a stronghold of externalism, is precisely to be sought in an internalist direction (Hinzen 2003, 2006a, 2007). It is the external relations that judgments of truth involve where mysteries abound, and no real progress has been made. Deflating the 'property' of truth should not be a path to ignoring these mysteries, which traditional metaphysical theories of truth rightly target.

7. Conclusions

Truth arises as an aspect of the mental organization of human beings—an evolved mental architecture that, ever since Skinner (1957), has proved hard to illuminate in externalist and physicalist terms. Its causes are internal and intrinsic to the development of the organisms we are. As this mental organization gets into place in human development, we come to apply a conception of truth to configurations of specific grammatical types. These configurations apparently have no externalist rationale and they only appear to be under weak external control. Arguably they reflect a more abstract, domain-general mode of cognition that transcends the ontological and structural differences implicit in core domain of knowledge that we share with other animals. As such, and if truth is an aspect of this novel format of thought, truth is not plural, notwithstanding the different ways in which different core domains of knowledge carve out the space of human experience. There appears to be no external property to which the truth-concept responds, either.

Given the above, it would be useful to study the origin of truth on an internalist basis, from a perhaps more Kantian stance, rather than departing from external relations. Such a study should not be made dependent on a notion of the physical, which I have argued naturalistic inquiry does not support. Neither should we pursue the search for external properties of the physical environment in order to understand what lends moral, linguistic, or aesthetic judgments the objective and alethic force that they clearly have.

References

Aikhenvald, A. (2004). *Evidentiality*. Oxford: Oxford University Press.
Blackburn, S. (1991). Just causes. *Philosophical Studies* 61: 11–15.
Carstairs-McCarthy, A. (1999). *The Origins of Complex Language: An Inquiry into the Evolutionary Beginnings of Sentences, Syllables, and Truth*. Oxford: Oxford University Press.
Chomsky, N. (1957/1985). *Syntactic Structures*. The Hague: Mouton.
Chomsky, N. (2000). *New Horizons in the Study of Language and Mind*. Cambridge: Cambridge University Press.
Chomsky, N. (2003). *Replies*. In L. Antony & N. Hornstein (eds.), *Chomsky and His Critics* (255–328). Oxford: Blackwell.
Chomsky, N. (2008). Approaching UG from below. In U. Sauerland & H.-M. Gärtner (eds.), *Interfaces + Recursion = Language? Chomsky's Minimalism and the View from Syntax-Semantics* (1–29). Berlin: Mouton de Gruyter.
Crow, T. (2008). The 'big bang' theory of the origin of psychosis and the faculty of language. *Schizophrenia Research* 102: 31–52.
Crow, T. (2010). The nuclear symptoms of schizophrenia reveal the four-quadrant structure of language and its deictic frame. *Journal of Neurolinguistics* 23: 1–9.
de Villiers, J. G. (2007). The interface of language and theory of mind. *Lingua* 117: 1858–1878.
Descartes, R. (1637/1984). *Discours de la méthode*, ed. E. Gilson. Paris: Vrin.
Fodor, J. A. (1998). *Concepts*. Oxford: Clarendon.
Fodor, J. A. (2000). *The Mind Doesn't Work That Way: The Scope and Limits of Computational Psychology*. Cambridge, MA: MIT Press.
Gallistel, R. (1990). *The Organization of Learning*. Cambridge, MA: MIT Press.

Gallistel, R. (2009). The foundational abstractions. In Piattelli-Palmarini, J. Uriagereka, & P. Salaburu (eds.), *Of Minds and Language: A Dialogue with Noam Chomsky in the Basque Country* (58–73). Oxford: Oxford University Press.

Gelman, R. (2009). Innate learning and beyond. In Piattelli-Palmarini, J. Uriagereka, & P. Salaburu (eds.), *Of Minds and Language: A Dialogue with Noam Chomsky in the Basque Country* (223–238). Oxford: Oxford University Press.

Gleitman, L. R., K. Cassidy, R. Nappa, A. Papafragou, & J. C. Trueswell. (2005). Hard words. *Language Learning and Development* 1: 23–64.

Harman, G. (1977). *The Nature of Morality*. Oxford: Oxford University Press.

Hauser, M., F. Cushman, L. Young, R. Kang-Xing Jin & J. Mikhail. (2007). A dissociation between moral judgments and justifications. *Mind and Language* 22: 1–21.

Hauser, M., N. Chomsky, & W. T. Fitch. (2002). The faculty of language: what is it, who has it, and how did it evolve? *Science* 298: 1569–1579.

Hauser, M. D. (2000). *Wild Minds*. New York: Holt.

Hinzen, W. (2003). Truth's fabric. *Mind and Language* 18: 194–219.

Hinzen, W. (2006a). Internalism about truth. *Mind and Society* 5: 139–166.

Hinzen, W. (2006b). *Mind Design and Minimal Syntax*. Oxford: Oxford University Press.

Hinzen, W. (ed.). (2006c). *Prospects for Dualism: Interdisciplinary Perspectives (special issue). Erkenntnis* 65: 1–4.

Hinzen, W. (2006d). Spencerism and the causal theory of reference. *Biology and Philosophy* 21: 71–94.

Hinzen, W. (2007). *An Essay on Names and Truth*. Oxford: Oxford University Press.

Hinzen, W. & J. Uriagereka. (2006). On the metaphysics of linguistics. *Erkenntnis* 65: 71–96.

Horwich, P. (1998). *Truth, 2nd ed*. Oxford: Oxford University Press.

Huang, J. T. (1995). Logical form. In G. Webelhuth (ed.), *Government and Binding Theory and the Minimalist Program* (125–176). Oxford: Blackwell.

Hume, D. (1841). *The History of England, vol. 6*. London: T. Cadell.

Jackson, F. (2006). Representation, truth, and realism. *Monist* 89: 50–62.

Leibniz, G. W. (1704/1996). *Neue Abhandlungen über den menschlichen Verstand*. Hamburg: Meiner.

Lenneberg, E. (1967). *Biological Foundations of Language*. New York: Wiley.

Lewis, D. K. (1983). Mad pain and Martian pain. In his *Philosophical Papers, vol. 1* (122–130). Oxford: Oxford University Press.

Lycan, W. (2003). Chomsky on the mind-body problem. In L. Antony & N. Hornstein (eds.), *Chomsky and His Critics* (11–28). Oxford: Blackwell.

Lynch, M. P. (2006). ReWrighting pluralism. *Monist* 89: 63–84.

Lynch, M. P. (2009). *Truth as One and Many*. Oxford: Clarendon.

Melnyk, A. (2003). *A Physicalist Manifesto*. Cambridge: Cambridge University Press.

Mendes, N. H., H. Rakoczy, & J. Call. (2008). Ape metaphysics: object individuation without language. *Cognition* 106: 730–749.

Mikhail, J. (2007). Universal moral grammar: theory, evidence and the future. *Trends in Cognitive Sciences* 11: 143–152.

Papineau, D. (1993). *Philosophical Naturalism*. Oxford: Blackwell.

Poeppel, D. & D. Embick. (2005). Defining the relation between linguistics and neuroscience. In A. Cutler (ed.), *21st Century Psycholinguistics: Four Cornerstones* (103–118). Mahwah, NJ: Lawrence Erlbaum.

Quine, W. v O. (1960). *Word and Object*. Cambridge: Cambridge University Press.

Rey, G. (2003). Chomsky, intentionality, and a CRTT. In L. Antony & N. Hornstein (eds.), *Chomsky and His Critics* (105–139). Oxford: Blackwell.

Scholl, B. J. (2007). Object persistence in philosophy and psychology. *Mind and Language* 22: 563–591.

Sebastián-Gallés, N. (2009). Individual differences in foreign sound perception. In Piattelli-Palmarini, J. Uriagereka, & P. Salaburu (eds.), *Of Minds and Language: A Dialogue with Noam Chomsky in the Basque Country* (344–351). Oxford: Oxford University Press.

Skinner, B. F. (1957). *Verbal Behaviour*. Acton, MA: Copley Publishing Group.

Spelke, E. S. (2003). What makes us smart? Core knowledge and natural language. In D. Gentner & S. Goldin-Meadow (eds.), *Language in Mind: Advances in the Investigation of Language and Thought* (277–311). Cambridge, MA: MIT Press.

Stromswold, K. (1999). The cognitive neuroscience of language acquisition. In M. Gazzaniga (ed.), *The New Cognitive Neurosciences* (909–932). Cambridge, MA: MIT Press.

Tarski, A. (1936/1983). Establishment of scientific semantics. In his *Logic, Semantics, Metamathematics: Papers from 1923 to 1938*, ed. J. Corcoran (401–408). Indianapolis: Hackett.

Terrace, H. S. (2005). Metacognition and the evolution of language. In H. S. Terrace & J. Metcalfe (eds.), *The Missing Link in Cognition* (84–115). Oxford: Oxford University Press.

Uriagereka, J. (2002). *Derivations*. London: Routledge.

Wright, C. J. G. (1992). *Truth and Objectivity*. Cambridge, MA: Harvard University Press.

Yolton, J. W. (1983). *Thinking Matter. Materialism in Eighteenth-Century Britain*. Minneapolis: University of Minnesota Press.

{ 12 }

On Describing the World
Dorothy Grover

> Now, what I want is, Facts. Teach these boys and girls nothing but Facts. Facts alone are wanted in life. Plant nothing else, and root out everything else. [. . .] Stick to the Facts, sir!
>
> DICKENS *(1854/1996: 1)*

1. Introduction

Pluralism is sometimes taken to be the view that there is more than one way of describing the world. Whether or not pluralism defined along these lines is defensible partly depends on the account given of descriptions. And so I begin this essay with a discussion of descriptions.

Descriptions we construct of the world vary from context to context. Across the sciences, dissimilar objects, states, and processes are identified. Black holes, electrons, climate change, and molecules feature in some sciences; living things, DNA, genes, species, hopes, fears, memories, and phobias, in others; societies, religious beliefs, political movements, wars, laws, numbers, tunes, and smells, in yet others. The structures of our descriptions also vary. Some are presented in rhyme, some use diagrams or models, while others have an axiomatic structure. There are many reasons for this variation: the world, background beliefs, background language, interests and needs, and the purposes of individual descriptions. So descriptions vary from context to context.

Reactions to this multiplicity have varied widely. Some have assumed there is a single complete description that will cover all the facts, finitely encapsulated. Some are skeptical a complete description is possible. Others claim there may be more than one unified complete description. Goodman (1978) argued that right descriptions and depictions make for many different worlds. I doubt the notion of a complete description is coherent. (I will not be defending this speculation in this chapter.)

If, for whatever reason, neither a single description nor a combination of descriptions do yield a complete description, what status do our descriptions have? I argue that though descriptions that inform us may not add up to a complete description, we need not be left with just a disparate assortment of descriptions. Rather, our different descriptions provide a necessary variety of perspectives on the world. These perspectives, in combination, provide information we use, or may potentially use, in rational decision making. This position is defended in §5.

Assuming this perspectival view of descriptions, I then assess the possibilities for pluralism, including alethic pluralism.

Background material is provided in §§2–4. An exploratory discussion of descriptions is given in §2. In §3, I present Anderson & Belnap's (1975) suggestion that there is value in having multiple perspectives, not only in the perception of physical objects, but also of formal structures. In §4, I briefly review portions of Millikan's (2000) seminal account of substances, and then appeal to that account in §5 in order to argue the case for multiple perspectives. As a way of honing in on the perspectival view of descriptions, in §6, I compare the perspectival view with views that hold a complete description of the world is the ideal possibility. Whereas on the perspectival view new perspectives are always invited, those in search of a complete description would hold the search comes to an end—once we have arrived at a complete description.

In §§7–9 I sketch some implications for pluralism of the perspectival view of descriptions. In §7 I argue that the perspectival view accommodates a version of Lynch's (1998) 'vertical pluralism', which he defined as the view that there are different types of nonreductive facts. Lynch also identifies 'horizontal pluralism' as the view that there are alternative ways of describing the world. Because on the perspectival view new perspectives are welcomed as potentially cognitively enriching, the challenge to find cases that would secure horizontal pluralism is greater for the perspectival view: cases Lynch uses in his defense of horizontal pluralism fail to work for the perspectival view. I discuss horizontal pluralism in §8, taking up Quine's (1986) suggestion that we might find an alternative way of describing the world in an 'irreconcilable' alien system. In the event such an alien system is a possibility, horizontal pluralism would be endorsed by the perspectival view; however, if all alien systems are reconcilable with our system, no defense of horizontal pluralism is forthcoming.

Given my defense of the need for different perspectives and acceptance of (at least) vertical pluralism, it may seem I would endorse the suggestion of a plurality of truth properties. However, it is my deflationary position on the role of the truth predicate that makes alethic pluralism a nonissue (§9).

I begin my project with a brief review of our *use* of descriptions. This leads to a focus on the status and structure informing-descriptions may take.

2. Descriptions

As Wittgenstein (1953) has famously pointed out, we do many things with language. We question, command, tell stories, justify, exclaim. . . . We also describe.

2.1 DESCRIPTIONS—VARIETIES AND PURPOSES

Descriptions are constructed sometimes for our own or another's understanding, sometimes because there's pleasure in learning, sometimes because we enjoy being curious. A description may also be used to amuse, promote empathy, change attitudes, encourage, or admonish. And a 'how-to' description can facilitate engagement with an everyday activity.

Different contexts and different reasons for assembling a description can mean references to different varieties of objects, states, and processes and the ascription of different properties. For example, nurses regularly refer to states (pain) or individuals (bacteria) that economists have few occasions to refer to; at the same time, nurses talk about some things economists also talk about (measurements). Neither have much occasion to talk of protons and electrons, or witches and ogres. Descriptions may also serve their purpose through the incorporation of significant creative moves, for advances in knowledge are sometimes made when an insightful new concept is used or a new substance identified. Examples include the introduction of *zero* early in the history of counting and calculation and Einstein's talk of *quanta* of light.

The context, including the purpose of a description, may also affect whether the sentences of a description should be true. On some occasions a most successful description may contain approximations or statistical generalizations.[1] But we place other requirements on fictional descriptions. Then there is the value we place on some false theories. Think of the respect we philosophers have for false philosophical theories.

Given the wide differences in context, purpose, and format of descriptions, there is no possibility I can provide a theory that covers all aspects of descriptions. I restrict my focus to those descriptions that inform us about the world.

---

[1] For this reason I will, somewhat vaguely, allow for the inclusion of 'near-truths', as well as truths, in true descriptions. See Wilson (2006: 185, 194) for perceptive discussions of the importance of approximations in the physical sciences.

Initially it might seem that what we want from an informing-description is a list of all the facts. But, at the very least, it must be supplemented, if it is to be of much use. Dickens (1854/1996) convincingly makes this case in *Hard Times*. A (mere) list of truths gives both not enough information and too much. An arbitrarily arranged complete list (if such were even possible) would contain too much information since it would be too long to be useful, given our limited cognitive capabilities. Furthermore, there is the clutter we would have to contend with, such as facts about the length of my toenails at each moment of each and every day—not to mention the length of your toenails. At the very least, we want a selection and arrangement of truths, or near truths, that facilitate practical decision-making. Also, just as we could not knowingly construct a list of truths without testing and application, so those using a list need an understanding of how such knowledge might be utilized in different contexts.

A suggestion for the construction of a description that more *usefully* conveys information is to find a way of unifying those facts we are interested in. In the history of philosophy, it has sometimes been assumed there is a 'key' to the universe; sometimes this has been expressed in a single principle, or sometimes in a selection of axioms with a set of foundational substances identified, for instance, God, foundational particles of physics. From these or out of these all else is speculated to derive. Identification of a such a 'key' would require that the world has a structure that on some basis we could recognize as 'ordered'.

But not everyone agrees the world has an orderly structure. Somewhat expansively Russell claimed, '[T]he most fundamental of my intellectual beliefs is that the [proposition that the world is a unity] is rubbish. I think the universe is all spots and jumps, without unity, without continuity, without coherence or orderliness or any of the other properties that governesses love' (1931: 98). Alternatively, it may be because of the nature of descriptions, as well as the complexity of the world, that a complete unified description is not in the realm of possibility.

However, my purpose here depends neither on challenging the key-to-the-universe assumption, nor on challenging the assumption that a complete description is possible. Rather, my focus is on the question: *What role may informing-descriptions have, if there is no key?* What role could informing-descriptions have if they are *not* headed in the direction of providing us with a complete unified description of the world?

In the case of sense perception, we must resource combinations of perspectives in learning about the world. I argue, by analogy, we resource combinations of descriptions in gaining even more information about the world. This brings me to my initial project: to work out a *perspectival view of descriptions*. This understanding of descriptions provides a basis for assessing pluralism.

In §2.2, I present an example of our use of informing-descriptions when making important decisions. I frequently revert to this example in later discussion.

2.2 AN EXAMPLE

I wish to draw attention to the variety of reading materials on *pain and its treatment* that were assigned to a group of surgical nurses completing an in-service training program.[2]

Nurses learn that unrelieved pain may cause serious damage to many parts of the body: pain can affect the circulatory system, the digestive system, psychological states, and so on. So it is medically important that pain is treated. From the physical and biological sciences, nurses learn how the surgeon's incision sensitizes nerve endings and causes inflammation. They learn that various physiological, chemical, and electrical changes occur, thereby generating the path from the incision to and through the spinal cord, and then to various parts of the brain. Descriptions from various sciences then give nurses an understanding of how different pain-relief combinations can interrupt this path.

If pain is to be treated effectively, the level of pain the patient feels must be assessed. Then there is the task of selecting an appropriate pain remedy. The effectiveness of the dosage administered must also be assessed. In making these decisions, nurses need to understand how patients' psychological states, cultural background, family influences, and beliefs about the effects of analgesics may all affect patients' expressions of pain and their receptiveness to treatment.

Nurses draw together information from the physical, biological, physiological, psychological, and social science disciplines when they make ongoing decisions as to interventions that can lead to good health. This example serves as a reminder that when we come to make important decisions, we frequently (always?) utilize descriptions from a variety of different avenues of inquiry.

If there is no theory that unifies such information in a complete description, how is it that such a seemingly piecemeal approach is a rational way to proceed? I believe an analogy used by Anderson & Belnap (1975) suggests an answer.

3. An analogy

Anderson & Belnap drew an analogy with perception in showing the theory of entailment is a formal system of substantial interest. This is because, like physical objects, the system may be viewed from a variety of perspectives: it can

---

[2] Thanks to Jan Grover for drawing my attention to this literature.

be presented through a Hilbert axiomatization, a Gentzen system of rules of inference, as a Fitch system of natural deduction, and through formal semantics. They argue as follows:

> We tend to think of systems as artificial or *ad hoc* if most of their formal properties arise from some *one* notational system in terms of which they are described. [. . . I]t looks as if the possibility of seeing a formal system from different perspectives contributes to our feeling that such a system is more like a tree than a pink elephant. [. . . A]mong the nicest firm formulations of an intuitive concept is the theory of computability, a theory which received formal treatment at the hands of Herbrand-Gödel as a new mathematical notion, from Turing as a new analysis of the way in which computers work, and from Church and Post as a new analysis of the way logical systems work. [. . .] If all these had turned out to be distinct, one might well have felt the differences hung on *notational* difference; but the fact that all turned out to be equivalent lends support to the attitude that there is something substantial there to view.
>
> It is difficult to say why this view is so commonly accepted, but we would like to hazard the conjecture that the indubitable substantiality of the mathematical theory of effective computability arises because the various perspectives make it look like a physical object, a pool table, say. (Anderson & Belnap 1975: 50–1)

The source analog cited by Anderson & Belnap is a situation where a sequence of perceptions leads to the judgment that the physical object presented to the viewer is a pool table with balls on it. Other examples could have been used as the source analog. For example, viewers in a desert see a body of water in the distance, but knowing of the existence of mirages, they only 'grow more convinced of the fact' when the initial perception is confirmed as they travel closer. Touch and taste lead to greater certainty.

What difference does the availability of multiple perspectives make? Before addressing this question, I review work of Millikan's (2000) that will be used in my argument that there are cognitive (and practical) benefits in our having access to multiple perspectives.

4. Epistemic benefits of identification

My brief review of Millikan's (2000) seminal account of substances pays special attention to her account of epistemic and pragmatic benefits of identifying and reidentifying substances. A subtle interplay between the epistemological and ontological is revealed.

Early in her discussion, Millikan drew attention to our evolved prelinguistic ability to distinguish between certain substances. We have the ability to distinguish between cats and dogs; cats and dogs also have that ability. This ability is useful when an identified substance is known to have properties *beyond* those initially perceived in the context of identifying it. If, for example, we perceive a particular furry, four-legged small animal as a cat, then we could be in a position to predict that it probably likes fish and is wary of dogs. The latter information will have been acquired through earlier perceptions of cats.

Millikan requires that projectable properties (*likes fish* and *is wary of dogs*) must be grounded in 'real' connections, not in mere correlations. Significantly, Millikan pointed out that, while substances are ontologically grounded, 'the category of substances, as I have defined it, is at root an epistemological category. What makes a substance a substance is that it can be appropriated by cognition for the grounded, not accidental, running of inductions, or projecting of invariants' (2000: 26). Indeed, her interest in ontologically grounded substances stems from the epistemic and pragmatic benefits to be gained following identification of a substance. For, if we can predict how things around us may behave, how they may interact with us or threaten us, then we have a better chance of survival. By contrast, there is no point in tracking a drunk's pink elephant, since it does not have projectable properties.[3]

Of special interest is a situation where the identification is made on relatively sparse information. An abundance of background information about the kind of substance involved may then give a basis on which to make predictions that go beyond the information used in the identification. I argue in §5 that an availability of multiple perspectives on the world enables similar epistemological gains.

Millikan's additional point that epistemic gain can lead to better decision-making (e.g., the identification and tracking of substances can make the difference between surviving and not surviving) reflects the more general fact that we value knowledge that can be *applied*. This fact has been highlighted by Wittgenstein (1939/1989) in a passage where he describes imagined apprentices who have been trained to reproduce proofs. They can write out the proofs even though they cannot do simple calculations, such as figuring the cost of six plums given the price of one. He then asked, 'would you say they had learnt mathematics or not?'[4] Similarly, if scientific theories were not accompanied by experiments and potential applications, we would not have the activity of science. We would have Star Wars 'science'.

While there are many reasons why we may value knowledge, it suffices for the arguments of the next section that knowledge that is useful in rational decision-making is knowledge that we value. My primary focus is on reasons why there is value in resourcing information gathered from multiple perspectives.

---

[3] However, we might draw conclusions about the person who sees the pink elephant.
[4] Thanks to Diane Proudfoot for drawing my attention to this passage.

5. Multiple perspectives

The main thesis of §5 is defended in §5.2. I show how multiple perspectives provide needed epistemological and practical benefits. But first, in §5.1, I offer some clarification on 'distinguishing between perspectives'. In §5.3 I consider whether there is 'logic' in the ways we work with different perspectives.

5.1 DISTINGUISHING BETWEEN PERSPECTIVES

In the prelinguistic case, different perspectives of macro-sized objects provide different information about an object. For example, an observer viewing a mountain from one position (in time and space) will have information about the mountain different from that which another observer occupying a different position would have. We learn more about the mountain from two perspectives than from one.

In my broader use of the term 'perspective', a wider range of factors (beyond position in space and time) is relevant to distinguishing between perspectives.[5] This is because many factors influence the construction of a description. When describing the world, people (including groups, like the group working in a scientific discipline) do so in the context of a language, interests, beliefs, and the world itself. Purpose will also be a factor in distinguishing between perspectives because purpose affects our choice in constructing a description. For example, there will be differences between the descriptions given of Smith by a doctor, a sport's team's selector, and an employer, even though one and the same person may occupy the roles of doctor, selector, and employer.

Accordingly, it is a variety of perspectives that surgical nurses resource when deciding how to treat a patient who is in pain. One perspective is provided by a nurse's visual examination: the nurse sees the patient grimacing, hears him groaning, tensing up, and so on. Nurses have access to the patient's perspective when he ranks the level of pain on a one-to-ten scale and provides the location, duration, and character of the pain. Various disciplines (physiology, psychology, chemistry, etc.) provide further perspectives on pertinent aspects of the complex situation of a person being in pain.

Note that I make no assumption that perspectives relevant to determining a course of action must zero in on 'same things'. Typically, they focus on aspects of constituents of the situation in question and/or on enveloping situations. Different goals or purposes have motivated the development of different disciplines with each discipline providing a perspective on different (though

---

[5] I borrow from Gupta's (2006: 76 ff) important notion of 'view'. Gupta's focus is 'the logical relationship of experience to knowledge', while mine is the status of our descriptions. Despite overlap in philosophical attitude, my use of 'perspective' is different from Gupta's use of 'view'.

possibly overlapping) objects and events. The physical sciences, for example, can tell us something of chemical changes in the body of a patient, while social sciences can tell us of influences from a patient's beliefs. Subareas of disciplines may likewise provide slightly different perspectives. Disciplines created across disciplines may initiate new perspectives, as in the case of psychoneuroimmunology.[6] Indeed, it would seem we have the prospect of a never-ending engagement with new perspectives, many of which may bring ever more information about the world.

The information gathered through the adoption of diverse perspectives will sometimes be viewed as quite distinct and sometimes not, because our interests, needs, and purposes vary from context to context. A portrait artist may make distinctions between perspectives that a nurse will likely find irrelevant. So I accept a degree of vagueness with respect to cases where two perspectives are different. Between two perspectives, a tiny difference in information may be significant; in other cases, the differences may not be significant. So sometimes we may need or want to distinguish between perspectives that on other occasions we would find burdensome. Sometimes we may want sharp lines drawn. For example, if in a situation we want the perspectives of *mature* people, we may, as in a legal context, decide on a cut-off point of, say, eighteen years. In other situations we may prefer vagueness because a vague boundary (including vagueness as to where the vagueness begins and ends) leaves room for adjustments according to the demands of local contexts.

5.2 BENEFITS OF ACCESSING DIFFERENT PERSPECTIVES

Access to multiple perspectives helps with the task of *identification*. For example, we may need more than one perspective before we can identify a mountain. Also, there can be better (more convenient, more reliable, etc.) opportunities to identify something if, in addition to our prelinguistic ways of perceiving, we gain information from other sources. For example, a health condition may be more finely identified if, in addition to observation of visible symptoms, information from blood tests and an MRI provide other perspectives.

Suppose identification has been made. Multiple perspectives may again provide *additional useful information*. This is because access to multiple perspectives provides us with the option of resourcing a greater breadth of information when we are making decisions as to what action to take. For example, while from a visual examination I can identify my cat and recognize it is lame, unless I also learn from the veterinarian's reports that the cat has injured its spine, I may inadvertently increase the harm the cat suffers. Similarly, a surgical nurse may through sense perception identify a person as the patient in

---

[6] Thanks to Megan Delehanty for this example.

pain, but *until* she gains information from scientific descriptions, the nurse will not be in a best position to treat the patient's pain. Through reading, the nurse gains a variety of useful information about people from the various perspectives that have been developed through fields of inquiry. It is such breadth that leads to the making of informed decisions.

A greater number of perspectives can also lead to a *greater range of options for effective action*. For among the 'most effective' choices we may have a choice between, for example, the easiest versus the cheapest option.

Closely allied perspectives are also beneficially utilized, as has long been recognized. There is the utilization of similar, but different, perspectives as a way of *protecting against bias*—useful, so long as clutter does not cloud the process. The value of a variety of similar, but different, perspectives is also assumed by those testing hypotheses. In this way, confirmation of a given hypothesis is shown to be confirmed with 'enough' generality.[7] In addition, we have seen that, in entertaining more than one perspective, *new perspectives* may be realized that, in their turn, provide new information about the world for yet further cognitive gain. Just as intertwining strands of a rope leads to a gain in strength, there are gains, cognitively, when we judiciously combine information gathered from different perspectives.

It is fortunate that there are many reasons why we seek to describe the world, since this has led to breadth of information gained from the variety of perspectives. We may resource this breadth for cognitive gain. More decisions that are better-informed and greater generality can be the result.

Support for my account of descriptions as providing us with needed multiple perspectives may be found in Wilson's (2006) groundbreaking work on the 'wandering significance' of predicates. A discerning search for an understanding of language in the development of science and in its application leads Wilson to argue that descriptions form a 'quilt-like' pattern. He calls these complexes of descriptions *façades*, where façades are 'linked, but nonetheless disjoint, patches' (2006: 179). A façade is a set of patches

> that are formally inconsistent with one another but are stitched together by 'for more details, see . . . ' linkages or other bridgework. Often the whole is fabricated in such a manner that, if we don't pay close attention to its discontinuous boundary joins and shifts in mathematical setting, we might suppose we are looking at a theory ready to be axiomatized [. . .]. (Wilson, 2006: 191–2)

Wilson is not suggesting there is a uniform axiomatic to be revealed, but rather, that the façades provide useful (true) information as they are. Compelling

---

[7] Note that I am not listing as an advantage the fact that a new perspective can provide *inspiration* in the search for knowledge. My focus is not on such accidental cognitive gains. (I return to this issue in §8.3.)

examples from the history of science are used to show there are good reasons for utilizing different patches in different contexts.

5.3 IS THERE LOGIC TO OUR UTILIZATION OF MULTIPLE PERSPECTIVES?

I have assumed throughout (as a working hypothesis) that there is no unified description in the offing. Accordingly, there is no reduction of a kind that reduces the facts identified through one perspective to facts of another (more 'basic') perspective.

There is also no requirement that the objects referred to in different descriptions are distinct. Indeed, there is 'overlap' among the objects and events identified by different perspectives. Consider the nursing situation again. There is the patient. Patients belong to families, religious groups, tribes, nations, and so on. Patients have beliefs, fears, goals, and pain; as well, they have bodies that have as parts brains, molecules, nerve pathways, inflamed tissue, and blood flow. Just as Millikan said of her substances, 'there is not one set of ontological "elements," one unique way of carving up the world, but a variety of crisscrossing overlapping basic patterns to be discovered there' (2000: 27).

Is there 'logic' in the ways we work with information gained from different perspectives? From one position in space and time, I gain information about the shape of one side of a mountain; but from this I can conclude little concerning the shape of the mountain on its 'other' side. Similarly, unless a nurse has background information, from her observation of a patient's behavior she can conclude little about the chemical changes occurring at an incision. No (deductively valid) logical connection need obtain between information from two perspectives.

However, there are good inferences that we can make based on what we have learned from observations from a variety of perspectives. There are, for example, the kinds of valid inferences involving more than one perspective that are cited in the literature on alethic pluralism.[8] Given background information, from just one perspective we may identify something as a cat; we may then conclude it has a heart. Empirical connections are also significant in more complex situations. With test results showing a patient has an infection, a nurse may infer a patient is in pain; further information (gathered from other perspectives) may lead to identification of the level and character of the pain.[9]

---

[8] For example, 'if you hold a prisoner indefinitely and without charge, you violate his rights. This prisoner has been held indefinitely and without charge. Therefore, this prisoner's rights have been violated' (Lynch 2008:125).

[9] In conversation, Mark Wilson has suggested (nevertheless) there may be little logic in our wide and varied utilization of information gained from different perspectives.

Just as lone sense perceptions have the potential to mislead, so, also, lone descriptions have the potential to mislead. The perception that a stick in water looks bent conflicts with how the stick feels in the water and how it looks out of water. Similarly, a nurse who has just come on duty may report that her patient is relaxed, laughing with guests, and showing no signs of pain. This report may initially seem in conflict with another nurse's report that the patient *is* in pain. In such cases, one perspective is weighed against the others. Sometimes this may involve a search for other perspectives. In the nursing case, the apparent conflict may be resolved by accessing a perspective of a psychologist who explains that distraction can temporarily relieve pain and/or the perspective of a physiologist who says endorphins increase when a person is engaged. In other cases (as where an astrologist's description is considered) discordant reports may be treated with suspicion.

As a way of providing a better understanding of the perspectival view of descriptions, I next compare the perspectival view with two other views of descriptions.

6. The perspectival view of descriptions

One position that the perspectival view may be contrasted with is a view of descriptions according to which a *complete unified description* (CUD) of the world is possible. Perhaps God's plan embodies a CUD. When I first arrived at graduate school in the 1960s, many philosophers seemed to assume physics would eventually provide a CUD.[10]

A less ambitious position, while rejecting the possibility of a CUD, holds a *complete unified description* is the *ideal* (CUDI). This position may be held on grounds that a CUD of the world is not logically possible, perhaps because the world doesn't cooperate, as would be the case if the world were all 'spots and jumps'; or perhaps on the grounds that a CUD is not possible because of the incompleteness of arithmetic. Alternatively, it could be for cognitive or pragmatic reasons that a CUDI view of descriptions is preferred to the CUD view. It might be claimed, for example, that given our limited cognitive abilities, the best we may achieve will be descriptions that come relatively close to being complete.

Insofar as standpoint theory promotes the position that there is an 'epistemically privileged' perspective on social issues without claiming the epistemically privileged position will provide the 'whole' truth, it does not endorse the CUD view.[11] Nor does it endorse assumptions of the perspectival view. For while standpoint theory accepts there are many perspectives on social issues, it does not accept that they are to be resourced *in combination* in rational

---

[10] If not a CUD of the world, then of the 'physical world'—but is the question then begged?
[11] Thanks to Megan Delehanty for discussing standpoint theory with me.

decision-making. So, between these options, standpoint theory would seem to endorse the CUDI view of descriptions of the social world. On the other hand, Strawson's (1985) position that we accept *both* the scientific and humanistic 'standpoints' is in line with the perspectival view.

There are other differences between the CUD and CUDI views and the perspectival view of descriptions. On the perspectival view, those descriptions that are true are so even though they are not part of a 'complete' description. On the CUD view, only descriptions that are part of a complete description or reducible to some part are true. Supporters of the CUDI view may hold that only descriptions that are part of an (ideal) complete description are true, or they may try adopting a notion of 'closer to the truth'.

On the perspectival view, a lone perspective cannot yield all information, so *further perspectives are always invited*. This is because the varieties of descriptions that arise from multiple perspectives, on the same or overlapping situations, may be resourced simultaneously to positive effect. This was illustrated in the case of nurses deciding on the best treatment of a patient in pain, where information from different perspectives may not only confirm an early diagnosis but eventually lead to new perspectives that may yield further information.

This contrasts with the CUD view of descriptions according to which inquiry would come to an end when a complete description had been reached. In the meantime, from among candidate descriptions the 'most promising' description may be sought for modification and development into a CUD, with other descriptions either absorbed into the chosen one through some form of reduction or rejected altogether. Alternatively, many perspectives may be explored in case the 'most promising' isn't the most promising.

To satisfy the *completeness* requirement of a (finite) CUD description, both objects and truths would need to be inductively specified, assuming there were infinite numbers of these. As there are no such requirements placed on the descriptions of the perspectival view, the structure of these descriptions may vary as best suits context and purpose. Some may utilize induction, some may not.

Further differences between these views will be reflected in their implications for pluralism. For reasons of space, I explore the implications of only the perspectival view. I consider the two versions that Lynch (1998) distinguishes: vertical pluralism (§7) and horizontal pluralism (§8). Alethic pluralism is discussed in §9 from the point of view of the prosentential account of the role of the truth predicate.

7. Vertical pluralism

Lynch's characterization of *vertical pluralism* runs as follows: 'vertical pluralism is the view that there is more than one type of fact to be had in the world, and hence that different "levels" of fact-stating discourse may not be reducible to a more basic discourse. Vertical pluralism is radically nonreductivist about facts' (1998: 6).

To establish vertical pluralism on the perspectival view of descriptions, I need to show that there are different types of (nonreducible) facts. I earlier pointed out that on the perspectival view of descriptions we gain new information when we resource information from different perspectives. Indeed, it is only when we have information from multiple perspectives (e.g., shape, smell) do we know there is a live rose in front of us. Similarly, I have supposed nurses utilize in productive ways a psychologist's (nonreductive) description of human behavior together with descriptions offered by physiologists and physical scientists. As my presentation of the perspectival view was partly motivated by the prospect of there being no prospect of a complete unified description, there is no assumption that information from the different perspectives is reducible to a 'basic discourse'.[12] If the assumption of such nonreductive facts suffices to establish that there are 'different types of facts' on the perspectival view, then the view embraces vertical pluralism as Lynch introduced the term.

Lynch said of vertical pluralism that the different types of facts would be 'autonomous', as in 'moral facts are autonomous from physical facts' (1998: 7). If Lynch used 'autonomous' to mean (only) *nonreductive*, then on the perspectival view the different types of fact are autonomous. However, 'autonomous' could suggest the different types of fact are *independent*. The 'types of facts' of the perspectival view could not then be characterized as autonomous, as the perspectival view assumes there are some connections (e.g., overlap, causal, statistical) between facts garnered from different perspectives (§5.3). Our practice of utilizing knowledge gained from multiple perspectives (§5.2) is based on an assumption that there are connections. For example, issues of physical maturity are sometimes factored in when describing social situations. Also, when seeking scientific knowledge of the physical world, measuring instruments are used by experimenters (so there is reference by scientists to macro-sized objects, including people), which in their turn raise issues of reliability and integrity when the observations are assessed. So, again, even when our focus is the acquisition of knowledge from just one perspective (from a perspective of a social science or subsection of physics), we resource knowledge from other perspectives (e.g., when using macro-sized objects when measuring). Such behavior is rational only if it is believed there are connections of some sort between the facts identified from the different perspectives. If this is right, the different types of fact on the perspectival view are not assumed to be autonomous, not if 'autonomous' signifies *independence*. Accordingly, the perspectival view implies only the version of vertical

---

[12] Note that I subscribe to the realist assumption that the perspectives are of one and only one world.

pluralism (there are different types of nonreductive facts) as initially defined by Lynch.

What, now, does the perspectival view of descriptions have to say of horizontal pluralism, the view that more than one description of the world is possible?

8. Horizontal pluralism

8.1 INCONSISTENCY?

Lynch introduced *horizontal pluralism* thus: 'horizontal pluralism [. . .] holds that there can be incompatible facts within a single level of discourse. Hence, a horizontal pluralist might hold that there can be equally correct moral facts or physical facts or facts about the nature of mind' (1998: 6–7). Horizontal pluralism allows for the possibility of a plurality of descriptions of moral facts, a plurality of descriptions of physical facts, and so on for each type of fact. Lynch's focus is horizontal *metaphysical* pluralism, where 'the facts in question concern the nature of reality—facts about God, mind, and the universe' (1998: 3).[13] He defends against the charge that a plurality of descriptions of "the nature of reality" would give rise to inconsistency. This opens the way, he argued, to the possibility of horizontal pluralism.

In his demonstration of where inconsistency is viewed as arising, Lynch considered a number of examples. These include apparently conflicting positions on personal identity, on substance, and on mathematical entities. A further example was borrowed from Putnam. The concern is that different answers may seemingly be given to the question, 'how many objects are there?' A person who counts only macro-sized objects will offer one count, while a mereologist, who counts macro-sized objects, combinations of these, and their parts, will offer another.

Lynch claimed to resolve the apparent inconsistencies by relativizing the claims of different descriptions to different conceptual schemes. While I am not persuaded by this move, I too believe the alleged inconsistencies are only apparent—unless certain assumptions are made—for I believe only issues of context sensitivity or ambiguity (possibly complex ambiguity) need be involved. Sometimes context makes clear enough which things are to be counted; on other occasions the addition of a sortal may suffice to remove ambiguity. A mother says, 'please pick up the things left scattered on the floor'. When the response is a quibble, she clarifies with 'toys'. 'Object' is no less in need of a sortal.

---

[13] Though Lynch did not mention this, I suspect he was thinking of complete descriptions. I think I have been able to sidestep that ambiguity.

Another suggestion for addressing such apparent inconsistencies was presented by Quine (1986), who attributed the idea to Davidson. The suggestion is to treat suspect terms as homonyms and then replace the coinciding terms by new terms. In the example I earlier cited from Lynch, this would mean replacing the term 'object' by, say, the terms 'object$_a$', 'object$_b$', etc. Likewise, in the personal identity case, 'person' could be replaced by 'person$_a$', 'person$_b$', etcetera. The now compatible claims could then be incorporated in the relevant descriptions after eliminating redundancies (if any).

In the case of the perspectival view of descriptions, if context fails to make usage clear, this would mean incorporating the word changes in the relevant descriptions. Descriptions arrived at from different perspectives could then be jointly resourced, in the event that would prove epistemologically fruitful.

So, given the assumptions of the perspectival view of descriptions, along with its welcoming attitude to new perspectives, there would seem to be no argument for horizontal pluralism—based on Lynch's examples. In the next subsection, I consider another prospect for horizontal pluralism.

8.2 IRRECONCILABLE DESCRIPTIONS

Quine (1986), in response to Gibson (1986) briefly discusses the possibility of there being distinct empirically equivalent 'systems'. He distinguishes two positions: the *secular* and the *ecumenical*. Quine was initially disposed to adopt the secular position, which 'deems' one position true and the other false. This, he says, is forced on him by his naturalism, according to which there is no God's-eye view that can adjudicate between them. Later, on the basis of his empiricism, he adopts the ecumenical position, according to which both are deemed true. But then, having wavered between the two positions, he finally favors the secular position.

With respect to the ecumenical position, Quine identified a couple of objections. He first considered the possibility that the two systems accepted as true contain contradictory claims. His resolution is the one aforementioned, according to which offending terms are treated as homonyms. The second objection to the ecumenical position supposes an alien system that cannot be reconciled with our own system. On a supposition that there are terms in the alien system that fail to have empirical content, Quine argued the alien system could not be coherently conjoined with ours. (Quine tentatively offered 'grace' and 'nirvana' as examples of terms that may fail to have empirical content.) For if a description containing terms that lack empirical content were added to our system, two problems arise: the conjoined system would fail Quine's empirical-content requirement of meaningfulness and it would not, as required, be economical. And so Quine claims to return to an acceptance of the sectarian position.

But, that's not the end of it. For having returned to the sectarian position, Quine wondered, '[w]hat if, we have somehow managed to persuade ourselves that the two [original systems] are empirically equivalent?' He expressed an inclination to oscillate between the two 'for the sake of an enriched perspective on nature', and continued, 'whichever system we are working in is the one for us to count at the time as true, there being no wider frame of reference' (Quine, 1986: 157).

In considering Quine's suggestion that we oscillate between the systems, rather than working with his assumptions of meaningfulness, I begin with an insight of Wittgenstein's, that language is inextricably tied to forms of life.

I suggest one way we could try thinking of an irreconcilable alien system would be to think of aliens who live a very different kind of life from ours. Inoue's (1991) detailed analysis of discrepancies between the Japanese and English versions of MacArthur's Japanese constitution shows how deep cultural differences can lead to a failure in communication. The differences between the cultures with respect to *individualism*, *familism*, and *individual dignity*, for example, had the effect that the parties agreed on the wording of translations often without being aware there was little agreement on content. It might be supposed that without a change in forms of life in one or both cultures, there will be descriptions of social practice offered by one society that would be irreconcilable with descriptions offered by the other society. As another alternative, we may consider an alien society that biologically has evolved differently from ours. Perhaps the beings of the alien culture have different senses and quite different needs and interests. In each of these cases, it might be supposed that we would not be able to add their system to ours since that would mean living a form of life incompatible with ours while still living our own form of life. So, in order to master the system of the alien, we must move into their society and try to live as they do, as Quine suggested.

I will suppose that the aliens use their language effectively in facilitating action; like us, not only may many survive reasonably well (or would, if we and they had the goodwill and understanding we are supposed to have) they also appear to make other choices effectively. Let's now consider Quine's suggestion that we oscillate between the alien system and our own and then his claim that 'whichever system we are working in is the one for us to count at the time as true, there being no wider frame of reference' (1986: 157).

Let's suppose '⌠⊥△√▼' is a sentence in an alien language. If we have no prospect of using their sentence '⌠⊥△√▼' in the context of our own language, we would have no basis, when working within our language, on which to determine whether ⌠⊥△√▼. For this alienated sentence is not just meaningless in our language, we are also supposing there is no way we could coherently add the sentence to our language—without drastically modifying our forms of life. So, just as we could not tell whether ⌠⊥△√▼, so, also, we cannot tell whether '⌠⊥△√▼' were true.

If such an 'irreconcilable' alien language with its cluster of (perspectival) descriptions were a coherent possibility, then it would seem the perspectival theorist would have grounds for endorsing horizontal pluralism.

But is it possible there could be an irreconcilable alien language? My examples do not convince as they stand. Inoue (1991) is able to guide English readers through the differences between the two cultures and how those differences generate problems for translators. Perhaps we just need greater effort than that exerted by those who constructed the translations of the Japanese constitution. Also, in the other case, I am not confident that beings who had evolved with different modes of perception could arrive at irreconcilable but equally successful sciences. For all I know, the suggestion of an irreconcilable alien system may be a fanciful suggestion. If so, horizontal pluralism could not thereby be shown a coherent possibility for a perspectival theorist.

With respect to an alien's perspectives that *are* reconcilable, they would be welcomed by us in the event they provide new information.

8.3 A NOTE ON 'ENRICHING' PERSPECTIVES

It is interesting that Quine thought that an irreconcilable system could provide an *enriched* perspective. What kind of enrichment could this be?

The enrichment could arise in any number of ways: enjoyment of a new art form, a new sport, new ways of interacting with others, or perhaps new intellectual challenges. Experience of the aliens' system may also provide psychological stimulus that prompts us to look anew at our own ways of acquiring knowledge, just as any out-of-the-blue events may sometimes prompt us to have inspirational thoughts. Or, if there are parts of the alien system we like, after shifting back into our own system we may be inspired to seek ways of modifying our practices. Modifications in our forms of life could lead to changes in the directions our search for knowledge may take and so to new perspectives. In any of these circumstances, the alien's perspectives could be a factor in aesthetically, morally, or psychologically enriching our own activity. Cognitive changes may occur as a result of such changes to our form of life.

But, on the supposition the alien system is irreconcilable with ours, there is no possibility we could directly process and utilize the actual information the aliens themselves gain from their perspectives—while we are still working within our original system. That is, the enrichment would not be (immediately) cognitive.

9. Alethic pluralism

Pluralism has been viewed as leading to the possibility of a plurality of truth properties. Am I committed to alethic pluralism by the perspectival view of descriptions?

Wright (2001) has suggested there may be a plurality of truth properties, given there are different discourses. He says of his so-called 'minimalist' theory of truth that it

> incorporates a potential *pluralism* about truth, in the specific sense that what property serves as truth may vary from discourse to discourse. [. . .] This potential pluralism is itself in opposition to the more traditional positions, insofar as they claim to uncover *the* universal nature of truth, something common to all truth-apt discourse. (2001: 752)

Likewise, Lynch (1998) has argued that the possibility of a plurality of truth properties would arise from pluralism and also from the 'fluidity' of language.

The perspectival view of descriptions recognizes there are different perspectives/discourses; at least one version of pluralism is endorsed. Elsewhere, I have argued that language is 'fluid' (Grover 2005),[14] I agree with alethic pluralists that we utilize inferences across discourses/perspectives (§5.3). I also agree that the complexities of meaning and truth ('what-is-true') may vary hugely from discourse to discourse. Given such breadth of overlap, the question certainly arises as to whether I should also entertain the possibility of a plurality of truth properties. The short answer is 'No'. I deny there is even one truth property.

The difference lies not in the perspectival view of descriptions or pluralism but in our different accounts of the role of the truth predicate. I subscribe to the prosentential theory of truth, first presented in Grover et al. (1975). The prosentential theory characterizes the truth predicate as a prosentence-forming predicate, not (as correspondence, coherence, and pragmatic theorists of truth would have it) as a property-ascribing predicate.[15]

Prosentences are used anaphorically, in ways similar to the ways pronouns are used—except pronouns occupy positions in sentences that nouns occupy, while prosentences occupy positions that sentences occupy. Just as pronouns may be used to refer to something previously referred to, so may prosentences be used to affirm (or consider, or deny, or hypothesize, or . . .) something said by a previous speaker. For example, the prosentence 'That-is-true' is used with anaphoric overtones in 'That-is-true. But do you realize the implications?' (I hyphenate to draw attention to the prosentential reading of the expression 'That-is-true'.) Suppose the previous speaker has claimed there is human-made climate change. In that context, 'That-is-true' is used to affirm that there is human-made climate change. The use of a term ('she') or of a sentence ('It-is-true') that utilizes anaphoric connections enables a speaker to implicitly acknowledge that something has been referred to, or said, by another speaker.

---

[14] I chose the term 'flexibility' because I sought to emphasize that languages are our ongoing creations, with flexibility essential in new or newly understood contexts.

[15] For more details see Grover (1992).

Just as we use pronouns (and individual variables) when generalizing, so also prosentences (and propositional or sentential variables) are used when we generalize with respect to sentence positions. The prosentence 'it-is-true' is so used in 'Everything the report says about the effects of climate change is such that it-is-true'.[16] This has instances like, 'if the report says that climate change will cause the oceans to rise then climate change will cause the oceans to rise'.

While some other deflationary theories begin with a 'metalinguistic' truth predicate and a version of the disquotational schema (e.g., 'p' is true if and only if p), the prosentential account does not.[17] The prosentential account *begins* with anaphoric connections. Natural language is the home of anaphoric connections and so the home of 'true' and 'false'. There, discourse typically (though not always) involves talk about extralinguistic things. That is, pronouns and prosentences are typically used when talking about extralinguistic things.[18]

If the prosentential sketch of the role of the truth predicate is on the right track, there seems no need to assume a property-ascribing role. So, how do alethic pluralists defend the assumption of a truth property and the possibility of several truth properties?

Some philosophers have claimed that because 'true' is used in explanations, the truth predicate must have an explanatory role. Perhaps, similarly, Wright suggests we need a truth property to explain 'substantial' matters. But, note, pronouns are used in explanations; yet that does not give them explanatory roles. Likewise, while 'true' is used in explanations, it may have a prosentential role rather than an explanatory property-ascribing role.

As for substantial issues, prosentential constructions enable us to ask big questions and express deep claims—such claims typically involve generalizations and for generalizations we need pronouns and prosentences. Take, for example, the question, 'what-is-true?' Read prosententially, this has instances like, 'is there water on Mars?' and 'Does pain inevitably follow surgery?' A philosopher's claim like, 'some beliefs that are warranted are false' has prosentential paraphrases like, 'there is at least one belief that is warranted and it-is-false'.[19] Instances include, 'the belief that pain undermines health is warranted, but pain doesn't always undermine health'.

Prosentences may also be used when we make claims about meaning, such as 'the meaning of a sentence is the same whether it-is-true or it-is-

---

[16] The paraphrases I use to highlight prosentential constructions are inelegant through my display of 'syntactically hidden' prosentences; for we normally exploit the subject-predicate sentence structure of English, which allows the breaking up of prosentences and the attachment of 'true' to nominal phrases beyond pronouns.

[17] For example, see Horwich (1990).

[18] Given the flexibility of language, such uses of 'true' can be extended in a metalinguistic context, as we see fit. See Grover (1998: 225–33; 2005: 201).

[19] 'False' provides a modified prosentence that inherits the modified content of its antecedent. 'That might be true' is another modified prosentence.

false', as well as in giving truth conditions (e.g., as when saying that, in conditions C_1, 'snow is white' is such that it-is-true; in conditions C_2, it-is-false). Prosentences can also be used to claim a distinction between assertion and what-is-true.

As well, property-theorists could assuage doubts by offering a characterization of a property or properties. Gestures have been made in that direction by alethic pluralists, but so often they contain words like, 'obtains', 'fact', 'reality', and 'defeated'. Can these terms be explained without circularity, that is, without an appeal to a truth property?[20] Interestingly, the prosentential account can provide paraphrases that do not appeal to a truth property. For example: for 'that p is a fact', substitute 'that p is a fact just in case it-is-true'. (That snow is white is a fact just in case snow is white.) For 'p is continually warranted without defeat' there is 'p is continually warranted, with no evidence showing that it-is-false'.

Given the range of claims that can be expressed using prosentences, a prosentential truth predicate would seem to serve us well in discourse that addresses substantive issues.[21]

Some alethic pluralists are challenged to explain 'preservation of truth', as used in describing valid inferences, when different premises exhibit different truth properties. This problem does not arise for the prosentential account. A prosentential rendering of 'An inference is valid just in case it preserves truth' can be given: an inference is valid just in case, if for each premise it-is-true, the conclusion is such that it-is-true. If, on the property view, multiple properties are in the offing, we hereby have yet another reason for endorsing the prosentential theory!

A summary

Alethic pluralism is a nonissue given acceptance of the prosentential account of the role of the truth predicate. However, this does not mean other kinds of pluralism must be rejected.

For the purpose of evaluating pluralism, I presented a perspectival view of descriptions. Our needs, interests, and contexts have meant we have taken a variety of perspectives on the world, and these have led us to descriptions of different types of facts. Because I began with doubts that a complete description of the world is possible, for the sake of this exploration, I assumed there is no set of 'basic' facts to which all such different types of facts may be reduced. I have shown there is much cognitive gain in resourcing the resulting variety of

---

[20] Are negative facts and cohorts being contemplated for true sentences like 'The cat is not on the mat'?
[21] These issues have been discussed in Grover (1998, 2001, 2005).

different perspectives. From there, I argued that a version of vertical pluralism is supported by the perspectival view of descriptions: the view affirms there are different types of facts that are nonreducible.

If it can be shown that an irreconcilable alien system is possible, horizontal pluralism would be affirmed by the perspectival view. If there is no irreconcilable alien system, horizontal pluralism is denied; but, then, all alien perspectives would be welcomed into the mix of perspectives, just in case information from their perspectives would prove useful in our rational decision-making.[22]

References

Anderson, A. R. & N. D. Belnap. (1975). *Entailment: The Logic of Relevance and Necessity, vol. 1*. Princeton: Princeton University Press.
Dickens, C. (1854/1996). *Hard Times*. Cologne: Könemann.
Gibson, R. F. (1986). Translation, physics, and facts of the matter. In L. E. Hahn & P. A. Schlipp (eds.), *The Philosophy of W. V. Quine* (139–154). La Salle, IL: Open Court.
Goodman, N. (1978). *Ways of Worldmaking*. Indianapolis: Hackett Publishing.
Grover, D. L. (2005). How significant is the liar? In Jc Beall & B. Armour-Garb (eds.), *Deflationism and Paradox* (177–202). Oxford: Oxford University Press.
Grover, D. L. (2001). The prosentential theory: further reflections on locating our interest in truth. In M. P. Lynch (ed.), *The Nature of Truth* (505–526). Cambridge, MA: MIT Press.
Grover, D. L. (1992). *A Prosentential Theory of Truth*. Princeton: Princeton University Press.
Grover, D. L., J. L. Camp, & N. D. Belnap. (1975). The prosentential theory of truth. *Philosophical Studies* 27: 73–125.
Gupta, A. (2006). *Empiricism and Experience*. Oxford: Oxford University Press.
Horwich, P. (1990). *Truth*. Oxford: Blackwell.
Inoue, K. (1991). *MacArthur's Japanese Constitution: A Linguistic and Cultural Study of its Making*. Chicago: University of Chicago Press.
Lynch, M. P. (2008). Alethic pluralism, logical consequence and the universality of reason. In P. A. French & H. K. Wettstein (eds.), *Midwest Studies in Philosophy: Truth and its Deformities, vol. 32* (122–140). Boston: Blackwell Publishing.
Lynch, M. P. (1998). *Truth in Context: An Essay in Pluralism and Objectivity*. Cambridge, MA: MIT Press.
Millikan, R. G. (2000). *On Clear and Confused Ideas: An Essay About Substance Concepts*. Cambridge: Cambridge University Press.
Quine, W. V. O. (1986). Reply to Roger F. Gibson. In L. E. Hahn & P. A. Schilpp (eds.), *The Philosophy of W. V. O. Quine* (155–157). La Salle, IL: Open Court.

---

[22] I am indebted to Diane Proudfoot, Philip Catton, and Ruth Millikan for help in the early stages; to Nuel Belnap, Heather Dyke, Elijah Millgram, Michael Perloff, Mark Wilson, and the editors of this volume, who generously provided comments on drafts. Thanks to all who asked questions or commented at presentations at the Universities of Canterbury, Calgary, Pittsburgh, and Illinois–Chicago. As always, such contributions have provided invaluable help toward a more coherent presentation of a work-in-progress project.

Russell, B. (1931). *The Scientific Outlook*. New York: Routledge.
Strawson, P. F. (1985). *Skepticism and Naturalism: Some Varieties*. London: Methuen.
Wilson, M. (2006). *Wandering Significance: An Essay on Conceptual Behavior*. Oxford: Oxford University Press.
Wittgenstein, L. (1953). *Philosophical Investigations*. Oxford: Blackwell.
Wittgenstein, L. (1939/1989). *Wittgenstein's Lectures on the Foundations of Mathematics, Cambridge 1939*, ed. C. Diamond. Chicago: University of Chicago Press.
Wright, C. (2001). Minimalism, deflationism, pragmatism, pluralism. In M. P. Lynch (ed.), *The Nature of Truth* (751–787). Cambridge, MA: MIT Press.

{ PART III }

Pluralism, Deflationism, and Paradox

{ 13 }

Deflationism, Pluralism, Expressivism, Pragmatism
Simon Blackburn

> "Yes, but has nature nothing to say here?" Indeed she has—but she makes herself audible in another way.
>
> WITTGENSTEIN, *ZETTEL*, §364.

The four words of my title form a set of cardinal points in current debates about semantic theory and the shape it should take. I should guess that in the contemporary debates most combinations are found and probably as many denials that those combinations can be motivated, or coherent, or even consistent. Yet it seems to me that there are reasonable readings of all of them on which these questions become focused and even capable of fairly definitive answers. It is the purpose of this chapter to lay out the landscape, as I see it, and to invite others to use my marks in the jungle when plotting their own routes.

Deflationism

For the purpose of this chapter I am going to take deflationism in the theory of truth to consist of three theses:

(A) That there is complete cognitive equivalence between Tp and p.
(B) That conforming to that equivalence is all that is required to manifest complete understanding of the truth predicate.
(C) That the utility of the predicate is therefore purely logical: it is a device for indirect reference and generalization.

I derive these from the seminal discussion in Paul Horwich's book *Truth* (1990), and I shall do no more than sketch some of their features.

The first is too familiar to need much introduction. Frege says 'It is really by using the form of an assertoric sentence that we assert truth, and to do this we do not need to use the word "true". (1897: 129). His view has been shared by many others, through Ramsey, Ayer, Quine, Davidson, and Brandom. Whether these writers have all absorbed the full message of Frege's insight will shortly concern us. But if we call the thesis in (*A*) the transparency property of truth, then few can be found to object, and I shall certainly not be calling it into question here.

The second thesis is slightly more elusive, and we shall find it queried. It makes a strong claim, for we can see it as issuing a bold challenge to would-be falsifiers: find a context that I cannot explain by use of the transparency property. Only then will this thesis be called into question. Horwich and others have done much to make this challenge formidable. But to see how they have done this, we need first to visit the third and final claim.

By saying that 'is true' is to be seen as a device of indirect reference and generalization, deflationists mean that there are many indirect methods of referring to what someone said and many ways of generalizing over actual and potential sayings. Again, there is widespread agreement that the truth predicate serves at least this logical function, and again, I shall take it for granted in what follows. It is more contentious whether it does more than serve this function, and this will occupy us in due course. But let me briefly indicate two thoughts that might seem inflationary, but that, clearly enough, the logical function enables the predicate to discharge.

The first is the place of truth in thoughts about explanation. We are successful, very often, because our beliefs are true. We would not be so successful were they not. This is undoubtedly so. But innumerable *individual* explanations of this form can be deflated. I was successful in seeing a nightingale because I believed they would be found here and my belief was true reduces, via the transparency property, to my being successful in seeing a nightingale because I believed they would be found here, and they are. We want to generalize the pattern, we have the device to hand, and this is what the generalization deploys. There is no *property* of truth intrinsic to the explanation, but only a vast array of explanatory stories of the identical form, none of which need use the predicate and none of which, therefore, requires the identification of any mysterious property or relation to which the predicate might be supposed to refer.

The second is the place of truth in thoughts about aims, goals, or normativity. 'You must take care that what you say is true' is a schema for collecting individual pieces of advice: 'you must take care that if you say that aardvarks amble, then it is true that aardvarks amble'. Again, the truth predicate can be knocked out of these individual statements with no change, for the same norm or aim is put by saying 'you must take care that if you say that aardvarks amble, then aardvarks amble', and again the generalization or schema of normative advice (or obligation or aspiration) introduces nothing more.

A threatened pluralism

These arguments for the adequacy of deflationism certainly make difficulties for any kind of pluralism that works in terms of different concepts of truth in different areas, or even, in Crispin Wright's preferred version (1992), different conceptions of one overarching concept of truth. If there is no property or relation in question and therefore no mode of presentation of a property or relation, how could there be room for different 'conceptions' of such a thing? And looking at the diagnostics Wright offered for understanding which conception of truth is in play in different areas, the deflationist response is very apparent. Wright advances such markers as 'width of cosmological role', involvement with our own potentially mutable responses ('Euthyphronic properties'), and the question of whether irresoluble disagreement implies a cognitive defect in one or another party ('cognitive command') as marking out the relevant distinctions. These might separate the conception of truth in play when we discuss scientifically heavyweight subject matter, such as the weight or shape of an object, from more lightweight matters, such as its color, or more contestable matters, such as its beauty.

The deflationist response is clearly that while these distinctions are no doubt very interesting and have a pedigree going back to seventeenth-century or even classical atomism, it is a kind of double counting to think that they strike at the conception of truth involved. They strike at the level of the proposition: they mark distinctions of subject matter and perhaps eventually distinctions of objectivity or the possibility of cognitively fault-free disagreement. But why add to a distinction of content, another, mirroring, distinction, one only applying to kinds of truth or conceptions of truth?

Frege's reaction

This would certainly have been Frege's reaction. Frege discussed where his work had left the concept of truth particularly in the brief posthumous paper, 'My Basic Logical Insights' (1915). Here Frege says roundly that 'the sense of the word 'true' is such that it does not make any essential contribution to the thought' (p. 251). He aligns the function of the term with the force of making an assertion, continuing:

> So the word 'true' seems to make the impossible possible: it allows what corresponds to the assertoric force to assume the form of a contribution to the thought. And although this attempt miscarries, or rather, through the very fact that it miscarries, it indicates what is characteristic of logic.

Frege famously made a sharp distinction of force from content. The same content can be put forward or presented with very different force, notably as asserted or only as conjectured (or hypothesized), or in contexts that take away the seriousness of assertion, for example on the stage or in other contexts of pretense.

Frege was acutely aware of this distinction. I interpret his remark about 'seeming to make the impossible possible' as indicating that at first appearance, the words 'is true' might—per impossible—function as an indicator of assertoric force. Indeed, in ordinary speech, something of the kind certainly happens, as when you say something, are challenged with some version of 'Surely you cannot be serious?' and reply along the lines: 'It's true, I am telling you'—signifying that your original saying was a genuine assertion. But of course Frege well knows that no word in a sentence can ensure that the thought presented is also asserted. He seems to be wrestling with the problem of the truth predicate seeming to try to occupy this impossible role in the last paragraph of his note (1915: 252):

> Now the thing that indicates most clearly the essence of logic is the assertoric force with which a sentence is uttered. But no word, or part of a sentence, corresponds to this; the same series of words may be uttered with assertoric force at one time and not at another. In language assertoric force is bound up with the predicate.

This is not entirely clear, since the last sentence seems to indicate some version of the very doctrine that the first part denies, nominating the predicate as some kind of privileged bearer of force. Even if Frege meant to say that in language assertoric force is bound up with the act of predication, the issue is still left unclear, since in at least one perfectly good sense, in indirect and unserious contexts, predication still occurs, yet assertoric force is lacking.

Deflationism compromised?

Thus far, I have laid out familiar defenses of deflationism and claimed the authority of Frege against a kind of pluralism that it seems to undercut. However, these familiar points do not mark the end of the story. To see why not, I shall present the argument as it is developed in a recent paper by Dorit Bar-On and Keith Simmons. They also take their cue from Frege. But, they claim:

> As we continue to reflect on or theorize about a language and its practitioners, we may turn to the speech act of assertion. We may say, following Frege, that to assert is to put forward as true. Here is the word 'true' again, appearing in the language in which we theorize. In our mouth, the word 'true' is not used as a disquotational or denominalizing or prosentential device. We are not even purporting to describe some sentence or thought. This is not a first-order use, and it cannot be disquoted away (2007: 77).

This is taking the equation that to assert is to put forward as true in an inflationary spirit. The idea is that while first-order uses of the truth predicate are susceptible of deflationist theory, when we step back and reflect on the basic act of assertion, we need an equation in which the notion of truth plays an indisputable role, yet one that cannot be seen either as a disquotation or in terms of the logical activities of indirect reference and generalization that are the deflationist's meat and drink.

It is certainly undeniable that we would like to say something about the speech act of assertion. And we would not be saying anything interesting by deflating truth as it occurs in the equation that to assert is to present as true. In usual deflationist fashion, we would approach this via the schema that to assert that p is to present p as true; we would analyze this as a summary generalization over cases such as 'to assert that aardvarks amble is to . . . what? . . . that aardvarks amble'—and the only term we could put in would be 'assert' or a synonym, giving us that to assert is to assert. Bar-On and Simmons say roundly that in their mouths the word 'true' is not susceptible of deflationist treatment. What we find instead is that it might be, but at the cost of the equation that to assert is to present as true reducing to the tautology that to assert is to assert.

It is clear, as well, that there is no other way of evading this collapse, if our resources begin with the presentation of a thought. As Bar-On and Simmons make very clear and as we can see from Frege again, to assert is not simply to present a thought, to imagine a state of affairs, or to do anything short of claiming truth. But are they right that this requires us to backtrack on all the deflationist insights that so far seem so promising? They themselves do not suggest that we take refuge in a thick or robust approach, ahead of which lie the impassable deserts in which correspondence, coherence, pragmatism and other landmarks prove to be nothing but mirages? There may be a different way out.

A normative approach

This way out would be to approach the nature of assertion in terms of the status and responsibilities accorded to one who asserts. The act is identified in terms of proprieties surrounding it and liabilities that are incurred when they are transgressed against. This is the approach championed by Robert Brandom (1994), and there is unquestionably something attractive about it. If you assert that p then you become liable to censures and reproaches if *not-p*, ranging from mild disappointment to utter ostracism, whereas if you had merely floated the thought that p, then you may escape the indictment (you may not entirely escape criticisms, for sometimes merely putting the thought into someone's head could constitute a malicious act. It was Iago's preferred modus operandi after all). Moreover, and centrally to Brandom's account, someone who asserts is making the kind of commitment that means he is liable to be asked for reasons but is also able to offer it in turn as a reason for other commitments. There are rules or norms, 'social deontic attitudes', governing both input and output.

Brandom presents his approach in terms of a generalized pragmatism, and it is part of a program of freeing our theorizing about language from some of the tyranny of ubiquitous semantic notions, such as truth and reference. But we have to move carefully here. Locating thinkers or speakers in a landscape in which we *only* answer to statuses accorded to us or denied to us by fellow thinkers and speakers risks distorting our positions. For we do not just answer to each other. We answer to each other because of what we get right or wrong *about* the things we are involved with—the things we are talking about. Substituting concern with each other for concern with the world is a mistake. If I am deciding whether an object is red or square or weighs five pounds, I am not primarily concerned with what other people will say in the case nor with predicting the penalties if I am out of step with them. To use an old analogy, it is not like tuning up with the orchestra, where my prime concern is to listen to whether my note is the same as the notes of other players.[1] We are not after democratic harmony but getting the judgment right. In the general case, I can make sense of the idea that most members of my community might themselves get the issue wrong, but when it is a case of simply being in step with others, this possibility does not arise: an individual may be out of step with others, but if the entire parade is marching the same way, there is nothing for them to be out of step with.

To see the importance of this point, consider a case not of assertion but of promising. We can use the same general normative terms about the act of promising. If I promise to meet you in Times Square at a given time, I take up a certain status: let us say I accord you the right to expect something of me or voluntarily put myself under a duty, and I am liable for social penalties if I fail or fail lacking sufficient excuse. All this is surely correct. But equally surely, it does not sideline or supersede the involvement of Times Square in the promise. It is not just any old actions that discharge my liability or show me failing to fulfill it. It is actions that result in my being or not being in Times Square. Similarly, if I make a bet with you I enter a 'normative space' of privileges and liabilities, but those privileges and liabilities are only triggered by whether some event occurs: the event referred to in the content of the bet. Our attention must be directed on the race, just as the attention of the promisee must be directed on Times Square.

Of course, Brandom's concentration on reasons gives him what he regards as a sufficient account of these foci of attention, in terms of harvesting input and output reasons for the various judgments that would

---

[1] See also Blackburn (1984: 83–87).

acknowledge the fulfillment or otherwise of the promise or settlement of the bet. This is the ambition of showing that his 'social-deontic attitudes' give us an entrée into the theory of content, and he would need, it seems to me, to show how they relate to such things as observation and attention on the input side and action, success, and failure on the output side. This is a very tall order, but here I make no judgment on its success or prospects for success.

For we can acknowledge the undoubted importance of rules and statuses in describing the speech-act of assertion without supposing that they give us any particular line on theory of the *content* of judgments made, nor therefore on whether in order to isolate that content we need to introduce such notions as reference and representation. For this is not the game we were chasing. We simply wanted a notion of assertion wide enough to embrace all sorts of content. And for this purpose, the notion of shifting status is entirely appropriate, just as it would be if we essayed a general account of promising or betting.

Bar-On and Simmons suggest in their paper that by saying a great deal about assertion, in terms of 'social-deontic attitudes', Brandom forfeits his claim to be deploying only a deflationist account of truth.[2] The idea is that if asserting is given a thick or robust story, then, since they are the same thing, so is 'presenting as true' and hence truth itself is inflated as part of the inflated compound. But this seems to me to risk asking for unreasonably clean hands. The question was whether, given that 'asserts' and 'presents as true' are synonyms, we read the equation left to right, supposing that assertion explains presenting as true, or right to left, supposing that presenting as true explains asserting. By reading it left to right, we give an account of a context in which the word appears and which otherwise might have been taken to be inflationary, but we show that the appearance is harmless or in other words that ingredients that are common property and that can do nothing to incite correspondence and the rest are sufficient to explain it. As a comparison, suppose the argument was played out in terms of 'doubting whether true' or the state of one who raises a doubt about truth. This is a particular state and could be given a fairly thick or robust treatment (there are norms for whether doubts are sensible, for instance). But since in any case doubting whether p is true is just doubting whether p, there is no reason to suppose that any thickness in the story *derived* from the presence of a synonymous phrase with the word 'true' in it. But that is what we would need to think in order to suppose that this is a strike against deflationism.

Deflationists do not, therefore, immediately succumb to Bar-On and Simmons's doubts. But it remains to be seen whether they can provide any useful theory of content without reinflating the notion of truth. Some of that emerges when we tackle our next topic, the prospects for pluralism.

---

[2] See Brandom (1994, ch. 5).

A different pluralism

When everything is above board, a person making an assertion is giving voice to a commitment of his own and intends that the person receiving it shares the commitment: either is already or becomes of one mind about the topic. There is responsibility involved because commitments are, taking on board ideas present in the work of Alexander Bain, preparations for action.[3] Even commitments that are apparently remote from the here-and-now, the environment that provides the immediate context of action and that punishes or rewards action with successes and failures, lay a trail that may lead to these things. It may be less important whether you are right about the date of Henry VIII's accession to the throne than about whether there is a bus bearing down on you. But the habit of accuracy, like the habit of sincerity, is itself a precious possession, and disapproval rightly follows assertions that show that you have not got it.

So we might put the moral of the last section in a slogan by saying that we should be looking not for truth makers but for assertion licensers. For the norm-abiding asserter needs the warrant he can cite, and somebody accepting the assertion as intended, which means welcoming it within his own repertoire of potential sincere assertions, will need to suppose that such warrant exists. In straightforward cases, he will suppose that the very warrant the original asserter would cite exists, but in less straightforward cases he may 'lay off', deploying his own resources rather than taking his informant's word for it. All this may suggest that we are moving toward something like a Dummettian 'assertibility condition' semantics rather than a truth-conditional one. But that is not at all clear, and in the light of our Fregean explorations of deflationism neither is the difference. For there will be no general contrast between incorporating an assertion into one's own repertoire and supposing it true.

All this may make the prospects for either pluralism or expressivism as a distinct view of various fields seem rather bleak. Are we poised to put up with a blanket notion of assertion and acceptance and corresponding to those a blanket notion of belief, smothering any of the differences that expressivists believed themselves to have found? I think we can get a clue to why this is not the upshot by looking at the kind of consideration that has been in play throughout the history of the subject. Let me start with Berkeley, a regrettably unsung hero of insight into how to do things with words, certainly compared with the more glamorous Hume. Berkeley writes:

> Besides, the communicating of ideas marked by words is not the chief and only end of language, as is commonly supposed. There are other ends, as

---

[3] See, e.g., Bain (1875: 505, 595).

the raising of some passion, the exciting to or deterring from an action, the putting the mind in some particular disposition—to which the former is in many cases barely subservient, and sometimes entirely omitted, when these can be obtained without it, as I think does not unfrequently happen in the familiar use of language. (1710: 83–4)

Berkeley applies this idea in at least five areas of his philosophy. They are the nature of the self, the nature of agency and force, the nature of normative and evaluative language, at least some theological sayings, and finally at least some mathematical sayings. About force Berkeley is particularly explicit: 'And if by considering this doctrine of force, men arrive at the knowledge of many inventions in mechanics, and are taught to frame Engines by means of which things difficult and otherwise impossible may be performed, and if the same doctrine which is so beneficial here below, serves also as a key to discover the nature of the celestial motions, shall we deny that it is of use, either in practice or speculation, because we have no distinct idea of force?' (1832: 503)

Hume shares Berkeley's view about force (under the topic of causation) and evaluative language and is not far away when it comes to the self and theological language. If we jump over two centuries, we come to Ramsey, who thinks the same about chance and probability, causation and evaluation, and then of course the later Wittgenstein, whose insistence that we pay attention to what is actually *done* with words infuses his discussions of necessity, mathematics, ethics, religious language, and psychological sayings. Wittgenstein also applies the doctrine to philosophical sayings themselves, in the doctrine that we should see them as injunctions or the laying down of grammatical rules.[4]

Now it is not presently my purpose to chart all the wrinkles in these different writers' treatments of these themes but to point to the surprising similarity of the lists. It is not too much to say that the shoe pinches in pretty much the same place across the generations. One suggestion, made by Hilary Putnam, is that an empiricist prejudice is at work, to the effect that if we cannot picture something then we cannot have a concept (or in the older terminology, an idea) of it. This might just about diagnose Berkeley and Hume, but it would be very difficult to see it as applying to Wittgenstein or for that matter to the many physicists from the time of Newton to that of Wittgenstein's idol Hertz, who found something especially problematic about the notion of force until eventually its eradication from a properly formed physics became a widely shared ideal. So is there a better principle explaining why the same suspects so constantly re-emerge?

---

[4] I shall not here rehearse the evidence for this strand in Wittgenstein. See Blackburn (1990) for details.

Putnam himself criticizes the empiricists for not understanding the way in which scientific theorizing engenders an understanding of theoretical terms, even when our ability to picture referents for those terms deserts us. Where we have an explanation, there we have an understanding of whatever has its necessary place in the theory doing the explaining. This may well be true and a just enough criticism, although the passage I quoted from Berkeley about force suggests he is perfectly aware of the shape of scientific theory, while treating it in an instrumentalist spirit. But in any case Putnam's diagnosis immediately suggests a more charitable explanation. If we associate representation not with the ability to *picture* so much as with the ability to *explain*, then even on Putnam's grounds we should start to sympathize with the thought that something else than simple representation is at work in these areas when we become baffled at explaining in any such terms why we go in for such sayings. Do we go in for asserting causal connections because we are responsive to and understand them? Do we go in for asserting evaluative and normative statements because we are responsive to values and norms and understand what it is to which we are responsive? And the same question presses for necessities in general (we are not responsive to distributions of properties across possible worlds because they do not affect us), for abstracta, for chances, for theological realms, and so on.

Because we—some of us—cannot find a satisfactory theory of our receptivity to these facts, we need to cast around for something else. And this is what Berkeley, Hume, Ramsey, or Wittgenstein gives us. We do not need to see ourselves as receptive to or responsive to any enchanted realities in order to explain what we do when we deploy these terms. We only need to think of our responses to the everyday and our needs as we tell each other of the way to cope with it. Hence we get a plurality of little or local pragmatisms: theories of use that eschew using the apparent denizens of the relevant theories (selves, necessities, forces, values, abstracta) as part of any explanation of why we ourselves are talking in these terms.

One way of pursuing such an agenda, to be sure, would be simply to go for a reduction of content. But by now it is notorious that such programs fail with a crashing inevitability. And they turn their backs on the obvious resource that the tradition leaves us. We may be doing something distinctive as we talk in the relevant terms, even if we need postulate no distinctive part of the world that we are describing, just as I am doing something distinctive when I make a bet or a promise or order you to shut the window, without in any way describing any special ways in which things stand.

The concentration on explanation makes a kind of expressivism almost inevitable as soon as we give our functional story of the reason why we have these pronouncements and commitments in terms that do not include mention of what, superficially, they purport to describe. For in the absence of reductions, anything other than expressivism would mean a fracture between the explanation and the truth of the output, which must surely render our own satisfaction with such pronouncements extremely vulnerable. Thus suppose a theologian who becomes convinced that the true explanation of the prevalence of religious sayings is emotional or social. But suppose he also sets his face against an expressive or functional story of what we are doing as we talk of the Holy Ghost and its structure. Then surely the dissonance between what explains the pronouncement and what the pronouncement appears to be about would be bound to suggest skepticism or an error theory. The whole business would have been exploded. On the other hand, if he can steel himself to admit that the sayings are expressive in intent, so that the words of the creed are, as it were, continuous with the organ music that precedes them or the feelings of reverence toward the world, love of fellows, or for that matter hatred of outsiders that they inspire, then there is no blanket error in sight. There would, of course, remain room for particular emotions and attitudes and mental postures to raise eyebrows, in this area as in all others.

Beliefs and their mental and social neighbors

Above, I took issue with Wright's transportation of distinctions of content into distinctions of conceptions of truth. The same strictures might seem to apply directly to transporting distinctions of content into differences in the act of asserting. But I think that would be wrong, for it may be that it is differences in the acts of asserting and accepting that play a role in explaining the identity of particular families of content, or propositions.

Consider, for instance, the simple English indicative conditional. I accept the view of Gilbert Ryle that the conditional 'if p then q' can best be explained by considering its cousin 'p so q'.[5] Putting this into public space, we assert p and we assert q, but it would be wrong to see us as having yet a third belief. Rather we also express allegiance to a movement of the mind from the one acceptance to the other. We issue, as Gilbert Ryle put it, an inference ticket, which others may decide to incorporate into their cognitive architecture or ways of dealing with the world, or may not. If we want to consider the merit of that ticket itself but without committing ourselves to p or q, we use the conditional form. Accepting the conditional is adopting a disposition to use the inference, or, on occasions when you want to speak your mind sincerely, to issue the ticket in one's own voice. We doubt the conditional if we have reservations about the movement in question or wish to hedge it or qualify it or contextualize it, or want to warn against being too confident in the consequent having accepted the antecedent.

---

[5] For details see Ryle (1950).

This functional story stands at some distance from one conducted entirely in terms of belief: a story that would begin and end by saying that we believe various conditional facts to obtain. I believe it has advantages over any such story, both in its ability to explain the puzzling relation between conditionals and the corresponding truth function of material implication and in its metaphysical economy, but I shall not defend that here.

Consider instead other things, such as metaphor. Wittgenstein says

> If we hold it a truism that people take pleasure in imagination, we should remember that this imagination is not like a painted picture or a three-dimensional model, but a complicated structure of heterogeneous elements: words and pictures. We shall then not think of operating with written or oral signs as something to be contrasted with the operation with 'mental images' of the events. (1979, 7e)

Here is one way of interpreting him. Romeo says that Juliet is the sun; suppose Mercutio agrees. It is surely flat-footed to begin and end with describing Romeo as expressing a belief and Mercutio as believing the same. Rather, Romeo has issued a kind of invitation to search for features of Juliet in a state of mind guided, as Wittgenstein suggests, by the thought of the sun or image of the sun. Mercutio accepts his invitation although he might do so even if his exploration does not issue in anything Romeo intended, for instance if dwelling on the salient fact that the sun is hot, he comes to suppose that Juliet is sexually athletic or enthusiastic. Here the distance from belief is more obvious, since what Romeo intended is insulated from what would normally be implications licensed by the syntactic form of what he said. For example, having announced that Juliet is the sun, if later in the day he also asserts that the sun is 93 million miles away, he cannot be faulted for refusing to infer or to believe that Juliet is 93 million miles away.

This compartmentalization is one of the things Wittgenstein highlights as a way of doubting whether what Hume called the 'somewhat unaccountable state of mind' of the religious adept fits easily into the category of belief.[6] Wittgenstein directs us to notice various ways in which the role of religious sayings is dissimilar in important ways from the role of other expressions of belief. Suppose the adept says, for example, 'The Holy Ghost, proceeding from the Father and the Son, is of one substance, majesty, and glory, with the Father and the Son, very and eternal God', where this for him is a serious use of language. In his mind, what he says requires saying. But Wittgenstein thinks that something would be out of kilter if, for instance, the adept affirms this, and I reply 'well I am not sure about that', treating it like other beliefs as a potential subject for discussion rather than an article of faith. More

---

[6] Hume (1757: 451).

importantly, the adept is also apt to discourage questions about specifics as missing the point or even blasphemous: God sees everything, but it would be crass to ask about the color of his eyes or shape of his eyebrows. Full inferential power is also lost: that is, the syntactic form of the saying would suggest certain inferences, which are in fact not made. Thus we get the phenomenon of compartmentalization. The Roman Catholic physicist feels no need to consider the implications of his Sunday commitment to transubstantiation when he returns to the laboratory on Monday. Again, the consequence of dissent or doubt here is different from that of dissent or doubt in normal cases: it is generally not a sin to doubt whether particular things exist, but in this domain it can be. In other words, when we look at the *function* of the affirmation in our 'stream of life', significant differences from more mundane cases of belief begin to show up.

We might add, as Wittgenstein does not, that the results intended by those who are professionally involved in transmitting the practice are somewhat different from those intended by those involved in teaching other beliefs. In the normal case, teachers want understanding, primarily shown by an independent ability to work through the implications of what is taught for what to expect and how to act. In the religious case, they cannot aim at that and are likely instead to want passivity or surrender. So long as the somewhat unaccountable state of mind issues in the right devotions, the right allegiances, or the right donations, that is enough. If it doesn't, then talk of heresy and sin raises its ugly head.

My final example, perhaps unsurprisingly, is that of evaluation. There is one fundamental thing to say about the proposition that X is good and its various embellished versions (X is as good as a . . . ; X is a good F; X is good for . . . ; X is good from such-and-such a point of view). This is that by asserting it you express approval or endorsement of X (perhaps as a . . . or for . . . or as seen by the occupants of some point of view). By putting approval or endorsement into public space, as something to be accepted by others, you also put yourself into a 'social deontic' space as well. You will be expected to back your endorsement with reasons, that is, by pointing out features of X that are themselves good bases for the attitude. Your selection of those features itself becomes a candidate for acceptance or rejection. This is a different issue, of course, for someone may share your approval of X but not approve of your reasons for that approval and substitute his own. Your view of the implications of what you say is assessable in the same way, and 'implication' here may include intention, choice, and action.

These thoughts, say expressivists, give us enough to explain the arrival of evaluative pronouncements in our repertoires and to explain what they do both when asserted directly and when occurring in indirect contexts. For since our own endorsements and approvals are among the things with good or bad inputs and good or bad outputs, they get into the domain of things to and from which inference tickets need issuing. Hence the appearance of the evaluative sentence in conditionals should not surprise us.

Truth again

So is it wrong to talk of believing that if you drink too much you will impair your balance; that the Holy Ghost, proceeding from the Father and the Son, is of one substance, majesty, and glory with the Father and the Son, very and eternal God; that Juliet is the sun; or that health is a good thing? For most purposes, not at all. We can usually get by using 'belief' and its associates, notably assertion and truth, as umbrella terms covering the acceptance of whatever is conveyed by indicative sentences. But that should not be thought to deny a finer grained taxonomy, one more adequate to the functional nuances and more adequate as well as the basis for an explanation of what we are doing. This finer grained taxonomy will distinguish beliefs from dispositions to make inferences, from being in the grip of a picture, from accepting or prompting invitations to see one thing in the light of another, or from attitudes such as endorsement and approval. This pluralism comes into its own when on its basis we can understand the behavior of the propositions believed or, if we like to put it this way, understand the role those propositions play in our mental and social economies.

It is natural to present this view, as I have done both here and in previous writings, in largely *contrastive* terms. One the one hand, there is belief, and here, on the other hand, there is, say, the issuing of an inference ticket. But we could maintain the pluralism while blurring, or in many cases disavowing, the contrast. Consider, for instance, everyday middle-sized dry goods. It is evident that believing that there is a chair here" is partly constituted by a variety of inferential dispositions: it includes being prepared to suppose that I will not be able to occupy some space without displacing the chair; that had you tried to occupy that space you would have met resistance; that without force being applied there will continue to be a chair there, and so forth. 'Belief' begins to look like a portmanteau including assent to inferences, counterfactuals, and other salient consequences or constituents of a world with a chair, there. The full truth would not be captured by a snapshot or single time-slice of reality.

I do not mind seeing such inferences not so much as contrasted with belief as partly constitutive of belief. The parallel in the case of evaluation would, I take it, be something like Hilary's Putnam's conception of Quine's world, which is grey with its blend of the white of analytic and the black of synthetic, as also pink with its blend of the red of evaluation and grey of fact. But just as the analytic chemist faced with a compound proceeds by analyzing out the constituent elements, so too, even if we too are faced with compounds, the path of progress may consist in finding in more detail what they are made of.

References

Bain, A. (1875). *The Emotions and the Will*, 3rd ed. London: Longmans, Green & Company.

Bar-On, D. & K. Simmons. (2007). The use of force against deflationism: assertion and truth. In D. Greimann & G. Siegwart (eds.), *Truth and Speech Act: Studies in Philosophy of Language* (61–89). London: Routledge.

Berkeley, G. (1843). *The Works of George Berkeley: including his letters to Thomas Prior, Dean Gervais, Mr. Pope, etc.: to which is prefixed an account of his life*, vol. 1. London: Thomas Tegg.

Berkeley, G. (1710). *A Treatise Concerning the Principles of Human Knowledge.* Reprinted in Berkeley (1843: 70–147).

Berkeley, G. (1732). *Alciphron: or, the minute philosopher: In Seven Dialogues Containing an Apology for the Christian Religion, against Those Who Are Called Free-Thinkers.* Reprinted in Berkeley (1843: 297–528).

Blackburn, S. (1990). Wittgenstein's irrealism. In R. Haller and J. Brandl (eds.), *Wittgenstein: Towards a Re-Evaluation* (13–26). Vienna: Verlag Hölder-Adler-Tempsky. Reprinted in Blackburn, S. (2010). *Practical Tortoise Raising* (200–219). Oxford: Oxford University Press.

Blackburn, S. (1984). *Spreading the Word*. New York: Oxford University Press.

Brandom, R. (1994). *Making It Explicit*. Cambridge, MA: Harvard University Press.

Frege, G. (1979). *Posthumous Writings*. H. Hermes, F. Kambartel, & F. Kaulbach (eds.). Oxford: Blackwell.

Frege, G. (1915). My basic logical insights. In Frege (1979: 251–252).

Frege, 1897. Logic. In Frege (1979: 126–151).

Horwich, P. (1990). *Truth*. Oxford: Blackwell.

Hume, D. (1779). *Essays and Treatises on Several Subjects by David Hume*, vol. 2. Dublin: J. Williams.

Hume, D. (1757). *The Natural History of Religion*. Reprinted in Hume (1779: 401–469).

Ryle, G. (1950). 'If', 'so', and 'because'. In M. Black (ed.), *Philosophical Analysis* (302–318). Ithaca, NY: Cornell University Press.

Wittgenstein, L. (1979). *Remarks on Frazer's Golden bough*. Edited by R. Rhees and translated by A. C. Miles. Atlantic Highlands: Humanities Press.

Wright, C. (1992). *Truth and Objectivity*. Cambridge, MA: Harvard University Press.

{ 14 }

Should We Be Pluralists about Truth?
Max Kölbel

Pluralism about truth can take several forms: first, it might be the claim that the truth predicate expresses several truth concepts, and second, it might be the claim that the truth predicate, even though it expresses a single concept, corresponds to several truth properties, in other words, that truth is realized by several distinct properties. Recently, following suggestions made by Wright (1992), a number of theorists have defended pluralist theses of the second form. They claim that while there is a single generic concept of truth with application in all areas of discourse, truth is nevertheless realized by different properties in different areas of discourse. In this chapter, I shall make some general observations about the way in which a pluralism of the second form can be motivated. Then I shall put forward some considerations in favor of the first sort of pluralism. Finally, I shall argue that pluralists of the second type cannot, without further ado, make use of standard frameworks of structured propositions, but rather need to rethink what type of entity, in their view, serves as truthbearer.

1. Methodological considerations: expressions, concepts, properties

EXAMINING CONCEPTS

There are many concepts. Concepts are abstract objects, individuated in terms of the rules that govern them. Some of the many concepts are employed by us in thought, some of them are expressed in language, and some of them are not employed in thought or not expressed in language, for each concept exists independently of there being any concrete episodes of thought and speech that could profitably be described as an employment of it. Concepts are in principle susceptible to a priori investigation. We can fix on a particular concept by laying down, in stipulative manner, by which conceptual rules the concept is to be governed. Alternatively, we can fix on a concept by describing it as the concept that is expressed by this or that expression in a particular public language or in a particular idiolect. Or we can fix on a concept by describing it as the concept employed by this or that person or persons in certain episodes of thought. Once we have fixed on a concept in one of these ways, we can start examining its properties. Some of these properties will be accessible to a priori methods; some may not be.[1]

Suppose we have fixed upon a concept by specifying a complete set of rules that govern it. Then we can directly move on to examine the a priori consequences of these rules. Such an examination may, for example, result in the finding that the concept is subsumed by another concept or that it subsumes another concept, if we have appropriate a priori information about these other concepts. It may result in the finding that the concept is definable in terms of certain other concepts (if the identifying set of rules didn't already come in the form of that definition). Alternatively, it may result in the finding that the concept is contradictory or that it fails uniquely to determine an extension. Even if we have fixed upon a concept by laying down the rules that govern it, the concept may have some properties that are susceptible only to empirical methods. For example, the question of whether a concept applies to anything will in many cases be an empirical question. If we have a sufficiently clear conception of a natural property or kind, we can also examine whether a concept's extension coincides with that of some natural property or kind, or maybe whether it does so necessarily.

Suppose we fix upon a concept by describing it as the concept expressed by a given expression in some public language. Then the question, 'By which rules is that concept governed?' may be answerable only by recourse to empirical or quasi-empirical investigation. Thus, if we examine a concept identified as the concept expressed by some expression in a language with which we are not competent, we will need to employ empirical methods to discover any conceptual rules governing that concept. This may involve observing the use competent speakers make of the expression in question. If we examine a concept identified as the concept expressed by some expression in a public language with which we are ourselves competent, then we can employ quasi-empirical methods to find out about the rules governing the concept. This may involve

---

[1] The approach to concepts described in this paragraph and assumed below is, of course, controversial. There are those, like Fodor (1975), Dretske (1981), or Laurence & Margolis (1999), who construe concepts as concrete psychological entities such as mental processes or mental symbols. This approach is often taken for granted in cognitive science. There are also those, who, like Dummett (1993), construe concepts as abilities. The current conception of concepts as abstract objects goes back to Frege's antipsychologistic theory of 'senses' (e.g., 1892), and is defended, for example, by Peacocke (1992, 2008) and Zalta (2001). I do not regard it as a foregone conclusion that the approach pursued in cognitive science is inconsistent, or even in genuine rivalry, with Fregean theories. For a defence of the role of abstract objects in theorizing about thought and speech, with which I sympathize, see Matthews (1994). Part of what I am assuming here is that concepts are governed and individuated by norms. This assumption is supposed to be neutral between a number of different construals of such norms.

relying on our own intuitions as competent users of the language in question. But even in this case we can make use of straightforwardly empirical methods by observing the use we and others make of the expression. Once we have an idea of the conceptual rules governing the concept empirically identified, the situation is as before with concepts stipulatively identified: we can again investigate those of the properties of the concept that are consequences of these conceptual rules using a priori methods, and we may investigate other properties using empirical methods.

Suppose, finally, that we are examining concepts that are identified as the concepts that this or that thinker or group of thinkers is employing in this or that situation. Again, it is in principle an empirical or a quasi-empirical matter to determine what the conceptual rules are that govern the concept. If the concept is identified as the concept the researcher him- or herself is employing in this or that situation, quasi-empirical methods involving memory and introspection can be used. If the concept is identified as the concept employed by this or that person distinct from the researcher, then the researcher has to resort to empirical methods such as the observation of verbal or other behavior in order to find out what the rules are that govern the concept. We can distinguish the case where the concept is identified as the concept employed by a group from the case where the concept is identified by the role it plays in the thought of an individual. Once the conceptual rules governing the concept are found, the situation is again the same as in the stipulative case.

EXAMINING PROPERTIES, KINDS, OR OBJECTS DENOTED BY CONCEPTS

Sometimes philosophers separate two questions, the question of whether a given concept applies to anything and the question of whether the concept applies to a (natural, real, etc.) property, a (natural, real, etc.) kind, or a (natural, real, etc.) object. This sort of question makes sense, I believe, only on a certain kind of background of assumptions and theoretical or explanatory interests. Let me explain.

Suppose we have an irreducible concept, that is, a concept that is not definable in terms of other concepts. Perhaps the conceptual norms involve certain perceptual criteria for the application of the concept as input conditions. Then the question of whether the concept has application at all will not necessarily require the employment of other concepts. Suppose that we have a concept that is definable in terms of other concepts that can be independently employed, such as the concept of a meat-eating plant. Then we will employ the concepts *meat-eating* and *plant* in adjudicating whether the concept has application and in which instances it can be correctly applied.

The question of whether a given concept corresponds to a property, a kind, or an object (I omit the qualifiers 'natural', 'real', etc. for ease of expression) is usually different. In this case, we have a concept c_1, from a system of concepts C, which may be either irreducible or definable in terms of other concepts c_2, c_3, ... from C, and we ask whether the extension of the concept constitutes or corresponds to a property, a kind, or an object. In order meaningfully to raise this question, we need to have some interesting separate system of concepts N = $\{n_1, n_2, \ldots\}$, in relation to which we are asking the question. The question is then whether c_1 is coextensional (or perhaps necessarily coextensional) with some concept $n \in N$.

N may be interesting for various reasons. For example, we might believe that the concepts in N are epistemologically privileged in some sense, perhaps because the methods used in employing these concepts are particularly well understood or reliable. In other cases, we might believe that the concepts in N are somehow ontologically or metaphysically privileged, perhaps in the sense that we accept the doctrine that there exist only properties, kinds, or objects that constitute the extension of some concept in N. Or perhaps N is ontologically privileged in the sense that the facts describable in terms of the concepts in N are sufficient to determine all the facts (supervenience). But no such extravagant significance need be attributed to N. Even someone who regards N as neither epistemologically nor ontologically privileged may still have a certain interest in finding out about the interrelation between the concepts in C and the concepts in N. Thus, she may for example be interested merely in establishing whether a reduction of c_1 in terms of the concepts in N is possible. Unlike a potential analytic reduction of c_1 in terms of c_2, c_3, ..., a reduction of c_1 in terms of $n_1, n_2, \ldots \in N$ might be an empirical (or at any rate nonanalytic or otherwise nonobvious) reduction that adds to our genuine knowledge. For example, a reduction of the concept of *heat* to concepts from thermodynamics (heat = mean molecular energy) or of the concept of *water* to concepts of elementary chemistry (water = H_2O) represent genuine gains in knowledge. Such findings can be valuable even in the absence of any general ontological or epistemological priority of N. It may, for example, help us develop methodological shortcuts or just satisfy our curiosity as to how things hang together.

One more specific concern that may spur our interest in a possible reduction of c_1 to some $n \in N$ is explanation. This may be related to the case where N is epistemologically privileged. Suppose we find that c_1 is coextensional (or necessarily coextensional) with some $n \in N$ (or perhaps merely that the extension of some $n \in N$ is contained in the extension of c_1). Suppose further that we have some theory or set of general principles that explain/predict why things fall under n. Then this will provide an explanation for, or explanatory understanding of, why things fall under c_1.

To summarize: it is important to keep in mind that any investigation as to which property, kind, or object, if any, a given concept corresponds to makes sense only on the background of some interesting set of reductive concepts that is used to individuate properties, kinds, or objects. In any such investigation, it will be useful to be clear about what the reductive set is and what kind of interest (epistemological, metaphysical, explanatory) we are pursuing in exploring the question.

THE CONCEPTUAL MESS WE ARE OFTEN IN

Usually, the issues are not as neatly separated as the last pages suggest. Very often, it is hard to make out whether in a particular philosophical debate about some issue, we are starting by identifying concepts stipulatively or whether we are identifying them in one of the empirical ways described above. Another difficulty is that the terrain often moves as we are exploring it. Suppose, for example, we are examining the concept expressed at some time t by an expression e of some public language. Empirical and quasi-empirical research suggests that at t, e expresses the concept specified by conceptual rules R. Further a priori research shows that that R is inconsistent. This result may now influence the way e is used subsequently; perhaps some aspects of R are now branded as mistaken. Thus after t, R does not govern the concept expressed by e (whichever way one wants to read the scope of 'after t').

Sometimes in philosophical debates everyone assumes that everyone is talking about the same concept or property, but some of the disagreements suggest that the disputing parties are pursuing different projects.[2] Thus, the different parties may all be employing the expression e when identifying the concept or property that is the assumed subject of the dispute. Their dispute presupposes that *e* is used with the same sense by everyone. However, one party may be basing their considerations on one set of a priori conceptual rules supposedly governing the concept expressed by e, while another party is basing their consideration on another set. It is now unclear whether we should say one of at least two things: either that each party is making stipulative or quasi-empirically correct assumptions about the conceptual rules governing the concept they each express by e, but they are simply wrong to assume that both are using e with the same sense (i.e., to express the same concept); or we say that given they are using e to express the same concept (since they take themselves to be disagreeing), one of them must be making mistaken claims about the conceptual rules governing that concept.

Let me illustrate some of the difficulties with an example. There is a philosophical debate about personhood. Locke, in the *Essay* (1689/1975), seems to start his examination from a certain view of what a person is. He says that a

---

[2] Kirkham argues that this has happened in the case of debates about truth; see Kirkham (1992/2001).

person is 'a thinking intelligent being, that has reason and reflection, and can consider itself as itself, the same thinking thing, in different times and places' (1975: II.27.9). He distinguishes persons from 'men' (i.e., human beings) and 'thinking substances.' Thus Locke seems to start directly from certain assumptions about the concept of a person, and he uses these assumptions to generate certain conclusions, for example about personal identity. Others, for example Derek Parfit (1984), use quasi-empirical evidence to establish what identity criterion the concept of a person involves. Thus Parfit will use imaginary situations and our responses to them in order to tease out certain features of the concept of a person. Locke is not bothered by certain counterintuitive consequences of his definition of a person. For example, it seems to be a consequence of Locke's view that if a sober man doesn't have appropriate memory links or any psychological continuity with the same man at an earlier time, when he was drunk, then the sober man is not the same person as the drunk man, even though they are the same man. Locke accepts this consequence. Why would we then punish the sober man for what the drunk man did, if they are different people? Locke bites the bullet and says that this is for pragmatic reasons only: it would be too easy to fake the condition of drunkenness (1975: II.27.22). By contrast Parfit, on his approach, has to take seriously our intuition that the drunk man and the sober man are the same person.

Now, should we say that Locke and Parfit are simply talking past one another? While Locke is talking about a concept of person as stipulatively defined, Parfit is talking about a concept of person that is expressed by the public language expression 'person' and that is employed by thinkers in certain contexts (otherwise his quasi-empirical methods would make no sense). There are reasons why this would not be a perfectly adequate portrayal of the situation. First, both philosophers are usually taken to be addressing the same issue. To proclaim that they are strictly addressing different questions would be to make a nonsense of much philosophical debate. Second, what concept we employ under the label 'person' is not independent of considerations, such as Locke's and Parfit's. For whatever consequences any of them derive may be taken as a motivation for revising our thinking and reasoning habits or our use of language. When we do change the way we use the expression 'person' as a result of philosophical reflection, are we changing the meaning of the expression? Are we adopting a new concept of a person, or are we merely revising a mistaken view of what that concept is and by what rules it is governed? Hard to say.

When we discover that certain a priori principles we employ are incoherent, are we discovering that some of those principles were after all erroneous? Or are we discovering that the concept we used is incoherent and that we should make a fresh start by adopting a new system of concepts? I am sure there are several different ways in which we can make sense of episodes like the philosophical debate about personhood. In the present context, I merely want to illustrate the mess we are in as philosophers.

Yet another dimension of confusion is added once we start considering whether our concepts correspond to any (natural, real, etc.) kinds or properties. Suppose our theory of the structure of human societies, or perhaps a theory of practical rationality, suggests that there are certain natural or social kinds. Then we might insist that our concept of a person must be construed in such a way that it can be taken to correspond to one of those kinds (perhaps we think that this is one of the conceptual rules governing the concept). In that case, we might regard certain a priori assumptions about the concept of a person or certain habits of language use (or concept employment) as mistaken.

A well-known example is that of our concept of jade. The concept JADE was well entrenched when, sometime in the nineteenth century, mineralogists discovered that there were two chemical (or mineralogical) kinds, all and only instances of either of which fell under the concept JADE: jadeite and nephrite. Did this show that our concept of jade, as previously employed, was somehow flawed? Not necessarily. Let's distinguish two cases: the concept JADE might have been governed by the conceptual rule that its extension is to correspond to a unique mineralogically uniform kind, or it might not. In the former case, the discovery of jadeite and nephrite would seem to have shown that we needed to abandon the concept as employed until then, because the discovery showed, precisely, that the original concept did not have application: nothing is both a mineralogically uniform kind and also answers to the criteria associated with the original concept. A revision would then have been called for: adopt a new concept, which either involves modified criteria or is not a concept of a mineralogically uniform kind. In the latter case, the discovery is just the empirical discovery that exactly two discreet mineralogical kinds constitute the extension of the concept JADE, and no revisions are called for.

The concept we were employing prior to the discovery seems to have been of the sort that does not aspire to reflect mineralogical kinds or at least to have been retrospectively reinterpreted in this way. For the concept JADE, including both JADEITE and NEPHRITE, continues in use. Under different historical conditions, we may have responded differently, for example by deciding that jadeite, but not nephrite, was the real jade, and that any conceptual rules that allowed nephrite to count as jade were mistaken. But as things are, we became *pluralists* (or more precisely: dualists) about jade: there are more than one (exactly two) different mineralogical kinds that count as jade. Our pluralism about jade is relative to mineralogical kinds. This is not pluralism about the concept JADE, for there continues to be just one concept, one that applies to exactly two mineralogical kinds, all and only the members of two different mineralogical kinds.

The concept of fish, as employed prior to modern biological classification, provides a contrasting example. This concept did not line up with a classification of kinds according to modern biology. As a result, we modified our conceptual framework. This can be characterized as the abandonment of the old concept FISH in favor of a new concept. Alternatively, it can be characterized as a case of coming to recognize that certain conceptual norms that had been assumed to govern the concept FISH were mistaken. The philosophical discussion of mental concepts such as BELIEF or PAIN seems to constitute yet another type of case. The presumption that there is no reduction of mental concepts to physiological or other material concepts has led eliminativists to deny the existence of mental states. Others draw the conclusion that in the absence of reduction, there is at least supervenience. Yet others deny even supervenience and accept dualism. Neither of these positions corresponds to the actual point of view regarding jade.

As I said above, the only way in which a question can arise as to whether, which, and how many properties or kinds a concept corresponds to is on the background of some alternative system of concepts that has some special significance. The answer to that question can range from empirical reduction (to one or more kinds) over supervenience to a claim of complete unrelatedness.

To summarize: we can examine concepts in a purely a priori manner by examining concepts identified in a stipulative manner. When we do this, we run the risk of examining concepts that no one ever employs or concepts that are not expressed by any expression. Thus, when examining concepts such as the concept of a person or that of truth, we may need, in order to avoid irrelevance, to pay attention to actual conceptual habits and language use. However, even clarity in principle about these issues does not always make things easier, for often it is very difficult to separate purely a priori considerations about concepts in the abstract from empirical issues concerning actual language use or actual concept employment. Moreover, sometimes we ask questions about how a given concept interacts empirically or nonanalytically with certain other concepts. We might assume that it must denote a (natural, real, etc.) property or kind, or perhaps several natural properties or kinds. In this case, we are basically expressing certain, possibly empirical, hypotheses or discoveries about how the concept we have identified interacts with certain other concepts we have in our repertoire and to which we attach special significance.

2. More than one concept of truth

In the case of truth, the conceptual mess we confront is considerable. The philosophical debate about truth is so old and so extensive that it would probably be impossible to separate pretheoretical from philosophically informed intuitions or judgments. We can start by postulating analytic principles concerning truth and then explore what follows from them. This is what some philosophers do. But of course if one philosopher postulates, say, a disquotational or equivalence schema as the basic conceptual rule concerning the concept of truth, and another philosopher starts from a different set of principles—say the idea that truth is what enquiry aims at or that truth is correspondence with objective reality—then who is to decide which of the two, if any, has started from the correct set of principles? There can only be genuine philosophical debate about truth where there is some common ground concerning the concept of truth.

I believe that one good way to avoid irrelevance or speaking at cross-purposes and to make sure that we know what we are talking about is to start by identifying the object of enquiry as the concept expressed by the predicate 'is true,' a concept that plays a certain role in actual reasoning.[3] Restricting ourselves to the English language would seem to be exaggerated, and I suspect that our findings concerning 'is true' and the concept thereby expressed will generalize to translations of the English predicate into other languages. However, we should in principle remain alert to the possibility that other languages may lack a predicate that works exactly like 'is true' in English.

We should carefully distinguish, first of all, the predicate 'is true' as used in ordinary discourse and the predicate 'is true' as used in semantic theorizing. In semantics, 'is true' usually figures as a predicate that applies to sentences, more specifically to ordered pairs of sentences and contexts or to ordered pairs of sentences, contexts, and circumstances of evaluation—often the latter are conceived of simply as possible worlds (see, for instance, Lewis 1970, Kaplan 1977). Not so in ordinary discourse, where 'is true' seems to be a one-place predicate that applies to what people say or think, not to sentences. Even those who, like Davidson (e.g., 1967, 1990), believe that semantic theorizing relies on our pretheoretical understanding of a primitive truth notion will have to admit that no one has ever pretheoretically thought of applying 'is true' to, for example, sentence-context pairs or to sentences as uttered by so-and-so at such-and-such a time. At the very least, the ordinary concept of truth undergoes some modification before it can figure in semantic theories in the way it does. There may well be some bridge principle that analytically links the semantic truth concept with our ordinary concept, and maybe therefore our understanding of the semantic truth concept does rely, as Davidson and others claim, on our understanding of ordinary truth. But it seems to me that we cannot avoid distinguishing the concept of truth employed in semantics from any ordinary concept, expressed in ordinary discourse by the predicate 'is true.'[4]

---

[3] Prompted by editorial comment, let me stress that I do not mean to denigrate other types of enquiry, such as the examination of broadly truth-related concepts expressed or employed elsewhere. All I am saying is that *one* way of avoiding the irrelevance of addressing concepts that no one uses and of speaking at cross-purposes is explicitly to address one of the several legitimate questions one might raise in the area, namely: what kind of concept (or concepts) is expressed by a certain range of uses of the English 'is true'.

[4] I have argued, in Kölbel (2001), that Davidson's claim that semantics relies on an understanding of the notion of truth is unfounded. See also Ludwig (2002) and Badici & Ludwig (2007). In Kölbel (2008a), I have also examined, in more detail than can be provided here, how the semantic truth predicate and the ordinary truth predicate are related.

Let us focus now on the concept expressed by the predicate 'is true' in ordinary nontheoretical discourse. Let us focus only on those uses where 'true' is applied to what people say or think, that is, the contents of thought and speech ('true' as in 'true friend' or 'true wheel' seem to me to express different concepts that we are not currently interested in). I have argued elsewhere that empirical and quasi-empirical considerations support the view that in fact the ordinary truth predicate expresses at least two different concepts and is therefore ambiguous (Kölbel 2008b). I shall here provide a brief summary of the view and its motivation.

We find two tendencies in ordinary usage of the truth predicate. On the one hand, we are quite happy to apply the truth predicate in any topic area. Whatever someone says, supposes, believes, or suspects, it is the sort of thing that we are liable to predicate 'true' of. Suppose someone uses an assertoric sentence, *any* assertoric sentence, to say something. We will always be prepared to say things like: 'That's true', 'That's not true', or 'I don't know whether that's true'. It seems also correct to say that whenever someone has said that p and someone else replies in one of the three ways just mentioned, then it is very hard to see any difference over and above style between these three replies and the following truth-free replies: 'p', 'not-p', and 'I don't know whether p'.[5] The two forms seem to have exactly the same consequences, commit the utterer to exactly the same things, and so on.

On the other hand, it is quite common for people to be more selective in their choice of candidates for truth-ascription. Thus, they may refuse to apply 'true' in certain topic areas, notably in the evaluative realm. They may well say things like: 'Statements about matters of taste can't be true or false.' People quite commonly and pretheoretically associate a connotation of objectivity with the truth-predicate, and insofar as they believe that in a certain area our beliefs do not admit of objective correctness, they would deny that claims, beliefs, judgments, and the like in this area are evaluable in terms of truth.[6]

The two different tendencies are, I believe, accessible to quasi-empirical evidence: competent users will, on the whole, agree that this usage is within the range of competent use. But there are also properly empirical data to back it up. On a one-page questionnaire, bona fide competent users repeatedly called the claim that Ali G is funny true (or false), but also denied that judgments

---

[5] One needs to be careful in the exact articulation of this principle: if someone says that she is hungry, and someone else answers 'That's true', the answer is obviously not equivalent to the answer that would have resulted from uttering 'I am hungry'.

[6] One may suspect that the second tendency is contaminated by the influence of philosophical theorizing. For example, Ayer and the logical positivists might be perceived to have brought about this tendency. However, I do not believe that it is useful to try to separate philosophical from nonphilosophical uses here. The first tendency could with equal right be suspected of being the result of philosophical influence, for wasn't it Aristotle who claimed that to say of what is that it is, and of what is not that it is not, is true? That seems to be a principle which applies across the board.

on what is funny can be true or false.[7] There may be disagreement as to the exact status of this usage—for example, to what extent it reflects literal meaning. However, even if we came to be convinced that one of the two tendencies reflected a nonliteral use of language to convey something pragmatically, there would still be two different concepts employed here.

The conclusion I draw from these observations is that 'is true' as employed in ordinary nonphilosophical contexts is ambiguous, or at the very least is used to express two different concepts.[8] Let us call the concept with the wide range of application 'TRUTHD' or 'DEFLATIONARY TRUTH', because it can easily be interpreted as a deflationary truth concept. And let us call the other concept, associated with the more restricted range of application, 'TRUTHS' or 'SUBSTANTIAL TRUTH'. The concept TRUTHD can easily be interpreted as a concept whose primary conceptual rule is that for any thought or speech content, in other words, proposition, p, the proposition that p is true is equivalent to the proposition that p.[9] Such a concept is a useful concept to have, for it allows us, for example, to think propositions such as the proposition that the first claim of section 3 is true, even when we do not know what that claim is. Similarly, it is useful to have a predicate that expresses that concept. In fact, if we didn't already have a concept like this and a predicate that expresses it, it would be high time to introduce and start using them.

TRUTHS, the concept in play when we are reluctant to apply 'true' across the full range of propositions, seems to be governed at least by some additional conceptual rules. It must be governed by an extra constraint of objectivity. Minimally, this might be the principle that whenever it is correct for anyone to apply TRUTHS to some proposition, then it is a mistake for everyone to deny the concept of that proposition. This would explain why some people are reluctant to apply TRUTHS to some evaluative propositions.[10] Now, it seems that even TRUTHS is subject to the equivalence principle within its more restricted range of application. Competent users of TRUTHS will infer the proposition that p from the proposition that the proposition p is trueS. And in the range of application of TRUTHS, competent users will infer the proposition that the proposition p is trueS from the proposition p.

This opens up the path for regarding the concept TRUTHS as subsumed under the concept TRUTHD, or in other words, that TRUTHS is a special case of

---

[7] The set-up is described in somewhat more detail in Kölbel (2008b).

[8] As I explain below, I believe this ambiguity not to be of the accidental kind exhibited, for example, by 'bank', 'bill', or 'premises', but rather I believe the distinct concepts expressed to be systematically related.

[9] This conceptual rule will generate contradictions if we allow that speech or thought contents such as the content that this very thought content is not true. Discovery of this problem will lead us to restrict the range of applicability of the rule or even to abandon the concept and replace it by a new one.

[10] Compare Richard (1997).

TRUTHD. I have suggested moreover, that TRUTHS can be defined in terms of the concept TRUTHD and some notion of objectivity:

(D) For all propositions p, p is trueS iff p is objective and p is trueD.

The thesis that 'is true' expresses two different concepts, TRUTHD and TRUTHS, in combination with the reductive definition (D), raises the question of why we are not aware of this ambiguity in our use of 'is true'—why, for example, we often do not feel that understanding an utterance involving 'true' requires disambiguation or why the term just doesn't seem ambiguous the way, for example, 'coach' seems ambiguous. However, there are examples of similar ambiguities. For example, most competent users would not at first have the impression that the nouns 'dog' and 'duck' are ambiguous.[11] However, when confronted with the following examples, they may change their minds:

(1a) Dogs are not allowed in the playground.
(1b) Mina is a bitch, not a dog.
(2a) Ducks like old bread.
(2b) Donald is a drake, not a duck.

It is clear that the intended meaning and the favored interpretation of 'dog' in (1b) and of 'duck' in (2b) are MALE DOG and FEMALE DUCK respectively. However, in (1a) and (2a), the intended meaning and favored interpretation of the same words are, respectively, DOG OF ANY SEX and DUCK OF ANY SEX. To be sure, we may argue about whether this is genuine lexical ambiguity or whether the b-examples merely express the gender-specific concepts in a pragmatic way. But what is hard to dispute is that the words 'dog' and 'duck' are used to convey two distinct concepts in these examples. Distinct, but related: just as in my ambiguity thesis concerning 'true,' one of the concepts subsumes the other and one is definable in terms of the other in a way analogous to (D).

Thus, just as one does not notice the ambiguity of 'dog' and 'duck' until one considers examples like (1b) and (2b), one will not notice any ambiguity in 'is true' until one considers examples like (3):

(3) It's true that Ali G is funny, though, actually, it's not true, because judgments concerning matters of taste do not admit of truth or falsehood.[12]

---

[11] Compare Lewis (1989: 130).
[12] Or, to preserve the analogy with (1) and (2), consider:

(3a) It's true that Ali G is funny if and only if Ali G is funny.
(3b) Ali G is funny, but it's not true that Ali G is funny (because that's not a matter of truth or falsehood).

It looks like both could be felicitously uttered, even by the same person. In that case, the best interpretation of (3a) will interpret 'true' as expressing a different concept from the one it expresses on the best interpretation of (3b). Thanks to the editors for this suggestion.

Those who regard (3) as incoherent will at least concede that one and the same person may, without change of mind and without irrationality or insincerity, utter 'That's true.' concerning the claim that Ali G is funny and also utter, perhaps in another context, 'Claims regarding what is funny can't be true or false'. Once this is conceded, I believe, it is conceded that 'true' is in ordinary discourse used to express two different concepts. My hypothesis is that these two concepts are TRUTHD and TRUTHS.

The advantage of the ambiguity thesis is that it allows us to make sense not only of ordinary thought and language, but also of the philosophical debate. Most philosophical debate about truth before the advent of deflationism seems to have concerned TRUTHS. A full-fledged deflationist who claims that 'true' only ever expresses TRUTHD will have to regard these debates as in some sense fundamentally misguided. However, acknowledging that 'true' can be used to express these two distinct but related concepts allows one to make sense of the traditional debate while still honoring the insights of deflationism about the so-called 'logical' point of a truth predicate and truth concept (see for example Horwich 1990/1998 and Wright 1992).

Some have warned against the thesis that 'is true' expresses distinct concepts in different topic areas on the basis that this would make it difficult to understand validity as truth-preservation and to treat connectives like 'and' or 'or' as truth-functional (Tappolet 1997; 2000). I believe that these worries have been satisfactorily addressed by Pedersen 2006. However, the current ambiguity thesis avoids these problems before they even arise: TRUTHD applies across the full range of propositions, so validity and truth-functionality can simply be construed in terms of TRUTHD, at least insofar as they need to be defined in pretheoretical language. Formal treatments of truth-functionality and validity will presumably in any case be couched within a formal semantics, employing its own distinct semantic truth concept.

My observations concerning the use of the truth predicate (assuming they are correct) do not, of course, conclusively demonstrate my ambiguity thesis. Let me briefly mention two alternative strategies for dealing with the observations and comment on one of them. One alternative, already touched upon, is to regard one of the two tendencies as mistaken, that is, to condemn as misguided either the tendency to apply the truth predicate across the board or the tendency to restrict its range of application. I regard this approach as unsatisfactory because both tendencies are, in my view, well entrenched and also justified by the usefulness and fruitfulness of each of the two truth concepts TRUTHS and TRUTHD. Another alternative, one that I would like to comment upon briefly, is to adopt what has been called a 'meaning-inconsistency approach' as it has been pursued in addressing liar and sorites paradoxes by, for example, Eklund (2002; 2007), Patterson (2006) Scharp (2007a; 2007b), as well as Badici & Ludwig (2007). According to this approach, there can be meaning-constituting principles that are false. This approach is in principle also available in response to the inconsistencies I observed in the use of the truth predicate (which are entirely independent of the liar problematic). Accordingly, instead of being ambiguous, the truth predicate is governed by inconsistent meaning-constituting principles.

I have three reasons why I believe this approach is less well suited to the current problematic. The first is that I do think that statements like (3) bring out a distinct feeling of disambiguation that resembles cases like (1a)/(1b) and (2a)/(2b). There is no such resemblance in the case of the liar or sorites paradoxes.

Second, I regard the meaning-inconsistency approach as a kind of last-resort response, which may well be appropriate in the case of the liar and possibly even the sorites paradox. But since there is a fairly simple solution available in the form of a credible ambiguity thesis, underpinned by a reduction of the form of (D), there is no need to adopt a meaning-inconsistency approach.

Third, it is not clear that a meaning inconsistency approach would avoid the conclusion that we are employing two distinct concepts of truth. For the meaning-inconsistency theorist needs to explain how we manage to use the predicate unproblematically despite the inconsistency in its meaning. This explanation will involve the thesis that we do not accept or follow the meaning-constituting principles or inferences. If we want to take seriously the observation that both the across-the-range uses and the restricted uses are well entrenched and fruitful, then the explanation would amount to the claim that we follow the relevant meaning-constituting principles selectively. That is: sometimes we follow the principles that accord with TRUTHS and sometimes we follow the principles that accord with TRUTHD. There are two possible interpretations of this: the first is to say that on all these occasions we are employing an inconsistent concept (constituted by the inconsistent principles), but avoid getting into a tangle by applying different principles case by case. This interpretation seems to me to be of dubious coherence, for what would justify the claim that it is the same inconsistent concept we are employing in different way on these different occasions? The second interpretation is that even though the meaning of 'true' is inconsistently governed by conflicting principles, the thoughts we express by means of it always involve only one of the consistent concepts, namely, either TRUTHS or TRUTHD (see Scharp 2007a; 2007b, who seems to argue for this). But this again seems difficult to accept, for what would justify the thesis that 'true' has this uniform inconsistent meaning in all the contexts in question, rather than being consistently ambiguous?

3. More than one truth property?

In recent years, a new brand of deflationism or minimalism about truth has become popular: pluralism about truth. Recent discussion of the view seems to take its departure from Wright (1992). It combines the claim that the ordinary truth-predicate expresses just one concept of minimal truth with the claim that there are nevertheless several distinct truth *properties*. The idea is, roughly, that while TRUTH is a concept that has application across the whole range of propositions,[13] there are nevertheless different properties of propositions that explain why a proposition falls under the deflationary concept of truth. More specifically, it is often suggested that the variety of truth properties corresponds to a variety in 'discourses' or domains of propositions, in other words, a variety of topic areas in which the concept of truth may be applied.

Thus, according to Michael Lynch, while the concept of truth expresses a single functional property, this property can be realized (2004), or manifested (2009) in a variety of different properties, such as the property of corresponding to reality and the property of being a member of a coherent system. Lynch compares his view with the functionalist view that the functional property of being in pain can be differently realized in different kinds of organisms. According to Nikolaj Pedersen (2006), the concept of truth may not even express any single property, but only a plurality of different properties in different domains of propositions. Gila Sher (2004) also argues that the concept of truth denotes a variety of different properties, though she argues that all these truth properties are correspondence properties.

Pluralism curiously reverses the direction of progress familiar from most of Plato's early dialogues. In these dialogues, Socrates' interlocutors often begin with a characterization of a plurality of kinds of virtue, of piety, of justice, and so on, and Socrates then asks them to provide a uniform account: What do all these things have in common? Contemporary pluralists about truth, by contrast, deem themselves already to be in possession of such a uniform account and go on to look for a plurality. Thus, Meno—one of Socrates' interlocutors—at one point proposes a form of pluralism about virtue. He says:

> First, if you want the virtue of a man, it is easy to say that a man's virtue consists of being able to manage public affairs and in so doing to benefit his friends and harm his enemies and to be careful that no harm comes to himself; if you want the virtue of a woman, it is not difficult to describe: she must manage the home well, preserve its possessions, and be submissive to her husband, the virtue of a child, whether male or female, is different again, and so is that of an elderly man, if you want that, or if you want that of a free man or a slave. And there are very many other virtues, so that one is not at a loss to say what virtue is. (2005: 71e)

---

[13] Wright claims not only that all assertoric content is truth-apt, but that he is also a minimalist about assertoric content in the sense that certain syntactic criteria, such as being capable of figuring as the antecedent of a conditional, suffice for assertoricity (1992: 36).

This is, of course, the type of account Socrates will dismiss in his usual fashion. In principle, however, Meno is attempting to provide worthwhile information. Even if he already had a uniform account of virtue in general, it would still be an interesting project to try to specify for various different types of people what virtue consists of for each type. He might even try to derive this information from the uniform account of virtue. (The fact that we are likely to disagree with the details of Meno's pluralism just goes to show that there can be nontrivial things a pluralist can say about different forms of virtue for different types of people.) I will therefore assume that in principle there is similar scope for an interesting pluralism about truth properties, even when one is already in possession of a uniform account of the concept of truth.

The four pluralists just mentioned seem to agree that there is a single unified truth concept that has application across all the domains, which is governed by principles such as compliance with the equivalence schema and perhaps normative principles such as the principle that one ought to believe or assert only truths. I have no quarrel with that (see §2 above). In addition, and this is what makes them pluralists, they claim that there is not just one, but several truth properties. As I pointed out in §1, the question of whether a concept denotes one or more properties (when this is understood to be separate from the question of whether the truth concept is instantiated at all) only makes sense against a background of some way of counting properties. Thus, in order to get a determinate question as to how many truth properties there are, we need a system of concepts N, which has some epistemological, ontological, explanatory, or other kind of interest for us, so that we can take the question to be the question whether the concept of truth is coextensional with a single concept $n \in N$, or whether its extension is perhaps the union of the extensions of several (noncoextensional) concepts in N. The schematic pluralist thesis is: the extension of the concept TRUTH is the union of the (nonempty) extensions of several concepts $n_1, n_2, \ldots n_n \in N$, where N is an interesting class of concepts. The condition that N must be 'interesting' is necessary because otherwise the pluralist thesis would be trivial. Take any concepts c with several instances: then there will always be an *uninteresting* set of concepts that subdivide the extension of n. Thus, in order to construe an interesting pluralism, we should identify an epistemological, ontological-reductive, explanatory, or whatever project that the pluralist is pursuing.

These constraints leave a lot of room for potentially interesting forms of pluralism about truth, and I am not in a position to be able to offer a comprehensive survey of all such forms. However, I would like to explore the possibilities for a certain restricted subclass of potential forms of pluralism about truth, one that is, I believe, prominent in the minds of many theorists. This is the subclass of pluralisms that construe the concept TRUTH as a concept that applies to propositions and also construe propositions as structured propositions in the manner of, for example, Russell (1956). I shall argue that there is a certain tension between (a) the claim that there is an explanatorily more basic set of concepts N, such that the *truth* concept is nontrivially coextensional with the union of several of the concepts in N and (b) the claim that *truth* applies generally to structured propositions only. The lesson will be that presumably the pluralist about the truth of propositions will have to postulate a variety of propositions that corresponds to the variety of truth properties she postulates.

Let us remind ourselves that the pluralist holds that there is a single truth concept that is expressed by the truth predicate. This concept is such that it conforms to a series of platitudes, such as the platitude that the proposition that p is true just if p and the platitude that believing or asserting a proposition is correct only if the proposition is true. Moreover, the pluralist is a minimalist about propositions: any declarative sentence expresses a proposition, that is, there is no discourse the declarative sentences of which fail to express propositions (as held by classical expressivists). There are, the pluralist claims, several distinct properties (from an explanatorily interesting class) in virtue of which this concept of truth can apply to a given proposition, and these distinct properties correspond to different discourses, in other words to different topic areas, such as mathematical discourse, discourse about medium-sized objects, moral discourse, and so on.

Suppose now that such a pluralist also holds that the truth concept applies to propositions, and that she construes propositions as structured propositions. Structured propositions, let us say, are complex entities that are constituted by particulars and universals, where universals include properties and relations of varying adicity, both first-order and higher-order. The construction of propositions from these constituents will be governed by certain rules, such as, for example: an n-ary first-order universal U, applied to a sequence $<o_1, \ldots, o_n>$ of n particulars makes a proposition; an n-ary first-order universal U, applied to a sequence $<o_1, \ldots o_{n-m}>$ of n−m particulars makes an m-ary propositional function; an n-ary second-order universal U, applied to an n-ary propositional function makes a proposition; an n-ary propositional connective C applied to a sequence $<p_1, \ldots, p_n>$ of n propositions makes a proposition; and so on.[14]

Now, there is one reductive explanation for which such theories of propositions were originally designed: a reduction of the truth of complex propositions to that of atomic propositions, and/or the reduction of truth in general to the notion of instantiation (as when a sequence of particulars or propositional functions instantiates a universal). Thus, the explanatory account explains what it is for a complex proposition to be true in terms of the more basic

---

[14] This sketch of a theory of structured propositions is supposed to be representative for a whole range of different such theories. I do not think that the details matter for the argument to come.

concept of atomic truth and/or explains what it is to be true in general in terms of the more basic concept of instantiation.

Now, the pluralists I am considering are interested in an explanation of what it is to be true in terms of several distinct truth properties, each of them corresponding to a certain topic area, such as propositions about medium-size objects, propositions about moral matters, the propositions of mathematics, and so on. However, as far as I can see, the only kinds of contrast of this sort that this framework provides for are two: the property of atomic truth versus the property of complex truth, and a subanalysis of the latter property into logical and nonlogical truth. Thus, at first sight, the framework of structured propositions does not lend itself to a pluralism that corresponds to the differences between different 'discourses' (compare Sher 1999, 2004). The set of concepts N with respect to which we are asking the question, 'How many properties of truth are there?' offers us instantiation and atomic truth as explanatory basics. However, these basics do not provide the tools to make the distinctions that our pluralist wants to make and for which she seeks an explanatory account.

In order to postulate further differences in the properties that realize truth in different discourses, the pluralist would need, presumably, to say that there are different kinds of atomic truth or different kinds of instantiation. This, however, is in tension with the idea of the framework of structured propositions. For the motivation for the framework lies precisely in its capability of offering a comprehensive reductive account of truth, that is, in the presumption that the basic notion (atomic truth and/or instantiation) is all we need to explain truth. Thus, a pluralist of the sort we are considering ought to develop a new or modified framework of propositions or other suitable truth bearers.[15]

References

Badici, E. & K. Ludwig. (2007). The concept of truth and the semantics of the truth predicate. *Inquiry* 50: 622–638.

Davidson, D. (1967). Truth and meaning. *Synthese* 17: 304–323. Reprinted in Davidson (1984: 17–36).

Davidson, D. (1984). *Inquiries into Truth and Interpretation*. Oxford: Oxford University Press.

Davidson, D. (1990). The structure and content of truth. *Journal of Philosophy* 87: 279–328.

---

[15] This chapter has been developed out of a presentation at a workshop on truth at the University of Connecticut in May 2009. I am grateful to the audience for useful comments and to the organizers for putting together a memorable conference. I am especially indebted to the editors, Nikolaj Jang Lee Linding Pedersen and Cory Wright, for their feedback on a highly unsatisfactory draft. Work on this chapter benefited from support by MICINN, Spanish Government, I+D+i programme, grant FFI2009-13436 and also CONSOLIDER INGENIO Programme, grant CSD2009-0056, as well as the European FP7 programme, grant no. 238128.

Dretske, F. (1981). *Knowledge and the Flow of Information*. Cambridge, MA: MIT Press.
Dummett, M. (1993). *The Seas of Language*. Oxford: Oxford University Press.
Eklund, M. (2007). The liar paradox, expressibility, possible languages. In Jc Beall (ed.), *Revenge of the Liar: New Essays on Paradox* (53–77). Oxford: Oxford University Press.
Eklund, M. (2002). Inconsistent languages. *Philosophy and Phenomenological Research* 64: 251–275.
Fodor, J. (1975). *The Language of Thought*. Cambridge, MA: Harvard University Press.
Frege, G. (1892). Über Sinn und Bedeutung. *Zeitschrift für Philosophie und Philosophische Kritik* 100: 25–50.
Horwich, P. (1990/1998). *Truth*, Oxford: Oxford University Press.
Kaplan, D. (1977/1989). Demonstratives. In J. Almog, J. Perry, and H. Wettstein (eds.), *Themes from Kaplan* (481–563). Oxford: Clarendon Press.
Kirkham, R. (1992/2001). *Theories of Truth*. Cambridge, MA: MIT Press.
Kölbel, M. (2001). Two dogmas of Davidsonian semantics. *Journal of Philosophy* 98: 613–635.
Kölbel, M. (2008a). Truth in semantics. *Midwest Studies in Philosophy* 32: 242–257.
Kölbel, M. (2008b). 'True' as ambiguous. *Philosophy and Phenomenological Research* 77: 359–384.
Laurence, S. & Margolis, E. (1999). Concepts and cognitive science. In E. Margolis & S. Laurence (eds.), *Concepts: Core Readings* (3–81). Cambridge, MA: MIT Press.
Lewis, D. (1970). General semantics. *Synthese* 22: 18–67. Reprinted in Lewis (1983: 189–232).
Lewis, D. (1983). *Philosophical Papers, vol. 1*. Oxford: Oxford University Press.
Lewis, D. (1989). Dispositional theories of value. *Proceedings of the Aristotelian Society, Supplementary Volume* 63: 113–137.
Locke, John. (1689/1975). *An Essay Concerning Human Understanding*. P. Nidditch (ed.). Oxford: Clarendon Press.
Ludwig, K. (2002). What is the role of a truth theory in a meaning theory? In J. Campbell, M. O'Rourke, and D. Shier (eds.), *Meaning and Truth: Investigations in Philosophical Semantics* (142–163). New York: Seven Bridges Press.
Lynch, M. (2004). Truth and multiple realizability. *Australasian Journal of Philosophy* 82: 384–408.
Lynch, M. (2009). *Truth as One and Many*. Oxford: Oxford University Press.
Matthews, R. (1994). The measure of mind. *Mind* 103: 131–146.
Parfit, D. (1984). *Reasons and Persons*. Oxford: Oxford University Press.
Patterson, D. (2006). Tarski, the liar and inconsistent languages. *Monist* 89: 150–177.
Peacocke, C. (1992). *A Study of Concepts*. Cambridge, MA: MIT Press.
Peacocke, C. (2008). *Truly Understood*. Oxford: Oxford University Press.
Pedersen, N. J. L. (2006). What can the problem of mixed inferences teach us about alethic pluralism? *The Monist* 89: 103–117.
Pedersen, N. J. (2010). Stabilizing alethic pluralism. *Philosophical Quarterly* 60: 92–108.
Plato. (2005). *Protagoras and Meno*. London: Penguin.
Richard, M. (1997). Deflating truth. *Philosophical Issues* 8: 57–78.
Russell, B. (1956). The philosophy of logical atomism. In R. C. Marsh (ed.), *Logic and Knowledge* (177–281). London: Allen and Unwin.
Scharp, K. (2007a). Alethic vengeance. In J. C. Beall (ed.), *Revenge of the Liar: New Essays on Paradox* (272–319). Oxford: Oxford University Press.
Scharp, K. (2007b). Replacing truth. *Inquiry* 50: 606–621.

Sher, G. (1999). On the possibility of a substantive theory of truth. *Synthese* 117: 133–172.
Sher, G. (2004). In search of a substantive theory of truth. *Journal of Philosophy* 101: 5–36.
Tappolet, C. (1997). Mixed inferences: a problem for pluralism about truth predicates. *Analysis* 57: 209–210.
Tappolet, C. (2000). Truth pluralism and many-valued logics: a reply to Beall. *Philosophical Quarterly* 50: 382–385.
Wright, C. (1992). *Truth and Objectivity*. Cambridge, MA: Harvard University Press.
Zalta, E. (2001). Fregean senses, modes of presentation, and concepts. *Philosophical Perspectives* 15: 335–359.

{ 15 }

Deflationism Trumps Pluralism!
Julian Dodd

1. Introduction

Let us define a *substantial, monistic theory of truth* as a theory that, if correct, explains what it is for any proposition to be true. This it will do by uncovering what truth *consists in:* a property F, common to all and only the true propositions, that allows us to say that the true propositions are true because they have F (David 1994: 65–6). The 'because' here is, I think, the 'because' of conceptual explanation; so the property F, if its possession by all and only the true propositions is to explain what it is for a proposition to be true, must be conceptually more fundamental than the concept of truth itself.[1]

Attempts to uncover the explanatory property F are familiar from the literature: historically significant candidates are *corresponding to an entity in the world*, *belonging to a coherent set of propositions*, and *being a belief that all investigators would share, if they investigated long enough and well enough*. But we are also familiar with two sources of skepticism concerning the very project of prosecuting a search for F. The first such source—*deflationism* about truth—has been around for a while, and has been variously adopted by philosophers such as F. P. Ramsey (1927), Ludwig Wittgenstein (1953: §§134–7), W. V. O. Quine (1970), J. L. Mackie (1973), Dorothy Grover and colleagues (1975), Hartry Field (1986), and Paul Horwich (1998). Deflationists accept that truth is monistic, but deny that it is substantial since, in their view, truth is not susceptible of the kind of analysis so beloved of seekers of a substantial theory: there is no property F that allows us to say that the true propositions are true *because* they have F.

---

[1] As Benjamin Schnieder reminds us, '[t]he direction of conceptual explanations seems to be owed to factors of conceptual complexity and primitiveness; in general, statements involving complex or elaborated concepts are explained in recourse to more primitive concepts' (Schnieder, 2006: 33).

This deflationary conclusion is usually drawn in the following way. 'True' would not be needed in our language were it not a certain kind of expressive device (Quine 1970: 11; Horwich 1998: 2–5): a device that facilitates the endorsement of propositions that we cannot explicitly formulate, either because we do not know what they are or else because there are too many of them (Quine 1970: 10–2).[2] That is, we only have need of 'true' in order to make indirect endorsements, as in

(1) What Wittgenstein just said is true,

and compendious endorsements, as in

(2) Everything Wittgenstein said is true.

Were it not for these uses, we would not need a truth predicate in our language at all, since to say that ⟨p⟩ is true is just to say that p. But now the deflationary thought is this: given that we only have need of the truth predicate in order for it to act as an expressive device, we have no reason to expect truth to be anything more than that whose expression in a language gives that language such a device; and, evidently, this does not require there to be any property F that truth consists in. So, for example, Horwich argues (1998: 5) that explaining how 'true' comes to play its expressive role requires us only to acknowledge that the following equivalence schema holds (at least, if the replacements for 'p' are not paradox-inducing):

(E) ⟨p⟩ is true if and only if p.

While not all deflationists offer precisely this account of what grounds the expressive function of 'true', all agree that explaining this function does not require us to view truth as substantial (Williams 2002: 148). For this reason, deflationists take themselves to be entitled to deny that there is anything that truth consists in until and unless it is demonstrated that this deflationary perspective is deficient in some way.

The second such source of skepticism about the prospects for a substantial, monistic theory of truth is a more recent phenomenon: *alethic pluralism*. Unlike deflationists, alethic pluralists accept that truth is substantial: there is always *something* in which the truth of a proposition consists (Wright 1996: 865). What pluralists deny is that this *something* is invariant between discourses. In their view, truth is *many* in the following sense: while there is no (non-disjunctive) property F in which truth consists across all discourses, there may be distinct domain-specific properties—F_1, F_2, F_3, and so on—in which truth consists in discourses D_1, D_2, D_3, and so on. Thus, Crispin Wright, who offered the first sustained defence of alethic pluralism, adopts the following position: while our

---

[2] Quine says 'sentences' where I say 'propositions', but this difference matters little in the present context.

concept of truth 'admits of a uniform characterization wherever it is applied', this monistic concept is also susceptible to what he terms 'variable realization', since truth may consist in different things in different discourses (1996: 924).³ Truth, he goes on to suggest, consists in superassertibility in certain (evaluative) discourses (1992: 142; 1996: 923),⁴ but in some sort of 'fit with an external reality' (1992: 142) or 'robust correspondence' (1996: 923) in others. Along the same lines, Michael Lynch claims that while truth is a matter of correspondence for propositions concerning the antics of physical objects, the same cannot be said, for example, of ethical truths (2009: 34). According to Lynch, the truth of an ethical proposition consists, not in its corresponding to a fact, but in its having the property of concordance (2009: 175).⁵

Alethic pluralism admits of many formulations.⁶ However, I shall abstract from the different forms pluralism may take in order to focus squarely on the benchmark claim made by any pluralist: namely, that truth consists in different things in different spheres of discourse (Wright 2001: 761). For it is the main contention of this paper that this benchmark thesis, however subsequently elaborated, has not been successfully motivated. To be more specific, I claim that a deflationary version of alethic monism is the default position in the theory of truth—the theory that must be accepted unless it is defeated—and that no pluralist arguments offered up to now have been sufficient to defeat it.

With a view to making good this claim, in §2 I explain why deflationism is prima facie correct, and then introduce the version of it that I take to be optimal. In §3 I employ a general counter against those with pluralist sympathies: namely, that the existence of differences between the truths of one domain and the truths of another need not be regarded as marking a difference in the properties that constitute truth in the respective domains. Having done this, and having thereby taken much of the wind out of the pluralist's sails, I complete my anti-pluralist case by explaining why a deflationist will not be moved by the specific attempts of Wright (§4) and Lynch (§5) to motivate pluralism. To clarify my position, I do not want to claim that resisting pluralism *requires* us to adopt deflationism. My claim is that (a version of) deflationism is prima facie correct, and that we have, as yet, no reason to abandon this position for alethic pluralism.

---

³ The distinction between deflationism and alethic pluralism is nicely captured by Wright's remark that '[t]ruth cannot admit of variable realization if, as for the deflationist, there is nothing substantial in which it *ever* consists' (1996: 925).

⁴ ⟨p⟩ is superassertible if and only if ⟨p⟩ is warranted without defeat at some stage of enquiry, and would remain so at every successive stage of enquiry (Wright, 1992: 48).

⁵ ⟨p⟩ is concordant if and only if: (i) ⟨p⟩ *supercoheres* with some framework of propositions Σ (i.e., ⟨p⟩ coheres with Σ at some stage of enquiry and would continue to do so without defeat, through all successive and additional improvements to Σ [Lynch, 2009: 171–172]); and (ii) Σ is itself 'durably coherent with the *external* coherence-independent facts—with whatever kinds of judgment are true, in other words, by virtue of corresponding to an extra-human reality' (Lynch, 2009: 175).

⁶ For a discussion of the varieties of pluralism on offer, see Lynch (2009: ch. 3–4).

2. A version of deflationary monism

Since I agree with Horwich both that 'true' is a genuine predicate (Horwich 1998: 2) and that this predicate is ascribed to propositions (Horwich 1998: 16–7), I also agree with the fundamentals of his account of how the truth predicate comes to serve as the kind of expressive device outlined in §1. It is the fact that (E) holds (at least, when the replacements for 'p' are not paradoxical) that enables the truth predicate to serve as a device for canceling the effect of propositional ascent, since its ascription to ⟨p⟩ is just a way of indirectly asserting that p. Consequently, the truth predicate comes into its own in precisely those situations in which we want to talk about reality by talking about propositions: that is, situations, as in (1) or (2), in which we want to endorse a proposition without formulating it or in which we want to make compendious such endorsements. For example, if what Wittgenstein just said is ⟨The world is everything that is the case⟩, the correctness of (E) guarantees that asserting (1) is just an indirect way of asserting that the world is everything that is the case.

Of course, a deflationist and a substantial monist may agree with this account of how 'true' is able to accomplish its expressive function. What distinguishes them is that the deflationist holds that truth is *nothing more than* that property whose expression in a language gives that language a device for canceling propositional ascent, and hence that there is *no more* to a proposition's being true than is supplied by the relevant instance of (E). For the deflationist, nothing more about truth need be assumed. There is no need to posit a property F that truth consists in.

To my mind, it is the demystificatory quality of this deflationary attitude toward truth that entails that its optimal manifestation (i.e., the most convincing available deflationary theory) is the default position on the subject, and for the reason briefly introduced in §1.[7] Since the truth predicate would not be needed in our language were it not a certain kind of expressive device, and since we can explain how the truth predicate acts as such a device without there being anything that truth consists in, considerations of theoretical economy demand that we refrain from positing such a property. We should call off the search for the fugitive property F until we have been shown that our concept of truth demands that there be such a thing. Consequently, inasmuch as the alethic pluralist presumes that truth always consists in something (even if this something may vary from discourse to discourse), she must provide compelling reasons why the supporter of the optimal deflationary theory of truth should abandon her position in favor of pluralism.

But what is this best deflationary theory of truth? Famously, Horwich eschews any attempt to capture the deflationary insight by means of either

---

[7] Similar sentiments are expressed by Michael Williams (2002: 153).

an explicit formulation or a finite compositional theory (Horwich 1998: 25–31), offering instead a *minimalist theory*—(*MT*)—that consists of the infinity of the (non-paradoxical) instances of (*E*). As a consequence, the biconditionals comprising (*MT*) are claimed by Horwich to be *explanatorily fundamental* in two respects (2001: 149). First, our underived inclination to accept these biconditionals is the source of everything else we do with the truth predicate and, as such, is what our grasp of the concept of truth consists in. Second, the biconditionals comprising (*MT*) explain all of the facts about truth (Horwich 2001: 150): there is no fact about truth that cannot be explained by (*MT*) alone or by its conjunction with facts not involving the property of truth.

But it is at this point that I part company with Horwich, preferring to follow Wolfgang Künne in his *modest account* of truth (2003: 333–74): an account that captures the infinity of the (non-paradoxical) instances of (*E*) in the following semiformal universally quantified proposition:

(*TD*) $\forall x$ (x is true if and only if $\exists p$ (x = $\langle p \rangle \wedge p$)) (Künne 2003: 337).

(*TD*) exploits both standard nominal quantification (i.e., quantification into name-position) and sentential quantification (i.e., quantification into sentence-position, in which the bound variables range over *ways things can be*). And it is this feature that enables (*TD*) to make the finitely stateable claim that can be glossed as follows: any entity x is true just in case, for some way things may be said to be, x is the proposition that things are that way, and things *are* that way.

So what has (*TD*) to be said for it? Two things, at least. First, since any instance of (*E*) can be proved by appealing to (*TD*) and some logical inference rules (Künne 2003: 353), (*TD*) is more fundamental than (*MT*). While it is the holding of (*E*) that explains how 'true' can fulfill its expressive function, the truth of (*E*)'s instances is ultimately explicable by means of (*TD*). Second, since (*TD*) is itself a universally quantified proposition, it avoids the debilitating *generalization problem* that afflicts (*MT*). In short, the generalization problem is this: since (*MT*) consists in the infinity of (*E*)'s (non-paradoxical) instances, it does not give us the means to explain our acceptance, and hence use, of any of the universal generalizations that we formulate using the truth predicate (Armour-Garb 2004: 494), including—irony of ironies—generalizations such as

(2) Everything Wittgenstein said is true.

True enough, if someone is prepared to accept any proposition provided Wittgenstein asserted it, then her possession of the inclination to accept each of (*E*)'s instances will thereby explain her potential acceptance of *each instance* of

(3) If Wittgenstein said $\langle p \rangle$, then $\langle p \rangle$ is true.

But since a universal generalization is not entailed by the set of its instances, what remains unexplained is an acceptance of (2) itself.[8] The neat thing about the modest conception is how it sidesteps this problem. It is because (*MT*) consists only of the *instances* of (*E*) that it is unable to explain our acceptance and use of generalizations such as (2). Since (*TD*) captures these instances in a universal generalization, it is not subject to the same explanatory lacuna.[9]

Of course, some have doubted whether the sentential quantification exploited in (*TD*) ultimately makes sense. Such quantification cannot be substitutional since it would render (*TD*), qua definition of truth, viciously circular (Horwich 1998: 25): on the usual way of understanding the substitutional reading of the quantifiers, '∀xFx' means that every substitution-instance of 'F . . . ' is true, while '∃xFx' means that at least one such substitution-instance is true. Hence, the deflationist, if tempted by the modest account, must regard (*TD*)'s sentential quantification as objectual. But now the charge commonly leveled at formulae such as (*TD*) is that they are malformed. Specifically, it is commonly claimed that bound objectual variables occupy places that are available exclusively to names and, as a result, must be understood to function like ordinary language pronouns (Quine 1970: 11–2). Clearly, if this is right, then the string 'x = ⟨p⟩ ∧ p' is ungrammatical: the second occurrence of 'p'—a place-holder for a name—can no more be a conjunct than can the pronoun 'it'.

But, as A. N. Prior (1963: ch. 33), Mackie (1973: 60–1), and Künne himself (2003: 360–5) have suggested, this dilemma is illusory. And the key to understanding why lies in seeing how the charge of malformedness rests on a groundless assimilation of sentential quantification to nominal quantification. Right enough, the sentential quantification in (*TD*) is fully objectual in the sense that it is quantification *over* ways things can be: its bound sentential variables have such ways as values. But what does *not* follow from this is that sentential variables take the place of names and, hence, must be taken to function as ordinary language pronouns do. For the quantification is into *sentence-position*, and sentences do not *refer* to ways things can be; they *express* them.

Consequently, rather than functioning like ordinary-language pronouns, the bound sentential variables in (*TD*) should, in fact, be given a *prosentential* reading (Künne 2003: 336): a reading that is achieved quite happily by using ordinary-language expressions such as 'things are that way' and 'that is how

---

[8] Horwich (2001: 156–158) attempts to answer this objection. For criticism of Horwich's reply, see Armour-Garb (2004).

[9] It should also be noted how neatly the modest account avoids another objection leveled at minimalism by Anil Gupta: namely, that (*MT*) is unable to explain why it is that only propositions (and not, for example, Julius Caesar) can be true (Gupta, 1993: 363–364). The modest account faces no such problem since (*TD*)'s righthand side says that something can only be true if it is a proposition.

things are'. On such a reading, 'x = ⟨p⟩ ∧ p' turns out to be perfectly grammatical: the final occurrence of 'p' should not be glossed pronominally, but prosententially; and since the variable is in this way syntactically akin to a complete sentence, it is suitable for serving as a conjunct. Someone could, I suppose, continue to insist that variables always function pronominally and that we cannot understand sentential quantifiers and variables in the way suggested; but in the absence of an argument for this restriction, we are entitled to regard such a point-blank refusal to countenance a prosentential reading of sentential variables as mere neo-Quinean prejudice: a stand that, to paraphrase Mackie (1973: 61), treats the symbols as our (first-order) masters rather than as our instruments.

The sentential quantification in (*TD*) is, I thus contend, perfectly in order; and what this means is that (*TD*)'s avoidance of the travails of Horwich's minimalism is not chimerical. The moral is this: we should not allow the well-known difficulties afflicting Horwich's version of deflationism to undermine our confidence in the deflationary project. In (*TD*) we have something fit for purpose as our default theory of truth.

3. Motivating alethic pluralism: a general problem

As David Wiggins has noted (1987: 332), theoretical parsimony demands that we regard alethic monism—whether this be elaborated along deflationary lines or not—as the default position pending disproof. Given, additionally, that the deflationary attitude toward truth enjoys similar default status and that (*TD*) is the most plausible version of deflationism on offer, what the pluralist must do is come up with a convincing reason for abandoning (*TD*) in favor of pluralism. The problem, though, is that this seems to be something of a tall order.

To see why, consider the following remark of Quine's:

> There are philosophers who stoutly maintain that 'exists' said of numbers, classes, and the like and 'exists' said of material objects are two uses of the ambiguous term 'exists'. What mainly baffles me is the stoutness of the maintenance. What can they possibly count as evidence? Why not view 'true' as unambiguous but very general, and recognize the difference between true logical laws and true confessions as a difference merely between logical laws and confessions? And correspondingly for existence? (Quine 1960: 131)

We should not let ourselves become distracted by the fact that Quine's explicit target here is the philosopher wont to treat 'true' and 'exists' as ambiguous, since his point generalizes beyond this crude formulation of the pluralist's intuition. What Quine, in effect, is saying here is this: before we accept that there are different *kinds* of existence or truth, different *ways* in which things can exist or be true, or different ways in which existence or truth can be *constituted*, we need to be told why the relevant differences uncovered are not really differences concerning *the things that are true* and *the things that exist*, as opposed to differences in the kind of existence or kind of truth enjoyed.

As Quine suggests and as Mark Sainsbury elaborates (1996: 900), when it comes to existence, the obvious thing to do is to offer a 'very general' (one might say 'deflationary') account of its nature, applicable across the ontological board, and then explain differences between what is involved in the existence of physical objects and what is involved in the existence of numbers as differences between physical objects and numbers. As for existence, so for truth. Here, by analogy, the natural thing to say is that truth admits of a uniform, general, and deflationary explanation, via (*TD*), and that the sorts of differences between truths described by pluralists can be construed, not as differences in *the way* these propositions can be true, but as differences in the respective *subject matters* of these propositions (Sainsbury 1996: 900).

With this strategy in mind, let us now consider the four ways in which Wright thinks that truths from variant discourses may differ (1992). First, certain spheres of discourse might, while others might not, contain truths that outrun *superassertibility* (where, roughly, for a proposition to be superassertible is for it to be assertible and to remain so no matter how much more information comes in) (Wright 1992: 77).[10] Presumably, even many convinced ethical realists will deny that ethical truths may transcend our recognitional abilities in this sense (Wright 1992: 9).

Second, and in an echo of the Euthyphro contrast, two discourses might differ with respect to the *direction of explanation* obtaining between a proposition's being true and its being superassertible (1992: 108–39): that is, it might be the case that in one discourse a proposition's being true provides the explanatory ground of its being superassertible, while in another discourse the converse obtains (Wright 1996: 86).

Third, it might be the case that truths from certain discourses do, while truths from other discourses do not, exhibit *cognitive command* (Wright 1992: 92–3): for example, while it is plausible to think it a priori that a difference of opinion over the truth of ⟨Heat is molecular motion⟩ can only be explained in terms of some kind of cognitive shortcoming on behalf of one of the disputants, even someone who takes evaluative propositions to be capable of truth might deny that they share this feature.

Fourth, while truths in certain domains have a *wide cosmological role*, there are other domains in which this seems not to be the case: for example, it might be thought that the truth of ⟨Heat is molecular motion⟩, but not the truth of an evaluative proposition, can feature in explanations of other facts besides speakers having certain attitudes toward such truths, and can feature

---

[10] For a more precise definition of superassertiblity, see n. 4 above.

in explanations in other ways than merely as the *objects* of such attitudes (Wright 1992: 196–9).

However, once we are armed with a Quinean 'very general', deflationary truth predicate, we can detach Wright's insights from his pluralism. First, the fact that the truths of discourse D_1 outrun superassertibility, but those from another discourse D_2 do not, does not entail that truth is constituted by different properties in D_1 and D_2. For the source of the relevant difference here is surely ultimately located in the two discourses' divergent *subject matters*: due to a difference in the kinds of facts they respectively state, in D_1 it can be the case that p even if it is not superassertible that p, whereas in D_2 this is not possible. This is not a difference in how truth is constituted between D_1 and D_2; it is a difference in the nature of the respective things the propositions of the two discourses are *about*. In the same vein, the fact that the propositions of D_1, but not those of D_2, are superassertible because they are true is perfectly compatible with deflationist monism, since the fact in question can be put thus: in D_1, but not D_2, it is *that p* that makes ⟨p⟩ superassertible, and not vice versa. Again, the relevant difference in the truths of D_1 and D_2 is ultimately a difference concerning the things in the world they respectively concern, not in how they are true. That we tend to formulate the issue in terms of the notion of truth is quite compatible with a deflationary understanding of the truth predicate, since such a formulation merely sees us exploiting the truth predicate's familiar expressive role. Finally, as is evidenced by Wright's own discussion of cognitive command and wide cosmological role, these features need not be formulated using the concept of truth at all (1992: 92–3; 196–9). Whether a discourse exhibits cognitive command and wide cosmological role is a matter, respectively, of *how disagreement is explained* and *how much is explained* by the facts the discourse expresses. Keeping (TD) in place, the fact that these questions might admit of different answers with respect to D_1 and D_2 is easily acknowledged. For the said differences will concern, respectively, whether faultless disagreement is possible and whether the discourse involves the explanation of mind-independent phenomena; and, once again, such differences will naturally be taken to have their source, not in differences in how truth is constituted across D_1 and D_2, but in differences in the two discourses' respective subject matters.

Oddly, Wright's response to the making of points such as these has tended to be concessive. Choosing to focus on rebutting the charge that his own version of pluralism treats 'true' as ambiguous, he has tended to deny that he has any quarrel with those critics who dispute the need to take up a pluralist position (Wright 1996: 925). One thing this reveals is the nature of Wright's priorities: he is more concerned to argue that he has uncovered the genuine cruces of realism/antirealism disputes than he is to make the case that these cruces require us to endorse alethic pluralism. But for our purposes, an important lesson has been learned. Someone seeking to make the case for alethic pluralism cannot proceed simply by pointing to the fact that the truths of one discourse possess different features than the truths of another. For, given that we can locate such differences in the respective subject matters of the divergent truths and given that we must distinguish differences in subject matter in any case (Jackson 1994: 169), theoretical economy demands that we acknowledge such differences without adopting pluralism.[11]

Consequently, if the pluralist is to stand any chance of converting the deflationist, she must come up with further arguments for her position. It is to the two most prominent such arguments that I now turn.

4. Wright on pluralism and realism/antirealism disputes

It was Wright (1992) who offered the first serious defence of alethic pluralism in analytical philosophy, so it is fitting that we first of all turn to him for an attempt to persuade us of this thesis. And on this matter Wright is admirably clear. The major motivation for alethic pluralism is, he claims, that its adoption is best placed to explain the nature of realism/antirealism disputes in such a way that their substantial nature is preserved. As Wright sees it, '[a] pluralistic conception of truth is . . . philosophically attractive insofar as an account that allows us to think of truth as constituted differently in different areas of thought might contribute to a sharp explanation of the differential appeal of realist and antirealist intuitions about them' (1999: 225). The problem for Wright, however, is that a deflationist about truth is herself fully able to account for the substantial nature of realism/antirealism disputes, so there is no pressure on her to abandon (*TD*) on this score. Let us see why not.

To start with, consider the following, wholly natural claim that realism about a discourse D is true just in case:

(4) D's declarative sentences express propositions (i.e., are truth-apt).[12]

---

[11] But perhaps I have been unfair. Elsewhere, Wright suggests that it is acceptable to talk of *identity* as variably realizable (1994: 174), arguing that we should recognize 'that what *constitutes* identity is subject to considerable variation in tandem with the change in the kinds of objects concerned' (1994: 174). So maybe, by analogy, we should think of truth as similarly pluralistic. But the intended analogy is of no help here, since Wright gives us no reason to accept pluralism about identity. True enough, if a and b are identical material objects, then they are spatially and temporally continuous, whereas the equivalent thesis does not hold if a and b are identical numbers. But it does not follow from this that *identity is constituted differently* in the material and numerical realms, since we can make what is now a familiar riposte: i.e., the self-same anti-pluralist riposte as that made by the alethic monist. For the monist about identity, leaning on considerations of theoretical parsimony, will insist that the differences between material and numerical identicals consist, not in differences in the respective *ways* in which they are identical, but in the differences between material objects and numbers. Whether a and b are material objects *or* numbers, they are identical in the same way, by sharing the same properties. Which kinds of properties these are depends on the ontological nature of a and b.

[12] Here I presume that propositions are, by definition, truth-apt.

(5) Some of the propositions expressed by declarative sentences of D are (nonvacuously) true.

The realist about D thus holds, from (4) and (5) respectively, that both noncognitivism about D and an error theory of D's sentences are false. Wright's claim is that if D is one of the areas that has been subject to a lively realism/antirealism dispute (for example, ethics, aesthetics, mathematics, intentional psychology, or theoretical science), then a commitment to what he terms the 'minimalist perspective' (1992: 140) toward truth and truth aptness establishes (4) and (5) all too quickly, and for reasons that are independent of the issues that have been seen by realists and antirealists alike to be the touchstones of such debates. This being so, Wright concludes that we have no choice but to conclude that the traditional characterization of realism/antirealism disputes has failed to identify what is really at stake. The only option for us is to reconfigure disputes as to realism in such a way as to give the antirealist at least a fighting chance of winning; and Wright's suggestion is that the best available such reconfiguration has it that they concern the *kind* of truth that the propositions of a contested discourse enjoy (1992: 78). If the truth predicate can vary in the 'metaphysical payload' (Wright 1992: 23) it carries from discourse to discourse, then what matters for establishing realism about D may turn out to be, not *whether* (some) of its declaratives can be (nonvacuously) true, but *the way* in which they are true. Wright's celebrated research project is that of giving substance to this idea by setting out 'a number of realism-relevant ways in which what is involved in a statement's being true may differ depending on the region of discourse to which it belongs' (Wright 1996: 865).

Now, before we get on to the details of Wright's thinking here, we must note at once that his discussion admits of complications along two distinct axes. The first such complication is that Wright draws a distinction between deflationism and what he calls 'minimalism'. Minimalism, in Wright's sense (as distinct from Horwich's) is deflationism 'unencumbered by the classical deflationist's claim that truth is not a substantial property' (1992: 24); and this claim that truth is minimal, yet not deflationary, can be explained, in turn, as the conjunction of two theses. First, the deflationist is wrong to think that truth is just that property that, when introduced into a language, gives us a device for canceling the effect of propositional ascent. According to Wright, 'is true' expresses a norm of our assertoric practice that is distinct from that of warranted assertibility inasmuch as satisfaction of one need not entail satisfaction of the other (1992: 16–21). But second, the deflationist is, nonetheless, right in her intuition that truth is not intrinsically a substantial notion and that what makes a predicate a truth predicate is its satisfaction of a set of platitudes. While the deflationist focuses on platitudes such as (*E*) or (*TD*), Wright takes the set of platitudes forming the touchstone of truth also to include the following: to assert is to present as true; any truth-apt content has a significant negation that is truth-apt; to be true is to correspond to the facts; and a statement can justified without being true, and vice versa (1992: 34).

The second complication in Wright's adoption of alethic pluralism involves the introduction of a distinction that is apt to be glossed over by talk of 'accounts of truth'. For Wright's thesis is *not* that a deflationary (or indeed, minimalist) account of truth *simpliciter* renders the truth of (4) and (5) too easily demonstrable for their conjunction to be the crux of realism. It is that this latter result is the product of a more general deflationary *perspective* that combines a deflationary (or minimalist) account of truth with a deflationary account of truth apt*ness*, where the latter thesis is that whether a sentence expresses a proposition can simply be read off from surface features of its syntax and use. Indeed, Wright's own favored deflationary account of truth aptness is 'disciplined syntacticism' (Jackson et al. 1994: 293): the thesis that a sentence's being declarative and being subject to *discipline* (i.e., 'firmly acknowledged standards of proper and improper use' [Wright 1992: 29]) jointly suffice for its expressing a proposition. So, to be clear, although Wright thinks that the deflationist (or minimalist) about truth will also be attracted to disciplined syntacticism (1992: 36), the two views are, strictly speaking, distinct (1996: 864); and it is the *combination* of these deflationary views that Wright regards as making (4) and (5) too easily achievable for their conjunction to be definitive of realism.

Having made these clarificatory remarks, let us now examine how Wright's argument is supposed to work. Unconvinced as I am by his claim that the would-be deflationist about truth should retreat to Wright's own doctrine of minimalism,[13] I shall put the differences between this latter doctrine and deflationism to one side. My focus will be squarely on the thesis that the deflationist about truth and truth aptness has no room to deny that (4) and (5) hold of disciplined discourses such as our ethical, aesthetic, and mathematical talk.

It is, of course, true that a deflationist about *both* truth and truth aptness must hold that (4) obtains for any disciplined discourse D. But we should notice, at once, that it is the deflationary account of *truth aptness*, not deflationism about *truth*, that does all the work here: *however* we think of truth, an acceptance of Wright's disciplined syntacticism leaves no future for noncognitivist treatments of our ethical and aesthetic discourses, for example. But this just goes to show that a deflationist about truth is only prevented from adopting a noncognitivist stance to a disciplined discourse, if she has no choice but to accept disciplined syntacticism. And this, as Wright in effect admits (1996: 864), is not the case. For deflationism about truth is in itself *silent* about what makes for truth aptness. To see this, note that (*TD*), while it claims that only propositions can be true, says nothing about what is required of a sentence to express a proposition (i.e., be truth-apt). For all (*TD*) says, there could

---

[13] Wright's argument for this conclusion is, I am convinced, unsound. For my reply to it, see my (1999) and (2000: 149–155).

turn out to be no ethical propositions at all. The ethical noncognitivist, for example, could turn out to be right.

It follows that deflationism about truth (as distinct from a Wrightian deflationary perspective on truth *and* truth aptness) is compatible with the following, decidedly *non*-deflationary, conception of truth aptness: a declarative, disciplined sentence is only truth-apt (i.e., only expresses a proposition), if it can be used to give the content of a *belief* held by someone who sincerely utters it (Jackson 1994: 165). The reason why this account of truth aptness is non-deflationary is that whether sincere utterers of a class of declarative sentences are giving voice to beliefs may be, to borrow Wright's own phrase, a 'potentially covert' characteristic of a discourse (1992: 35). For what makes a given psychological state a genuine belief-state is that it plays the kind of functional role distinctive of beliefs: minimally, it must be a representational state that serves to fit the world, that combines with desires to guide us around the world, and that is susceptible to change in the wake of recalcitrant information (Jackson et al. 1994: 296). And whether the sincere utterers of a certain class of declarative sentences are in states occupying this functional role is not determined merely by whether this class of sentences is 'disciplined' in Wright's sense. Consequently, such an account of truth aptness, wholly compatible with (*TD*), in no sense guillotines the traditional debate between realists and noncognitivists in ethics. Noncognitivists will argue that our ethical convictions do not so much guide us around the world in conjunction with desires as provide the motivational push distinctive of desires. Realists will either deny that ethical judgments are intrinsically motivational or else insist that their motivational character does not compromise the thought that an agent sincerely uttering an ethical declarative counts as giving voice to an ethical belief.[14]

It is, of course, one thing to point out that there is conceptual space for a deflationist about truth to adopt a non-deflationary account of truth aptness, but quite another to argue that deflationists should adopt the latter position. However, such a non-deflationary account of truth aptness is in itself eminently sensible. Wright himself accepts that a platitude linking truth aptness and belief is the following: if someone sincerely utters a sentence, then she has a belief whose content can be characterized by means of the sentence used (Wright 1992: 14). All that our substantial account of truth aptness amounts to is a coupling of this platitude with a (necessarily) non-platitudinous account of what a belief is.

Naturally, Wright's reply to this line of thought is to insist that the above account of belief is an unwarranted hijacking of the notion. According to Wright, '*any* attitude is a belief which may be expressed by the sincere endorsement of a sentence which complies with the constraints of syntax and discipline imposed by [disciplined syntacticism]' (1994: 170). And, true enough,

---

[14] David Brink (1989), for example, takes the first option; John McDowell (1979) takes the second.

the folk unreflectively describe ethical convictions and aesthetic opinions as 'beliefs' (Wright 1994: 171). But two points beg to be made at this stage. First, the fact that ethical and aesthetic opinions tend to be described in this way no more shows that utterances of such sentences give voice to genuine beliefs than does the folk's tendency to describe computers as 'intelligent' show that computers can think (Jackson et al. 1994: 297). In both cases, our everyday talk is loose talk, which is not surprising given that a perspicuous grasp of the nature of our concepts is not required for much everyday discourse.

Second, our practice of ascribing beliefs actually embodies the possibility that someone may sincerely utter a declarative sentence without holding the corresponding belief. If the prime minister sincerely says to his Cabinet colleagues, 'I am merely first among equals', the said colleagues may nonetheless come to the conclusion that the prime minister does not really *believe* this if, for instance, he consistently overrules his fellow ministers and generally behaves in a dictatorial fashion.[15] The prime minister's colleagues may conclude that even though he is sincere in his utterance, he does not really believe what he is saying; and the reason for this would be, I take it, that he does not occupy a state with the kind of links to behavior definitive of the belief in question. But if this is right, and if someone can sincerely utter a disciplined declarative sentence and yet not have a belief whose content can be captured by the said sentence, then there is clearly room for truth aptness to be the potentially covert feature of a discourse that the noncognitivist trades on. And if this is correct, then noncognitivism concerning our ethical discourse remains a live, albeit controversial, option for the deflationist.

It is not true, then, that deflationism about truth settles the case against noncognitivism. What I want to point out now is this: even if the deflationist were to accept disciplined syntacticism, and thereby close off the possibility of adopting the noncognitivist form of antirealism about, say, our ethical discourse, she would not thereby be debarred from adopting an error theory concerning it. Wright seems to think otherwise, however. For while he argues that his own brand of minimalism faces a problem of *motivating* such an error theory (1992: 86–7), he seems to regard this particular antirealist paradigm as simply *ruled out* by a deflationist who accepts that the discourse in question is truth apt.[16] So consider, once more, the ethical domain. According to Wright (1992: 85–6), an error theorist will accept both that there exist standards of

---

[15] This is an example inspired by Jackson et al. (1994: 297).

[16] To be sure, Wright is less than explicit on this issue. Nevertheless, he distinguishes his brand of minimalism from deflationism by saying that the former, unlike the latter, takes truth to be a 'genuine property . . . which warranted assertions are therefore not guaranteed to possess': something that, in turn, he takes to show that his minimalism (*unlike* deflationism, presumably) does not 'immediately shut down all room for the sort of charge of massive mistake which is the error theorist's stock in trade' (1992: 35). This certainly suggests that Wright endorses the argument in the main body of the text for the thesis that deflationism *does* in this way shut down all room for adopting an error theory.

warrant for the assertion of this discourse's propositions *and* that many ethical propositions—propositions such as ⟨Torturing people for fun is wrong⟩, for instance—meet these standards. Consequently, if an error theorist is to defend the thesis that ⟨Torturing people for fun is wrong⟩ is false, she must be able to point to a 'shortfall between the standards of warrant that actually inform the discourse in question, and the notion of truth that actually applies therein' (Wright 2003: 128–9). In other words, in order for such an error theory to be an option, it must be possible for ethical propositions to be warrantedly assertible and yet fail to be true. But, so the Wrightian argument continues, precisely this distinction looks to be unavailable to the deflationist. For if 'true' is nothing but a device for making indirect or compendious assertions, then 'the only norms operating in assertoric practice are norms of warranted assertibility, and . . . the truth predicate can mark no independent norm' (1992: 18). And if this is right, then the deflationist must say that the propositions that meet the standards of warrant operative within the discourse *just are* true. The deflationist seems not to have the requisite room for maneuver in order to endorse an error theory of our ethical talk.

But such an argument rests on a false lemma; and the lemma in question is that an error theorist will accept that certain propositions of the contested discourse are, in fact, warrantedly assertible. Let us reconsider the ethical case for a moment. The error theorist about our ethical talk, as represented in print by J. L. Mackie (1977), holds that when we make ethical judgments, we thereby ascribe properties to things that they simply could not have: namely, *objectively prescriptive properties*: in other words, properties whose instantiation imposes demands upon us to act in certain ways (Mackie 1977: 38–40). But insofar as the error theorist takes the making of such judgments to embody this metaphysical superstition, she will insist that we in fact *lack warrant* for making them. Since, she will argue, we are not warranted in believing in the existence of objectively prescriptive properties, we cannot be warranted in making judgments that entail their existence (Jackson 1994: 167). The point generalizes. Error theorists about D will deny that any of D's (nonvacuously true) propositions are warrantedly assertible, and they will do so because they hold that such propositions carry the implication of metaphysically preposterous entities (Mackie 1977: 87): moral properties, aesthetic properties, numbers, or whatever.[17]

This being so, the apparently impossible task Wright sets for the would-be deflationist who wishes to adopt an error theory—namely, that of explaining how a proposition can be warrantedly assertible without being true—turns out to be bogus. Since an error theorist about D denies that any of D's (nonvacuously true) propositions are warrantedly assertible, there is nothing for her to explain here. The *explanandum* disappears. And what this means is that such

---

[17] In making this point I have been influenced by the work of Daly & Liggins (2010).

an error theory, whatever its independent merits, is by no means ruled out by deflationism.

The moral of the story is this. In §3, we saw that the details of Wright's own proposals for reconfiguring realism/antirealism debates can be detached from their pluralist setting. What we know now is that the deflationist should dispute the need for any such a reconfiguration in the first place, thereby undermining Wright's claimed motivation for pluralism at source. As long as we couple our deflationism with a non-deflationary account of truth aptness, noncognitivist strains of antirealism remain live options; while an error theory of a disciplined discourse D will always be open to a deflationist as long as such an error theory is understood to insist that D's implication of metaphysically preposterous entities prevents its disciplined declaratives from being warrantedly assertible. Pace Wright, there is no reason for us to abandon deflationism for alethic pluralism in the course of prosecuting a much-needed reconfiguration of realism/antirealism disputes. Deflationists can happily regard such disputes as being in fine working order as they stand.

5. Lynch on 'the scope problem'

Lynch's more recent attempt to persuade us toward alethic pluralism fares no better. As Lynch sees it, the basic problem to which pluralism is the solution is what he calls 'the scope problem' (2009: 4): namely, that it seems that for any candidate property F that truth supposedly consists in, there are classes of proposition that are capable of being true while lacking F (2009: 4).[18] The depth of this problem is revealed, Lynch supposes, when we consider the case of the most historically significant candidate for F: correspondence.[19] For it is correspondence, supposedly, that the truth of the propositions of the natural sciences, as well as the truth of propositions concerning how things stand with 'middle-sized dry goods' (Lynch 2009: 32), consists in; and so correspondence would seem to be the most plausible candidate property to be an alethic common denominator. But according to Lynch, at least three classes of truth—evaluative truths, arithmetical truths, and legal truths—are insusceptible of such an analysis.

The reason why Lynch takes this to be so is that he presumes a correspondence theory of truth to be inevitably situated against a naturalistic background. A correspondence theory, Lynch contends, does not merely take a proposition to be true just in case its components 'stand in certain representational relations to reality and that reality is a certain way' (2009: 23–4); it

---

[18] This problem has also been called 'the common denominator problem' (Sher, 1999: 133; Wright, 2005: 1).

[19] Hence Lynch's tendency to refer to the scope problem as 'the correspondence puzzle' (2009: 79).

also cashes out these subpropositional denotation relations in a naturalistic style: that is, either causally or teleologically. So Lynch has it that a correspondence theorist will claim that the propositional constituent ⟨a⟩ either denotes: (i) whatever object causes, under appropriate conditions, mental tokenings of ⟨a⟩; or (ii) whatever object it is the biological function of ⟨a⟩ to be mentally tokened in the presence of (2009: 25–6).

According to Lynch, once such a naturalistic picture of correspondence is in place, the idea that evaluative, legal, or arithmetical propositions can be correspondence-true is severely undermined. For the causal or teleological accounts of denotation to hold, it must be the case that the things denoted are found in the world and can prompt mental tokens of them (2009: 32–3); but when it comes to arithmetical truths, evaluative truths, and legal truths, this condition seems not to be met. Arithmetical truths, so Lynch claims (2009: 34), cannot be correspondence-true because their subject matter, numbers, are *abstracta*: items that lie outside the causal nexus. And the same goes for ethical truths: ⟨Torturing people for fun is wrong⟩, though true, cannot be true by virtue of corresponding with reality because the property denoted by 'is wrong' is not a natural property with which we can causally interact (2009: 34): it is neither in itself physical nor supervenient on the physical (2009: 1).[20] Finally, legal truths, he says, fail to be correspondence-true because legal facts are not denizens of the mind-independent natural world, but items ontologically dependent upon laws, and hence themselves mental constructions (2009: 35).

What this reasoning shows, if Lynch is right, is that there is no prospect of truth consisting in correspondence across the board: correspondence cannot be the fugitive property F sought by the philosopher who presumes truth to admit of a substantial, monistic analysis. But Lynch takes the putative failure of the correspondence theory to extend to the evaluative, arithmetical, and legal domains to be illustrative of a deeper point: for while propositions from these discourses can be true, they are 'radically different in subject and function' (2009: 2) from the kinds of truths for which a correspondence theory seems appropriate; and these differences are best explained as being differences in the *ways* in which these propositions are true. So, for example, since we understand that nothing would be legal or illegal if there existed no legal systems, we do not regard legal truths as having the mind-independence of the truths of physics; and this, Lynch believes, is ultimately a difference in the kind of truth for which the respective classes of propositions are assessable (2009: 34–5). The key motivation for alethic pluralism thus turns out to be this: adopting such a position does maximal justice to the fact that the various kinds of propositions

---

[20] Lynch appears not to appreciate the controversial nature of this claim: 'Cornell realists', such as David Brink (1989), Richard Boyd (1988), and Peter Railton (1986), all deny it. Having said this, I do not want to quarrel with Lynch over this point, for my claim is that *even if* Lynch is right to characterize moral properties in this contested way, this does not justify the adoption of alethic pluralism.

we express are both diverse and unified: diverse inasmuch as these kinds of propositions may differ in their subject and function; unified inasmuch as they are all open to being true (2009: 2).

Clearly, Lynch's scope problem—inasmuch as it presumes truth to be substantial—will be regarded by the deflationist as little more than a mildly diverting irrelevance. But before I get on to this and before I discuss Lynch's arguments against deflationism, it is important to note that even a dyed-in-the-wool correspondence theorist need not feel threatened by it. For a sophisticated correspondence theorist has two possible avenues of response to Lynch's claimed counterexamples. First, and entirely plausibly, she may drive a wedge between the correspondence theory and naturalism, thereby giving herself room to insist that the apparently recalcitrant propositions Lynch highlights really are correspondence-true.[21] For it is tempting to think that all that is essential to the correspondence conception is a commitment to the thesis that truths need truthmakers (Dodd 2000: ch. 1; Künne 2003: 149ff.). Nothing about the correspondence theory *per se* commits its supporter to either a naturalistic account of denotation or to the thought that only mind-independent, concrete items can be truthmakers. Indeed, Armstrong, who remarks that '[t]ruthmaker theory is a correspondence theory' (2002: 30), also says both that the relation between a truth and its truthmaker is *not* causal (1997: 115) and that states of affairs—his favored candidates for truthmakers—have, at the very least, a spatial location that is 'strange and ambiguous' (1991: 195). Given that this is so, there is no reason why we should think arithmetical, evaluative, or legal truths to be beyond the correspondence theory's scope, even if they commit us to the existence of entities of which a thoroughgoing naturalist would disapprove.

Second, the correspondence theorist, if impressed by noncognitivist or error-theoretic treatments of the supposedly problematic discourses, may simply deny what Lynch regards as a simple datum here: namely, that there are (nonvacuous) arithmetical, evaluative, and legal truths. Lynch has only come up with counterexamples to the correspondence theory, if it *really is* the case that these discourses offer up truths that are not correspondence-true; and it is open to a correspondence theorist to make use of familiar expressivist or error-theoretic arguments either to deny that the disciplined declaratives of the problematic discourses express propositions at all or else to deny that the propositions they express can be nonvacuously true. Either way, there is plenty of metaphysical space for the correspondence theorist to deny Lynch's claim that there are true propositions of a kind that cause trouble for the correspondence theory.

Lynch considers objections of these kinds, but what he has to say in reply cuts little ice. For one thing, while he is right in thinking that watering down

---

[21] This kind of response, although not put in quite this way, is made by Sher (2005: 323).

the correspondence theory into the claim that 'a proposition corresponds to reality just when things are as that proposition says they are' gives us a 'vacuous platitude' (2009: 35), that is not the proposal made by the correspondence theorist's first line of response. The claim that truths need truthmakers—things whose existence guarantees their truth—is not platitudinous.[22] And besides this, Lynch's claim that expressivist or error-theoretic accounts of disputed discourses are 'somewhat tired' (2009: 2) is little more than an unsupported assertion. Insofar as we can recover a philosophical thesis beyond the rhetoric here, it would seem to be this: the adoption of either of these antirealist paradigms could only be ad hoc, since making such a move 'is just to acknowledge that representational theories of truth fail to be plausible in some domains' (2009: 35). But this claim is false. Expressivists, as we have noted already, seek to make their case by, first of all, arguing for a robust account of what it is for a disciplined declarative sentence to express a proposition, and then pointing to a feature of the said discourse from which it is supposed to follow that its declaratives do not express propositions. Error theorists, meanwhile, construct arguments designed to show that the world does not offer up the kinds of entities required for the discourse to contain any non-vacuous truths. In the one case, the focus is on the nature of the speech-acts we perform; in the other case, the issue concerns whether entities of a certain kind really exist. Whether such arguments ultimately succeed will depend upon the specifics of the cases made, but the crucial point is that the only principles about truth required by these arguments are uncontroversial instances of (*E*); and what this means is that the said arguments may be endorsed by a correspondence theorist non-question-beggingly. There remains plenty of room for the correspondence theorist to wriggle out of the clutches of the scope problem.

But, of course, I am no correspondence theorist and so will draw the sting from the scope problem in a more direct way. As I explained in §2, rather than agreeing with Lynch that the monistic theory of truth occupying default status is the correspondence theory, I take this position to be occupied by (*TD*). And from this perspective, the scope problem is simply bogus. There is no more to a proposition's being true, in *any* discourse, than is supplied by (*TD*), and yet saying this is quite compatible with the existence of disciplined discourses susceptible either to expressivist or to error-theoretic, antirealist analyses. Consequently, the deflationist can acknowledge the substantial nature of antirealist challenges without being forced into construing such a challenge as requiring commitment to the pluralistic claim that the contested discourse's disciplined declaratives are true in a different way to those of discourses meriting a realist treatment. What this goes to show, once more, is that realism/antirealism disputes are not situated *within* the theory of truth: their cruces

---

[22] As is explained by, among others, Daly (2005), Dodd (2002), Hornsby (2005), Lewis (1992; 2001), Liggins (2008), and Rodriguez-Pereyra (2005).

are discrete issues in metaphysics, the philosophy of mind, and the philosophy of language. Once we become clear on the nature of truth, we realize that the issues that seem to interest Lynch the most are located elsewhere.

Although Lynch fails to notice the compatibility of deflationism with the familiar antirealist paradigms,[23] he nonetheless appreciates that the deflationist will resist the premise upon which the scope problem is founded: namely, that there is a property in which truth consists in the sense introduced in §1, even if it turns out that this property may vary from discourse to discourse. This being so, it is incumbent upon Lynch to close this deflationary escape route, if he is to succeed in motivating alethic pluralism. But now the problem is this: neither Lynch, nor any other pluralist, has added anything to the debate as to the cogency of deflationism that has not already been rebutted in the literature. Lynch himself gives two reasons for rejecting deflationism: first, since deflationists regard truth as having no genuinely explanatory role, it follows that they cannot give a truth conditional account of the nature of meaning and content (2009: 114); second, deflationists are unable to do justice to the normative nature of truth: the fact that we should believe ⟨p⟩ only if ⟨p⟩ is *true* (2009: 111–3).[24] But as we shall now see, both replies miss their mark.

On the first matter, it does, indeed, follow from deflationism that knowledge of a sentence's meaning cannot *consist in* knowledge of its truth conditions: for knowledge that

(6) 'Lions roar' is true if and only if lions roar

to be knowledge of the quoted sentence's meaning, we must know already what it is for something to be true; in which case, pace deflationism, understanding (6) cannot constitute our grasp of what it is for the quoted sentence to be true. But as Horwich makes clear (1998: 68–9), this just shows that we should deny that understanding a sentence *consists in* knowing its truth conditions. Just to be clear, this is not to deny that an interpretational, Tarski-style truth-theory can serve as a theory of meaning for a language (i.e., a theory of *what* we understand when we understand its sentences). After all, the reason why truth is what a theory of sense is a theory of is that the predicate 'is true' is a devise for canceling the effect of semantic ascent (McDowell 1976: 8): nothing more about truth need be assumed. What *is* ruled out is a certain conception of *how* we come to understand a language's sentences: a conception that pictures such grasp as the bringing to

---

[23] According to Lynch, if deflationism is correct, then '[t]ruth, or rather 'true' ... is an honorific that all propositions therefore compete for equally' (2009: 4). If this remark attributes to the deflationist the view that all discourses are on a par when it comes to whether they are truth apt and whether they express propositions that are true, this attribution is false.

[24] Lynch's version of this claim says 'if and only if', but this difference between us does not affect the discussion that follows.

bear of the appropriate interpretational truth-theory in such a way as to deduce the relevant theorem. But then so much the worse for this latter claim. Our use of language is the unreflective exercise of a collection of techniques and capacities; our understanding of language is a matter of unreflective perception (McDowell 1977: 118). It can be no objection to deflationism that it blocks the endorsement of a questionable conception of what it is to understand a language.

It is, though, the claim that the normative dimension of truth eludes deflationism that has been more influential within the circles in which alethic pluralists move.[25] But here, once more, the debate has moved on. Lynch, in effect, points to the correctness of

(NB) It is prima facie correct to believe something only if it is true,

and then asks, rhetorically, how a deflationist can explain this normative fact (2009: 111). But the response to this worry is familiar by now: (NB) does not express a normative fact about truth at all; 'true' just appears in (NB) in its familiar role of facilitating generalization on sentences in such a way as to avoid sentential quantification (Dodd 1999: 294–5). The normativity we are concerned with—a norm of *belief*, not truth—lies in the following schema in which 'true' does not appear:

(B) It is prima facie correct to believe that p only if p.

'True' only enters the scene in (NB) because we need to capture (B)'s content in a single, universally quantified proposition; and a convenient way of doing this is to produce, in (NB), a proposition with the following logical form:

(BL) $\forall x$ (it is prima facie correct to believe x only if x is true).

But the occurrence of 'true' in (BL) does not show that (B) is really a norm of truth, since 'true' only shows its face in (BL) in order to facilitate its familiar role of cutting a long story short: a role it plays by virtue of being a device for canceling the effect of semantic ascent. Indeed, were we more inclined to allow ourselves the use of sentential quantification in our ordinary discourse, 'true' would not put in an appearance at all. (NB) could instead be replaced by

(NB*) It is prima facie correct to believe that things are a certain way only if things are that way,

the logical form of which is represented as

(BL*) $\forall p$ (it is prima facie correct to believe that p only if p).

---

[25] That the truth predicate expresses a norm is the premise upon which Wright's claimed refutation of deflationism depends (1992: 16–21). Cory Wright has also dismissed deflationism on the grounds that it fails to account for truth's normative dimension (2005: 5).

It is only an accident of our linguistic practice—namely, that we tend not to use sentential quantification—that gives 'true' any role whatsoever in the kinds of normative claim to which Lynch draws our attention.

Lynch has three responses to this line of argument (2009: 112). First, he claims that the mere fact that (B) does not employ the truth predicate does not entail that it is not really *about* truth. In his view, since (B) is a good paraphrase of (NB), (B) must preserve (NB)'s ontological commitments, and this means that (B) is no less about truth than (NB). Second, he states that it is more plausible to regard both (NB) and (B) as telling us something about truth *and* belief because '[b]elief and truth are interrelated concepts': 'belief's standard of correctness is truth . . . and truth is the standard of correctness of belief' (2009: 112). Finally, Lynch claims that, since individual normative prescriptions are justified by general normative principles, our acceptance of the instances of (B) is only explicable by our being committed to (NB); and this he takes to demonstrate that (NB) is 'in the epistemic driver's seat' (2009: 112).

However, none of these replies succeeds. First of all, pointing out that (B) must share (NB)'s ontological commitments is a non sequitur. Let us grant Lynch's claim that (B) is *about* truth because (NB) is. The crucial issue is not whether (NB) and (B) involve the property of truth, but *how* the property of truth is involved. And on this score the deflationist's point is that the truth predicate only appears in (NB) to facilitate generalization on sentences: a role it plays merely by virtue of its being a device for canceling the effect of semantic ascent. So while 'true' enables us to *express* a norm, truth is not itself normative: (NB), though it involves truth, is not *about* truth in the sense of laying out a normative feature of it. Consequently, we may harmlessly grant that (B) is about truth too. But all this means is that the final occurrence of 'p' is equivalent to '⟨p⟩ is true'; and this displays, not that (B) is a norm of truth, but that the truth predicate is a device for canceling the effect of propositional ascent.

Having clarified this point, we can see that Lynch's second reply is question-begging. Belief and truth are, indeed, interrelated concepts, but only in the following, minimal sense: believing that ⟨p⟩ is true is just a way of believing that p. And what this shows is, not that truth is what we aim at in belief, but that truth is *too thin* a notion to constitute belief's standard of correctness. A deflationist precisely *denies* that (NB) 'tell[s] us something about truth' (Lynch 2009: 112): it merely displays that 'true' serves to cancel propositional ascent.

This is not to say, however, that the deflationist need deny that there is a general normative principle that justifies our acceptance of (B)'s instances. (NB) is, indeed, in the epistemic driver's seat. It is just that (NB)'s occupancy of this position does not entail that (NB) expresses a norm of truth. For, since 'true' only figures in (NB) for the purpose of enabling the norm to be *articulated*, it follows that it is not *truth* that is the goal of belief. The nature of the general norm in question is, in fact, clarified by (*NB**). Take any proposition you like: one should believe it only if the way it represents things is the way they are. This is the norm of belief that Lynch misidentifies as a norm of truth. He has conflated the norm with the means by which we express it. And what this means is that, ultimately, Lynch has given us no reason for abandoning a deflationary theory of truth—namely, (*TD*)—that neatly sidesteps his scope problem.

6. Conclusion

As we saw in §3, the pluralist cannot properly motivate her position simply by pointing to differences between truths across domains of discourse. Such differences can be explained away as differences, not in how truth is constituted in the various discourses, but in the divergent subject matters with which the respective discourses are concerned. This being so, pluralists must offer arguments for construing such differences in their terms; and what we have seen is that the arguments of Lynch and Wright do not succeed in this regard. Perhaps there will be other arguments that fare better. Let us wait and see. For the time being, though, we should just stick with our favored version of deflationism.[26]

References

Armour-Garb, B. (2004). Minimalism, the generalization problem, and the liar. *Synthese* 139: 491–512.
Armstrong, D. (1991). Classes are states of affairs. *Mind* 100: 189–200.
Armstrong, D. (2002). Truths and truthmakers. In R. Schantz (ed.), *What is Truth?* (27–37). Berlin: Walter de Gruyter.
Armstrong, D. (1997). *A World of States of Affairs*. Cambridge: Cambridge University Press.
Boyd, R. (1988). How to be a moral realist. In G. Sayre-McCord (ed.), *Essays in Moral Realism* (181–228). Ithaca: Cornell University Press.
Brink, D. (1989). *Moral Realism and the Foundations of Ethics*. Cambridge: Cambridge University Press.
Daly, C. (2005). So where's the explanation? In H. Beebee & J. Dodd (eds.), *Truthmakers: The Contemporary Debate* (85–103). Oxford: Oxford University Press.
Daly, C. & Liggins, D. (2010). In defence of error theory. *Philosophical Studies* 149: 209–230.
David, M. (1994). *Correspondence and Disquotation*. Oxford: Oxford University Press.
Dodd, J. (2000). *An Identity Theory of Truth*. Basingstoke: Palgrave.
Dodd, J. (1999). There is no norm of truth: a minimalist reply to Wright. *Analysis* 60: 291–299.

---

[26] Many thanks to Chris Daly, David Liggins, and Cory Wright, who each gave me very helpful comments on previous drafts.

Field, H. (1986). The deflationary conception of truth. In G. MacDonald & C. Wright (eds.), *Fact, Science and Morality* (55–117). Oxford: Blackwell.

Grover, D., Camp, J., & Belnap, N. (1975). The prosentential theory of truth. *Philosophical Studies* 27: 73–125.

Gupta, A. (1993). Minimalism. In J. Tomberlin (ed.), *Philosophical Perspectives* 7: 359–369.

Hornsby, J. (2005). Truth without truthmaking entities. In H. Beebee & J. Dodd (eds.), *Truthmakers: The Contemporary Debate* (33–47). Oxford: Oxford University Press.

Horwich, P. (2001). A defense of minimalism. *Synthese* 126: 149–165.

Horwich, P. (1998). *Truth, 2nd ed.* Oxford: Clarendon Press.

Jackson, F. (1994). Realism, truth and truth aptness. *Philosophical Books* 35: 162–169.

Jackson, F., Oppy, G., & Smith, M. (1994). Minimalism and truth aptness. *Mind* 103: 287–302.

Künne, W. (2003). *Conceptions of Truth*. Oxford: Clarendon Press.

Lewis, D. (1992). Armstrong on combinatorial possibility. *Australasian Journal of Philosophy* 70: 211–224.

Lewis, D. (2001). Forget about the correspondence theory of truth. *Analysis* 61: 275–280.

Liggins, D. (2008). Truthmakers and the groundedness of truth. *Proceedings of the Aristotelian Society* 108: 177–196.

Lynch, M. (2009). *Truth as One and Many*. Oxford: Oxford University Press.

Mackie, J.L. (1977). *Ethics: Inventing Right and Wrong*. Harmondsworth: Penguin.

Mackie, J.L. (1973). *Truth, Probability and Paradox*. Oxford: Clarendon Press.

McDowell, J. (1977). On the sense and reference of a proper name. Reprinted in A. W. Moore (ed.), *Meaning and Reference* (111–136). Oxford: Oxford University Press, 1993.

McDowell, J. (1976). Truth conditions, bivalence and verificationism. Reprinted in his *Meaning, Knowledge and Reality* (3–28). Cambridge, MA: Harvard University Press, 1998.

McDowell, J. (1979). Virtue and reason. *The Monist* 62: 331–350. Reprinted in his *Mind, Value and Reality* (50–73). Cambridge, MA: Harvard University Press, 1998.

Prior, A. (1963). *Objects of Thought*. Oxford: Clarendon Press.

Quine, W. (1970). *Philosophy of Logic*. Englewood Cliffs, NJ: Prentice-Hall.

Quine, W. (1960). *Word and Object*. Cambridge, MA: MIT Press.

Railton, P. (1986). Moral realism. *Philosophical Review* 95: 163–207.

Ramsey, F. P. (1927). Facts and propositions. *Proceedings of the Aristotelian Society (suppl.)* 7: 153–170.

Rodriguez-Pereyra, G. (2005). Why truthmakers. In H. Beebee & J. Dodd (eds.), *Truthmakers: The Contemporary Debate* (17–31). Oxford: Oxford University Press.

Sainsbury, M. (1996). Crispin Wright: *Truth and Objectivity*. *Philosophy and Phenomenological Research* 56: 899–904.

Schnieder, B. (2006). Truth-making without truth-makers. *Synthese* 152: 21–46.

Sher, G. (2005). Functional pluralism. *Philosophical Books* 46: 311–330.

Sher, G. (1999). On the possibility of a substantive theory of truth. *Synthese* 117: 133–172.

Wiggins, D. (1987). *Needs, Values, Truth*. Oxford: Blackwell.

Williams, M. (2002). On some critics of deflationism. In R. Schantz (ed.), *What is Truth?* (146–158). Berlin: Walter de Gruyter.

Wittgenstein, L. (1953). *Philosophical Investigations*. Oxford: Blackwell.

Wright, C. D. (2005). On the functionalization of pluralist approaches to truth. *Synthese* 145: 1–28.

Wright, C. (2003). Comrades against quietism. In C. Wright, *Saving the Differences: Essays on Themes from Truth and Objectivity* (125–150). Cambridge, MA: Harvard University Press.

Wright, C. (2001). Minimalism, deflationism, pragmatism, pluralism. In M. Lynch (ed.), *The Nature of Truth: Classic and Contemporary Perspectives* (751–787). Cambridge, MA: MIT Press.

Wright, C. (1996). Précis of *Truth and Objectivity* and response to commentators. *Philosophy and Phenomenological Research* 56: 863–868, 911–941.

Wright, C. (1994). Response to Jackson. *Philosophical Books* 35: 169–175.

Wright, C. (1992). *Truth and Objectivity*. Cambridge, MA: Harvard University Press.

Wright, C. (1999). Truth: a traditional debate reviewed. In S. Blackburn & K. Simmons (eds.), *Truth* (203–238). Oxford: Oxford University Press.

{ 16 }

Deflated Truth Pluralism
Jc Beall[*]

In this chapter I present what I call *deflated truth pluralism*. My aim is not to argue for a particular version of deflated truth pluralism, but rather only to illustrate the sort of view involved. This sort of truth pluralism is deflated in at least two senses: it essentially revolves around 'deflationary' truth; and it acknowledges only deflationistically kosher truth predicates in the plurality. After presenting the view and motivation for it, I close by briefly responding to a few objections and/or questions about deflated truth pluralism.

1. Background terminology

Let me fix terminology. Throughout, L is any language, where, for present purposes, a *language* may be thought of as any set of interpreted or meaningful sentences; and $\ulcorner \, \urcorner$ is an operation that takes sentences of L to names of those sentences.

1.1 CAPTURE AND RELEASE

A unary predicate H(x) is said to *capture for L* (or *play* capture for L) just if A entails H($\ulcorner A \urcorner$) for all sentences A in L.

---

[*] I am very grateful to Michael Lynch and Aaron Cotnoir for feedback and suggestions. Section 7 is largely due to their useful suggestions. I'm also grateful for an early workshop at St Andrews, where Crispin Wright, Graham Priest, and—again—Michael Lynch were very helpful. Probably, Patrick Greenough was also helpful, in which case he would deserve thanks too. Finally, Nikolaj Pedersen and Cory Wright deserve many thanks for their patience, and Nikolaj for providing very, very good feedback on early drafts.

Similarly, we say that a unary (sentential) operator H plays capture for L just if A entails HA for all sentences A in L. A familiar example from English is *it is possible that*. This is an operator in English that plays capture *for* English.

A unary predicate H(x) is said to *release for L* (or *play* release for L) just if H($\ulcorner A \urcorner$) entails A for all A in L. And similarly for a unary operator. A familiar example from English is *it is known that*.

1.2 CAPTURE-RELEASE PREDICATES

A unary predicate H(x) is said to be a *capture-release* predicate for L just if it plays captures and release for L. And similarly for a unary operator.

2. Truth predicates

On my terminology—and, I think, the terminology prominent in logical studies—a predicate H(x) is said to be a *truth predicate for L* just if it is a capture-release predicate for L. Tighter constraints on being 'the fundamental truth predicate' or 'the real truth predicate' or enjoying some such privileged status may be—and, in discussion of truth pluralism(s), often are—imposed. The capture-release condition is advanced as a simple necessary and sufficient condition for counting as a truth predicate.

3. Truth pluralisms

Now that the notion of *truth predicate for L* is in place, a variety of truth pluralisms jump out. My focus is on what I shall call *language-wide truth pluralism*—for short, *truth pluralism*. The distinction is as follows.

3.1 LANGUAGE-RELATIVE TRUTH PLURALISM

Here is one easy way to get truth pluralism: begin with a truth predicate T for L, and consider each restricted predicate $T_i(x)$ defined as follows for each (proper) fragment L_i of L:

$$T_i(x) := T(x) \wedge x \in L_i$$

Then we have a plurality of truth predicates, one for each given fragment of L. No such restricted predicate plays capture and release for L itself (i.e, none are truth predicates for L); however, each plays capture and release over its appropriate fragment L_i.

This sort of truth pluralism arises from changing the language (or, strictly, fragment) for which the truth predicate plays capture and release. In a slogan: truth pluralism via language (or fragment) pluralism.

Deflated Truth Pluralism

This sort of language-relative pluralism need not be philosophically uninteresting. Indeed, if one thinks of philosophically interesting proper fragments of English—for example, 'moral discourse', 'scientific discourse', or the like—one might find motivation for versions of language-relative truth pluralisms. But my interest is not in language-relative truth pluralism; my interest is in language-wide truth pluralism.

3.2 LANGUAGE-WIDE TRUTH PLURALISM: *TRUTH PLURALISM*

In contrast with language-relative truth pluralism (understood per above), language-wide truth pluralism requires a plurality of truth predicates for L itself—for one and the same language. This is what, for present purposes, I shall call *truth pluralism*.

One might think that truth pluralism, so understood, is at least hard to motivate. After all, suppose that T_1 and T_2 are both truth predicates for L, in which case both play capture and release for L, and so—assuming a transitive consequence relation—we have the equivalence of these predicates in at least the following bi-implication (or bi-entailment) form:

$$T_1(\ulcorner A \urcorner) \dashv\vdash T_2(\ulcorner A \urcorner)$$

That A is true-1 (so to speak) implies that it's true-2, and that A is true-2 implies that A is true-1. But, then, what work might one predicate do that can't be done by the other?

Rather than answer such questions in the abstract, I turn to a particular sort of truth pluralism for illustration: deflated truth pluralism.

4. Transparent truth

A unary operator H is said to be *transparent* (*in L*) just if HA and A are inter-substitutable in all (nonopaque) contexts, for any sentence A (of the given language). Such an operator is formally modeled via identity of semantic values: namely, HA and A have the same (i.e., identical) semantic value.

A truth *predicate*, versus operator, is especially important on the 'transparency' conception of truth (Beall, 2009; Field, 2008; Leeds, 1978; Quine, 1970) and similar 'merely logical' conceptions of truth (Horwich, 1998).[1] The idea

---

[1] I note, in passing, that with a truth predicate (or, at least, a 'transparent' one, discussed below), one can define an appropriate predicate H corresponding to any (sentential) operator H. Example: where T is the given truth predicate, define predicate H(x) via H and T thus: HT(x). Going in the other direction (e.g., beginning with only a truth *operator* and trying to define appropriate predicates) doesn't work. (If this is not clear, Tarski's theorem makes it clear. The theorem rules out any truth *predicate* in classical languages, but there are truth *operators*, as §5 briefly notes.)

here is a familiar 'deflationary' one. In short, our *fundamental truth predicate* is (only) a logical device that exists only for its logical, expressive work: it affords valuable generalizations (e.g., 'Everything in such-and-so infinite theory is true,' etc.) that, for practical reasons (viz., our finitude, so to speak), we could not otherwise express. (I assume familiarity with this 'deflationary' idea. See any of the works cited above for elaboration.)

A *see-through* or *transparent* predicate H is one such that H($\ulcorner$A$\urcorner$) and A are intersubstitutable in all nonopaque contexts: the result of substituting an occurrence of one for the other in any (nonopaque) context is logically equivalent to the original unsubstituted form. The transparency conception of truth maintains that our fundamental truth predicate is nothing more than such a device: a see-through truth predicate.

4.1 TRANSPARENT TRUTH AND DEFLATIONISM

A see-through truth predicate can be, and often is, used to voice many important claims about the world—normative, epistemic, moral, ontological, religious, political, whathaveyou—but it is only a logical device used in voicing such claims; it doesn't name a property that figures in *explanations* of such phenomena.

If for nothing more than fixing terminology (if only for the present chapter), let us say that a *deflationist* about truth—specifically, a transparent truth theorist—is one who holds that the see-through device is our *fundamental* truth predicate, and other truth predicates, if any there be, are logical derivatives: they're built from the fundamental truth predicate and other logical resources. (This rather strict criterion for deflationism might be too strict by some lights, but I use it only to illustrate 'deflated truth pluralism' in a simple from.)

A *deflated truth pluralist* is a deflationist who recognizes at least two (logically distinguishable) truth predicates.

4.2 TRANSPARENT TRUTH AND INFLATIONISM

Recognizing the existence of a see-through device is insufficient for a deflationary philosophy of truth. One might acknowledge a transparent truth predicate (a see-through device) but also other truth predicates that are not definable out of (only) the see-through device and other logical resources: *extralogical* truth predicates, ones that express extralogical properties—perhaps something along the lines of a *correspondence* property that essentially involves extralogical notions of *representation* or the like. One candidate for this sort of truth pluralism might be Vann McGee (1991; 2005), whose truth theory involves both a see-through truth predicate and something closer to 'correspondence' that does the work that truth-conditional semantics seems to require (e.g., at the very least, an *explanatory* notion of truth that illuminates meaning).

Deflated Truth Pluralism

My aim is not to evaluate theories of truth that involve 'inflated' notions of truth in addition to a logical, see-through notion. I note such theories only as sample options of *non-deflated truth pluralisms* in the running sense.

My main question, to which we now turn, concerns the motivation for a *deflated* truth pluralism.

5. From paradoxes to nonclassical logic

How do we get truth *pluralism* from the transparency conception of truth? What motivates it? While a variety of answers are available, each pointing to different features of (fragments of) discourse, I shall focus on a very simple—though important—one: paradoxes.

At least on the transparency conception, our language enjoys its own (transparent) truth predicate—a capture-release predicate in the language and for the language. What Tarski (1936) showed is that such a language cannot be a classical language; its logic is nonclassical.[2] The problem, in short, is paradox.

5.1 BASIC PARADOX

The liar paradox arises from a sentence L equivalent to its own negation ¬L. By way of concrete example, think about a name b that denotes the sentence ¬T(b), so that we have the true identity

$$b = \ulcorner \neg T(b) \urcorner$$

as a premise—and we assume standard *substitution* principles governing identity. In addition, we assume various classically valid principles or rules, including *excluded middle* and *explosion*, respectively, where amounts to absurdity:

(LEM) ⊢ A ∨ ¬A

(EFQ) A ∧ ¬A ⊢ ⊥

Additionally, we assume a *conjunction principle* (viz., *adjunction*), namely,

(CP) A and B jointly imply A ∧ B.

and the following *disjunction principle* (viz., *reasoning by cases*):

(DP) if each of A and B individually implies C, then A ∨ B implies C.

---

[2] Of course, classical languages enjoy a truth operator. For example, letting ⊤ be any logical truth (e.g., any classical tautology), the operator 𝕋, defined 𝕋A := A ∧ ⊤, is a truth operator (or, on a dual spelling, A ∨ ⊥, where ⊥ is unsatisfiable); it plays capture and release for any classical language. But such operators do not play the generalizing role that a see-through *predicate* affords.

With all of this in hand, we can think of the following form of the liar paradox. From (*LEM*), we have

$$T(b) \vee \neg T(b)$$

This gives us two cases:

1. Case one:
   (a) $T(b)$
   (b) Substitution yields: $T(\ulcorner \neg T(b) \urcorner)$
   (c) Release yields: $\neg T(b)$
   (d) (*CP*) yields: $T(b) \wedge \neg T(b)$

2. Case two:
   (a) $\neg T(b)$
   (b) Capture yields: $T(\ulcorner \neg T(b) \urcorner)$
   (c) Substitution yields: $T(b)$
   (d) (*CP*) yields: $T(b) \wedge \neg T(b)$

(*DP*), in turn, delivers $T(b) \wedge \neg T(b)$ from $T(b) \vee \neg T(b)$. But, now, (*EFQ*) delivers $\bot$ from $T(b) \wedge \neg T(b)$. Outright absurdity.

Enjoying a truth predicate in and for our language requires a nonclassical logic. While the nonclassical options are legion, a few different paths are prominent. In what follows, I simply gloss two familiar nonclassical logics that underwrite two standard responses to paradox. I avoid details, which may be found in cited works.[3]

5.2 PARACOMPLETE

A *paracomplete* theorist—so-called because she advocates a truth theory that is *beyond (negation-) completeness*—rejects (*LEM*). While many statements of the form $A \vee \neg A$ may be true, they're not *logically* true—not true just in virtue of logic. Indeed, it may be that many—most—instances of excluded middle are true; a paracomplete theorist rejects that they're *all* true. And liar-like phenomena are a good example of abnormal phenomena where the relevant instance of excluded middle 'fails.'

5.2.1 Sample framework: K3

A simple model of a basic paracomplete language goes as follows (Kleene, 1952).[4] We expand our set of semantic values, used in classical semantics,

---

[3] I should also emphasize that I am sliding over many subtleties throughout. For example, the nontransparent-truth theory of Gupta & Belnap (1993) is more or less classical (subject to caveats concerning so-called metarules such as our (*DP*)). Field (2008) provides a good discussion of the details of Gupta–Belnap truth theory. And for a more leisurely discussion of the following logical frameworks, see any of these works: Beall (2010); Beall & van Fraasen (2003); Priest (2008); Restall (2005).

[4] For a model of how exactly truth might work in this setting, see Kripke's well-known 'outline' (1975).

Deflated Truth Pluralism

from $\{1, 0\}$ to $\{1, .5, 0\}$, with the middle value thought of as the 'abnormal' cases.[5] In turn—and, for simplicity, focusing on the propositional level—we assign semantic values to all sentences via (total) valuations $v: L \to \{1, .5, 0\}$ that obey the following familiar (indeed, classical) clauses:

(*Negation*) $v(\neg A) = 1 - v(\neg A)$.

(*Conjunction*) $v(A \wedge B) = \min\{v(A), v(B)\}$.

(*Disjunction*) $v(A \vee B) = \max\{v(A), v(B)\}$.

We say that a valuation v *satisfies* A just if $v(A) = 1$. We say that v is a *counter-example to the argument* $\langle \{A_1, \ldots, A_n\}, B\rangle$, B just if v satisfies each of the A_i but fails to satisfy B. With all this in hand, the logic—that is, the K3 consequence relation—may be defined in the familiar way:

$A_1, \ldots, A_n \vdash B$ iff there's no counterexample to $\langle\{A_1, \ldots, A_n\}, B\rangle$.

That (*LEM*) fails in this framework is clear: a counterexample is found by setting $v(A) = .5$, in which case $v(\neg A) = .5$, and so $v(A \vee \neg A) = .5$, and so $A \vee \neg A$ unsatisfied; hence, $\nvdash A \vee \neg A$.

Without (*LEM*), one requires an extralogical argument for the initial liar premise $T(b) \vee \neg T(b)$. Paracomplete theorists maintain that no good argument along these lines is forthcoming. Paradox-driven absurdity is avoided, and the coherence of transparent truth preserved.

5.3 PARACONSISTENT

By contrast, a *paraconsistent* theorist—so called because she advocates a truth theory that is *beyond (negation-)consistency*—rejects (*EFQ*). Such theorists maintain that some statements of the form $A \wedge \neg A$ may be true, but they reject that all statements are true. A good example of the abnormal statements is the liar: it is a true falsehood—a truth with a true negation.

5.3.1 Sample framework: LP

A simple model of a paraconsistent language is as follows (Asenjo, 1966; Priest, 1979). In short, leave everything as per the K3 framework (above) except 'designate' the middle semantic value by defining satisfaction thus: a valuation v satisfies A just if $v(A) \in \{1, .5\}$.

That (*EFQ*) fails in this framework is clear: a counterexample is found by setting $v(A) = .5$, in which case $v(\neg A) = .5$, and so $v(A \wedge \neg A) = .5$, and set

---

[5] NB: I'm concentrating on the paradoxical cases because they're the simplest to see. Clearly, other phenomena might be thought of as 'abnormal,' from vague discourse to moral discourse to religious discourse to philosophical discourse to more.

$v(\bot) = 0$. This is a case in which $A \wedge \neg A$ is satisfied while $\bot$ is not satisfied, and so $A \wedge \neg A \nvDash \bot$. Unlike the paracomplete K3 framework, (*LEM*) stands firm: $\vdash A \vee \neg A$. (Proof: for an instance of $A \vee \neg A$ to be unsatisfied, both disjuncts would need to have value 0, but this is impossible given clauses for negation.)

The liar derivation, in this setting, goes up to—but stops short of—absurdity. We get the contradiction $T(b) \wedge \neg T(b)$, but this does no further damage, since (*EFQ*) is invalid. Hence, paradox-driven absurdity is avoided and the coherence of transparent truth preserved.

6. And truth pluralism?

What we have so far is that the transparency conception of truth motivates a capture-release predicate—that is, a truth predicate—in and for our language. But standard paradoxes have long taught that languages containing their own truth predicates are not classical languages: they're nonclassical, languages whose logics are nonclassical. While there are many (many) nonclassical options, two standard routes are paracomplete and paraconsistent. For concreteness, I have focused on the two most familiar such frameworks: K3 and LP.

But what does any of this have to do with truth pluralism? We've gone nonclassical to keep our truth predicate from incoherence. But how does this motivate truth pluralism—and, in particular, deflated truth pluralism?

A full answer requires details of particular theories, and this chapter is not the venue for that. A general idea, however, can be sketched. The motivation arises from abnormal (e.g., paradoxical) discourse; the resources for pluralism are logical.

6.1 TALK ABOUT ABNORMAL

Consider the paracomplete theorist. There are some sentences that are 'gappy' in the sense that their instance of (*LEM*) is 'not true' (in some sense), that is, some sentence A is such that neither A nor ¬A is true. But how does the paracomplete theorist truly say *that*? The obvious thought is that her claim amounts to this:

$$\neg T(\ulcorner A \urcorner) \wedge \neg T(\ulcorner \neg A \urcorner)$$

But given the transparency of T, this claim is equivalent to

$$\neg A \wedge \neg \neg A$$

which, in the K3 framework, implies absurdity via (*EFQ*).[6]

---

[6] This is not peculiar to K3. The same applies to logics that have been thought to be natural candidates for paracomplete truth theories.

What, then, does the paracomplete theorist's claim amount to? The *truth-pluralist* idea is that her claim involves a different truth predicate, something at least less see-through than transparent truth; she is using some different truth predicate Tr when she (truly) says of some appropriate A that ¬(A ∨¬A) is not true:

$$\neg \text{Tr}(\ulcorner A \urcorner) \wedge \neg \text{Tr}(\ulcorner \neg A \urcorner)$$

And because—we're supposing—this is not equivalent to ¬A ∧ ¬¬A, absurdity is avoided.

But where does this other truth predicate come from? How does it work? Here is where theories will differ; and precise details are not the aim of this discussion. For present purposes, I sketch one route toward enjoying such a predicate Tr and mention a different one—much more sophisticated (but beyond the scope here).

One route (Beall, 2002) finds the additional truth predicate via additional logical—in particular, negation-like—resources.[7] Suppose that, in addition to the K3 resources, we also have what is sometimes called an 'exhaustive' or 'external' negation-like connective modeled thus:

$$v(\dagger A) = \begin{cases} 1 & \text{if } v(A) \in \{.5, 0\}, \\ 0 & \text{otherwise.} \end{cases}$$

What is important to see is that in such a language, we automatically have a nontransparent truth operator:[8] namely, let $\mathbb{T}A$ be defined as ¬†A.

- $\mathbb{T}$ is a truth operator:
  - Capture: let v(A) = 1, and so v(†A) = 0, and so v(¬†A) = 1.
  - Release: let v(¬†A) = 1, and so v(†A) = 0, and so v(A) = 1.
- $\mathbb{T}$ is not transparent: ¬$\mathbb{T}$A is *not* equivalent to ¬A, whereas v(HA) = v(A) for any transparent operator H. (See §4 for terminology.)

Finally, letting Tr be the corresponding predicate for $\mathbb{T}$, where Tr is true of A just if $\mathbb{T}A$ is true, we have a predicate that plays the target role for the paracomplete theorist. In particular, the sense in which A is 'gappy' or 'neither true nor false' may be understood as invoking the nontransparent truth predicate; the sentence

$$\neg \text{Tr}(\ulcorner A \urcorner) \wedge \neg \text{Tr}(\ulcorner \neg A \urcorner)$$

is true when A is a 'gap' (e.g., the sample liar sentence above).[9]

---

[7] Note well: for the usual paradox-driven reasons, the following ultimately requires moving into a paraconsistent framework (though it can remain paracomplete in some sense). I discuss details elsewhere (2005), where the semantic values are expanded to four values and † is fixed at one of them, and for more recent discussion see (2009: ch. 5). I ignore all of these complexities here, concentrating instead only on the general picture of additional truth predicates in a deflated pluralist picture.

[8] A corresponding truth *predicate* can be defined as usual using the see-through predicate. See footnote above or discussion below.

[9] Again, I am ignoring complexities involving paradoxes arising from the additional machinery—paradoxes that may be avoided in this context by allowing gluts in addition to gaps. But I omit further

Having the additional 'exhaustive' negation-like connective † is only one simple example of how additional logical truth predicates may emerge. A much more sophisticated approach is the paracomplete truth theory advanced by Hartry Field (2008). Field's theory admits a great plurality of additional logical truth predicates, all defined from logical resources, notably, from a nonclassical, nonmaterial conditional, →, and from ⊤, where ⊤ is any logical truth:

$$\mathbb{T}A := A \wedge (\top \to A)$$

That $\mathbb{T}$, so understood, is a capture-release (i.e., truth) operator falls out immediately from the logic involved (2008), but I skip details here. Moreover, that a plurality—indeed, a vast plurality—of distinct truth operators (and, in turn, predicates) emerges from this approach, arising from features peculiar to the given conditional: for example, A → (A → A) is not equivalent to A → A, and generally such embedded contexts resist the given sort of 'collapse' or 'contraction,' thereby affording many nonequivalent operators via embedding.

My aim is (obviously) not to cover details of Field's or any other theory, but simply flag it as an important example of how a variety of truth predicates may emerge in the context of a transparent truth theory.

What we have in the foregoing examples are transparent truth theories that are also truth-pluralist theories in the target *deflated* fashion. We have transparent truth but also nontransparent truth; this is the pluralism. All such truth predicates are either mere logical tools (e.g., the see-through predicate) or built from purely logical tools; and this is deflationism.

6.2 TALK ABOUT NORMAL

Perhaps not surprisingly, the (dual) paraconsistent theorist has motivation for pluralism from a dual problem. Because the issues are so similar, I merely note the point here, leaving the details to the cited works.

Unlike the paracomplete theorist, the paraconsistent theorist may easily talk about the abnormal sentences; she can simply use her transparent truth predicate and say of such A that they're gluts: $T(\ulcorner A \urcorner) \wedge T(\ulcorner \neg A \urcorner)$ or, more simply (and equivalently, given see-through-ness), $A \wedge \neg A$. No problem.

What about the *normal* sentences? Well, these sentences are not gluts: $\neg(T(\ulcorner A \urcorner) \wedge T(\ulcorner \neg A \urcorner))$. But given transparency, this is equivalent to $\neg(A \wedge \neg A)$, which, in LP (or similar target logics), is simply equivalent to $A \vee \neg A$, which is logically true—and, hence, true of *all* sentences. So, if the idea of being a *non-glut* is to be more than vacuous, some other notion of truth

---

discussion here, since my discussion aims only to illustrate not-uncommon avenues toward forms of 'deflated truth pluralism.'

must be in play when the paraconsistent theorist (truly) says of A that it is not both true and not true.

The issues here are delicate, and different responses to the problem(s) have been offered (Beall, 2009; Brady, 2006; Field, 2008; Priest, 2006). For present purposes, I simply note a route (Beall, 2009: ch. 3 appendix) similar to one mentioned above. In particular, suppose that we have some sentence T that is 'true and normal,' that is, a 'non-glutty truth' in the target sense (assuming that there is coherent sense in our sights). As with the proposal above in a paracomplete setting, if we have a conditional with the right features then a nontransparent truth operator will do the trick here:

$$\mathbb{T}A := \tau \to A$$

Whether this does the trick depends, of course, on the details of the logic in question, and I skip details here.[10] The important point is that, once again, there is motivation for more than a transparent truth predicate (and so motivation for pluralism), but the more may be achievable via merely logical resources (and, so, deflated pluralism).

6.3 DEFLATED TRUTH PLURALISM

I've given examples (though not exact details) of deflated truth pluralism. Beginning with a transparent truth predicate, which we enjoy via a nonclassical logic setting, at least the standard paradoxes—if not other phenomena—motivate different (nontransparent) truth predicates. Truth pluralism, on my usage, requires at least two such truth predicates for a language. Deflated truth pluralism, on my (perhaps somewhat strict) usage, requires that any such predicates reduce to logical resources. The examples above, notwithstanding details, count: paradox pushes pluralism, and the box of logical tools keeps the pluralism suitably deflated.

7. Objections, questions, and replies

In this chapter, I have tried only to highlight one sort of truth pluralism that, I think, is both natural and perhaps not uncommon (at least when paradoxical discourse is taken into account). This section is offered by way of answering a few questions or objections that may remain, and also, perhaps, flagging other avenues of exploration.

---

[10] I note that, while exact details matter (e.g., if there's extra machinery going on), this sort of approach does work in the general logical frameworks advanced by Priest (2006), Beall (2009), and, I think, Brady (2006), as well as in Field's framework (2008).

7.1 QUESTIONS

Question. How does this compare with prominent versions of truth pluralism—for example, Lynch (1998; 2009) or Wright (1992)?

Reply. This volume gives an excellent taste of the prominent versions of truth pluralism, and I largely leave the reader to compare deflated truth pluralism with those versions. (An aside: I should note, on the word 'prominent,' that deflated truth pluralism is likely prominent in its own right, though probably more in logical studies in which it is less controversial than in metaphysics.) But one comment, perhaps on the most salient issue, may be useful.

As I understand them, such prominent truth pluralisms disagree with me on what it takes to be a *truth predicate*. They think that more than capture-release features is required. I remain unconvinced. What do we lose by accepting that whatever is expressed by a capture-release predicate is a truth property? Prominent truth pluralists might say that we lose the essential normativity of truth or the like. But why think that that's essential to all truth properties—particularly when, for example, it is hard to say as much about logical properties such as transparent truth, which—except for the insistence on 'essential normativity' or the like—is hard to strip of the title *truth property*.

In the end, we have a very simple criterion for being a *truth* predicate: namely, being a capture-release predicate (where, recall, capture and release are defined over the entire language). While metaphysics, morals, and more might be used to lobby against the sufficiency of capture-release for *truth* (i.e., for a capture-release predicate expressing *truth*), such lobbying—by my lights—is not useful. Imagine, for example, that we had exactly one predicate that played capture and release for our language L. In that case, would there really be controversy over whether it were a—and, by hypothesis, *the—truth* predicate? Perhaps there's no obvious answer without further details, but my guess is that the answer is 'no.' One longstanding feature of truth is its capture-release behavior. If nothing else in the language behaved that way (over the entire language), there'd be no reason to think it *truth*.

Question. If all it takes to be a truth predicate for L is to play capture and release for L, what is to prevent there being a predicate that expresses some robust/explanatory property that also plays capture and release for L? If there were such a predicate in our overall language, it would seem to be bad for your *deflated* pluralism. Are you committed to the claim that no predicate expressing a robust/explanatory property plays capture and release over the whole language? (This, after all, is a classic motivation for both deflationism and language-relative pluralism.)

Reply. A truth predicate for L is a capture-release predicate for L. Anything less is not a truth predicate for L. Being a capture-release predicate for L is not incompatible with expressing an explanatory (or more-than-logical) property. But if there is some such more-than-logical truth predicate in (and for) the language, then the deflated truth pluralist, as I've (strictly) drawn the position, is undermined. (One could take a middle road here: a capture-release *predicate* is a truth predicate, but not all truth predicates express truth properties. I prefer a simpler framework: truth predicates express truth properties. Sometimes, of course, as in the case of color predicates, we classify a predicate in terms of the properties/relations that it expresses: H is a color predicate just if H expresses a color. But on my view, to express a truth property is to be a capture-release predicate. Unlike in the case of color, where we look at the property to determine whether the predicate is a color predicate, here we look at the logical behavior of the predicate to determine whether the predicate is a truth predicate—and, in turn, whether it expresses a truth property.)

Question. The operator *it is a fact that* (similarly, corresponding predicate) plays capture and release for our language. Hence, by your account, it is a truth operator (similarly, corresponding predicate). But FACTHOOD is an explanatory, more-than-logical notion. But, then, isn't deflated truth pluralism undermined?

Reply. Not surprisingly, I agree that *it is a fact that* is a truth operator (similarly, predicate), but disagree that it's more than a logical device. In fact, I agree with Quine (1987) that the capture-release 'fact' talk likely reduces to standard talk spelled with 'truth.' (Whether it's *transparent* is a different but, in the present context, not-clearly-relevant issue.) While I do not have an argument, I conjecture that if there is some notion of facthood that proves to be essential to our best overall explanation of the world, it probably fails to capture and release (over the entire language).

7.2 OBJECTIONS

Objection. Surely none of this makes sense. Truth is just one thing, and so these so-called 'truth predicates' are really just truth-like predicates: they share logical features of *the* truth predicate, but they fail to be a *truth* predicate because they don't express the—one and only—truth property.

Reply. I've already addressed this above. If this is not to boil down to mere terminological quibbles, there must be a principle that determines a (supposed) *unique* truth predicate. What principle? Lynch (2009), perhaps more than anyone else, has presented principles that purport to narrow the field to exactly one truth predicate (via one truth property). I remain unconvinced by the proffered principles. The debate is sincere, but currently at a standstill as far as I can see. Where Lynch (or others along Lynchian lines) argue that such-and-so is *essential* to being *truth*, I myself tend to see the supposed essential ingredients as features (e.g., normativity in some respects) that have nothing to do with truth. The tie to truth (or, as I'd say, truth predicates) is only expressive in the usual way: truth is used to *voice* such claims, but it is not itself essential to the various phenomena at issue.

Objection. One reason that a truth predicate can be seen as non-deflationary is that it figures in explanations of other phenomena but in a more than expressive role. The paracomplete and paraconsistent nontransparent truth predicates you detail could be said to satisfy this. In particular, both might serve to explain why such-and-so claims should be (or, simply, are) rejected: they're not *true* (in one of the various nontransparent senses of 'true').

Reply. It's true that the (say) paracomplete theorist uses 'stronger,' nontransparent truth predicates to say of certain (e.g., gappy) sentences that they are not true; and such claims figure prominently in a variety of explanations—for example, rational acceptability (or rejectability, as it were) of various theories. And so, as the objection pushes, these notions of truth have explanatory work to do. And now we have a choice—as the objection makes clear. Do we define *deflationary* along the *only built from logical properties* route, or along the *no explanatory role route*—or both? For present purposes, I've taken a stand on the former route, but a comment on the latter route may be useful. In short, the details of the explanatory materials are important. In particular, when our paracomplete (or other target nonclassical) theorist says that they reject A because A is a gap in the given sense, that is,

$$\neg Tr(\ulcorner A \urcorner) \wedge \neg Tr(\ulcorner \neg A \urcorner)$$

where Tr is the nontransparent truth predicate constructed along something like the §6.1 lines, they are indeed using the given nontransparent truth predicate to offer an explanation. What is not happening, though, is an appeal to some more-than-logical property that, *when analyzed*, affords an explanation that goes deeper than what was said—deeper than that, well, A is neither true nor false, where this reduces to a claim using only logical resources (e.g., some sort of conditional, etc.).

Objection. Another reason we might say a capture-release predicate is not deflationary is that it has a different meaning from the paradigmatic deflationary truth predicate: namely, the transparent truth predicate. Not being transparent, the additional truth predicates you discuss do have different meanings. Therefore they are not deflationary.

Reply. I agree that this is a clean way to carve out the family of deflationary predicates, but I think that it is unnecessary. We have clean terminology for *the* transparent truth predicate. The notion of *deflationary truth predicates* seems to be wider—involving, as above, either a reduction to logical resources or absence of certain sorts of explanatory work. (Ultimately, this may be mere terminological debate. If so, I am happy for what I've called *deflated truth pluralism* to be labeled something else. But I do think that it falls squarely within standard conceptions of 'deflationary' views.)

Objection. Linked argument: where T′(⌜A⌝) is not equivalent to *A* in nonopaque contexts, they have different meanings (content). The best explanation of this fact is that the predicate T′ denotes an additional property whose nature cannot be known just by grasping all instances of release and capture.

Reply. I agree. What's required for grasping the 'nature' of T′ (scare quotes are very important in this context) is a grasp of the logical machinery out of which T′ is constructed. This machinery delivers capture-release behavior; the capture-release features are not themselves the underlying logical ingredients of T′ that constitute the 'nature' in question.

References

Armour-Garb, B. & Beall, Jc (eds.). (2005). *Deflationary Truth*. Oxford: Oxford University Press.
Asenjo, F. G. (1966). A calculus of antinomies. *Notre Dame Journal of Formal Logic* 16: 103–105.
Beall, Jc. (2002). Deflationism and gaps: untying not's in the debate. *Analysis* 62: 299–305.
Beall, Jc. (2005). Transparent disquotationalism. In Jc Beall & B. Armour-Garb (eds), *Deflationism and Paradox* (7–22). Oxford: Oxford University Press.
Beall, Jc. (2009). *Spandrels of Truth*. Oxford: Oxford University Press.
Beall, Jc. (2010). *Logic: The Basics*. Oxford: Routledge.
Beall, Jc & van Fraassen, B. C. (2003). *Possibilities and Paradox: Introduction to Modal and Many-Valued Logic*. Oxford: Oxford University Press.
Brady, R. (2006). *Universal Logic, vol. 109*. Stanford, CA: CSLI Lecture Notes.
Field, H. (2008). *Saving Truth from Paradox*. Oxford: Oxford University Press.
Gupta, A. & Belnap, N. (1993). *The Revision Theory of Truth*. Cambridge, MA: MIT Press.
Horwich, P. (1998) *Truth*. Oxford: Blackwell; first published, 1990.
Kleene, S. C. (1952). *Introduction to Metamathematics*. Amsterdam: North-Holland .
Kripke, S. (1975) Outline of a theory of truth. *Journal of Philosophy* 72: 690–716. Reprinted in Martin (1984).
Leeds, S. (1978). Theories of reference and truth. *Erkenntnis* 13: 111–129. Reprinted in B. Armour-Garb and Jc Beall (2005: 33–50).
Lynch, M. P. (1998). *Truth in Context*. Cambridge, MA: MIT Press.
Lynch, M. P. (2009). *Truth as One and Many*. Oxford: Oxford University Press.
Martin, R. L. (ed.) (1984). *Recent Essays on Truth and the Liar Paradox*. New York: Oxford University Press.
McGee, V. (1991). *Truth, Vagueness, and Paradox*. Indianapolis, IN: Hackett.
McGee, V. (2005). Two conceptions of truth? *Philosophical Studies* 124:7 1–104.
Priest, G. (1979). The logic of paradox. *Journal of Philosophical Logic* 8: 219–241.
Priest, G. (2006). *In Contradiction, 2nd ed*. Oxford: Oxford University Press; first printed by Martinus Nijhoff in 1987.

Priest, G. (2008). *An Introduction to Non-Classical Logic, 2nd ed.* Cambridge: Cambridge University Press; first published, 2001.
Quine, W. v. O. (1970). *Philosophy of Logic.* Englewood Cliffs, NJ: Prentice-Hall.
Quine, W. v. O. (1987). *Quiddities.* Cambridge, MA: Harvard University Press.
Restall, G. (2005). *Logic: An Introduction.* New York: Routledge.
Tarski, A. (1936). Der Wahreitsbegriff in den formalisierten Sprachen. *Studia Philosophica* 1: 261–405. Reprinted in English in Tarski (1956).
Tarski, A. (1956). *Logic, Semantics, Metamathematics: Papers from 1923 to 1938.* Translated by J. H. Woodger. Oxford: Clarendon Press.
Wright, C. (1992). *Truth and Objectivity.* Cambridge, MA: Harvard University Press.

{ 17 }

Pluralism and Paradox
Aaron J. Cotnoir

1. Introduction

The semantic paradoxes are as much of a problem for pluralists about truth as they are for any other theory of truth. Alethic pluralists, however, have generally set discussion of the paradoxes aside.[1] In what follows, I argue that considerations involving the paradoxes have *direct* implications for alethic pluralism.

More specifically, alethic pluralism has bifurcated into two main types: *strong* and *weak*. Weak theories accept a truth predicate that applies to every true sentence (a *universal* truth predicate) in addition to the many other truth predicates, $T_1, \ldots, T_n$. Strong theories reject a universal truth predicate in favor of $T_1, \ldots, T_n$.[2] This chapter has two parts. The negative part (§2) shows that *both* types of theories suffer from paradox-generated inconsistency given certain plausible assumptions. The positive part (§3) outlines a new, consistent way to be a strong alethic pluralist. The trick to avoiding paradox is rejecting infinitary disjunction, something we already have pluralism-independent (but paradox-motivated) reasons to reject. In §4, I conclude by comparing this theory with a Tarskian hierarchical view and discuss some directions for future research.

---

[1] There are one or two exceptions. The only pluralist theories that handle paradoxes are those who have come to alethic pluralism *as a result* of dealing with paradoxes. Hartry Field (2008) endorses a plurality of 'determinate' truth predicates in order to handle certain *revenge* charges. Jc Beall (2008b) discusses a strong falsity predicate to avoid a *revenge* charge as well. See Beall (2013), for more details.

[2] Strictly speaking, there are more types if one considers the predicate/property distinction. Pedersen (2006) is quite careful about this. In this chapter, however, I focus merely on truth predicates rather than truth properties. This is for three reasons. First, regardless of one's theory of truth *properties*, one will need truth *predicates* to express them. Second, paradoxes arise most straightforwardly for predicates; although there may be parallel (Russell-like) paradoxes for truth properties, whatever they may be. Finally, I am unclear what considerations would make a property a *truth* property; that is, I am somewhat sympathetic to deflationary theories of truth. In order not to prejudge any of this, I stick to predicates throughout.

2. Problem: universal truth and paradox

Pluralists endorse many truth predicates $T_1, \ldots, T_n$. Usually, each predicate is a truth predicate *for* a certain 'domain of discourse.'[3] Here, domains are not what first-order quantifiers range over. For our purposes, we may treat them simply as *fragments* of a language, where fragments of a language are disjoint proper subsets of the sentences of that language.[4]

What does it mean to be a truth predicate *for* a domain? Pluralists have endorsed certain minimal constraints.[5] One such minimal constraint is the T-scheme:

(TS) $\vdash T_i(\ulcorner \alpha \urcorner) \leftrightarrow \alpha$ for all sentences α in domain$_i$.

Here 'T_i' is a truth predicate for domain$_i$. '$\ulcorner \alpha \urcorner$' just signifies the code for sentence α generated some adequate coding scheme; any arithmetization that yields a language rich enough to 'talk' about its own syntax will do. And '$\leftrightarrow$' is constructed in the normal way from any conditional that satisfies modus ponens ($\alpha, \alpha \to \beta \vdash \beta$), identity ($\vdash \alpha \to \alpha$), and transitivity ($\alpha \to \beta, \beta \to \gamma \vdash \alpha \to \gamma$).

Pluralists have endorsed many other constraints, but let me focus only on (TS). Weak alethic pluralists—those pluralists who endorse a universal truth predicate $\mathbb{T}$—must decide whether this universal predicate obeys the T-scheme. That is, does the weak pluralist accept (FULL-TS)?

(FULL-TS) $\vdash \mathbb{T}(\ulcorner \alpha \urcorner) \leftrightarrow \alpha$ for all sentences α.

If the answer is 'yes,' then it is straightforward to derive a paradox. We have assumed an adequate coding scheme; this is guaranteed if the language has the expressive resources of first-order arithmetic. So, standard diagonalization techniques guarantee that any expression with one free variable will have a Gödel sentence that is equivalent to that expression predicated of itself. In this case, $\neg \mathbb{T}(x)$ is such an expression; call its Gödel sentence 'λ.' But then λ is equivalent to $\neg \mathbb{T}(\ulcorner \alpha \urcorner)$, and so we can prove (GS).

---

[3] This is how both Wright (1992; 2001) and Lynch (2001; 2004; 2009) set up their theories. But see Horgan (2001), who thinks truth predicates are true of sentences relative to 'contexts.'

[4] Domains are difficult to pin down. Lynch (2004) writes, 'Intuitively, a propositional domain is simply an area of thought. . . . Propositional domains are individuated by the types of propositions of which they are composed. Propositions are in turn individuated by the concepts we employ in thinking about different subject matters' (399–400). But in order to type propositions in this way we must already have a clear taxonomy of types of concepts. Lynch himself believes that concepts often cannot be individuated in a determinate manner. He admits, 'Here, like everywhere else, types of concepts shade off into one another' (2001: 731). Thus, we have reason to think these propositional domains will be (in some cases) indeterminate. But this conflicts with Lynch's (2004: 400) assertions that every atomic proposition is a member one and only one domain (and essentially so). See Sher (2005) and C. D. Wright (2005) for more objections, and Lynch's essay in this volume for an attempt to address them.

[5] Wright and Lynch both endorse a *platitude*-approach to alethic pluralism. For Wright, the platitudes define the concept of truth; for Lynch, they define the functional role of truth.

Pluralism and Paradox

(GS) $\vdash \neg \mathbb{T}(\ulcorner \lambda \urcorner) \leftrightarrow \lambda.$

And in the presence of (*FULL-TS*) we have it that $\vdash \mathbb{T}(\ulcorner \lambda \urcorner) \leftrightarrow \lambda$. But this, combined with (GS), gives us the paradox: $\vdash \neg \mathbb{T}(\ulcorner \lambda \urcorner) \leftrightarrow \mathbb{T}(\ulcorner \lambda \urcorner)$. Unless the logic is *extremely* nonclassical, these paradoxes will explode into triviality. It will turn out that *everything* is true, which is hardly desirable for a theory of truth.[6] None of this is anything novel or controversial. It is surprising, then, that alethic pluralists would endorse (*FULL-TS*). But nearly all weak alethic pluralists have, including Wright, Lynch, and Sher.[7]

So, I claim that the weak alethic pluralists, if they wish to avoid paradox, ought to reject (*FULL-TS*). If there *is* a universal truth predicate, it better not satisfy the T-scheme unrestrictedly. Should the weak pluralist endorse (*TS*) for each truth predicate $T_1, \ldots, T_n$? That is, can each domain-specific truth predicate satisfy the T-scheme restricted to its own domain? If weak pluralists accept this, this puts them in a sufficiently similar position as the strong alethic pluralist who endorses TS for the truth predicates $T_1, \ldots, T_n$. So let us turn to this option now.

2.1 STRONG PLURALISM AND THE LIAR

The strong alethic pluralist accepts many domain-specific truth predicates $T_1, \ldots, T_n$, yet rejects any universal truth predicate. Now, the strong pluralist must also decide whether each truth predicate satisfies the T-scheme (*TS*). If so, however, each T_i needs to satisfy (*TS*) only for all α in domain$_i$. This also would appear to run straight into semantic paradox.

Consider the liar-like sentence λ_1 constructed via diagonalization using the truth predicate T_1.

$$\lambda_1 : \neg T_1(\ulcorner \lambda_1 \urcorner)$$

Since λ_1 is the Gödel sentence of the open expression $\neg T_1(x)$, we can prove the following:

(GS1): $\vdash \neg T_1(\ulcorner \lambda_1 \urcorner) \leftrightarrow \lambda_1.$

If we endorse (*TS*), we are committed to $T_1(\ulcorner \alpha \urcorner) \leftrightarrow \alpha$ for all α in domain$_1$. But then we can show that $\vdash \neg T_1(\ulcorner \lambda_1 \urcorner) \leftrightarrow T_1(\ulcorner \lambda_1 \urcorner)$, on the assumption that λ_1 is in domain$_1$. And that's bad.

---

[6] I should note that I have some sympathy for nonclassical truth theories. See Caret & Cotnoir (2008) for a defense of one paracomplete option.

[7] See Wright (1992; 2001: 760); Lynch (2001: 730; 2009: ch. 4, §1). Sher (2004) is not explicit, but her discussion of the *unity* of truth raises serious suspicion that she endorses (*FULL-TS*) (see pp. 26–35). To be fair, none of these pluralists are undertaking any discussion of the paradoxes. But, in this chapter, I am claiming that they should.

Contrary to the above derivation, however, the strong alethic pluralist has available a novel response to these paradoxes. The derivation depends crucially on the assumption that the λ_1-liar is actually in domain$_1$. But the pluralist, of course, is free to reject that λ_1 is in domain$_1$. If λ_1 is *not* a sentence of domain$_1$, then we do not have to commit to $T_1(\ulcorner\lambda_1\urcorner) \leftrightarrow \lambda_1$. Thus, we do not arrive at the paradoxical consequence that $\vdash \neg T_1(\ulcorner\lambda_1\urcorner) \leftrightarrow T_1(\ulcorner\lambda_1\urcorner)$.

Here is another way of stating the point. As strong pluralists, we are free to claim that λ_1 is *not* true$_1$. Of course, λ_1 actually says of itself that it is not true$_1$. And so intuitively, it ought to be true! But if λ_1 is actually in domain$_2$, it may very well be true$_2$. We can endorse $T_2(\ulcorner\lambda_1\urcorner)$ without paradox.

Of course, we will be able to define a *new* liar, λ_2, by diagonalization using T_2.

$$\lambda_2 : \neg T_2(\ulcorner\lambda_2\urcorner)$$

But notice that λ_2 is *not* the same sentence as λ_1. Indeed, the two use different truth predicates. Here again, the pluralist is free to reject that λ_2 is in domain$_2$, but rather in, say, domain$_3$. This process can continue, and the result is that the pluralist can consistently endorse (*TS*) for T_i over domain$_i$ for every natural number i.

2.2 STRONG PLURALISM AND REVENGE

There is trouble lurking with the above proposal. And the trouble is tied up with the fact that is more difficult to avoid a universal truth predicate than one might initially think. Given the resources of disjunction, one can always define a universal truth predicate thus:[8]

$$(\textit{T-DEF}) \quad \mathbb{T}(\ulcorner\alpha\urcorner) := T_1(\ulcorner\alpha\urcorner) \vee T_2(\ulcorner\alpha\urcorner) \vee \ldots \vee T_n(\ulcorner\alpha\urcorner).$$

In the case where the number of domains is countably infinite, we simply require infinite disjunction to yield the definition.

$$(\textit{T-DEF*}) \quad \mathbb{T}(\ulcorner\alpha\urcorner) := \bigvee_{i \in \mathbb{N}} T_i(\ulcorner\alpha\urcorner).$$

Notice that (*T-DEF*) and (*T-DEF**) are genuinely universal truth predicates, in that $\mathbb{T}$ will be true of α regardless of its domain.[9] It turns out that it is difficult to be a *strong* alethic pluralist.

More troubling, however, is that if T_i satisfies (*TS*) for each $i \in \mathbb{N}$, then $\mathbb{T}$ will satisfy (*FULL-TS*). Suppose $\vdash T_i(\ulcorner\alpha\urcorner) \leftrightarrow \alpha$ for all α in domain$_i$, for each

---

[8] In (2009), I defined such a truth predicate to show that the proposal in Edwards (2008) did not avoid one. Nikolaj Pedersen (2010) used the same technique to formulate the 'linguistic instability challenge.'

[9] Here I assume that each truth predicate is true of only of sentences in its domain. Pluralists may wish to reject this assumption. If so, then (*T-DEF*) needs an additional constraint: sentence domains must be made explicit. So, $\mathbb{T}(\ulcorner\alpha\urcorner) := (T_1(\ulcorner\alpha\urcorner) \wedge \ulcorner\alpha\urcorner \in D_1) \vee (T_2(\ulcorner\alpha\urcorner) \wedge \ulcorner\alpha\urcorner \in D_2) \vee \ldots \vee (T_n(\ulcorner\alpha\urcorner) \wedge \ulcorner\alpha\urcorner \in D_n)$ will do the trick. See Pedersen & Wright (2013), this volume, for discussion of this issue.

$i \in \mathbb{N}$. Then $\vdash (T_1(\ulcorner \alpha \urcorner) \vee T_2(\ulcorner \alpha \urcorner) \vee \ldots T_n(\ulcorner \alpha \urcorner)) \leftrightarrow \alpha$ for all α irrespective of the domain; or, more generally,

$$\vdash \bigvee_{i \in \mathbb{N}} T_i(\ulcorner \alpha \urcorner) \leftrightarrow \alpha$$

will hold for any sentence α. But the lefthand side just is the definition of $\mathbb{T}(\ulcorner \alpha \urcorner)$, and so we have $\vdash \mathbb{T}(\ulcorner \alpha \urcorner) \leftrightarrow \alpha$ for any sentence α. We have used (infinitary) disjunction to construct a universal truth predicate satisfying (FULL-TS). So any strong pluralist who thinks $T_1, \ldots, T_n$ must satisfy (TS), is actually a *weak* pluralist that endorses (FULL-TS). The two positions actually collapse into the same view.

And now notice that $\neg \mathbb{T}(x)$ is an open expression of the required kind for diagonalization. So we will have its Gödel sentence, call it λ_ω, such that $\vdash \neg \mathbb{T}(\ulcorner \lambda_\omega \urcorner) \leftrightarrow \lambda_\omega$. But in the presence of (FULL-TS), we get the paradox: $\vdash \neg \mathbb{T}(\ulcorner \lambda_\omega \urcorner) \leftrightarrow \mathbb{T}(\ulcorner \lambda_\omega \urcorner)$. To put the point plainly, given infinitary disjunction, we can construct a sentence that says of itself: 'I'm not universally true.' That sentence is λ_ω, equivalent to $\neg \mathbb{T}(\ulcorner \lambda_\omega \urcorner)$.

That is just an abbreviation for

$$\neg \bigvee_{i \in \mathbb{N}} T_i(\ulcorner \lambda_\omega \urcorner).$$

But given that we have DeMorgan negation, that is equivalent to

$$\bigwedge_{i \in \mathbb{N}} \neg T_i(\ulcorner \lambda_\omega \urcorner).$$

So, intuitively λ_ω is a sentence that says of itself that it is not true$_1$, *and* not true$_2$, *and* so on.

The point has failed to be noticed. I, myself, failed to notice this result in (2009) where I argue that Edwards's (2008) solution to the problem of mixed conjunction has a universal truth predicate. Edwards's solution would require infinitary disjunction and hence necessitates $\mathbb{T}$. As a result of the above, Edwards's solution is outright inconsistent if it accepts (TS).

But others have failed to notice the point as well. Consider, for example, Pedersen (2010), who uses a construction similar to (T-DEF) to argue that strong alethic pluralism collapses into weak pluralism.[10] Regarding (TS), he says,

> According to pluralists [...] what makes a given predicate a truth predicate is that it satisfies a series of platitudes, or truisms, which delineate the truth

---

[10] More accurately, he argues that it does so given a principle of 'linguistic liberalism' regarding language expansion. He seems to assume that the predicate $\mathbb{T}$ must be *added* to the language, and that such additions need to obey certain principles. However, given that $\mathbb{T}$ is defined merely out of linguistic items we already have available, the language needs no expansion. We may wish to add the symbol '$\mathbb{T}$' to our syntax, but we are stuck with the universal truth predicate even if no such symbol is added.

concept. A non-exhaustive list would include as platitudes that 'p' is true if and only if p ('disquotational schema') [. . .]. (2010: 99))

While Pedersen's argument does not require the platitude approach, he fails to note that the strong pluralist simply cannot, on pain of paradox, introduce $\mathbb{T}$. He claims,

> Nothing prevents us from introducing $\mathbb{T}$. It is syntactically well-formed and disciplined, as any legitimate predicate should be[. . .]. $\mathbb{T}$ is a universal truth predicate because it applies to *exactly* those sentences to which one of $T_1, \ldots, T_n$ applies. (2010: 99])

And again, regarding $\mathbb{T}$ he writes,

> It is syntactically well formed, and comes with a condition of application [the T-scheme]. In the light of this, there is simply no further question whether $\mathbb{T}$ is a legitimate addition[. . .]. Hence, I see no way to resist the introduction of $\mathbb{T}$. (2010: 99)

There *is*, however, something that prevents us from introducing $\mathbb{T}$—doing so introduces paradox and inconsistency. There *is* a further question about whether $\mathbb{T}$ is a legitimate addition.[11]

The alethic pluralist has three options. First, one may endorse a nonclassical logic to avoid paradox. Any such theory will have to be significantly different from usual pluralist theories; indeed, it will represent a significant departure from classical logic.[12] The second option is to reject that (TS) holds for some truth predicate T_i. On pain of paradox, the pluralist must admit that there is at least one T_i that fails to satisfy the T-scheme. The last option is to reject the linguistic resources for introducing $\mathbb{T}$, to reject infinitary disjunction.

3. Solution: rejecting infinite disjunctions

Alethic pluralists—both strong and weak—may respond to this problem by rejecting that (TS) serves as a constraint on being a truth predicate for a domain. Or they may respond by adopting a nonclassical logic that can handle such paradoxes. These are just the usual, well-explored responses found in literature regarding monistic theories of truth. I argue, however, that both

---

[11] These considerations apply equally well to the disjunctivist theory endorsed by Pedersen (with Cory Wright) in chapter 5 of this volume.
[12] Contrary to some, the nonclassical option is not the 'easy way out' of the paradoxes. Two nonclassical pluralist theories, along with the difficulties surrounding them, are given in detail in Beall (2008b) and Field (2008).

Pluralism and Paradox

of these options are unnecessary. Instead of rejecting (TS) as a constraint on truth, one only needs to reject infinitary disjunction. Such a rejection is already well motivated by Curry's paradox. Moreover, the considerations that motivate such a rejection will apply to almost any nonclassical option for handling the paradoxes. And obviously, the *strong* alethic pluralist—who thinks there is no universal truth predicate—will have a vested interest in rejecting any method for constructing one.

The liar is not the only semantic paradox that proves difficult for truth theories. Curry's paradox, formulated by Haskell Curry (1942), relies on the conditional rather than negation. Given the usual diagonalization techniques, we can arrive at a self-referential sentence κ that is equivalent to $T(\ulcorner \kappa \urcorner) \to \bot$, where $\bot$ is some falsehood like "0 = 1."

Here is the problem. Assume for conditional proof $T(\ulcorner \kappa \urcorner)$. By the left–right direction of (TS), we get κ, which is just equivalent to $T(\ulcorner \kappa \urcorner) \to \bot$. By modus ponens, we have $\bot$. So, we have proved $T(\ulcorner \kappa \urcorner) \to \bot$. But then we've really also proved κ because they are equivalent. The right–left direction of (TS) gives $T(\ulcorner \kappa \urcorner)$. And we use this, by modus ponens, to yield $\bot$. But $\bot$ can't be true!

Greg Restall (2008) has given a general argument, based on very minimal constraints, on the difficulties that Curry's paradox brings. Here are the requirements:

(TRAN) $\vdash$ is transitive.

(CONJ) $\alpha \vdash \beta$ and $\alpha \vdash \gamma$ if and only if $\alpha \vdash \beta \wedge \gamma$.[13]

(DISJ)   Infinitary disjunction is available in the language.[14]

(WEAK-TS) $T(\ulcorner \alpha \urcorner) \wedge \tau \vdash \alpha$ and $\alpha \wedge \tau \vdash T(\ulcorner \alpha \urcorner)$ where τ is any true sentence.

The assumptions are quite plausible, even for the nonclassical theorist. Moreover, the version of the T-scheme here is extremely weak. In fact, (WEAK-TS) requires only that from $T(\ulcorner \alpha \urcorner)$ *and* some conjunction of true background constraints τ, we can infer α. This is even weaker than what is sometimes called the 'rule-form' T-scheme.

The derivation of $\bot$ is a bit involved, but a few important points should be highlighted.[15] The reason we need infinitary disjunction is that it can be used as a *residual* of conjunction. A connective $\odot$ is the residual of conjunction if it satisfies (RES).

(RES) $\alpha \wedge \beta \vdash \gamma$ if and only if $\alpha \vdash \beta \odot \gamma$.

---

[13] This amounts to the algebraic constraint that $\wedge$ must be a greatest lower bound with respect to $\vdash$.
[14] Finite conjunctions satisfying (CONJ) must also distribute over infinitary disjunction. Algebraically, then, this requires the logic to be a distributive lattice, which is nearly always the case.
[15] For the full derivation, see Restall (2008: 265).

Many conditional connectives satisfy (RES), which is why conditionals are often used to generate Curry paradoxes. So the nonclassical option for the alethic pluralist will have to include only non-(RES) conditionals. But in the presence of infinitary disjunction, we can define a residual thus:

(∨-RES) $\beta \odot \gamma := \bigvee \{\alpha \mid \alpha \wedge \beta \vdash \gamma\}$

(∨-RES) defines a connective satisfying (RES).[16] And so, any theorist accepting (TRAN), (CONJ), (DISJ), and (WEAK-TS) will fall prey to Curry's paradox. Of these options, I think the lesson of this version of Curry is that (DISJ) must go.

Recall, however, the lessons of the liar. There were three rival options for the alethic pluralist: (i) rejecting (TS) for some truth predicate T_i; (ii) moving to a nonclassical logic; and (iii) rejecting infinite disjunctions required for constructing $\mathbb{T}$. However, Restall's Curry shows more.

First, for option (i), it will not be enough simply to reject (TS) for some truth predicate T_i. They must reject (WEAK-TS) for some T_i. That is, not even an *enthymematic* version of the 'rule-form' T-scheme can count as a necessary condition on being a truth predicate for a domain. That is a fairly drastic limitation, especially given the alternative options.

Secondly, consider option (ii): nonclassical logic. The choice to reject (WEAK-TS) will completely undermine the reason for going nonclassical when faced with the liar. So, the nonclassical alethic pluralist, too, will have to reject either (TRAN), (CONJ), or (DISJ). The former two are arguably essential features of validity and conjunction.[17] It is intriguing to note, however, that nonclassical pluralists might have an advantage over nonclassical monists: pluralists might endorse nonclassical logics as restricted only to a 'paradoxical' domain. While this route is intriguing, I will not explore it here.[18]

These results should cause the alethic pluralist to seriously consider option (iii). The pluralist can retain (TS) for each T_i by rejecting infinite disjunction given by DISJ. She can retain her uniquely pluralist response to the liar. Rejecting DISJ also solves the problem of Curry paradoxes constructible using

---

[16] *Proof* (due to Restall): For the left–right direction of RES, assume $\dot\alpha \wedge \beta \vdash \gamma$. Since $\dot\alpha \in \{\alpha \mid \alpha \wedge \beta \vdash \gamma\}$, we have it that $\dot\alpha \vdash \bigvee\{\alpha \mid \alpha \wedge \beta \vdash \gamma\}$. For the other direction, assume $\dot\alpha \vdash \bigvee\{\alpha \mid \alpha \wedge \beta \vdash \gamma\}$. So, $\dot\alpha \wedge \beta \vdash \beta \wedge \bigvee\{\alpha \mid \alpha \wedge \beta \vdash \gamma\}$. Distributing, we have $\dot\alpha \wedge \beta \vdash \bigvee\{\alpha \wedge \beta \mid \alpha \wedge \beta \vdash \gamma\}$. But obviously, $\bigvee\{\alpha \wedge \beta \mid \alpha \wedge \beta \vdash \gamma\} \vdash \gamma$, and so by transitivity of $\vdash$ we have the result.

[17] Neil Tennant (1994) has endorsed non-transitive systems of logic. However, none of his systems will help with Curry paradoxes. It should be noted that Alan Weir (2005) has argued for restricting a generalized cut rule, related to transitivity in order to avoid Curry paradoxes. His system is also nonclassical in other ways; it is paracomplete, and adjunction fails—$\alpha, \beta \nvdash \alpha \wedge \beta$.

[18] While distinct from the logical pluralism of Beall and Restall (2006), Lynch (2008) provides philosophical motivations for this domain-relative logical pluralism. In (forthcoming), I give a formal semantics consistent with this approach. I fully expect, however, that there will be expressive difficulties for such a pluralist. It may be hard to isolate the paradoxical sentences from the normal ones, for similar reasons as given in Beall (2013). See also the essays in Beall (2008a).

infinitary disjunction. Curry paradoxes constructed from the classical material conditional will take a form similar to $T_i(\ulcorner \kappa \urcorner) \supset \bot$. This is classically equivalent to $\neg T_i(\ulcorner \kappa \urcorner) \vee \bot$. But these paradoxes can be handled identically to liars: while κ is not true$_i$, it may well be true$_j$ for some j ≠ i. Barring future and unforeseen paradoxes, the alethic pluralist may adhere to a fully classical logic.

The above considerations suggest that the alethic pluralist would do well to avoid infinitary disjunction. As I showed in §2, the *strong* alethic pluralist must deny infinitary disjunction in order to avoid a universal truth predicate. Moreover, the *weak* alethic pluralist is faced with limited options if she decides not to reject it.

4. Conclusion: looking ahead

The response above has some similarities to a Tarskian hierarchical view of truth (Tarski, 1983;[19] 1944). So it is worth pausing briefly to compare and contrast the views. At the start, one obvious difference between the two views is that a Tarskian view relativizes truth to a *language*, whereas the pluralist relativizes truth to a *domain* (defined here as disjoint proper subsets of a language). The Tarskian theory is constrained by the fact that languages are arranged hierarchically; language $\mathcal{L}_n$ is a proper subset of the distinct language $\mathcal{L}_{n+1}$. Domains, however, share no sentences in common, since they are disjoint from each other. Moreover, on the Tarskian view, truth-in-$\mathcal{L}_n$ is only well-defined in $\mathcal{L}_{n+1}$; that is, no two languages may share the same truth predicate. By contrast, domains may share the same truth predicate. There might be multiple domains for which, say, correspondence is the correct truth property.

This feature of the Tarskian theory is tied to a second difference between it and the pluralist theory outlined above. According to the Tarskian theory, Liar sentences are ruled out on *syntactic* grounds. No language can contain a truth predicate that applies to sentences in that language. So if T_0 is the truth predicate for language $\mathcal{L}_0$, then any sentence containing the predicate T_0 cannot be a sentence of L_0. A fortiori, no liar sentence $\neg T_0(\ulcorner \lambda_0 \urcorner)$ is well-formed in L_0. According to the pluralist view, however, liar-like sentences arise at the syntactic level. Indeed, a sentence like $\neg T_1(\ulcorner T_1(\ulcorner \lambda_1 \urcorner) \urcorner)$ is syntactically well formed. The only constraints regard which sentences can belong to which domains.

Third, one must consider why liar sentences involving a truth predicate T_i must be in domain$_j$ where i ≠ j. Remember that for the Tarskian theory, truth-attribution involves semantic ascent. A pluralist, however, need not claim that truth-attribution requires *ascent* to a 'higher' language. She is free

---

[19] After this chapter was in press, Shapiro (2011) briefly suggested a similar approach.

to claim that a truth-attribution of a sentence in some domain must always be in a distinct, but not 'higher,' domain. Since a pluralist (usually) individuates domains by the what a sentence is about, the pluralist can claim that while a sentence like 'Torture is wrong' is about moral concepts, the sentence "'Torture is wrong' is true" is about the semantic properties of a sentence. This general answer extends straightforwardly to all sentences of the language, including paradoxical ones.[20]

Finally, it is worth noting that some alethic pluralists like Horgan (2001) think truth is relative not to domains, but to contexts. Pluralists of this stripe have very close ties to contextualist approaches to the semantic paradoxes. Rejecting (DISJ) could be seen as a consequence of rejecting absolutely unrestricted quantification,[21] the main difference being that pluralists view different contexts as inducing distinct truth predicates; this is something contextualists explicitly deny.[22]

If an alethic pluralist takes the recommended route, by rejecting infinite disjunctions and a universal truth predicate, there is still work to be done. To be sure that the proposal is completely free of any unforeseen paradoxes, it would be desirable to have a full consistency proof.

Second, since the rejection of infinite disjunctions blocks the most obvious route to a universal truth predicate, it can serve as a response to Pedersen's (2010) 'instability challenge' for strong alethic pluralism. Precise details would have to be given, including an explanation as to why the strong pluralist rejects the infinitary disjunction to generalize over the truth predicates she accepts.

Thirdly, the instability challenge is not the only problem to be answered; the problems of mixed compounds and mixed inferences pose difficulties to alethic pluralists. Indeed, strong alethic pluralism appears to be underpopulated in part due to these problems.[23]

Responses to each problem would have to be formulated. Fortunately, there are already some options on the table. In the last section of (2009), I outlined a solution to the problem of mixed compounds that avoids a universal truth predicate. It is compatible with the strong theory proposed above. Jc Beall (2000) appeals to designated values in many-valued logic to solve the problem of mixed inferences. It should be noted that Christine Tappolet (2000)

---

[20] Michael Lynch has pointed out in conversation (also in his essay in this volume) that such a view will clash with deflationary theories of truth, who generally accept that α and T ($\ulcorner\alpha\urcorner$) have the same semantic content.

[21] See Rayo and Uzquiano (2006), and in particular Glanzberg's (2006) for arguments that could be marshaled in favor of the above approach.

[22] See, for example, Glanzberg (2004).

[23] The problem of mixed inferences is originally due to C. Tappolet (1997). The problem of mixed compounds is probably due to Tim Williamson (1994). Michael Lynch (2001; 2004; 2009) has given weak pluralist responses. For another proposed solution, see Edwards (2008); but see my (2009) and Edwards's (2009).

responded to Beall's solution by arguing that the notion of 'designatedness' amounts to a universal truth predicate, which apparently undermines the proposal. In order for the notion of designatedness, however, to be expressible in the object language, one would need the resources of infinitary disjunction. And so Tappolet's objection will not be a problem for the current proposal.[24]

To the alethic pluralist who is not sympathetic to rejecting infinite disjunctions: it is my hope that this chapter will lead the way for pluralists to discuss the semantic paradoxes and the uniquely pluralist options available. At the very least, they should not continue to be ignored.[25]

References

Beall, Jc. (2000). On mixed inferences and pluralism about truth predicates. *Philosophical Quarterly* 50: 380–382.

Beall, Jc. (ed.). (2008a). *Revenge of the Liar*. Oxford: Oxford University Press.

Beall, Jc. (ed.) (2008b). *Spandrels of Truth*. Oxford: Oxford University Press.

Beall, Jc. (2013). Deflated truth pluralism. In N. J. L. L. Pedersen & C. D. Wright (eds.), *Truth and Pluralism: Current Debates* (323–338). New York: Oxford University Press.

Beall, Jc & Restall, G. (2006). *Logical Pluralism*. Oxford: Oxford University Press.

Caret, C., & Cotnoir, A. J. (2008). True, false, paranormal, and 'designated'? A reply to Jenkins. *Analysis* 68: 238–244.

Cotnoir, A. J. (2009). Generic truth and mixed conjunctions: Some alternatives. *Analysis* 69: 473–479.

Cotnoir, A. J. (Forthcoming). Validity for strong pluralists. To appear in *Philosophy and Phenomenological Research*.

Curry, H. (1942). The inconsistency of certain formal logics. *Journal of Symbolic Logic* 7: 115–117.

Edwards, D. (2008). How to solve the problem of mixed conjunctions. *Analysis* 68: 143–149.

Edwards, D. (2009). Truth-conditions and the nature of truth. *Analysis* 69: 684–688.

Field, H. (2008). *Saving Truth From Paradox*. Oxford: Oxford University Press.

Glanzberg, M. (2004). A contextual-hierarchical approach to truth and the liar paradox. *Journal of Philosophical Logic* 33: 27–88.

Glanzberg, M. (2006). Context and unrestricted quantification. In A. Rayo and G. Uzquiano (eds.), *Absolute Generality* (45–75). Oxford: Oxford University Press.

Horgan, T. (2001). Contextual semantics and metaphysical realism: Truth as indirect correspondence. In M. Lynch (ed.), *The Nature of Truth* (67–95). Cambridge, MA: MIT Press.

Lynch, M. (2001). A functionalist theory of truth. In M. Lynch (ed.), *The Nature of Truth* (723–750). Cambridge, MA: MIT Press.

---

[24] Moreover, I have argued elsewhere (Caret & Cotnoir, 2008) that for purposes of the semantic paradoxes, designatedness need not be expressible. I give the problem of mixed inferences full treatmeant in my (forthcoming). See also Pedersen (2006) for another strong pluralist option.

[25] Thanks to Jc Beall, Colin Caret, Doug Edwards, Michael Lynch, Patrick Greenough, Nikolaj Pedersen, and Crispin Wright for many helpful discussions.

Lynch, M. (2004). Truth and multiple realizability. *Australasian Journal of Philosophy* 82: 384–408.
Lynch, M. (2006). ReWrighting pluralism. *Monist* 89: 63–84.
Lynch, M. (2008). Alethic pluralism, logical consequence and the universality of reason. *Midwest Studies in Philosophy* 32: 122–140.
Lynch, M. (2009). *Truth as One and Many: A Pluralist Manifesto*. Oxford: Oxford University Press.
Pedersen, N. J. L. (2006). What can the problem of mixed inferences teach us about pluralism? *Monist* 89: 103–117.
Pedersen, N. J. (2010). Stabilizing alethic pluralism. *Philosophical Quarterly* 60: 92–108.
Pedersen, N. J. L. L., & Wright, C. D. (2013). Pluralism about truth as alethic disjunctivism. In N. J. L. L. Pedersen & C. D. Wright (eds.), *Truth and Pluralism: Current Debates* (87–112). New York: Oxford University Press.
Rayo, A., and Uzquiano, G. (eds.). (2006). *Absolute Generality*. Oxford: Oxford University Press.
Restall, G. (2008). Curry's revenge: The costs of non-classical solutions to the paradoxes of self-reference. In Jc Beall (ed.), *Revenge of the Liar* (262–271). Oxford: Oxford University Press.
Shapiro, S. (2011). Truth, function and paradox. *Analysis* 71: 38–44.
Sher, G. (2004). In search of a substantive theory of truth. *Journal of Philosophy* 101: 5–36.
Sher, G. (2005). Functional pluralism. *Philosophical Books* 46: 311–330.
Tappolet, C. (1997). Mixed inferences: A problem for pluralism about truth predicates. *Analysis* 57: 209–210.
Tappolet, C. (2000). Truth pluralism and many-valued logics: A reply to Beall. *Philosophical Quarterly* 50: 382–385.
Tarski, A. (1944). The semantic conception of truth and the foundations of semantics. *Philosophy and Phenomenological Research* 4: 341–375.
Tarski, A. (1983). The concept of truth in formalized languages. In J. Corcoran (ed.), *Logic, Semantics, Metamathematics* (152–278). 2nd ed. Indianapolis: Hackett.
Tennant, N. (1994). The transmission of truth and the transitivity of deduction. In D. Gabbay (ed.), *What is a Logical System?* (161–177). Oxford: Oxford University Press.
Weir, A. (2005). Naive truth and sophisticated logic. In B. Armour-Garb & Jc Beall (eds.), *Deflationism and Paradox* (218–249). Oxford: Oxford University Press.
Williamson, T. (1994). A critical study of truth and objectivity. *International Journal of Philosophical Studies* 30: 130–144.
Wright, C. (1992). *Truth and Objectivity*. Cambridge, MA: Harvard University Press.
Wright, C. (2001). Minimalism, deflationism, pragmatism, pluralism. In M. Lynch (ed.), *The Nature of Truth* (751–787). Cambridge, MA: MIT Press.
Wright, C. D. (2005). On the functionalization of pluralist approaches to truth. *Synthese* 145: 1–28.

{ INDEX }

Alethic deflationism, 11, 69, 230–234, 263–265, 298–299, 301–304. *See also* Truisms about truth; Truth pluralism
  and knowledge of meaning, 317–318
  as the minimal theory (MT), 302
  and noncognitivism, 309–313
  and the normativity of truth, 71–77, 266–269, 318–320
  as prosententialism, 255–258
  and warranted assertibility, 71, 74, 76, 308
Alethic disjunctivism, 4, 30, 87–111
  and manifestation functionalism, 98–101, 106–108, 109–110
  and second-order functionalism, 97–98, 104–106
  and strong truth pluralism, 103–104
Alethic functionalism, 25–27, 42–68
  and the concept of truth, 23–31, 42–45, 56, 60, 75–77, 79, 84, 90–94
  definition of truth, according to, 60–65
  and manifestation functionalism, 110
  and multiple realizability, 42, 47
  and the normativity of truth, 69–84
  as proto-functionalism, 139–140
  as realizer functionalism, 28–29, 128–129, 134–135, 299–300. *See also* Truth pluralism, modes of
  second-order, 29–30, 63–65
  and the truth-role, 25–26, 34–37, 42–65, 93–94
  as a version of specifier functionalism, 61
Anderson, Alan Ross, 239, 242–243

Barnard, Robert, 7–9, 168
Bar-On, Dorit, 12, 266–267, 269
Beall, Jc, 14–15, 133, 348
Belnap, Nuel, 239, 242–243
Berkeley, George, 270–274
Blackburn, Simon, 12–13
Brandom, Robert, 12, 264, 267–269
Brink, David, 310 n. 14, 314 n. 20

Chomsky, Noam, 126, 217
Cognition
  adaptive, 218
  human, 160–161
  moral, 215, 224

  objective, 223
  response-dependent, 224–225
  truth-theoretic, 215, 219–220, 227–230, 234–235
Conceptual analysis, 90–92, 278–285
Conceptual framework, 188, 197, 203–205, 284
Correspondence
  degrees of, 202
  direct and indirect, 159–164, 168–178, 182–196
  as an ideologically mediated relation, 182–196
  intuition, 225–227
  mathematical, 168–174
  pluralism about corrrespondence truth, 158–196
  principles, 159, 161–162
  semantic standards governing, 182–196
  theory of truth, 7, 9–10, 22, 22 n.3, 24, 27, 34, 47–48, 87–88, 124, 158–211, 214, 223, 225, 313–316
Cotnoir, Aaron, 15
Curry, Haskell, 345–347

David, Marian, 5–6, 33 n. 10, 94 n. 14
Davidson, Donald, 3, 125, 253, 286
Descriptions, 238–259
  complete unified, 249
  informing-, 240
  perspectival view of, 10–11, 238–259
Dodd, Julian, 13–15
Domains, 32–34, 49–50, 55–58
  of cognition, 224
  ideological commitments of, 184, 192
  pluralism about, 10, 265, 273–276, 304–307
Dummett, Michael, 69, 71, 84, 124, 145, 211, 270

Edwards, Douglas, 4–5, 135–137, 139, 145–152
Engel, Pascal, 6
Expressivism, 12, 188 n. 17, 270–276

Frege, Gottlob, 12, 91, 129–130, 263–267, 270, 279
Fumerton, Richard, 9, 11, 199, 204

Grounding
  and pluralist truth theories, 4, 95–102
  weak principle of, 34–38
Grover, Dorothy, 10–11

Hinzen, Wolfram, 10, 15
Horgan, Terence, 7–9, 108, 168, 176, 348
Horwich, Paul, 69, 72–73, 138 n. 10, 231, 263–264, 301–304, 317

Immanence, 31, 91 n. 10, 95–99, 160

Jackson, Frank, 128

Kant, Immanuel, 219, 235
Kim, Jaegwon, 28
Kölbel, Max, 12–14

Lewis, David, 28, 128
Lynch, Michael, 1–7, 14–15, 42–68, 70, 76–84, 87–110, 119–121, 125–128, 131–135, 138–145, 313–320, 335

Manifestation, 3, 6, 31–36, 65–68, 95–101, 141–145. *See also* Grounding
Manifestation functionalism, 31–39, 141–145. *See also* Alethic disjunctivism; Simple determination pluralism
  and domains, 32–34
  and plain truth, 34–39
Millikan, Ruth, 243–244, 248
Minimal realism, 9, 181–182

Naturalism, 213–237
  metaphysical vs. methodological, 220–224
Network analysis, 128–129, 134–136, 143, 149–151

O'Connor, David, 88 n. 4, 94 n. 15
Ontology, correct, 181–187, 182 n. 5, 183 nn. 6–7, 185 n. 9, 190–192, 195

Pedersen, Nikolaj, 4, 30 n. 16, 119–120, 125, 292, 343–344, 348
Pluralism, 238
  horizontal, 252–255
  pragmatist, 12, 270–277
  about truth concepts, 75, 265, 285–295
  vertical, 250–252
Predication, 129–131, 265–266
Price, Huw, 73–78
Properties
  abundant conception of, 103–104, 131, 133, 150–1
  cardinality, 170
  determinable and determinate, 95, 140–144, 199
  disjunctive, 4, 92–110
  explanatory, 334–335
  immanent, 31
  metaphysically transparent, 38
  moral, 10, 215–216, 220–224
  more-than-logical, 334, 336

  natural, 314
  second-order, 63, 77, 119–120
  semantic, 216–217
  sparse conception of, 103–104, 131
  substantive, 69, 78–79, 151, 308
  truth-determining, 2–6, 28–29, 53, 77, 94, 117–120, 139–140
  winning-determining, 114–115
Putnam, Hilary, 252, 271–272, 276

Quine, W.V.O., 11, 13–14, 125, 239, 253–255, 276, 299–306, 335

Rattan, Gurpreet, 91 n. 10
Russell, Bertrand, 134, 241

Scope problem, 6–7, 14, 48, 214–216, 265, 313–317
Semantic paradoxes, 14–15, 290–291, 326–333, 339–349
  and nonclassical logics, 327–333
Sher, Gila, 7–8, 10, 90 n. 8, 91, 95 n. 17, 160
Shapiro, Stewart, 34–39, 96
Simmons, Keith, 12, 266–267, 269
Simple determination pluralism, 113–122
  and alethic disjunctivism, 119–120
  and domain-specific (Edwards) conditionals, 4–5, 115–118, 145–152
  and manifestation functionalism, 120–121
  and second-order functionalism, 119–120
Smith, Michael, 128
Strawson, Peter, 199, 250
Superassertibility (superwarrant), 21, 32–33, 75, 135–137, 149–152, 305–306

Tappolet, Christine, 132, 158, 164–167, 290, 348–349
Tarski, Alfred, 3 n., 13, 214, 327, 347–349
Truish features, 25–40, 46–47, 106–110
  and the truish relation, 55
T-schema, 340–345
Truisms about truth, 23–25, 43–52, 75–77, 79–84, 116, 134, 158
  core, 25–26, 42, 90–92
  and deflationism about truth, 308–309
  formulation of, 135–138
Truth
  analytic, 188
  antirealism about, 211
  coherence theory of, 205–211
  about comedy, 124, 287–289
  deflationary concept of, 73–77, 288–291. *See also* Alethic deflationism
  about fictions, 209
  legal, 208–209
  logical, 100–101

Index

mathematical, 168–178, 211
monism about, 88–90
naturalistic analysis of, 213–237
necessary, 37–38
nominal essence of, 23–26, 143–145
pragmatist theory of, 210–211, 268–273
relativism about, 203–205
as structural, 227–230
substantial concept of, 288–291
substantivism about, 88–90, 298
theory of, 23–25, 195
transparency of, 264
Truth pluralism, 21, 27, 48, 164, 293, 299. *See also* Pluralism
and conferral, 138–152
deflated, 14, 323–338
and deflationism about truth, 11, 38–39, 88–90, 304–307
and disquotationalism, 30–31
and the disunity of truth, 158–168, 180–196
family resemblance, 127–129. *See also* Truth pluralism, modes of
language-relative, 324–325
language-wide, 325
and mixed inferences, 116 n. 8, 132–133, 158–159, 164–168, 192–194, 348–349
and mixed propositions, 28–30, 34, 49 n. 9, 54 n. 14
and mixed sentences, 132–133, 158–159, 164–168, 348–349
modes of, 126–152
one-level vs. many-level, 97
Quine-Sainsbury objection to, 13, 265, 304–307
and realism/antirealism disputes, 307–313
simple (alethic), 126–127, 131–135. *See also* Truth pluralism, modes of
strong, 3, 65, 89, 285–291, 339
and structured propositions, 293–295
and the unity of truth, 232, 180–196
weak, 3, 48, 89, 138–152, 339. *See also* Truth pluralism, modes of
Truth predicates
as capture-release predicates, 323–324
domain-specific, 340
fundamental, 326
monism about, 12, 14–15, 48, 89 n. 6, 129 ff., 158, 165, 286, 294, 301–302, 334, 342
pluralism about, 12, 14, 323–338, 339
transparent and non-transparent, 14, 325–333, 336–337
universal, 339–349
Truth-aptness
according to disciplined syntacticism, 309–311
and monism about truth, 87 n. 1
Truth-conditions, 124–125, 172–174, 326
Truth-role, 3, 5–6, 26–31, 33–34, 33 n. 20, 36, 38–39, 42–68, 77–83, 93–95, 98, 105–106, 108. *See also* Alethic functionalism

Wiggins, David, 304
Wilson, Mark, 247–248
Wittgenstein, Ludwig, 124, 127–128, 240, 244, 254, 271–275
Wright, Cory, 4, 26 n. 12, 89 n. 6, 91, 318 n. 25
Wright, Crispin, 4–5, 14–15, 28, 49, 69, 71–79, 84, 116, 157–159, 226, 257, 307–313